ONE WEEK LOAN

D1342326

Roman Jakobson
Linda R. Waugh

The Sound Shape
of Language

Assisted by Martha Taylor

Third edition, with a new preface by Linda R. Waugh

Mouton de Gruyter
Berlin · New York   2002

Mouton de Gruyter (formerly Mouton, The Hague)
is a Division of Walter de Gruyter GmbH & Co. KG, Berlin.

Second Edition: 1987.

This work was originally published in 1979
by Indiana University Press, Bloomington and London.

♾ Printed on acid-free paper which falls within the guidelines
of the ANSI to ensure permanence and durability.

Die Deutsche Bibliothek – CIP-Einheitsaufnahme

Jakobson, Roman:
The sound shape of language / Roman Jakobson ; Linda R. Waugh.
Assisted by Martha Taylor. – Berlin ; New York : Mouton de Gruy-
ter, 2002
  ISBN 3-11-017285-2

Typesetting: Georg Appl, Wemding.
Printing and binding: Werner Hildebrand, Berlin.
Cover design: Sigurd Wendland, Berlin.
Printed in Germany.

What fetters the mind and benumbs the spirit
is ever the dogged acceptance of absolutes.

Edward Sapir, 1924
*The Grammarian and His
Language*

CONTENTS

VIII

ILLUSTRATIONS

ACKNOWLEDGMENTS

For support of our work on this book, we thank the Ford Foundation and its director, McGeorge Bundy.

For gracious assistance in the preparation of our study, thanks are due to the Massachusetts Institute of Technology; Cornell University; Ossabaw Island Project and its president, Eleanor Torrey West; Perception Technology Corporation and its director, Hüssein Yilmaz; the Bryggen Museum in Bergen, its director, curator Asbjörn Herteig, and Aslak Liestøl, curator of the Universitetets Oldsaksamling in Oslo; the Department of Indo-Pacific Languages at the University of Hawaii; Stanford University Phonology Archives; Harvard University Interlibrary Loan; and the National Library of Medicine, Bethesda, Maryland.

For valuable advice and suggestions we are gratefully indebted to our friends and colleagues: Milada Blekastad, Sheila Blumstein, Robert Blust, Dwight Bolinger, the late Jacob Bronowski, Noam Chomsky, George N. Clements, Helge Dyvik, Samuel Elbert, Donna Erickson, Rachel Erlich, Sigurd Fasting, Charles Ferguson, Eli Fischer-Jørgensen, Ivan Fónagy, Joseph Greenberg, Morris Halle, Einar Haugen, Charles Hockett, Marcia Howden, Andrew Kerek, Michael Krauss, Peter Ladefoged, Alvin Libermann, Björn Lindblom, André Malécot, Robert H. Maurer, Sven Öhman, Colin Painter, Donald Preziosi, Ronald Scollon, Michael Silverstein, Edward Stankiewicz, Kenneth Stevens, Michael Studdert-Kennedy, William S.-Y. Wang, Calvert Watkins, David Waugh, Roger Wescott, Dean S. Worth, and in particular Gunnar Fant and the late Pierre Delattre. Permission to reproduce illustrations and texts was kindly granted by Doreen Kimura and *Cortex*, by S. Blumstein and K. Stevens, by Harcourt Brace Jovanovich, by Granada Publishing Limited, and by Chappell Music Company.

NOTE ON TRANSCRIPTION

For the vowels we use the official IPA system, except that *ü* (and not *y*) designates the high front rounded vowel corresponding to *i.* Long vowels are noted by a macron (e.g., ā), nasal vowels by a tilde (ã).

For the consonants we use the symbols t, d for dental or dentialveolar stops where there is no further distinction. If there is a difference, t and d are usable for the dental stop, and t° and d° for the alveolar. For the palatal consonants – stops, fricatives, nasals – we use the principle used by Slavistic literature and going back to the spelling system established by Jan Hus for Czech: a ˘ is placed over or at the top right of the corresponding dental: t̃, d̃, š, ž, ň, č, and ǰ. The last two are palatal affricates corresponding to the dental affricates c and ʒ. (In some systems of transcription quoted here š and ž are rendered as ʃ and ʒ.) ř is a strident r (as in Czech). θ and ð are the tense (voiceless) and lax (voiced) interdental nonstrident continuants. Secondary modifications of consonants are noted in the following manner: palatalization by ' (e.g., t'); rounding, velarization, or pharyngealization by ° (e.g., t°); retroflexion by ˌ (e.g., ţ); aspiration by ʰ (e.g., tʰ); glottalization by ˀ (e.g., tˀ); devoicing by ₀ (e.g., ḑ); syllabicity by ˌ (e.g., ṛ).

PREFACE TO THE THIRD EDITION

> This third edition is dedicated
> to the memory of Roman Jakobson and to the
> furtherance of his intellectual legacy

Roman Jakobson and I began our work on what was to become *The Sound Shape of Language* in January 1977. This third edition, published as part of the jubilee celebration of the merger of Mouton and de Gruyter, appears, therefore, on the 25th anniversary of our writing the first paragraphs about spoonerisms, sense discrimination, homonymy, doublets, and so on. The book, as it emerged from our collaboration, changed from a technical monograph (much like Jakobson's earlier *Preliminaries to Speech Analysis* [Jakobson, Fant, Halle 1952] and *Fundamentals of Language* [Jakobson, Halle 1956]) on the acoustic definitions of "the ultimate constituents of language" (our first, provisional title for the work), to a shorter work on the distinctive features and their structural interrelations, to the present book with its insistence on both the structural and the functional aspects of sound and on the propensity of distinctive features to signal meaning directly (as discussed, in particular, in Chapter Four). Ultimately, our aim was to address the vast scope of issues relevant to the understanding of these smallest units of sound and their combinations (phonemes), while taking account of new, relevant research of the 1960's and 1970's on acoustic phonetics, speech perception, language and the brain, neurolinguistics, the genetic code, language change, language variation, language universals, the sound systems of little known languages, child language acquisition, sound symbolism, synesthesia, anagrams, children's play with language, mythopoeic usage and other uses of language where sound seems to cast a "spell" on its users. At the same time we paid homage to our predecessors, from antiquity to the first half of the 20th century, whose insights into the sound pattern of language we hailed as precursors to the present work.

Jakobson often claimed that it took twenty-five years for many of his most original ideas to be heard and understood. Recent interest in functionalist, emergentist, corpus, laboratory-phonological, discourse-pragmatic, interactional, anthropological, sociological and socio-cognitive approaches to language is, I hope, a sign that this third edition of *The Sound Shape of Language* will find new sympathetic readers.

Linda R. Waugh
Tucson, Arizona

PREFACE TO THE SECOND EDITION

Since the first edition of *The Sound Shape of Language*[1] is out of print and the demand for copies continues, this second, augmented edition is being published. Minor, mostly typographical changes were made in the text itself; and an index of names has been provided. I have added a second appendix, my "On the Sound Shape of Language: Mediacy and Immediacy". This article, which was written in 1979, after this book went to press, reviews one cluster of its basic findings.

Roman Jakobson died on July 18, 1982. This second edition is dedicated to his memory.

In general, it could be said that this book represents the fourth (and final) stage in Jakobson's quest to uncover the function and structure of sound in language. In the first stage (1920's and 1930's), he collaborated with the linguist Nikolai S. Trubetzkoy. Together, they developed the concept of the phoneme as a functional element and adumbrated various structural patterns which underlie phonological systems. Their fundamental concepts were based on invariance and contextual variation. Thus, phonemes are defined by those constant characteristics which relate them to other phonemes of the same system; and these common denominators are related to the various alterations which a phoneme manifests as it is used in different contexts. Moreover, Jakobson and Trubetzkoy showed that there are different types of phonological systems: e.g., triangular (a) vs. quadrangular (a ae) vocalic systems.

Structural relations were also discerned among phonemes; the most important of these were binary opposition (markedness relations) and

---

[1] Published in 1979 by Indiana University Press and prepared with the assistance of Martha Taylor.

implicational laws, especially asymmetric implication (X→Y but not vice versa). These new concepts were applied to language synchrony, language typology (types of systems), and language diachrony (change). Jakobson was also able to show that these structural patterns and relations determine the order of acquisition of phonemes in children: in general, simpler structures tend to be learned before complex ones (unmarked before marked, triangular before quadrangular, Y before X [if X→Y]).

In the second stage (late 1930's and 1940's), Jakobson developed the notion of binary distinctive features as the minimal building blocks of language. He argued that phonemes are complex since they are combinations of distinctive features, and that it is these features which underlie the different types of phonological systems. Moreover, he came to the general conclusion that distinctive features are signs whose *signatum* is "mere otherness" or pure differentiation; thus language is a completely semiotic system, from the largest components (texts) to the smallest ones (distinctive features).

In the third stage (1950's and 1960's), Jakobson collaborated with the acoustician C. Gunnar Fant and his student, the linguist Morris Halle, in developing acoustic definitions of the distinctive features which function to differentiate words perceptually. They also promulgated the theoretical concept that there is a small set of features which underlies the phonological systems of all the languages of the world. They found that they could unify in one acoustic feature a variety of articulatory properties (e.g., the feature of flatness encompasses labialization, rounding, velarization, and pharyngealization). And they developed a more relational account of invariance: for example, the /a/ in triangular systems is structurally, and thus linguistically, different from the /a/ in quadrangular systems.

The fourth stage is marked in particular by the present book (written in 1977-78, but in preparation for a few years before that). In it we attempted to give as broad a coverage as possible to the continuity of Jakobsonian thought. But there are new themes as well – or new perspectives on old ones. In general, this work underscores the importance of functional concerns in the analysis of sound. Thus, there is a recognition that everything in the speech sound plays some linguistic role and that, therefore, there are redundant, configurative, expressive and physiognomic features in addition to the distinctive ones. In fact, the sound shape as a whole is a linguistic creation, and oppositions such as (phon)etic vs. (phon)emic are outmoded. All of

this is shown to be corroborated by modern research on the hemispheric specialization of the brain. Each of the distinctive features is
discussed in turn and redefined as rigorously as possible. In addition,
we further develop properties of feature systems: for example, the nature and interconnection of the two basic axes, compact ⌣ diffuse and
grave ⌣ acute; the interrelation of the tonality features (grave ⌣ acute,
flat ⌣ plain, sharp ⌣ plain); consonantal correspondences to the prosodic (vocalic) features; glides as prime examples of zero phonemes.

Many of these themes are developed, at least in part, as a reaction
to the work of other phoneticians and phonologists of our time, many
of whom were responding in turn to Jakobson's earlier work. This is
particularly true of generative phonology and of its leading practitio-
ners, Noam Chomsky and Morris Halle, and of their book, *The
Sound Pattern of English* (1968). In certain ways, the present book
provides a (usually implicit) corrective commentary to the generative
trend. Examples abound on almost every page. The most salient are
the following. We object to the abandonment of the notion of phoneme: even though the distinctive features are primordial, the phoneme has its place in language structure. Various attempts to replace
the original set of distinctive features proposed by Jakobson are evaluated and rejected. It is affirmed that invariance is crucial to any
analysis of sound and is to be applied rigorously at the level of the
feature. Features are defined in acoustic terms: articulatory means
are to be seen only in the light of their ends, namely their use to distinguish perceptually words which are different in meaning. The concept of markedness is given a relational definition such that either
pole of an opposition (+ or −) is marked, depending on the context
in which it is found. This is correlated with the order of acquisition in
children, language change, and language typology and universals, especially implicational laws. And sound systems are defined as dynamic, heterogeneous, multiform structures in which time (older and
newer forms) and space (social and geographical variants) have a
semiotic value. Moreover, the interlacing of learning and innate structures in language acquisition is affirmed, with emphasis on the former; as is the centrality of dialogue for learning and usage, even for
our own inner speech (thinking).

Perhaps the most important tendency within current linguistics
which we sought to address is the widespread disregard for the functional, pragmatic, social, and communicative basis of sound (and of
language in general). This was particularly evident in the abandon-

ment by generative phonology of the fundamental division between two different functions of the distinctive features. The first is their use to keep apart words which differ in meaning. This is distinctiveness proper, which serves as the basis for the set of distinctive features given here. It is primary in all languages of the world and exhibits regular patterns across languages. The second function, which is built on the first, includes the study that Jakobson and Trubetzkoy originally called morphonology. But actually it encompasses questions not only of the alternations of a word (or a morpheme), but also the information that features supply about derivational and inflectional structure and lexical and grammatical meaning. This is called "sense-determination": sound is necessarily linked with, and thus informs about, meaning. The ways in which this is accomplished exhibit great diversity across languages.

This distinction is crucial to an understanding of the diverse ways in which sound functions in language. However, in much generative phonology, these two functions have been collapsed into one, called "distinctive"; and their study has been called "phonology". Because of this, we once again attempt to define "distinctive" through the synonymous expression "sense-discriminative": the capability of signaling, with a probability near to 1.0, the semantic likeness or nonlikeness of two meaningful verbal units. And we avoid the words "phonology" and "phonological" – terms which Jakobson himself had helped to launch decades earlier with Trubetzkoy – because we felt that their meaning had become too blurred.

The important, but widely neglected, theme of the relation between sound and given units of meaning, which in our original plan occupied only a few lines in Chapter One, eventually became the topic of Chapter Four. Our concern was to relativize the popular notion of arbitrariness. This led to the definition of a new antinomy, namely, mediacy vs. immediacy: the tendency for sound to have an indirect, or mediated, relation to meaning (sense-discrimination) versus its tendency to have direct, and thus immediate, signification. In the former, the distinctive features connect sound and meaning solely by virtue of contiguity; but in the latter, the sound symbolism inherent in these features sustains a similarity relation between sound and meaning. As evidence of the "spell" which the sound shape may cast over the language user, we explore domains as widespread as synesthesia, word affinity relations, taboo substitutions, and glossolalia. But nowhere is the direct interplay of sound and meaning more salient than in poetry, which is based on similarity (and equivalence) at all levels. In fact, poetry is the fullest accomplishment of the synthesis between contiguity and similarity and the most important locus of linguistic creativity. Thus we endeavor to affirm that any science of language must find a proper place for the mutual implication of the two inseparable universals: *Language* and *Poetry*.

Linda R. Waugh

CHAPTER ONE

SPEECH SOUNDS AND THEIR TASKS

> A thing without oppositions
> *ipso facto* does not exist.
> Charles Sanders Peirce
> *Collected Papers*, 1.457

I. SPOONERISMS

"May I sew you to another sheet?"
This is a joking substitute reportedly originated by the Reverend William Spooner (1844–1930) for the familiar question: *May I show you to another seat?* The mere exchange of two initial sibilants, one hushing and the other hissing, or in other words, a metathesis of the two opposite terms of the feature compact ~ diffuse, changes the meaning of two words (*show* to *sew* and *seat* to *sheet*) and creates a comic effect. In like fashion, the interchange of the two liquids *r* and *l* in *blade of grass* produces the unusual *braid of glass*. Algernon Charles Swinburne wrote in the 1890s to his cousin Mary Gordon Leith, the dark lady of his ballads, in a childish code: *"By Merest Dozen"* instead of *My Dearest Cousin,* using a playful metathesis of the initial consonants: M.D.K. > B.M.D. Such reversals, labeled 'Spoonerisms', frequently occur as simple slips of the tongue (cf. MacKay 1970a), but are also widely used as intentional, "laboriously fabricated" humorous constructions, customary in English (see Robbins 1966) and even more so in French, where this device is known under the name *contrepèterie* (see, e.g., Etienne 1957). Spoonerisms transposing separate features, such as the metathesis of compactness and diffuseness (velarity and labiality) in Fromkin's (1966) example, *"plear glue sky"* in place of *clear blue sky,* are one of the clear-cut testimonies for the free play of 'distinctive features'. The punlike metathesis of distinctive features may serve to weld together words etymologically unrelated but close in their sound and meaning, as in the chapter title of a scholarly book, "Identification of Roles and Rules", which playfully confronts the sound and meaning of the last two nouns. Wordplays recorded from unwritten languages often cling to the same principle.

II. SENSE DISCRIMINATION

Indisputably, the grammatical pattern of the sentence, the verbal context of the words at issue, and the situation which surrounds the given utterance prompt the hearer's apprehension of the actual sense of the words so that he doesn't need to pick up all the constituents of the sound sequence. Still, the degrees of expectancy are variable and the addressee may suddenly be faced with a message requiring him to pay full attention to the various distinctions possible:

> *It shows   the strange zeal of the mad sailor with neither mobility*
> *" showed "   "   deal " " bad tailor "   " nobility*
> *nor fashion.*
> *" passion.*

Such attention to single features is needed in order both to grasp the vocabulary (words and lexical morphemes) and to assign to the grammatical morphemes such as affixes their meaning. It is true that in the latter case listeners may find a substantial cue in the syntactic arrangement of the sentence, but the choice between, for instance, the present tense suffix [z] and the preterit suffix [d] in the utterance quoted still is not helped by the syntactic context, and thus cannot be derived from other representations of the sentence, notwithstanding the hearer's knowledge of the grammatical rules. Given the two basic operations – selection and combination – one may, when dealing with a construction such as *children showed,* conclude from the preceding word *children* that *showed* and not *shows* is in question, but the subject *it* would not constrain the selection. In this way, the 'paradigmatic' (selectional) axis keeps its relevance independently of the 'syntagmatic' (combinational) axis.

Such components as those which in the sentence discussed enable the perceiver to distinguish *zeal* from *deal, shows* from *showed,* and *sailor* from *tailor,* or *mad* from *bad, mobility* from *nobility,* and *fashion* from *passion* are termed 'distinctive features'. But the attribute 'distinctive', apparently introduced by the astute English phonetician Henry Sweet, is unfortunately sometimes confused with 'distinct'. "Distinctive", that is "discriminative", "having the ability to distinguish", has often been misinterpreted as "discriminable", "distinguishable", "capable of being easily perceived". It is true that "discriminative" components of speech are readily perceivable, but not all particulars "distinguishable" in the speech sounds by the language-user may effect the distinction of meanings.

III. HOMONYMY

The primary task of distinctive features is the discrimination of verbal meanings. It is, so to speak, their *raison d'être* in the makeup of language. Sometimes the (sense-)discriminative role is questioned by the-oreticians whose chief argument against this function is provided by the existence of homonyms. It is *a priori* clear, however, that a language devoid of homonyms is conceivable, whereas a purely homonymic language is a *reductio ad absurdum*. By differing in sound shape and meaning, the surrounding words as a rule serve for the disambiguation of homonyms and thus for their correct semantic interpretation by the listener. When a language, such as Chinese, radically reduces the number of distinctive features and of their simultaneous and sequential combinations and confines words to a uniform, monosyllabic model, the number of homonyms among simple (noncompound) words increases excessively (e.g., an *i* in the 'fourth tone' offers no less than thirty-eight words of totally noncognate meanings). But the question "How is it in practice possible to use a language having so many homophones?" finds an exhaustive answer in Bernhard Karlgren's classic study (1962). The language frames such simple words into different types of "elucidative compounds" by adding to a given monosyllable a synonymous or generic apposition (cf. the Chinese pidgin English *look-see*), by accompanying the monosyllabic verb with its tautological object (cf. *I eat food*), or finally by prefixing the noun with a semantic 'classifier' (such as "mouth" as a classifier for objects with a round opening or "branch" for long objects). (See also Klima 1975: 262 ff.) In all such cases the basic goal of these devices is the buildup of a wider range for a possible application of the sense-discriminative features, in order to overcome any annoying ambiguity.

When no help is given by the verbal context (cf. Appendix I), it is often the nonverbalized situation which provides the clue. Homonyms within a spoken sentence can have a double sense for the listener in such sentences as *The children had a* [pɛr]. Three words may remain ambiguous: *my children*, or *some children* in general? *ate*, or merely *possessed*? *pair*, or *pear*? The reason for the ambiguity lies in the elliptic character of this example, translatable into such explicit sentences as *My children* (or *the children I know*) *each ate* (or *possessed*) *a pear* (or *a pair of shoes* or *pants* or *socks*, and so on). Most of the questions of verbal ambiguity cited by linguists belong to various degrees of elliptic speech. The phenomenon of ellipsis remains largely minimized or disregarded in the science of language, despite the insistent and repeated suggestions of the sixteenth-century Spanish linguist Franciscus Sanctius Brocensis, who clearly viewed explicitness and ellipticity as two extreme aspects of linguistic operations. They may be seen as two poles of the verbal code, because the scale of transitions from the explicit makeup of language to the elliptic offers a set of ordered rules. Rules of gradual omission have a specific order in each language, just as they differ in such customary patterns as folkdress. In contradistinction to some Western habits, Russian rural tradition allowed people to go outdoors barefoot; however, a married woman was required to have her head covered and a man to wear a belt when outside. This explains such pejorative Russian verbs as *raspojásat'sja* ('to stay ungirdled, throw aside all restraint') and *oprostovolósit'sja* ('to make a fool of oneself', literally referring to an improperly bared woman's head).

The convenience of the omission of linguistic elements which are redundant for the comprehension of the message is by no means the sole impetus for ellipsis. Socially or individually tabooed words and expressions are currently censored and excluded from speech, or are at least camouflaged, for instance by being distorted in their sound shape (cf. below, pp. 211 f.), and it is worthy of note that words tabooed and omitted by a patient may be deemed highly significant when recovered by psychoanalysis (cf. Lacan 1966).

We are constantly faced with elliptic structures, and thorough orders of rules underlie the different degrees of ellipticity on each level of language, from discourse through syntax and morphology and finally to reductions in sound sequences and concurrences of distinctive features. The elliptic abbreviation of the English conjunction *and* first entails the reduction of the initial vowel, then the abolition of the final *d*, next the loss of the vowel (with concomitant syllabification of *n*) after a terminal consonant of the preceding word, and finally, in a postvocalic position, the possible loss of *n* with the assignment of nasality to the final vowel of the preceding word.

Some linguistic ambiguities cited by scholars are actually confined to the elliptic variety of oral language and may find support in the written form, which does not take into account intonational and pausal distinctions characteristic of explicit oral speech but omissible in elliptic style. Hence, in the instructive example discussed by Noam Chomsky (1972: 104 f., 162 f.) – *"John is certain that Bill will leave"*, and *"John is certain to leave"* – a pause may occur after "is certain" in the first sentence but before the same words in the second; thus in their explicit oral shape the so-called "superficial similarity" of these two sentences disappears.

Any elliptic message is translatable by the speaker into a more explicit statement and vice versa. Thus, with respect to its two varieties, the elliptic and the explicit subcodes, the overall code may be characterized as 'convertible'. François Dell (1973b), who pays close attention to "styles of diction", namely 'careful style' (*"diction soignée"*) on the one hand and 'casual speech' (*"conversation familière"*) on the other, cites the curious example of two French phrases *à votre tour* and *à votre retour*; in elliptic style they become *avottour* and *avotretour* respectively, so that the elliptic variant of the phrase *à votre retour* coincides with the explicit form of the other phrase. The allegro variety of American English is full of such elliptic phonations as the frequently quoted *ten min sem* 'ten minutes to seven', or *jijčɛt* 'did you eat yet?' and produces numerous homonyms, such as *gone* and *going, put him* and *put them, allude* and *elude, affect* and *effect*, homonyms normally disambiguated in lento speech.

One is apt to designate the explicit variety of language as the optimal facet of the code. It is in fact optimal with respect to the plenitude of informational distinctions; however, on the other hand, explicitness risks carrying too much redundant information in the flow of speech when the topic of discourse is familiar to the interlocutors. In such situations the economy of the tersely elliptic exchange of messages is preferred by both addressers and addressees.

Besides codified, conventionalized elliptic omissions, there are occasional, individual inadvertences in both the speaker's and the listener's performance. One could label the latter 'elliptic perception', which causes a loss of features, words, and syntactic units in the reception of the message; some of the signals omitted by the speaker as well as by the hearer are restored and correctly identified by the latter thanks to the context which he succeeds in picking up, while others remain unconstrued or even misunderstood. Familiar words or even larger wholes are easily recognized in spite of emissive or perceptual ellipsis and hence enable the recipient of the message to apprehend immediately and directly many higher units without the need for prior attention to their components.

IV. DOUBLETS

Besides homonyms, another peculiarity of language has sometimes been drawn in as evidence against the generality of the sense-discriminative function of the distinctive features: namely, in single rarissime cases, which Ferdinand de Saussure (1857–1913) in his Geneva lectures used to call 'linguistic dust' (*"poussière linguistique"*), as his student Karcevskij recalled, there occur among the tens or even hundreds of thousands of vocables of a given language a handful of sporadic doublets with no semantic difference. Yet the occurrence of lexical doublets such as the two noticeable examples discussed by Sebastian K. Shaumyan (1965: 24f.) are quite exceptional. Particularly rare (probability near zero) is the use of the two doublets by one and the same member of the speech community without any semantic or at least stylistic differentiation. Of the instances cited by Shaumyan, the pair *škap/škaf* ('cupboard, wardrobe', etc.) goes back to two different borrowings from German; with respect to the latter form, the /f/ is still felt to be a foreign phoneme at the end of Russian nouns (cf. RJ I: 728 ff.), and individual use tends to differentiate both forms. The other pair, *okolótok/okolódok* ('ward'), both with the same cluster [tk] in the genitive, etc., seems, whatever its origin, to be based on two different folk etymologies, the first alluding to a fence (cf. *kól* 'stake, picket', *okolotít'* 'to fence') and the second to a heavy barrier (cf. *kolóda* 'log, block' and the association between *okolódočnyj* 'police officer' and *kolódki, -dok* 'shackles, fetters, stocks'; cf. also *zakolódit'* 'to shackle').

Usually such coexisting doublets belong to different dialectal varieties, as is emphasized in the jocular song by Ira and George Gershwin:

You say eether [ī] and I say eyether [ay],
You say neether [ī] and I say nyther [ay];
Eether [ī], eyether [ay], neether [ī], nyther [ay],
Let's call the whole thing off!

You like potato [ē] and I like potahto [a],
You like tomato [ē] and I like tomahto [a];
Potato [ē], potahto [a], tomato [ē], tomahto [a]!
Let's call the whole thing off!

＊　＊　＊

So, if you like pajamas [æ] and I like pajahmas [a],
I'll wear pajamas [æ] and give up pajahmas [a].
For we know we need each other,
So we better call the calling off off.
Let's call the whole thing off!

Such doublets as *either* [ay]/[ĩ] are felt by speakers as proceeding from different dialects, or else, when used by the same speaker, take on differing emotional tinges. For instance, some users of both varieties feel that *either* with [ay] is the more prestigious variant and is thus endowed with a more elevated significance. Within the same dialogue by the same speaker one would rarely find the use of doublets different in their sound shape but with no functional difference in their application. The minimal differentiation of the two similar forms is their dissimilation within a narrow context. When such an interdialectal doublet is enrooted in the use of one speech community, the meaning-giving capacity of the distinctive features endeavors to assign two different lexical meanings to the members of the doublet: e.g., Polish *dziewka, dziwka,* the former, with an [ɛ], meaning 'girl' or 'servant girl', the latter, with an [i], taking on the specialized designation of 'whore'. Curiously enough, Czech uses the two corresponding variants of the same word in the opposite semantic distribution: *dívka* ([ī]) 'girl' - *děvka* ([ɛ]) 'whore'. Cf. *bába* 'grandmother, grandma', and *baba* 'old crone, old woman, old hen'. As in most of the essential questions of linguistic analysis, we must when dealing with the semantic uses of distinctive features operate with usability, the capacity to be utilized, as a concept which implies certainty (probability 1.0), whereas the actual use of any features for semantic discrimination can admit apparent exceptions and thus displays a probability less than but very near to 1.0.

V. EARLY SEARCH

The international quest for the ultimate constituents of language able to serve to discriminate meaning has endured through millennia. Its first steps are manifested in the history of writing systems, with their gradual dissociation of the speech sequence into words, syllables, and finally the shortest successive segments. This last step was first attained over three thousand years ago in the Aramaic and subsequently in the Greek alphabetic script. "It has been rightfully stated that in the oldest Greek inscriptions there occur but a few abbreviations as compared for example with Latin, and that early Greek writing shows no disposition to ligatures; each letter remains separate and retains its atomic character, its own place, its individual validity" (Patočka 1964: 48). The consistent segmentation of the Greek alphabet into single sound units was a powerful inspiration for the theory of ultimate, discrete verbal constituents.

In the Greek philosophical literature indivisible sound units capable of forming meaningful strings were termed STOICHEIA, 'the underlying primes of sounds and letters'. The sound shape of language and correspondingly its alphabet were viewed as a joint coherent system with a limited number of discrete and interconnected formal units. This concept proved to be so persuasive that Democritus (fragment A6; cf. Diels and Wilpert) and his adherent Lucretius, in searching for an analogy which might confirm their theory of the atomic structure of the physical universe, cited STOICHEIA as the minimal components of speech. Thus Lucretius, in his philosophical poem *De rerum natura* (Liber II, verses 694 ff.) teaches:

> Sic aliis in rebus item communia multa,
> Multarum rerum cum sint Primordia longe
> Dissimili tamen inter se consistere summa
> Possunt: ut merito ex aliis constare ferantur
> Humanum genus, ac Fruges, Arbustaque laeta.

> ("So likewise in other matters, many elements,
> as they are the primary principles of many things,
> may yet exist in dissimilar combinations among
> themselves; so that the human race and the fruits
> of the earth and the rich groves may justly be
> considered to consist each of distinct original-
> particles.")

Just as in Antiquity the term STOICHEION, used originally for linguistic elemental units, was extended to the physical world, in a similar way, but reversely, linguistic theory of the last hundred years in its quest for the ulimate constituents has appealed in turn to the model of atomic physics.

In Plato's *Dialogues* and Aristotle's writings some focal concepts and problems of modern discussions on the theory of language (cf. Koller 1955, 1959; Burkert 1959; Moravcsik 1960a; Gallop 1963; Demos 1964; and Patočka 1964) are anticipated. The verbal STOICHEIA are "distinguishables not detachables; abstractables not extractables" (see Ryle 1960: 436). To the cardinal tasks pointed out by Plato with regard to the STOICHEIA belong their identification, recognition, classification within the system, and an exact rendering of their compatibility and interwovenness (namely the hierarchy of the rules for their combinability into meaningful sequences). In his dialogue *Philebus* Plato states that none of us could learn any STOICHEION by itself without learning all of the members of the given SYSTEMA and their mutual bonds. Both the account of the distribution of elements in the sequence (SYMPLOKE) and, first and foremost, their underlying classification on the basis of their distinctive properties (DYNAMEIS) are foreseen in Plato's attempt "to discriminate the DYNAMEIS of the STOICHEIA" (*Kratylos*, D 424). The STOICHEION as such is for the philosopher a relational unit denoting otherness and, to cite Julius Moravcsik's comment on the dialogue *Sophist* (1960a: 48 f.), "whatever is 'other', it is always other than something else." According to Plato, it is the art of grammar that enables us to recognize the elements, to separate them from each other, and to discern their appropriateness for combinations.

In the theory of language richly and widely developed for many centuries by the Sanskrit grammarians, the concept of *sphoṭa*, interpreted as the relation between form and meaning in language on its various levels, occupied a pivotal position (cf. Brough; Ruegg; and Iyer) and gave rise to vivid and broad discussions producing such major achievements as the treatises of Patañjali in the second century B.C. and Bhartṛhari in the fifth century A.D. - that fixed attention to empirical data which was proper to the Indic linguistic tradition finds a patent expression in Patañjali's 'minimal pairs test', according to the current American terminology - *yūpa/cūpa/sūpa* (see Allen 1953: 81) - and on the other hand this scholarly tradition daringly touched upon the fundamental puzzles of linguistic theory such as the perennial antinomies between permanence and mutability or between real percepts of the language user and heuristic constructs imposed by grammarians upon the verbal material, and it was Indic theory that brought to discussion the paradoxical status of units which by themselves are devoid of meaning but at the same time are endowed with an indispensable significative value.

The problems of the relationship between a verbal sound shape and its meaning, far from being abandoned, gave rise to inquisitive theoretical approaches in the philosophy of the Middle Ages (cf. RJ 1975: 292 f.) and to new, striking examples of concrete experimentation with script. Thus an ingenious insight into the discrete ultimate segments and their autonomous sense-discriminative value is characteristic of the Old Norse tradition. Besides the entangled sound/meaning problems hidden in skaldic poetry and poetic treatises, one may quote a few simple examples. One of the terse medieval runic texts recently unearthed in Bergen (see Liestøl 1964: 18 f.) constitutes a set of seven seven-letter words differing only in their initial consonant – *mistill, tistill, pistill, kistill, ristill, gistill,* and *bistill* – written in such a way as to point out the difference of the initials and the identity of each further segment, i. e., a 'commutation test' with a magical purpose (see Figure 1):

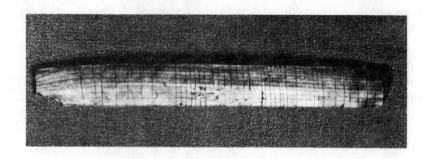

Figure 1.
Magic runes from Bryggen (Bergen, Norway).
mtpkrgb iiiiiiissssssstttttttiiiiiiilllllll

An anonymous Icelandic grammatical treatise of the twelfth century arguing for a revised adaptation of the Latin alphabet for the local language resorts, as is shown in the excellent edition by Einar Haugen (1972[2]), to the device of 'minimal pairs' in order to establish the repertory of sense-discriminative vowels, each of which, because of the function it performs, requires a separate graphic designation. Thus, to split off vocalic "distinctions [*grein*] each of which changes the meanings", the author places each of the numerous vowels he finds in his language "between the same two consonants" in order to show which of these vowels "placed in the same position make[s] a different sense". The next step of the treatise is to distinguish those vowels which are "spoken in the nose" by placing a dot above them, because this vocalic distinction appears to him to be systematic and to show "that it too can change the meaning". Exemplifying sentences are used to justify this attempt: "*har* ['hair'] grows on living creatures, but *hár* ['shark'] is a fish", etc. Another "distinction which changes the meaning" is the division of vowels into long and short ones; the treatise proposes to "mark the long ones with a stroke to distinguish them from the short ones", and again minimal pairs and illustrative sentences follow: "*far* ['vessel'] is a kind of ship, but *fár* ['danger'] is a kind of distress". In this way, as the author states, all thirty-six distinctive vowels of the Icelandic language are taken care of in a new "alphabet for us Icelanders". On the other hand, the treatise makes use of one and the same letter for cognate sounds without distinctive capacity, e.g. for the voiced and voiceless interdentals.

Many remarkable theoretical and empirical assertions of the past, after suffering long-term disregard and oblivion, reappear, often with no reference to the original model, and turn into new, effective propositions. Such was, for instance, the historical destiny of the 2000-year-old Stoic thesis which treated the sign, sēmeion, as an entity constituted by the two correlatives: the sēmainon ('the signifier') and the sē-mainomenon ('the signified'). In the last semester of his series of courses in linguistic theory, Saussure took over and emphatically recommended this formula – "le signifiant et le signifié sont les deux éléments composant le signe" (1916: 152; cf. Gołębiewski) – and it entered into his posthumous *Cours de linguistique générale,* compiled by Saussure's disciples Charles Bally (1865-1947) and Albert Sechehaye (1870-1946) and published in 1916. This thesis, often mistakenly viewed as an invention of the Genevan, is unsurpassed because of its clear ascertainment of the two semiotic constituents, one (sēmainon, 'signans', *signifiant*) directly given and the other (sēmainomenon, 'signatum', *signifié*) prompted by the first. Both abstract and concrete questions of the relationship between *signans* and *signatum* in the realm of signs (*signa*) and especially in the various aspects of language belong to the continuously increasing penetrations into the cultural life of humanity which engender ever-new solutions and ever-new puzzles.

VI. INVARIANCE AND RELATIVITY

Consistent efforts toward the delineation and identification of those further-indivisible constituents of language which serve to differentiate fundamental linguistic units endowed with their own meaning such as words and their meaningful components ('morphemes') was begun in the 1870s by a few young pioneers scattered throughout different countries. Three of these far-sighted scholars, all three born in the mid-1840s – the Englishman Henry Sweet (1845-1912), the Pole

Jan Baudouin de Courtenay (1845-1929), and the Swiss Jost Winteler (1846-1929) - resolutely advanced the basic question of the relationship between sound and meaning. From 1877 on, Sweet outspokenly separated the "independently significant" sounds which may correspond to differences of meaning from all other "differences which are not significant and cannot alter the meaning" (cf. RJ II: 456 ff.). As early as 1869 Baudouin broached the subject of the differences in sounds which are "used to differentiate meanings" (see 1974: 258), and the elaboration of "connections between sounds and meaning" became the main concern of his research and teaching through the next decades (see 1963 I; cf. RJ II: 394 ff.; Stankiewicz 1972). In his thesis of 1876, Winteler unswervingly distinguished variations labeled "accidental features" from "essential properties", sense-discriminative invariants on the sound level of language. In order to extract and identify these invariants he made deliberate use of minimal pairs (cf. RJ 1972) and was followed in this technique by Sweet.

No matter whether there was a convergence in thought or whether linguists received a new impetus from mathematics, the seminal idea of invariance developed into the dominant principle for both fields of knowledge, especially in the 1870s. In either case, according to Felix Klein's (1849-1925) Erlanger Programm of 1871-72, "the 'given' is a multiplicity and within it a transformational group; the patterns to which this multiplicity is related have to be investigated with respect to those properties which remain unaffected by the transformations of the group" (1921: 463).

This view found a series of close correspondences in the broad aims and purposes outlined in Baudouin de Courtenay's introductory lecture, published at the same time as the Erlanger text (see 1963 I: 47 ff.), and in the comprehensive programs of Baudouin's linguistic courses, delivered chiefly during the next ten years and printed in the same *Bulletins* (see 1963 I: 78 ff.) of Kazan' University in which half a century earlier Nikolaj Lobačevskij had issued his epochal sketch of a non-Euclidean geometry. Baudouin stated that "we have to put aside the divergent, accidental properties of individual sounds and substitute a general expression for the mobile sounds - an expression that is, so to speak, the common denominator of these variables" (1963 I: 120). The linguist's aim was to discover the relational invariants in the flux of speech, with its countless contextual and optional sound variations. He predicted also that the acoustic correlates of these linguistic invariants would be more precisely determined when speech analysis could utilize such technical achievements as the telephone, microphone, and electricity and could obtain a visual portrayal of sound waves (Baudouin 1881–82: 4f., 61f., 65). This prediction, which up to our time is still objected to by regressive dogmatists, found a convinced advocate in Leonard Bloomfield (1887–1949), who in 1934 foresaw that "the physical (acoustic) definition of each phoneme of any given dialect can be expected to come from the laboratory within the next decades" (see Twaddell 1935: 23).

Both to Baudouin and to the prematurely deceased Mikołaj Kruszewski (1851–1887), Baudouin's omniscient disciple and uncompromising collaborator (cf. RJ II: 428 ff.), it was clear that every linguistic unit occurs in diverse modifying environments and that all its occurrences are equivalent to each other: i.e., in the terms of 'Group Theory', they are merely different expressions of one and the same linguistic essence. Baudouin approached this extracted, purely relational unit as an indivisible phonetic particle (or 'phoneme' in his later terminology), comparable with the atom as the unit of matter and with 1.0 as the unit of mathematics.

Since both penetrating Polish explorers, Baudouin and Kruszewski, were aware of invariances in relationship, the connection between the initial aspirated p^h of English and the final unaspirated p, parallel to an equivalent connection between the other initial and final stops within that language, quite naturally authorized the assignment of both variants to the same phoneme. The identical relation between the aspirated initial stops and the unaspirated final stops cannot serve in English to discriminate meanings of two words because the two sounds do not occur in the same position (in contradistinction to those languages, such as the Swiss-German dialect described by Winteler (1876), in which [t^h] and [t] appear in the same position and carry a sense-discriminative capacity). On the other hand, the feature distinguishing [p^h] from [t^h] or [p] from [t], all other things being equal, is capable of signaling such lexical pairs as *pot* and *tot*, *top* and *tot*, *pill* and *till*, *pick* and *tick*, *lip* and *lit* in English, and thus [p] and [t] function as two different phonemes.

Both Baudouin and Winteler, when dealing with sound patterns of diverse languages, invoked verbatim the principle of "relativity [*otnositel'nost'*] of sound categories" (Baudouin, see 1963 I: 80), since relativity and invariance are necessarily two complementary concepts, or as physicists say, "the reverse side of invariance ⟨...⟩ is called relativity" (Morgenau 1961: 82). Gunnar Fant's insistent reminder (1973: 163) to

speech sound analysts of different training – "the invariance is generally relative rather than absolute" – becomes more and more oppor-
tune. From the early 1870s Baudouin detected and pointed out "sets of
parallel sound oppositions [*protivopoložnosti*]" and emphasized "the
intimate connection of such oppositions with the meaning of words
and of their constituents" (see 1963 I: 80). Both Baudouin and Sweet
developed the same approach in similar ways not only in intralingual
but also in interlingual analysis. Thus, as stated in the program of Baudouin's university course for 1876–77, "within different languages
physiologically identical sounds may possess different values in con-
formity with the whole sound system, i. e. in correspondence with their
relations to the other sounds. Their scales are unlike" (1963 I: 90).
Sweet taught in 1876 not only that each language utilizes only a few
sound distinctions for differences of meaning, but moreover that there
are universal restrictions. Thus, if two vowels are "formed in a totally
different way" but are "never employed together in the same language
to distinguish the meanings of words ⟨...⟩ they may be considered as
variations of the same vowel". Herewith the extraction of invariants
from intralingual variations is supplemented by a search for interlingual, universal variations and for corresponding invariants.

   Saussure, obviously inspired by Kruszewski's and Baudouin's example, concentrated on problems of the relation between sound and
meaning during the final, Geneva period of his academic activities. In
his comprehensive sketch for a phonetic treatise, drafted in the 1890s
and now part of the Harvard manuscript collection (see RJ I: 743 ff.),
Saussure developed the view of speech production as a programmed,
intentional, anticipatory activity with an auditory, perceptual effect.
Correspondingly, he discussed the different aspects of phonemes and
advanced the thesis that "Phonèmes = Valeur sémiologique", or, in
other words, that the leading role is played by the "rapport entre le son
et l'idée". Briefly, phonemes were treated here as simple signs which
endow "acoustic oppositions" (*"oppositions acoustiques"*) with a
"sense-discriminative value" (*"une valeur pour l'idée"*). Therefore, such
solely positional differences as the divergence between the syllabic
and nonsyllabic *i* in Indo-European proves to be "devoid of any semiotic value" (*"sans valeur sémiologique"*) and both "semiotically equivalent" specimens are to be assigned to one and the same phoneme and
may be transcribed by the same letter. In another note of this same
time, Saussure added that in the forms *srutos, sreumen, sreuo,* "the
phoneme 'u' appears in two acoustic forms" and reveals a "unity in di-

versity". He emphasized that this identification should not be viewed as a mere scientific construct. Herewith Saussure attempted to inaugurate a new discipline, "semiologic phonetics", which later was tentatively renamed "phonology" by his follower Albert Sechehaye in his book of 1908, and this label, adopted in the early 1920s by the Prague linguists, has entered into international use.

Thus, the astute warning of the young Baudouin de Courtenay against "an unjustified and paralogical jump" from the treatment of such semantic units as sentences, words, and their minimal grammatical components ("morphemes" as he named them) to the gross sound matter without any regard for its semiotic function has been corroborated by decades of linguistic research, and the question of the relationship between the two sides of verbal signs – the *signans* and the *signatum* – has finally been extended to the sound units of language as well. Saussure's view that any linguistic constituent is "une entité à deux faces" and that "any material unit only exists through the sense, the function it is endowed with", has been echoed, discussed, and worked through in the subsequent development of linguistics.

Habent sua fata libelli: as one the landmarks in linguistic research based on the conjunct concepts of relation and invariance, Saussure's *Cours de linguistique générale*, in the version elaborated by his devotees Bally and Sechehaye, appeared in 1916, the same year as the first edition of Einstein's *General Theory of Relativity*. It is noteworthy (see RJ 1972: 74) that in 1895, while Albert Einstein was a student of the cantonal school at Aarau near Zurich, he was a boarder in Jost Winteler's household and was treated as a member of the family. Until the end of his life Einstein paid high tribute to the memory of the "clairvoyant Papa Winteler" and when as an Aarau student he started those experiments which gradually led him to the theory of relativity, he was aware of the principle of "situational relativity" (*Relativität der Verhältnisse*) enunciated in Winteler's historic dissertation of 1876.

"Sound Patterns in Language" (1925 [see 1949]) was Edward Sapir's momentous contribution to the first issue of the first volume of the review *Language*, published by the newborn Linguistic Society of America. This first American pathfinder (1884–1939) in the theoretical insights into the sound shape of language said that "a speech sound is not merely an articulation or an acoustic image, but material for symbolic expression in an appropriate linguistic context"; and it was on "the relational gaps between the sounds of a language" that Sapir put the chief emphasis. Similarly, the topological idea that in any analysis of structure "it is not things that matter but the relations between them", an idea which found a manifold expression in contemporaneous sciences and arts, was a main guide for the exponents of the Prague Linguistic Circle, founded in 1926. They endeavored to derive the characteristics of phonemes from the interrelations of these units and in the "Project of Standardized Phonological Terminology" of 1930 they defined a 'phonological unit' as a term of an opposition. The concept of 'opposition' took on fundamental importance for the inquiry into sound differences able to serve in a given language for the differentiation of cognitive meanings. The question of the relationship between the sense-discriminative units became the necessary requirement for any delineation of functional sound systems.

VII. QUEST FOR OPPOSITIONS

In the 1920s the analysis of sense-discriminative constituents of language did not go beyond the successive segments of the sound sequence; in other words, phonemes were viewed as those terms of oppositions which cannot be dissociated into smaller oppositions (see for instance RJ I: 8). This view was a corollary of the traditional, especially the enduring Saussurian, thesis ascribing a mere linearity to the sounds of language which are measurable in one dimension only: "c'est une ligne" (1916: 157). This principle is based on a vicious circle: sounds defined as segments of a temporal sequence are not supposed to be perceived as simultaneous. The striking successivity of sound units tempted one to disregard the simultaneity of their components, even though hints about the idea of simultaneous features of sounds, each of these elements carrying a sense-discriminative capacity, at times must have attracted the attention of experts. Thus, Baudouin noticed that "phonemes are not separate notes but chords composed of severals elements" (1910) and later added in his Petersburg University lectures that a semantic and morphological role is carried out not by total and indivisible phonemes, but only by their fractional motor-auditory "constituent elements", for which he coined a special Russian label, *kinakema* (see 1963: 290). Similarly, Saussure's lectures in general linguistics stressed the need to resolve the phonemes into their differential elements while taking into account the participation of negative factors as distinguished from positive ones, for instance the absence of nasal resonance in opposition to its presence (1916: 110).

The Preparatory Committee of the First International Congress of Linguists, held in The Hague in 1928, raised the question of the methods appropriate to a comprehensive view of a given language; a proposition sent in answer from Prague outlined a particular class of significative differences, namely a phonological correlation "constituted by a set of binary oppositions all of which are defined by a common criterion conceivable apart from each couple of opposites": comparative phonology was entrusted with the formulation of general laws which underlie the interconnection of these correlations within any given sound system. The division of the couples in question into the *principium divisionis* and the common substratum which unifies the two members of any opposition meant the first step in the componential analysis of phonemes into their distinctive features. The first concrete application of this prerequisite, the successful effort of Nikolaj S. Trubetzkoy (1890–1938) to approach the vowel patterns of languages from such a point of view, appeared in the first volume of the *Travaux du Cercle Linguistique de Prague* (1929), which was dedicated to the First International Congress of Slavists held that year in Prague.

After the intense discussions on the foundations of phonology at the two aforementioned congresses, and then in a more comprehensive way at the Prague International Phonological Conference of 1930, the necessity for a consistent dissociation of a phoneme into its simultaneous components was made increasingly clear. At the beginning of the 1930s, the Praguians designated the phoneme as a "set, bundle, totality of those concurrent sound properties which are used in a given language to distinguish words of unlike meaning". These properties were tentatively labeled differential or distinctive qualities or attributes and later were called 'distinctive features'. The English term emerged in the American linguistic literature of 1933, when it was used by Edward Sapir in his encyclopedia article "Language" (see 1949: 25) and by Leonard Bloomfield, who in his book *Language* oscillated on one and the same page (1933: 79) between the earlier conception of the phoneme as "a minimum unit of distinctive sound-feature" and its newer, innovative definition as a "bundle of distinctive features". (On contradictions in Bloomfield's use of the term 'distinctive feature' see Twaddell 1935: 19 ff.) With reference to the Praguian work on the dissociation of phonemes into 'binary oppositions', Zellig Harris brought to the attention of American linguists the fact that the focus of interest had been shifted "toward discovering what are the differences among the phonemes in terms of the relative speech-feature categories" (1951:

146 ff.), and the principle of basing such an analysis upon a relative approach met with his express approval.

Saussure's basic definition of differential units as "negative, relative and oppositive" has been seminal. The idea of opposition as the primary logical operation universally arising in humans from the first glimmerings of consciousness in infants and from youngsters' initial steps in the buildup of language was viewed as the natural key to the inquiry into verbal structure from its highest to its lowest levels. The inalienable property of opposition which separates it from all other, contingent differences is, when we are dealing with one opposite, the obligatory copresence of the other one in our minds, or in other words, the impossibility of evoking *long* without a simultaneous, latent idea of *short*, or *expensive* without *cheap*, 'voiced' without 'voiceless', and vice versa, as was for the first time (1938, 1939) brought to light and lucidly demonstrated by the Dutch theoretician of language Hendrik Pos (cf. below pp. 176 f.). When contending in the 1930s with the idea of opposition, linguists were unacquainted with Charles Sanders Peirce's (1839–1914) writings, which offer an astute insight into the "particular features of language" and into the concept of opposition: "The natural classification takes place by dichotomies" (Peirce I.437); "A dyad consists of two subjects brought into oneness" (I.326); "Essential dyadic relation: existence lies in opposition merely" (I.457). In Peirce's parlance "a dual relative term, such as 'lover', 'benefactor', 'servant' is a common name signifying a pair of objects". Every "relative has also a converse, produced by reversing the order of the members of the pair. Thus the converse of 'lover' is 'loved' " (III.238 & 330).

Curiously enough, some American linguists insisted on the replacement of the allegedly un-American term 'opposition' by the less telling and more ambiguous label 'contrast', despite the remarkable commentary on opposition given by this most prominent American thinker. It becomes a fundamental, operational concept not only for language (cf. Ivanov 1974), but also for social structure in general (cf. Lorrain 1975; Lévi-Strauss 1958: 37 ff., 93 ff., 257 ff., 1963, and 1971: 240 ff., 498 ff., 539 f.; Parsons & Bales 1955; Blanché 1966; Fox 1974, 1975, 1977). François Lorrain opens his research on social systems by arguing for "the privileged place of binary oppositions in the human mind" (p.17). In his dense essay on intellectual structures, R. Blanché (p.15) insists on the importance of such oppositional structures: they should not be underestimated, and in particular the organization of concepts by adversative couples appears to be an original, permanent form of thought (cf. Ungeheuer). In Wallon's formulation, "le couple, en même temps qu'il oppose, unit" (I: 117; cf. 75).

Saussure's and earlier Baudouin's (see above, p.20), recourse to the idea of opposition was an efficacious event; however, this device was not applicable to phonemes as wholes. The question "what is the opposite of the English [m]?" makes no sense. There is no unique opposite. But the feature nasality finds its true and single opposite in the absence of nasality, as Saussure anticipated (see above, p.22): all other things being equal, the nasality of [m] has its self-evident opposite in the nonnasality of [b], or of [n] in [d], or of (French) [ɔ̃] in [ɔ]. Step by step it became clear that from the dichotomous analysis of 'correlations' it was possible and indispensable to proceed to a similar, binary dissociation of all phonemes into distinctive features. The direction of inquiry was quite natural and had been foreseen in diverse patterns of spelling, for instance in the diacritic signs used by the above-mentioned (see above, p. 15 f.) Icelandic treatise (with strokes for the long vowels and dots for the nasal ones), in the treatise on Czech spelling by the many-sided reformer of the fifteenth century Jan Hus, who distinguished the palatal (compact acute) set of consonants by an inverted circumflex in contradistinction to the corresponding diffuse consonants (e. g., *ť, ď, ň, č, š, ž*), and especially in Enmun, the Korean vernacular script of the same epoch with its radical division of letters into particular strokes referring to the distinctive constituents of the native phonemes.

A systematic search for what later, in the early 1950s, was metaphorically described as the "elementary quanta of language" (cf. e. g. RJ II: 224) was devoted chiefly to the decomposition of consonants habitually aligned in the phonetic textbooks according to their place of articulation from the bilabials to the uvulars and laryngeals. This linear arrangement obstructed any questions of conceivable oppositions. It was impossible to ask: "what is opposed to the dentality of [t] or to the bilabiality of [p]?" or "what is in dichotomous terms the relation between labials and velars?" However, despite a striking distance on the string of their point of articulation, labials and velars often show their close connection in the history of phonetic changes from velars into labials and vice versa.

Particularly familiar are mutual changes between the velar and labial continuants – [x] and [f] and the corresponding voiced [ɣ] and [v] – such as Jespersen's example of the English "jump" *enough*; or the Celtic change of [ft] into [xt] (cf. Irish *secht* 'seven' with [pt] > [ft] > [xt]);

and the Dutch shift to [xt] from [ft] with *achter* for *after* (Kaiser 1929: 119); or – for stops – the Celtic change of *vesper* into *fescor*; or the interchange between [f] and [x] in various Slavic dialects, for instance in Polish *na ftórym, xtorek* and Slovenian *kožuch> kožuf, chruška> fruška, krxka> krfka, plexko> plefko*, and the reverse Czech substitution of the labial preposition by a velar one, [x] before voiceless obstruents: *ch Turnově, chpravit, ch Čechách* and [ɣ] before voiced ones: *hběhnou, h Vysokým, h Jablonci*, or Russian dialectal forms with velars instead of labials: *déxka, verëxka, xlex kúzox, x čérkox (v cerkov), krox, oxtórnik*, and a corresponding change of [v] into [ɣ]: ɣ *lése*, ɣ *uɣlú (v uglu)*, ɣ *nuk*, ɣ *dovéc*, ɣ *dom*, as well as reverse changes of velars into labials: *fto, lefkó, if, fodít', fájat'*. The Russian dialectal changes of [g] or [ɣ] into [v] may be exemplified by the masculine genitive ending of adjectives and pronouns, *-ovo*, and also by such forms as *povóst* from *pogóst* or *mnóvo* from *mnógo*, as well as the exchange between [x] and [f] in words of foreign origin, such as *kufárka* instead of *kuxárka, xrancús* instead of *francús*, and *xrukt* instead of *frukt*. In some Indonesian (namely Eastern Toba-Batak) dialects, [p] in general changes into [k]: for instance *piso* 'knife' > *kiso* (see Meillet & Cohen 1924: 418 f.). Also typical are the Czech dialectal variant *kařez* instead of *pařez* and such children's oscillations between velars and labials as Czech *telefon* and *vousy* changed into *exon* and *xosi* or in Peking Chinese *xuŋ* from *fuŋ* (see Ohnesorg 1959: 30, 44).

It was especially in this and similar connections that the question of a property joining labials with velars in opposition to the common feature of dentals and palatals, as well as the question of the feature common to labials and dentals in contradistinction to that of velars and palatals, was brought into consideration, especially since each of these paired groups displays characteristic interchanges in the history of world languages. The preliminary solution to this complex of questions and to the problem of interconnections between the consonantal and vocalic patterns was presented for discussion at the Third International Congress of Phonetic Sciences in Ghent in 1938 (See RJ I: 272 ff.), on the eve of the world events which put an end to the Prague phonological deliberations and in general radically changed the topography of international scientific activities.

Any notion of opposites is inseparable from the notion of opposition as such and neither of the two opposites can function in the neighborhood of other concurrent or successive features if such a neighborhood excludes the appearance of the other opposite. If instead of the explicit designation of an opposition, for example nasality ~ nonnasality, we use the abbreviation 'the nasality feature', ambiguities cannot arise, because the feature is present only in those contexts where both members of the opposition – nasal and nonnasal – are admissible. In Russian the opposition of voiced and voiceless obstruents functions only before phonemes other than obstruents; therefore the voicelessness of the word-final consonant in [luk] loses its distinctiveness, and the nominatives of the two nouns whose datives are [lúku] 'to the bow' and [lúgu] 'to the meadow' become homonymous. The sound-form [d'étkə] corresponds to both *d'etka* 'kid' and *d'edka* 'grandpa'; and in the sentence – highly improbable precisely because of its flagrant homonymy – *èto ne* [*d'étkə*] *a* [*d'étkə*] *prokazit* 'it's not the youngster but the grandpa (or not the grandpa but the youngster) who plays tricks', the question of the detected trickster remains ambiguous. Compare cognate derivatives with an initial vowel of the second, antecedent suffix, such as [d'étuškə] 'kiddy' and [d'éduškə] 'grandpa'. It is self-evident that to look for a distinctive feature in positions where no distinction is possible is a gross contradiction in terms. If in certain contexts only one of the opposites can appear, the feature loses its distinctiveness and becomes inactive and disabled. The opposition is alive when both opposites are able to occur in the same context, given, that is, the identity of concurrent and adjacent features.

The question of whether the dichotomous scale is inherent in the structure of language or whether it is only a profitable principle for inquiry into that structure, a device imposed by the analyst upon the linguistic material, has been repeatedly raised. The Russian linguist Vjačeslav V. Ivanov has devoted several penetrating studies to binary relations as an intrinsic qualitative property "permeating the entire system of language and enabling one to describe it as a monolithic whole and not an accumulation of scattered data" (1972). Far from being a mere heuristic guide, the question of binary choices faces any interlocutor, for example whenever it is necessary for the addresser to bring to the knowledge of the addressee whether in the sentence cited near the beginning of this chapter, *deal* or *zeal*, *showed* or *shows*, *tailor* or *sailor*, etc., are meant. A choice between the two alternatives, stop or continuant, through the recognition of the appropriate one, is of course demanded not only from the linguistic inquirer, but first and foremost from the listener of the message, regardless of whether the identificational process is conscious or subliminal (cf. Muljačić 1977; Mel'čuk 1977: 292 ff.).

The difference between a single and a multiple distinction is palpable for the speakers. Thus, there is a single binary distinction between *seal* and *zeal*; similarly, the distinction between *seal* and *feel* is single but that between *seal* and *veal* is double, a simultaneous pair of two binary distinctions; between *zeal* and *dill* there is a sequentially double distinction – one in the initial consonant and the other in the vowel. Finally, the discrimination of *sill* and *bill* is based on a triple concurrent distinction. And again we must say that the difference between a single and a multiple distinction and between a simultaneous and a sequential one is a palpable operation both for linguistic analysis and for actual interlocutors. Lev Tolstoj acknowledged that he endowed some characters of *War and Peace* with generally known aristocratic Russian family names, which he changed only slightly, so that they would sound familiar to his readership. In each case he played with one single featural distinction: he made *Bolkonskij* from *Volkonskij* and *Drubeckoj* from *Trubeckoj*. These names sound quite natural, whereas with a double distinction they would have become grotesque, for instance *Dolkonskij* or *Polkonskij* or *Zrubeckoj*. Children also show an acute feeling for single distinctions. As Čukovskij (1966) reported, a Russian child complained about the word *došlyj* ('shrewd'), which he felt to be too close to *doxlyj* ('putrid'). Among various characteristic examples, Willem Kaper (1959) quotes a four-year-old Dutch boy who amused himself with the sound-meaning differences between the rhyming words *peertje* 'little pear' and *beertje* 'little bear'. Another Dutch boy, according to Kaper's report, announced with pleasure to his mother that both *Piet* (proper name) and *biet* 'beet' really exist. A similar pleasure is felt by children in the juxtaposition of an extant word with an invented one distinguished by a single feature: *pink is bink, bink is pink*.

Of course, any speech sound exists for its producer as well as for the perceiver both as a whole and as a concurrence of those parts which are imposed by the code of their language and imply single distinctions. The parts are exemplified for the consonant [s] by its distinctions from [z], [t], [f], and [š] in French and also from [θ] in English and from palatalized [s'] in Russian. In an analogous way, *seal* exists simultaneously for speakers of English both as a lexical whole and as a sequence of its speech sounds, just as in turn a whole conventional sentence, such as *take it easy*, necessarily coexists in the mind of speakers both as a phraseological whole and as a set of single words. When discussing the pattern of features (1973), the adept analyst of speech Gunnar Fant rightly viewed their pattern as "a matter of coding convenience only", but the code and its conveniences are much more enrooted in the users of language than in its explorers despite the fact that the users of the verbal code may be unaccustomed to taking its conveniences into deliberate examination. For the sake of efficiency the perception of the sense-discriminative cues naturally has recourse to the polar differentiators facing the native decoder with a set of bare yes-or-no decisions between any two members of binary oppositions. In this way, the need for maximal simplicity, not only in the scientist's approach to the sound pattern of language, but first and foremost in the daily strategy of the language user, is fulfilled, especially since the number of oppositions in any given language is prefabricated and strictly limited for the apprehension of its speakers and perceivers.

VIII. FEATURES AND PHONEMES

It has been questioned whether linguistic operations with phonemes would not be more advantageous than those dealing directly with their ultimate constituents. The comparison of phonemes and distinctive features with respect to the most productive concept of opposition shows, as mentioned above (pp. 25 f.), that this concept, consistently applicable to the distinctive features, cannot be extended to the phoneme. A phoneme, being a bundle of distinctive features, proves to be an ever important but derivative unit, a complex, simultaneous construct of a set of elementary concurrent units. It can be compared in this respect to the syllable, which is a constructive complex unit within the verbal sequence. However, it is to be noted here that the sequence implies concurrence, while the reverse is not always the case. For instance, French vocabulary offers such homonymous words as /u/ 'where' and /u/ 'or'. And the Latin imperative /i/ 'go' may function as an entire utterance.

The difficulty or even the impossibility of a consistent segmentation of a sequence into phonemes has again and again been confirmed by instrumental studies both on the motor and on the acoustic level. The process of multifarious coarticulation was first thoroughly pursued by Paul Menzerath (1883–1954) and was impressively demonstrated by him with the help of an X-ray sound film at the Rome International Congress of Linguists in 1933. Through manifold experiments and instrumental observations of the articulatory process of speech, he came to the conclusion that "a speech sound has no position; speech is a continuous, uninterrupted movement, irregardless of whether the sounds are vowels, diphthongs, or consonants, even plosives. All of them are gliding sounds ⟨...⟩ A sound sequence in an articulatory sense does not exist. The parts combined into a word prove to form not a chain but an interweaving. An acoustically later sound may begin articulatorily before the acoustically earlier sound" (Menzerath & Lacerda 1933).

These observations have recently been supplemented by the comprehensive acoustic, primarily spectrographic data of Haskins Laboratories. Yet, these impediments disappear as soon as we go from the level of phonemes to the segmentation of the speech sequence into the succession of distinctive features. The diverse features can exhibit different limits of duration in the sequence, for they often capture a large portion of the preceding phoneme or on the contrary begin in the middle of the phoneme to which they belong; they may spread over into the next phoneme or cease in the middle of their own phoneme. The relative order of these features, however, usually remains the same, apart from rare and insignificant digressions. As a rule, the divergence between the limits of the implementation of different features does not cancel their concurrence in a certain at least minimal segment of the string, so that localization of their co-occurrence is usually preserved, except in the negligent, elliptic variant of speech. Thus, the segmentation of a sequence into successive features permits its further segmentation into phonemes. The temporal order of phonemes remains an undeniably significative factor – cf. Russian *rvu* 'I tear' vs. *vru* 'I lie', or Czech *vře* 'boils' vs. *řve* 'shouts' vs. *řev* 'roar'.

One cannot but agree that "we are a long way off from a really well-developed model of the speech perception process" (cf. Pisoni 1975: 98), yet indeed direct recourse to "the basic primes" defended by Sheila Blumstein and William Cooper (1972: 208) is indispensable, for "within any language system every phoneme is characterized by the minimum number of features needed to distinguish it from all other phonemes of that system", and such direct recourse ensures the most exact application of those two vital principles of relativity and invariance which underlie any present scientific task. The strategy of these fundamental tasks will be touched upon below, but the direct approach to the listener's experience seems to be often a simpler pathway than the search for the speaker's commands to the articulatory muscles, especially since "we cannot at the present time observe those processes nor can we directly measure their output" (Liberman, Cooper, et al. 1967: 446 ff.); moreover, "when the temporally overlapping gestures for successive phonemes involve more or less adjacent muscles that control the same structures, it is of course more difficult to discover whether there is invariance or not". In a recent survey volume edited by Ljudmila Čistovič on theories of speech perception, the motor theory is said to have been very popular some ten years ago; although this theory gave hope for finding the key to speech perception by detecting the "motor commands", the unjustified assumption of their standard nature was superseded by proof of their high variability. It became obvious that "in order to describe and model the process of governed speech production, it is necessary to turn to such a notion as the aim of the motor act, and the solely evident aim is the production of a definite acoustic effect accessible and 'understandable' to the listener" (Čistovič et al. 1976: 31 ff.).

At the beginning of our century, one of the most perspicacious phoneticians of his time, Alexander Thomson (1860–1935), again and again rejected the still ineradicable efforts to exaggerate the articulatory criteria for the listener's speech interpretation: "It is not the movements of the speech organs but the speech sounds themselves which are primary in language. The sounds are a more uniform and more constant element in language." Deprived of acoustic analysis, the "physiology of any sounds whatever remains incomprehensible, since the articulation is only a means to an end". Through the analysis of consonants, Thomson brings to light the fact that "the dorsal or coronal way of articulation, a difference which fallaciously is highly regarded, is by itself quite inessential for the sound and the choice is chiefly determined by the height of the tone assigned to the noise" (Thomson 1909 and 1934).

An additional reason for following the path of analysis from the features to phonemes and not vice versa and for the advantages of a featural transcription over a simple notation of mere unanalyzed phonemes is the possibility of an unambiguous answer to the question of the presence vs. absence of a given distinctive feature in its two terms, whereas the makeup of a phoneme is different according to the context. Thus for instance, in the Russian adverb *zdes'* 'here', the initial consonant lacks two distinctive features proper to the phonemes /z/, /z'/, /s/, and /s'/ in prevocalic position, e.g. *zad* = [zat] 'back', *zjat'* = [z'at'] 'son-in-law', *sad* = [sat] 'garden', *sjad'* [s'at'] 'sit down'. Hence the initial sibilant appears here as an 'incomplete phoneme', because before obstruents the normally distinctive opposition of voicing and voicelessness is canceled and likewise the opposition of palatalized and nonpalatalized dentals is discarded before another dental. The question of rendering such 'incomplete' phonemes in transcription creates unavoidable complications and disagreements as long as spelling is based not on features themselves but on entire phonemes. The distinction between such tense and lax consonants as /t/ and /d/ or /s/ and /z/ is lost in English after obstruents (cf. the final [d] and [z] in *ribbed* and *ribs* and the final [t] and [s] in *ripped* and *rips*). In German dialects where only [z] occurs initially and only [s] finally, the phonemes /s/ and /z/ do not display the tense ~ lax distinction in other than some internal positions (e.g., *weisse* and *weise*) and this distinction remains valid only as long as the antecedent diphthong [ay] in relation to the following consonant does not carry its own significant distinction. In those positions where the tense ~ lax distinction is not operative, the German hissing sibilant phoneme is quite incomplete: nondistinctively lax in a prevocalic and nondistinctively tense in a postvocalic position. Cf. *Saus* [zaʊs] 'rush', gen. *Sauses* [zaʊzəs].

IX. SPEECH SOUNDS AND THE BRAIN

The frequent French designation of distinctive features as *traits pertinents* easily leads to misconceptions; besides distinctive features the sound shape of language contains a few other kinds of likewise pertinent, functional features. Only the degree and not the fact of their pertinence can be questioned. One may be an adamant 'featurist', but one should not disregard the manifest copresence and functioning of classes of features other than the distinctive ones. It should not be forgotten that speech sounds are tools of verbal communication and that their entire makeup is an ensemble of diverse types of features, all of which fulfill an interplay of tasks essential for communication. In the process of communication, none of these features remains insignificant or immaterial. The obsolete but recurrent view of a phonetic description of articulatory and physico- and psycho-acoustic phenomena as one which disregards their role in language and their communicative significance not only inhibits inquiry, but above all arbitrarily suppresses the fundamental question of the manifold goals that these phenomena pursue.

Such lack of respect for the multifold significance of sound shapes causes a dangerous truncation of the analyst's task and curbs rational classification. Particularly vain is psychoacoustic, perceptual speech analysis if done without regard for those diverse linguistic values of the sensory stimuli which are picked up by the native perceiver, whose selectional response to such stimuli depends precisely on their informational cues, most of them socially codified.

In light of the functional load of these sensory elements, which all fulfill some semiotic duty, the view of phonetics as *abstraction faite de fonction* now appears to us to be outdated, unrealistic, and emasculated. More and more we realize that speech sounds as a whole are an artifact built precisely for speech and are thus self-evidently goal-directed. The idea of "gross, raw" phonic matter, "amorphous substance", is a fiction. Discrete articulated sounds did not exist before language, and it is pointless and perverse to consider such "phonic stuff" without reference to its linguistic utilization. The growth of language and the development of the human supralaryngeal vocal apparatus are interconnected innovations (cf. Lieberman 1975: 35); in particular the hominid dental evolution turned the oral cavity into the best resonating chamber for linguistic use (Sheets 1977). And it is for their verbal purpose that speech sounds were formed and submitted to a special hierarchical organization.

The Old Indic theoreticians of language made a clear-cut distinction not only between *varṇa sphoṭa*, the sense-discriminative constituent in speech sounds, and *dhvani* 'speech sound' in general, but also between the latter and *śabda* 'nonspeech sound'. Any individual uttering of a speech sound, which Bhartṛhari named *vaikṛta-dhvani* 'modified sound', presents differences of diction, but behind these fluctuations inherent in given messages there is a codified, fixed sound-design, *prakṛta-dhvani* 'primary sound', encompassing all those sound properties which are normally produced by the speakers and perceived by the listeners of a given speech community. Only some of these integral properties, those connected with meaning, pertain to the *varṇa sphoṭa*.

Thomas Aquinas opposed speech sounds, *voces*, to sounds emitted *naturaliter* by animals. The former he characterized as *voces significantes, ex institutione humanae rationis et voluntatis*. His definition of speech sounds as *significantia artificialiter* and given *ad significandum* appears to be the most valid one, especially now that a radical division between speech and nonspeech sounds is becoming increasingly evident (cf. Manthey 1937). Sapir taught that "speech sounds exist merely because they are the symbolic carriers of significant concepts and groupings of concepts" (1921: 184). In his study of 1925 cited above, he compared the candle-blowing "wh" with the externally similar speech sound [hw] (*wh*), pointing to the essential difference between the two sounds, the latter of which is "'placed' with reference to other sounds" and to "relational gaps" between all of them, whereas its candle-blowing homonym is "not spaced off from nor related to other sounds – say the sound of humming and the sound of clearing one's throat." In his later, 1933 paper on the psychological reality of phonemes, Sapir presaged that "it may even be seriously doubted whether the innervation of speech sound articulation is ever actually the same type of physiological fact as the innervation of 'identical' articulations that have no linguistic context" (see 1949).

Since the early 1960s (Kimura 1961, 1967; cf. also Broadbent 1954) the widespread, constantly progressing and developing experiments with dichotic hearing, that is, with listening to different stimuli presented simultaneously to both ears, have proved the privileged position of the right ear and correspondingly of the left (dominant) hemisphere of the brain for the perception of speech sounds within real, meaningful words, synthetic nonsense syllables, and even in speech played backwards (see Mattingly et al. 1971). On the other hand, the left ear and correspondingly the right (nondominant) hemisphere of the brain showed a greater capacity for all other auditory stimuli, such as musical tones and melodies (both unknown and familiar), sonar signals (see Webster & Chaney 1967), and environmental noises such as a car starting, the sharpening of a pencil, water running, and oral emissions apart from speech – coughing, crying, laughing, humming, yawning, snoring, sniffling, sighing, panting, or sobbing (see Figure 2).

Doubts expressed at the outset of these experiments as to the advantage of the right ear for discerning separate vowels were dispelled by the confirmation of this laterality whenever isolated vowels were pronounced at the average speed of spoken language or when the fact that they pertain to speech had been anticipated by the listener (Spellacy & Blumstein 1970; Haggard 1971; Lisenko 1971; King & Kimura 1972). The greater efficiency of the contralateral auditory pathways in comparison with the ipsilateral direction, as well as the dependence of speech recognition and discrimination on left temporal acuity, were powerfully proved by these significant experiments, which disclose not only the divergent treatment of speech constituents from all other sound matter, but also the relative perceptual recognizability and dis-

LEFT HEMISPHERE   RIGHT HEMISPHERE
    (DIGITS)   (MELODIES)

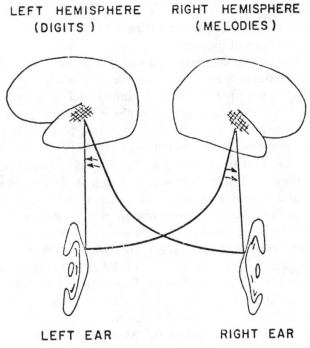

LEFT EAR   RIGHT EAR

Figure 2.
Neuroanatomical schema for the auditory asymmetries.
From D. Kimura,1967, in *Cortex* 3, p. 174.

criminability of diverse categories of speech sounds. While some initial hints at further insights into these matters may be found in extant reports (cf. for instance Studdert-Kennedy & Shankweiler 1970; Berlin et al. 1973; and Darwin 1971), and while material other than English is beginning to attract the attention of experimenters (cf. Kok et al. 1971; Shimizu 1975), more active cooperation with linguists in this search and in the interpretation of the results may throw further light on these critical problems. Although so far only the first steps in the linguistic analysis and interpretation of the dichotic listening technique have been ventured (cf. particularly Blumstein 1974), it is already evident that speech sounds, at least from the moment they are perceived by the listener, occupy an obviously particular place directly opposite to all other aural percepts; therefore, in view of this new criterion, the earlier attempts to include speech and nonspeech sounds in a common classificatory table can no longer be justified. Previous surmises that "the controlling mechanisms of non-speech sounds are quite similar to those of speech sounds" (cf. Pike 1943: chap. 2, sec. 8) are invalidated by the research on the different pathways of speech and nonspeech sounds to the brain of the listener.

Split-brain studies connected with section of the cerebral commissures of epileptics have been pursued since the 1960s (see Gazzaniga & Sperry 1967). They show that speech, writing, and calculation depend almost exclusively on the major hemisphere. In his rich, critical summary of experiments with split-brain subjects, Stephen D. Krashen concludes that after left lesions only stereotyped, automatic language remains (1976: 176) and he refers to the convincing case of left hemispherectomy described by A. Smith: after surgery, the patient suffered from global aphasia but preserved his ability to curse and swear. Attempts have been made to analyze responses to natural speech stimuli recorded from scalp electrodes symmetrically placed over the two cerebral hemispheres simultaneously (see Wood, Goff, & Day 1971; Morrell & Salamy 1971; Cohn 1971; Neville 1974; Molfese, Freeman, & Palermo 1975; Harnad et al. 1977). This research has contributed to grasping the functional specialization of the two hemispheres and in particular the respective ways in which they treat auditory stimuli – both linguistic and nonlinguistic (cf. Mosidze & Akbardija 1973, as well as the surveys in the 1977 Segalowicz & Gruber volume).

However, through the last ten years it has been the intensive Russian investigation of changes – in both perception and execution – manifested by schizophrenic and depressive patients during the first few minutes after unilateral applications of electroconvulsive therapy which has given the deepest and most consistent insight into the speech and hearing capacities of the two hemispheres. The very promising results of the systematic inquiry into the far-reaching differences between the functions of the two hemispheres and into their vital complementarity have been instructively outlined in Lev Balonov and Vadim Deglin's absorbing Russian monograph of 1976, *Hearing and Speech of the Dominant and Non-Dominant Hemispheres* (with an exhaustive bibliography). The comprehensive content of this book gives evidence of a continuously growing understanding of the part played by each of the two hemispheres in the organization of speech production and perception.

The temporary inactivation of the left hemisphere causes a proclivity toward a "desemantization" of words and reduces the comprehension and active mastery of words and phrases as well as the intelligibility of phonemes. The perception and reproduction of single speech sounds is severely inhibited. Selective attention to words and their components breaks down. This is not a disintegration of hearing as such, but the loss of speech hearing only (cf. Traugott & Kajdanova 1975); the categorial apperception of phonemes and of their distinctive features is shaken. According to a pertinent remark by Balonov & Deglin (1976), the paradigmatic frontiers between phonemes undergo a kind of "erosion" (p.160f.). The orderly hierarchical organization of sense-discriminative elements and of their bundles into phonemes is judiciously viewed by the two authors as a "supra-sensory formation" (p.144). Under the inactivation of the left hemisphere this network of distinctive features loses its stability and equilibrium, but the disintegration of this system in turn reveals a hierarchical order in the deficits suffered by patients. The authors are right in their assertion that the featural composition of phonemes remains the decisive symptom at all stages of the patients' responses. The most common types of confusion between phonemes are limited to one single distinctive feature, and the various features manifest different degrees of resistibility. Thus, the vocalic opposition compact ~ diffuse (see below, pp. 101 ff.) and the optimum of compactness, /a/, are the steadiest constituents, whereas the distinction /o/ ~/e/ and /u/ ~/i/ easily disappears (Balonov & Deglin 1976: 132, 142, 181). It is noteworthy that shock therapy of the right hemisphere has proved that "the perception of vowels when they are close in duration to vowels in the ordinary speech stream is performed by the left hemisphere" (p.141).

The comparison of such disruptions with spontaneous aphasic disturbances suggests itself, especially since "aphasic disorders in general result essentially from lesions on the left hemisphere" (Hécaen 1969: 308). Pathologists of language have maintained that 'sensory' aphasia with its decoding impairments is tied to posterotemporal lesions of the cortex, whereas frontotemporal lesions are responsible for 'motor' aphasia with its encoding impairments (cf. Luria 1958: 27 ff.; RJ I: 289-305). The current inquiry into the effects of unilateral electric shocks with respect to the difference in the left-side position of the convulsive electrodes reveals that their posterotemporal location effects mostly syndromes of sensory aphasia with disturbances in the perception of speech sounds. On the other hand, the frontotemporal placement of electrodes most frequently results in syndromes of motor aphasia and in a lowering of speech activity (see Balonov & Deglin: p.191). Briefly, there appears an instructive analogy between the localization of electrodes in shock therapy and that of brain lesions in aphasiology, an analogy which opens new vistas to the cerebral topography of diverse linguistic manifestations.

No doubt the gradual restoration of the disturbed system at the end of the short-lived aphasic stage caused by the electric shock must attract the special attention of observers and inquirers into the patient's linguistic experience. And indeed it had already been noted in 1940–41 in analogous cases of insulin shock that the gradual recovery of speech corresponds in its relative chronolgy to the progressing sound pattern of children's language (see RJ I: 370). In one such case, Professor B. I. Jacobowski, director of an Uppsala psychiatric clinic, asked a schizophrenic who was recovering from insulin shock and had started to regain his speech capacity to recite the Swedish alphabet. Beforehand, the medical assistants were given copies of the alphabet with marginal indications by RJ (prompted by his linguistic experience with children) as to what spelling names would be omitted or distorted at first by the patient and what the order of their restitution would be at his repeated performances. The expected order of mistakes and their corrections, based on the analogy between children's acquisition and patients' reacquisition of the speech sound pattern, for the most part was confirmed.

The recognition of all auditory stimuli outside of language is supervised solely by the right hemisphere (Balonov & Deglin: p.77 ff.). Its inactivation affects neither speech sounds nor word units, but has a totally destructive effect on all other auditory stimuli: noises of humans and animals, of industry, transport, and of natural forces, as well as musical tones, chords, and melodies (cf. Gordon 1970; Mindadze et al. 1975), even when these auditory stimuli are quite familiar to the patient. Subjects with a temporarily inactivated right hemisphere were helpless when faced with a succession of the following auditory stimuli, which were perfectly recognizable as long as this hemisphere remained active: the ringing of a clock, singing birds, splashing water, neighing horses, a howling snowstorm, a roaring lion, a crying child, the clatter of crockery, peals of thunder, a grunting pig, the clank of metal, the call of a rooster, snoring, a barking dog, a lowing cow, the sound of a furnace, footsteps, a cooing dove, the rumble of a plane, cackling geese, a ringing telephone, the thundering of waves at high tide (Balonov & Deglin: p.77). During the inactivation of the right hemisphere, the noise of applause was actually taken for the winnowing of grain, laughter for crying, thunder for an engine, the squeal of a pig for the noise of a caterpillar tractor, the honking of geese for the croaking of frogs, a dog barking for the cackling of hens, the noise of a motorcycle for that of an animal, etc. (pp. 80 ff.).

On the other hand, with respect to language the right hemisphere acts as a "brake" or "censor"; it exerts a "damping" influence on the language centers of the left hemisphere (pp.145 f., 182 ff., 186; for the role of the right hemisphere as a 'speech framer' see below, pp. 49 f.).

The recent copious report of Eran Zaidel of the California Institute of Technology about the verbal conduct of split-brain patients (1978: 229 ff.) corroborates the signal results of the electrotherapeutic experiments reported by Balonov & Deglin. Unlike the left hemisphere, which performs a consistent "distinctive feature analysis", the right hemisphere, with its "reduced efficiency" and poor discriminatory ability, fails particularly "to analyze correctly long non-redundant sentences in which order is important and the context is not helpful". According to Zaidel, this "limitation may be attributed to a restricted (perhaps as small as a 3-item) short-term verbal memory" (p. 269). The right hemisphere proves to be "3 times" less efficient in sound pairs that differ in two features than in pairs differing in one feature (p. 243), and it recognizes more easily the unmarked varieties than their marked counterparts, e. g. plosives and orals than the marked continuants and nasals (p. 241). Finally, once again it was made evident that the motor theories of speech perception "are not physiologically necessary to account for comprehension" (p. 258). The endeavor of the international research to separate out the activities of the two hemispheres has actually succeeded in bisecting the brain, *cere comminuit brum*, according to the audacious word figure of Quintus Ennius (239–169 B.C.; see Vahlen 1854: 85), and herewith has opened a broad outlook for an insight into the brain and its language mechanisms.

X. REDUNDANCY

Redundant features occupy a considerable place in the sound shape of speech and must be accounted for by speech analysis. Rather than being superfluous and useless, as the age-old term "redundancy" infelicitously suggests, they serve to support and enhance the distinctive features, yet must at the same time be carefully distinguished from them. The auxiliary role of redundancy is to provide complementary information about the identity of contiguous distinctive features which are either adjacent (preceding or subsequent) in the sequence or concurrent with the redundant features. We may quote a still valid remark by the psychophysicist Stanley Smith Stevens (1906-1973): "The fact of redundancy increases the reliability of speech communication and makes it resistant to many types of distortion. By limiting the number of discriminations required of the listener and by assisting his choice through the redundant coding of information, we make talking to one another a reasonably satisfactory business" (1950: 690).

Both a lack of attention on the analyst's part to the framework of redundant features and the danger of intermingling distinctive features with redundancies without respect for the obvious, natural hierarchy of the two classes must be prudently avoided in order to allow an adequate description and hierarchic explanation of linguistic wholes and parts. Against the aprioristic doubts of detached onlookers (cf. Bar-Hillel 1957: 326 f.), an objective and exhaustive examination of linguistic data unfailingly shows that the discrimination of distinctive and redundant features is an intrinsic task. The difference between the "independently significant" (in Sweet's terms) distinctive features and the redundant ones is objectively contained in the data, notwithstanding the hypotheses of critics who are unfamiliar with technical linguistic requirements but prone to interpret the delimitation of distinctive and redundant features as an arbitrary decision and terminological contrivance on the part of linguists.

The lucid example of vocalic nasality in such American English vocables as *win, whim,* and *wing* shows that, in contradistinction to the consonants, where nasality occurs not only in postvocalic but also in other positions, the nasal vowels are always bound to the nasal consonants that follow, whether the latter are fully or at least allusively implemented. (Cf. p. 10 above, and Malécot 1960.) Consequently, consonantal nasality in English is independently significant, whereas vocalic nasality is a mere redundancy anticipating the ensuing nasal consonant, notwithstanding the fact that at times, especially in elliptic speech, this anticipatory redundant feature may nearly take over the discriminative function of the consonantal nasality.

The independently significant opposition of palatalized (sharp) and nonpalatalized consonants in Russian occurs both with and without a following vowel, and especially at the end of a word. The opposition is supported in prevocalic consonants by a redundant difference between a more advanced and a more retracted articulation of vowels after palatalized and after nonpalatalized consonants respectively. Hence, for instance, the front [i] and the back [ɯ] prove to be two contextual implementations of one and the same phoneme and their difference is a redundant feature signaling the opposition between the antecedent presence or absence of palatalization; however, in other positions the same distinction of these two kinds of consonants is deprived of this redundant support: cf. *kel't* [t] 'Celt' and *sel'd'* [t'] 'herring'; *košt* [št] 'living expenditures' and *vožd'* [št'] 'leader'.

The opposition of voicing and voicelessness carries its independently sense-discriminative capacity in Russian obstruents when a vowel either follows immediately or is separated from the obstruent by a nasal, a liquid, or a /v/ (see RJ 1978). In all other situations, the voicing or the voicelessness of these obstruents is redundant; it can merely point to a subsequent voiced or voiceless phoneme, as for example in the case of the initial continuants *žgut* und *škura*. With /č/ and /c/ the lack of voicing before a vowel is a redundant feature: it points to the concurrent distinctive features which build the affricate (abruptness combined with stridency) and in this way it underlines the difference between such words as *cýkat'* 'hush' and *zýkat'* 'shout', *cugovój* 'harnessed one before the other' and *dugovój* 'bow-shaped'. A feature occuring in Russian as redundant solely is tenseness. For example, the tense [e] in contradistinction to the lax [ɛ] occurs at present only between two palatalized consonants, e.g. [m'ɛl] 'chalk' and [m'el'] 'shoal'. Among consonants, the difference lax ~ tense is a redundant feature which in Russian only accompanies the actual distinctive feature voicing ~ voicelessness (see chap. 3). The redundant feature reinforces a given distinctive feature, but only in the latter's sense-discriminative function, and not in the sense-determinative role. In this regard the loss of the opposition voicing ~ voicelessness at the end of a word in Russian can cancel a word distinction, as we see for example in the nominative [ab'ɛt] 'dinner' or 'vow' versus some other case form of the same nouns, such as dative [ab'ɛdu] ~ [ab'ɛtu] respectively.

XI. CONFIGURATIVE FEATURES

Since Trubetzkoy's guiding initiative of the early 1930s, summed up later in his posthumous *Principles of Phonology (Grundzüge der Phonologie)*, linguists (such as Bloomfield 1939; Harris 1951 and 1963; Chomsky & Halle 1968; and others) have paid increasing attention to the complex class of configurative features, which, as is generally known, "signal the division of the utterance into grammatical units of different degrees of complexity", namely into phrases, words, and their diverse morphological components. The integration and delimitation of words and their constituents are achieved either by particular rules for the use of distinctive features and of their combinations or by other, quite special signals. To exemplify the utilization of distinctive features for delimitation, let us note the widespread difference between the repertory of phonemes and of their groupings at the beginning, at the end, and in the interior of words and smaller grammatical units. We may cite, as a means of integration, the use of so-called 'free' stress in those languages where its position is not in a unilateral dependence on the word boundary: here the opposition of stressed and unstressed vowels fulfills both a sense-discriminative and an integrational, namely culminative, function. For example, in Russian, stress distinguishes the meanings of *pláču* 'I cry' and *plačú* I 'I pay'; even in long words such as *presmykájuščiesja* 'reptiles', one single stress signals the unity of a word. Another device which fulfills such an integrating role is known as vowel harmony and, according to Baudouin's favorite metaphor, serves to "cement" all the syllables of words or of smaller grammatical units (see below, p. 149).

In languages with a fixed word-accent, for instance in Czech, where stress falls on the first syllable of the word, the difference between stressed and unstressed vowels is not a distinctive, but merely a configurative means. It serves only for the demarcation and integration of words and separates them both from the neighboring stressed words and from the proclitic conjunctions (cf. the word group *alogický a logický* 'illogical and logical', with the stress on the initial vowel of both adjectives). There is an essential functional difference between the distinctive and the configurative features which is comparable to the hierarchical difference between letters and punctuation marks. The absence of commas and even, as ancient scripts testify, the total omission of spaces between words do not hinder the comprehension of the texts, as the complete lack of letters would obviously do. Thus the role of sense-discriminative items is primary as compared to the subordinate implementation of the configurative features.

It has been emphasized that grammatical units and their boundaries exist for the speaker and listener even if they are not expressed. For a wider scrutiny of fixed and free accent from this point of view, see the comparative study of Czech and Russian verse (RJ 1923) and particularly its argumentation: "May the word boundaries serve as a factor which conditions certain sound phenomena or is it on the contrary

Czech stress that determines the word boundaries? In the latter case Czech stress would unquestionably be a meaningful, innerly conditioned element. Yet the word exists in the linguistic mind irrespective of indispensable acoustic limits." In American linguistics, in reply to some endeavors to attach boundary signals to the class of phonemes as a subsection of "secondary phonemes" (Bloomfield 1933), Chomsky has adopted the traditional Praguian viewpoint: "The phrases are 'abstract' in the sense that neither their boundaries nor their categories need be physically marked" (1975: 32). The relative primacy of the sense-discriminative elements of the speech sounds is thus duly acknowledged.

XII. STYLISTIC VARIATIONS

So-called 'free' or, to be more precise, 'stylistic' variations are, to a high degree, ways of coloring and diversifying speech by digressing from neutral style to emotive varieties of the overall code. To such subcodes belong the slowed-down or on the contrary the slurred, the exclamatory or the softened, the excited or the subdued styles of expression which apply the diverse devices of prolonging or reducing the tempo of articulation and of strengthening and heightening or weakening and lowering various sounds. "There is", as the phonetician Daniel Jones (1881–1967) thought, "what we may call the 'ordinary' or 'slow conversational' style, there are very rapid familiar styles, and there is formal style used for instance in reciting or reading aloud to a large audience, and there are styles intermediate between these. With some speakers ⟨...⟩ the differences are considerable and may involve the use in formal and in very rapid styles of sounds not occuring at all in the 'ordinary' style" (1962: 197). In his once-renowned manual of natural stage speech, S. Volkonskij warned actors and reciters not to impart to their diction the tinge of one particular vowel, for instance in tragic style the habitual shift of [a] toward [ɯ], e.g. *zn[ɯ]eš li*, or in a tone of elegant ease the shift of [a] to [ɛ], e.g. *[dɛrɛ]gój i[vɛ́]n i[vɛ́]novič*. He also condemned the [u] or [uo] nuance of the mincing feminine Moscovite style: *n[u] št[ú] èto tak[ú]e* (1913: 55). A similar labialization of vowels in the "sweet prattling" of Latvian women has been noted (Rūķe-Draviņa 1952: 68 ff.). The *manière affectée* of pronouncing [ə], [a] almost as [œ], [æ] by many Parisian ladies was observed by Passy (1891: 248).

Such effects are ordinarily superposed onto the distinctive features of a given language without conflicting with them. Thus for instance, according to Georg von Gabelentz, in those dialects of Saxony which do not have the front rounded phonemes /ü/, /ø/, and /œ/, these sounds occur when one is talking about gloomy and deep things – "von einer tüfen Fünsternüss" (1891: 362). If a language has at its disposal a distinction between long and short vowels, usually only the long ones may undergo further lengthening and only the short ones are subject to an expressive shortening. But the strong intervention of an emotive tinge is able to threaten the distinctive oppositions themselves. When approaching such variations of English as the use or omission of the prevocalic glottal catch between words in close syntactic interdependence, one observes that the occurence of this sound belongs to a style seeking a sharper segregation of words within a sequence.

"Lumps" of emotive function, such as interjections, tend to use sounds and clusters otherwise alien to a given language or to language in general; cf. English examples such as the interjections conventionally spelled (especially in comic strips) *tut,* described by Webster's as "placing the tip of the tongue against the alveolar ridge and suddenly sucking in air – used to express disapproval or disbelief"; *brr,* a bilabial trill; and *phooey.* Dwight Bolinger quotes such conventionally written exclamations as *uh-huh* and *hunh-uh* ("the latter with a distinctive glottal stop"), *phew,* and *hynah-hynah,* in addition to the warning [ˀəˀˀəˀ] (1963: 122f.).

The emotive features superimposed upon notional speech differ from the distinctive features by their gradual, rather than binary, oppositional character: the emphasis can be of different degrees. Moreover, these features are not necessarily confined to a single segment of the speech sequence and show a tendency to expand and cover a longer section. For instance, we observe durational variations in several successive speech sounds. The distinctive features are compulsory elements of the linguistic code, whereas emotive features occur as an optional property of individual speech performances. Emotive features are socially coded rather than mandatory; therefore, examples of their salient misinterpretation by members of an alien speech community are quite frequent. Since Gyula Laziczius (1896–1957) drafted his groundbreaking remarks on the emotive and conative ingredients in the sound shape of language, both cognate sets called 'emphatica' by him (1935; cf. Trubetzkoy in 1939a: 14ff.), much remains to be done in this still fecund field (cf. Stankiewicz 1964).

In his "Introduction to the Study of Speech" (1921: chap. 1), Sapir asserted that "ideation reigns supreme in language", while "volition and emotion come in as distinctly secondary factors". However, the author's broad view of language in his prescient essay of 1927 enabled him to overcome the ingrained assumption "that the task of language is a pure denotive one", and to bring up those "peculiar characteristics of language" which have not as yet been "sufficiently understood" and are likely to be overlooked by linguists. In fact,

> the denotive function of speech is always compounded with certain expressive factors ⟨...⟩ which are always present in the actual life of language. It is impossible to pronounce even so indifferent a word as "horse" without a lesser or greater show of interest, without some change of emotion. This expressiveness may relate to our attitude toward the person that we are speaking to or thinking of, or to our general state of mind. ⟨...⟩ In the course of our speech activities we are really doing two rather distinct things, though these are never to be completely sundered except by a process of abstraction. [1927: 425 f.]

As Ivan Fónagy has newly demonstrated, "each concrete sound necessarily contains two pieces of information differing profoundly both at the level of content and of expression". To specify the rules of procedure, he has shown "the mechanism for the acoustic encoding of emotions analyzed by two x-ray films containing neutral and emotional variants (anger, hate, sadness, joy, tenderness, irony) of six Hungarian phrases. Each attitude is expressed by an articulatory pattern peculiar to it. This oral gesture can be seen as superimposed on the neutral articulation" (1976: 31 ff.).

XIII. PHYSIOGNOMIC INDICES

Finally, the physiognomic indices ('identifiers') which enable the addressee to identify the sex, the age, the areal, social, and ethnic origin, and the personality of the addresser, including his kinesthetic type – in other words, a kind of vocal ID or "passport" – may, along with the discrimination of the speech content, be the focus of the addressee's attention. Here he may find highly informative signs to be interpreted; and we have to discern which of these signs depend on the will and purpose of the addresser. For example, in their ways of articulation and even in their voices, men and women may be interested in underlining or dissimulating their age or sex. The process of a speaker's conforming his voice to the volume and strength of the listener's voice is a widespread adaptational behavior, going as far back as prelinguistic infancy. Geographically or socially dialectal elements may be deliberately effaced by the speaker or, on the contrary, proudly emphasized. Ladefoged's & Broadbent's assessment of the information conveyed by vowels has enabled them to put forward the tentative hypothesis that "sociolinguistic information does not depend on the absolute values of the formant frequencies, but is like linguistic information, a matter of the relative formant structure of vowels", whereas "the personal information conveyed by vowels does seem to depend on the absolute values of the formant frequencies" (1957: 103; cf. also Sievers 1924). Calls to pursue and extend the investigation of all these factors should be responded to by a wide recognition of this socio- and psycho-linguistic program and of its strictly systematic fulfillment (cf. Ladefoged & Broadbent) and at the same time by a resolute methodological warning against any confusion of these questions with the nuclear and omnipresent sound-meaning problem.

XIV. THE DISTINCTIVE FEATURES IN RELATION TO THE OTHER COMPONENTS OF THE SPEECH SOUND

If the analyst accounts for the different constituents of speech sounds, no conflict can arise between the study of linguistic and physical units, since any physical unit must be defined in intimate association with the role it fills in the perception of language. Any *signans* should be approached in relation to its *signatum* (see above, p. 17). The preoccupation with the entire variety of features and their tasks must in no case conceal the profound, hierarchical, and multilateral difference between the distinctive features and all other features carried by the speech sounds. The striking divergence between these "independently significant" features and the rest of the features can be exemplified in various ways.

The emotive use of vocalic lengthening does not help a speaker whose native language lacks the long ~ short opposition to acquire such a distinctive feature when confronted with a language endowed with it. And the occurence of interjectional clicks in a speaker's mother tongue does not facilitate his learning of, for example, South African sense-discriminative clicks. The occurence of redundant nasality in English vowels is of little help to Americans seeking to master the

French category of nasal vowels. The sense-discriminative distinction in Russian between consonants with and without palatalization, easily grasped by any native from earliest childhood, creates great difficulties for most Western listeners and speakers. When faced with the minimal pair /jer/ and /jer'/ (spelling names of two Russian letters), West European, for instance Norwegian, listeners apparently apprehend no difference between them or else assign the difference to the distinction of the lower vs. higher openness of the preceding /e/, a variation which for an ordinary Russian observer is nearly imperceptible. At the same time, certain consonants at the end of Norwegian words are definitely palatalized, but the average Norwegian speaker remains deaf to the Russian distinction of the noun *sáxar* 'sugar' and the imperative *sáxar'* 'sweeten!', especially in connected speech. And he proves to be unaware even of his native configurative feature when pronouncing the six final [r']'s in the following two lines from the national anthem:

> Elske[r'], elske[r'] det og tænke[r']
> på vo[r'] fa[r'] og mo[r'].

The chief difference between the distinctive features and all other kinds of features lies in the fact that the distinctive features are the only ones which, according to Sapir's concise formulation, have "no singleness, or rather primary singleness, of reference" (1949: 34). The nasality of the initial consonant in the word *mill* signals that, all other things being equal, another word beginning with the corresponding consonant without nasality will, with a probability near to 1.0, not have the same meanings as the word with the nasal consonant. The same relationship exists between *nil* and *dill,* or between *rim* and *rib.* The sole *signatum* of any distinctive feature in its primary, purely sense-discriminative role is 'otherness'; as a rule a change in one feature confronts us either with a word of another meaning or with a nonsensical group of sounds: cf. *mesh* and **besh.* Distinctive oppositions have no positive content on the level of the *signatum* and announce only the nearly certain unlikeness of morphemes and words which differ in the distinctive features used. The opposition here lies not in the *signatum* but in the *signans:* phonic elements appear to be polarized in order to be used for semantic purposes. Such a polarization is inseparably bound to the semiotic role of distinctive features.

In the Danish science of language of the middle of this century, so-called 'glossematic' theory, developed and propounded by Louis Hjelmslev (1899-1965), argued against feature analysis as a new jump

from linguistic form to physical substance; but as Eli Fischer-Jørgensen (1966) rightly sensed, the artificial separation of substance from the
plane of linguistic form does not account for the buildup of oppositions as a manifestly formal, logical operation profoundly inherent in
the verbal code. Moreover, the idea itself of a sound substance independent of linguistic patterning disregards the fact that speech sounds,
made solely for the needs of language, are adapted to its purpose (cf.
above, p. 33 f.). The dichotomy of substance and form proves to be fic-
titious.

All features other than the distinctive features are invested with a
"singleness of reference". The positive *signatum* of a redundant feature is the presence of a certain contiguous distinctive feature. Thus in
French the point of constriction between the postdorsum of the tongue
and the palatovelar arch is sharply affected by the adjacent vowel, and
before front vowels such a consonant "can be almost palatal" (Delattre
1968 a: 204). This palatal proclivity is a redundant feature unambiguously signaling the distinctive palatal feature of the ensuing vowel, e. g.
in *quitter* versus the velar vowel of *côuter*. And yet, in Macedonian (see
Lunt 1952: 10, 12) the velar and palatal varieties, spelled *k* and *k′,* carry
a sense-discriminative opposition grave ~ acute (*kuka* 'hook' - *kuk′a*
'house', plur. *kuki* - *kuk′i*), and the difference between the palatal and
velar characters signals nothing else than the high probability of be-
longing to semantically distinct words.

A configurative feature may signal the limit or the unity of a word.
Emotive features import to the addressee certain feelings of the addresser. As a rule, physiognomic features ('indices') such as a soprano
voice indicate a female speaker. In all these cases, there is a much more
immediate path from the *signans* to the *signatum* than there is in dealing with distinctive features. This lack of immediacy, as well as the
usual orientation of the listener toward the ideational content of the
message, requires him to concentrate his chief, mostly subliminal, attention on the distinctive features in contrast to all other types of features. From this angle Sapir was right in having come "to the practical
realization" that among the sound phenomena which face "the naïve
speaker, he hears above all phonemes" (1949: 47) and (as we may now
specify) their distinctive features.

Recent studies by Blumstein & Cooper (1972, 1974) clearly show
that the intonation contours which encompass, diversify, and characterize sentence types point with surprising consistency to left-ear superiority, in contradistinction to the sense-discriminative word tones of a

polytonic language like Thai (investigated by Abramson and Erickson). The tones of this language, according to the dichotic data collected by van Lancker & Fromkin (1973), are perceived more readily by the right ear, "since here pitch is used linguistically to distinguish one lexical item from another". Russia's recent scientific experience with unilateral inactivations of the brain hemispheres has confirmed and enhanced these findings on dichotic hearing. The inactivation of the left hemisphere sharply obstructs the recognizability and the reproducibility of speech sounds and the accentual design of the word, but leaves intact the recognition and reproduction of the sentence intonations, whereas the inactivation of the right hemisphere preserves intact the structure of the word for a speaker or a listener undergoing electric shock, but sharply renders the patient unable to recognize or even notice sentence intonations. The affective intonations are particularly likely to disappear. (For a detailed comparative survey of "psychoacoustic syndromes" which follow from the inactivation of the two hemispheres, see Balonov & Deglin: Table 21.)

The strict hemispheric distribution of these two classes of linguistic phenomena has indeed been surprising and revealing, but the significant linguistic difference between the two sets in question was presumable in advance (cf. Bolinger 1964; Nikolaeva 1977). Nearly forty years ago in a Copenhagen University discussion, it was noted that such sound elements as

> sentence intonation, sentence accent, sentence pauses, etc., may play within the limits of the referential function merely a dividing and subordinating role. ⟨...⟩ In referential speech the sequential sound devices serve merely for delimitation, segmentation, and gradation of meanings but not for their semantic differentiation as is the case with the distinctive sound devices within the frame of the word. ⟨...⟩ Perhaps one would guess that the interrogative intonation prompts a special meaning of the sentence, but it could hardly be justified to view the interrogative sentence as one of the kinds of reference. The interrogative sentence is not a reference but only a kind of appeal for reference. [RJ I: 289]

In short, interrogative intonation announces the end of an utterance and at the same time a requirement addressed to interlocutors for a continuation of the discourse; in contradistinction to mediators of meaning such as phonemes and distinctive features, the interrogative intonation stands like any conative or affective expression in a direct, immediate relation to its *signatum*.

One can differentiate those constitutive elements of linguistic signs which serve either independently or as a redundant auxiliary to discriminate the meanings of morphemes, words, and their syntactic constructions from the contoural, framing properties of the verbal messages. It is to these properties that the sentential prosody and the emotive factors of speech belong. All these framing components are regulated by the right hemisphere, and the specifically physiognomic properties of discourse belong to the same kind of components. It is highly characteristic that patients submitted to a temporary inactivation of the right hemisphere lose the ability to distinguish between men's and women's voices or to tell whether two utterances belong to one and the same speaker or to two different people, as well as to identify even the most familiar individuals by sound only; moreover, the patient also loses the ability to regulate his own voice in accordance with a given emotional situation (see Balonov & Deglin: pp. 164 ff., 171 ff.).

Furthermore, as has been pointed out, a mere hum *(mmm, uh)* can be modulated with different intonations to transmit intelligible messages. "Question intonation symbolizes the question independently of the content of the sentence. The interrogative intonation can even do without any words and be implemented by a mere murmur." In newspaper style this type of bare question is often symbolized by - ?- (RJ I: 289; cf. Stokoe 1975). In a similar way, the subjects of dichotic experiments perceive, notice, and understand only the interrogative intonation itself, while characterizing the words as sounding like the "muffled" vocalization of "someone speaking into a can" (Blumstein & Cooper 1974: 151).

Whereas sentence intonation proves to be controlled by the right hemisphere, the sound pattern of the word is still supervised, let us repeat, by the left hemisphere, even if the listener is presented with speech played backwards, as long as he feels it consists of intended, though distorted, speech sounds. In concluding their monograph, Balonov & Deglin venture an ingenious hypothesis, plausible both phylogenetically as well as ontogenetically: "The mechanisms of sound production and the auditory functions of the right hemisphere prove to be considerably older than the mechanisms of sound production and the auditory functions of the left hemisphere which secure speech articulation and the discrimination of speech sounds on the basis of distinctive features" (p. 194). The asymmetric arrangement of the human brain and in particular the development of the left, dominant hemisphere have been apparently interconnected with the origin and growth of language. An uncommon case has been systematically examined by Victoria Fromkin et alii. When a fourteen-year-old girl who had been deprived of all language was found and given careful education, she showed a very limited capacity for language acquisition and no prospect for its further development. The investigation testified that "the inadequate language stimulation during her early life inhibited or interfered with language aspects of left hemisphere development", and due "to a kind of functional atrophy of the usual language centers", the right hemisphere, as experiments proved, was "doing all the work" in her linguistic rudiments (1974: 98 ff.; cf. Curtiss 1977: 213, 216 f., 234). This experience adds new proof in favor of the hypothesis concerning the relative age of the two hemispheres.

In the hierarchy of percepts the distinctive feature dominates all other features. However, none of the other types of features remains unperceived. In fact, the entire makeup of a speech sound is apprehended by the naïve speaker with regard to the ensemble of featural functions. Therefore a scholarly observer of the linguistic sound shape who abstracts the shape alone from all the diverse functions it carries displays, in Sapir's terms, the "reverse of a realistic point of view" (1949: 46 f.) and appears to be much more arbitrary than the naïve speaker. As Claude Lévi-Strauss underscored in a well-timed remark, "both the natural and the human sciences concur to dismiss an outmoded philosophical dualism. Ideal and real, abstract and concrete, 'emic' and 'etic' can no longer be opposed to each other. What is immediately 'given' to us is neither the one nor the other, but something which is betwixt and between, that is already encoded by the sense organs as by the brain" (1972). If in the customary scientific parlance one confines 'emic' to distinctive features, ignoring all the rest, and excludes from the notion 'etic' all references to the goal of the sound phenomena observed, the dyad emic ~ etic loses its applicability to the present-day science of language. In particular, such an 'etic' level, in Lévi-Strauss's words "too long taken for granted by mechanistic materialism and sensualist philosophy", becomes a curtailed construct. On the one hand phonology, which stops at phonemes and their distinctive components, and on the other hand speech analysis, which discards all question of purpose, seem equally obsolete in their narrow isolationism and futile abstractionism.

A perceptual constancy enables interlocutors to go beyond particular contexts and, either consciously or subliminally, to extract the invariant cues from the different featural environments of concurrent features and surrounding phonemes. Two auditory percepts are felt to be equivalent. Thus, members of the Russian speech community identify the opposition between palatalized (sharp) and nonpalatalized consonants within varied phonemic contexts, despite the considerable difference between the physicomotor implementation of diverse palatalized consonants in different surroundings. Studies (cf. Bondarko & Zinder 1966) have pointed out the salient particularities displayed by the palatalization of Russian consonants in its dependence on the presence or absence of various neighboring vowels and on the concurrence of this palatalization with other features of the phoneme in question; thus, there are differences between the palatalization of sibilants, labials, and dental stops. The opposition of the presence or absence of palatalization remains the categorial invariant of perception throughout all the transformations of the sequential and concurrent environment.

Difficulties in the analysis of linguistic sound shape into distinctive features occur only if the inquirer takes as his point of departure not the mutual relation of opposites (e.g., that between sharp and nonsharp), but each opposite in and of itself; a strictly relational sequence of operations is here the only one able to grasp the speaker/listener's goal. Thus, for example, as long as the three sound units of Gilyak, the strong, aspirated [kʰ], the weak [k], and the continuant [x], were treated as three separate entities, we were faced with two relations, one between stops and continuants and the other between two stop varieties. Yet if we realize that in the initial, strong position the strong [kʰ] is opposed solely to the weak [k], and that the noninitial, weak position [k] is confronted only by the continuant [x], we are forced to recognize the equivalence of the two oppositions between strong and weak, a relation which in the strong position is implemented as a stronger occlusion vs. a weaker one and in the weak position as the presence of occlusion vs. its absence. It is noteworthy that in the strong position the [k] functions as the weak member and in the weak position as the strong member of one and the same opposition: here we face an eloquent example of what has been erroneously taken for the imaginary "overlapping of two phonemes" (Bloch 1941). In a consistently relational approach, the subjective, uncontrollable notion of similarity has been deliberately replaced by the more compelling principle of equivalence, inseparably connected in science with the concepts of relativity and invariance. Moreover, the complementarity between the extraction of invariance and the determination of variables shows up clearly

in the Gilyak example: the aspiration of [kʰ] and the continuant char-
akter of [x] signal the initial and noninitial position respectively.

It has been emphasized by Jakobson & Halle (see RJ I: 468 f.) that

> since the differentiation of semantic units is the least dispensable among
> the sound functions in language, speech participants learn primarily to re-
> spond to the distinctive features. It would be deceptive, however, to believe
> that they are trained to ignore all the rest in speech sounds. Besides the dis-
> tinctive features, the speaker has at his command other types of coded in-
> formation-bearing features which any member of a speech community has
> been trained to manipulate and which the science of language has no right
> to disregard.

While attending to the whole complex of all these diverse features,
the listener perceives the distinctive features as different from the other
functional constituents of speech sounds. They are discrete percepts
which, according to neurobiologists, are changed into categorial concepts through a polarization method used by the nervous system.

XV. THE IDENTIFICATION OF DISTINCTIVE FEATURES

In debates about distinctive features the question of their recognizability by supposedly "naïve" speakers has given rise to a number of
controversies. The 'commutation test', to use the term proposed by
Louis Hjelmslev, enables the linguist to give an unambiguous answer
to this question, but proves to be a shaky device for dealing with an in-
experienced native informant. As Hockett suggested (1955: 144f.), the
question of whether two speech events sound "the same" or "different" puts a native speaker in a perplexing situation because different
shades of meaning, in particular emotive variants deprived of a sense-
discriminative value, may be rightly appraised by him as "sounding
different". Even if we change the question and ask whether the two utterances "mean the same or not", a misunderstanding can easily occur
because the verb "mean" for the informant may cover emotive differences as well.

The once proposed replacement of "sounding same or different" by
"rhyming or not" would lead the native even more astray because the
rhyme conventions in most oral and written traditions cancel some distinctive oppositions. Thus, for instance, in Serbo-Croatian poetry vowels with rising or falling accent rhyme with each other and long vowels

rhyme with short ones. It suffices to compare, for example, the codes of Chinese rhyming, the so-called "generic" rhymes of Irish medieval poetry (cf. Murphy 1961 and Ó Cuív 1966), and Scandinavian rhymes to see how different and artificial the rules of sound equation are in diverse conventions of rhyming technique. As Janos Lotz (1913–1973) summarized, rhyme "is a culture-bound phenomenon" and in various poetic patterns "admits diverse and often substantial deviations from requirements of identity" (1972: 20).

The question of so-called 'differential' (same or unlike) meaning posed to the naïve speaker is insufficient, and additional information must be requested: "What in fact is the meaning of each of the two distinguished utterances?" The native informant is even less effective in treating the problem of the equivalence between distinctive oppositions in different sequential or simultaneous contexts of features. The decision concerning the equivalence of a relation such as initial t:initial d ≡ final t:final d, or further such as t:d ≡ s:z, can be made only by the analyst via a search for the invariant contained in the variables.

Rather than being a mere contrivance of the linguist, such invariants are intrinsic to the objective code or, in other words, to the actual, albeit unconscious, competence of the members of the speech community. Despite the motor-acoustic difference between initial and final *p, t, k,* the reduplication of one and the same entity in such vocables as *tit, tot, pap, pup, pip, kick, keck* is "intuited" by the ordinary speaker, according to Sapir's favorite locution (1949: 548).

Among the proofs for the manifest givenness of equivalent distinctive oppositions is the fact that the productive device of 'vowel harmony', which is widespread in diverse languages and prohibits the use of two opposite classes of vowels within one and the same word unit, resorts to one or two (even three) of all the inherent oppositions existing in the vocalic patterns of the world: back ~ front, or in more relative terms retracted ~ advanced (grave ~ acute); rounded ~ unrounded (flat ~ nonflat); high ~ low (diffuse ~ compact); lax ~ tense; nasalized ~ nonnasalized (cf. pp. 149 ff. below). Moreover, verse systems make use of the oppositions long ~ short and stressed ~ unstressed, and the poetry of some tonal languages displays so-called 'tonal counterpont', a wordplay based on an opposition between two polar tones, typical particularly of Yoruba poetry (Bamgboṣe 1970: 112); see for instance the variation between the high tone of /kú/ 'die' and the low tone of /kù/ 'remain':

Ẹni tí yó. kú yó. kú	"Those that will die will die
Ẹni tí ó. kù ó. kù	Those that will remain, will remain
Ẹni tí ó, kù ni a kò mò	It is those that will remain that
	we do not know"

The variety of vowel harmony which opposes lower (compact) vowels to higher (diffuse) ones - /o/ to /u/, /e/ to /i/ - implements the pair of retracted unrounded vowels as (1) an /a/ actually lower than /o/ or /e/ and (2) its opposite either as /ə/ ('schwa'), actually lower than /u/ and /i/, or as /ɯ/ parallel to those vowels in height. These two varieties of the vocalic pattern are also spread among languages lacking this type of vowel harmony or even devoid of vowel harmony altogether (cf. Havránek 1932: 31 f.):

	a				a	
o	ə	e		o		e
u		i		u	ɯ	i

In the strictly relational terms of distinctive features, only the equivalence of the relations between the two opposites within each of the three pairs matters, so that both variants of patterning are merely two implementations of one and the same system:

o	a	e
u	ə/ɯ	i

A persual of the manifold material on the vocalic systems of the world by Sedlak (1969) reveals a striking divergence between the seemingly asymmetric, disorderly vocalic patterns constructed from absolute articulatory data and the strongly regular structure of the consistent relational laws of distinctive features which underlie the languages in question. Thus, in the four-vowel systems (p. 32) comprising /e/ and /i/ as the lower and higher advanced vowels and /a/ and /u/ or /o/ as the corresponding retracted vowels, the difference between the /u/ and /o/ implementations is irrelevant. Even the four-vowel system with /e/ and /i/ as advanced and /o/ and /ɯ/ as retracted vowels is relationally equivalent. In a language with /o/ and /u/ on the one hand and /a/ and /u/ on the other, the system is constructed in the same way, but the opposition advanced ~ retracted is replaced by unrounded ~ rounded. The physically "asymmetric" Czech pattern, with its set of consonantal pairs carrying the opposition voiced ~ voiceless, implements the voiced opposite of the velar /x/ as a voiced laryngeal /ɦ/ and thus offers another argument for the relativist cause.

The search for both compulsory and probabilistic distributional rules is a pertinent task within the study of distinctive features, but it is neither self-sufficient nor even achievable without constant recourse both to the sound matter and to the semantic facet of any feature. Stubborn arguments intended to vitiate the indispensability of both of these aspects have been raised repeatedly in linguistic literature.

The distinctive features consist of formal oppositions specified and individualized by the phonic prerequisites they are built of. Radical partisans of glossematics have endeavored to extract the system of primitive constituents with no reference to sound substance at all. On May 26, 1959, in a lively discussion in the Copenhagen Linguistic Circle, a staunch partisan of glossematics, which presumed to liberate 'form' from 'substance', attacked the Praguian views of language (cf. Fischer-Jørgensen 1966: 26 ff.). For an artificial language with such formatives as *a, pa, ta,* and *at,* this discussant believed he had found a practicable way to extract the vowel *a* by characterizing this constituent as the only one able to appear by itself. Such an operation, however, presupposes the knowledge that the [a]'s of this whole series implement one and the same entity. If all reference to the phonic matter is prohibited, the idea of the four equated [a]'s appears to be, as was polemically stated in a methodological argument, "bought on the black market of sound substance". Such contraband, uncontrolled use of sound material unsubjected to analytic operations which would transmute this raw material into a linguistic form, creates an illegitimate, unbridgeable chasm between form and inarticulate substance.

On the other hand, attempts have been made to determine the phonemes of a given language through purely distributional criteria. Thus, for instance, Polish voiced obstruents were tentatively defined as consonants which do not occur at the end of a word. Such methodological tentatives gave rise to a witty definition popular a while back among American linguists: "a dining car is a car which cannot occur between two freight cars." We cannot use this definition as a point of departure in an analysis of the train's composition because in order to state this distributional law we must know beforehand which of the train's constituents may be identified as freight cars and which as dining cars, and we must recognize the specific tasks of these two kinds of cars (which even gave rise to their names, referring to "freight" and "dining"). The primary function of a dining car is to serve meals, just as the primary aim of the feature voiced ~ voiceless is to serve as a device for the distinction of verbal meaning (and this task brought about the addition of the attribute 'distinctive' to the noun 'feature'). Both a dining car which is not destined to provide meals and a distinctive feature which does not serve to differentiate meanings are contradictions in terms. The distributional rules applied to the features specify the latter's sense-discriminative role, the constraints on this role, and the interplay between the distinctive, redundant, and configurative features, but such rules can hardly underlie the definition and specification of the distinctive features. This situation implies the primacy of the features over the rules which limit the operativeness of distinctive oppositions. It is the existence of a system of such oppositions which enables sounds to carry a meaning and language to fulfill its functions. "Traffic rules" help to regulate communication, but without vehicles there would be no traffic.

XVI. SENSE DISCRIMINATION AND SENSE DETERMINATION

One must keep in mind both functions of the distinctive features. The obviously primary function, the sense-discriminative (purely distinctive) one, assigns to the feature the capability of signaling – with a probability near to 1.0 – the semantic likeness or nonlikeness of two meaningful verbal units. The second task, which necessarily presupposes the first, is a sense-determinative or, in the terminology launched by the Prague Circle, 'mor(pho)phonological' function; the arrangement of features supplies information about the derivational and/or flexional structure and grammatical meaning of the units in question. The delimitation of the two interconnected but still discriminable functions of phonemes (and likewise of distinctive features) was already accomplished by Baudouin de Courtenay from the beginning of his concern with the question of sound and meaning and with the diversified morphological utilization of the significant sound differences. He repeatedly posited a clear-cut difference between two employments of phonemes: lexicalized (i.e., sense-discriminative) on the one hand and grammaticalized (i.e., sense-determinative) on the other. Discussions about the relation between these two different functions of phonemes have continued in Russian linguistic tradition for a century (cf. Reformatskij 1970). For any given language, the interconnection of the two heterogeneous and at the same time kindred tasks of phonemes "is to be translated into a set of exact rules," as the Praguians emphasized from the time of the First Congress of Linguists. As Trubetzkoy stated in a message of 1930 (see 1975: 153), "along with the actually general structural laws of phonology, there exist laws constrained by a particular type of morphological (and perhaps also lexical) structure of languages. Since language is a system, a close connection between the grammatical and phonological structure consequently must exist."

The question of the interdependence "between the phonemic and grammatical facets of language" was scheduled for a plenary meeting of the Sixth International Congress of Linguists, held in Paris in 1948, and the report (cf. RJ II: 103 ff.), summing up the numerous contributions, stated that "neither does the autonomy of these two linguistic aspects mean independence nor does their coordinate interdependence imply a lack of autonomy". The report expressly warned against all attempts "to confine oneself to a simple inventory of the distinctive features and of their simultaneous and successive configurations without any grammatical specification of their use". Different configurative arrangements of distinctive features used to mark morpheme and word boundaries were cited, as were examples of sets of features circumscribed for certain classes of grammatical units, such as the Russian rule limiting the admissibility of monophonemic morphemes in inflected words: only grammatical desinences may consist of one single vowel and only pronominal (thus also grammatical) roots may be limited to one single consonant. Likewise, consonantal stem alternations in Russian are confined to conjugational paradigms as opposed to declensional ones. The truncation of verbal stems with a final vowel before the vowel of the inflectional suffix is one of the manifestations of this rule.

A further characteristic example is furnished by the limitation of final consonants in English inflectional suffixes to one single series of obstruents - [d] and [z] (with their contextual, automatic substitution by [t] and [s]) and [n] in unproductive forms, while the velar nasal [ŋ] of the -ing desinence tends to disappear in this function (likin' vs. Viking). Even more explicit information is furnished in English by the confinement of the initial lax (voiced) interdental /ð/ to purely grammatical, mainly deictic words "of demonstrative and relative meanings", judiciously defined in this respect by Leonard Bloomfield as "words whose meaning resembles that of a pointing gesture", such as this, that, they, their, thee, thou, then, there, thus, than, though, the. In a similar way, /hw/ figures as a characteristic constituent of the English interrogatives *what, which, where, when, why, whether, how* (with an inversion), and *who* (with a merger of [w] und [u]).

The sense-determinative role of distinctive features is brought to the foreground by such examples as the appearance of nasality, either consonantal or vocalic, in all the various desinences of the Polish instrumental - /-em, -ami, -im, -imi, -õ/. In the Russian declensional desinences, *m* occurs solely in the three marginal cases - instrumental, dative, and locative (for further examples, see RJ II: 178 f.). The process of the inquiry into the sense-determinative function of distinctive features promises an ever deeper analysis of subjects such as the makeup of morphemes, their selection and combinations, so that morphology will evolve into a phonological description of "grammatical processes" indissolubly connected with a semantic scrutiny of corresponding "grammatical concepts", according to Sapir's application (1921: chap. 4) of these two correlative terms. For the last hundred years, up until recently, most efforts to uncover the grammatical utilization of the sound pattern of a given language have been almost uniquely, and in any case chiefly, preoccupied with the variability in the makeup of grammatical units, primarily stems. Much has been done toward the adequate interpretation of such diverse and quite differently founded alternations, such as those in the Russian root of the verb *vedu* 'I lead' - [v'id-] in *vedú*, [v'id'-] in *vedët*, [v'is'-] in *vestí*, [v'ó] in *vël*, [v'ét-] in *vétši*, [vad'-] in *vodít'*, [vód'-] in *vódit*, [vót-] in *uvód*, [važ-] in *vožú*, [váž-] in *vážival*, [važd'-] in *voždí*, and [vóšt'] in *vóžd'* - while the constructional rules in invariable morphemes (and some languages exclude alternations) require a much greater attention from investigators than they have received in the past.

XVII. AUTONOMY AND INTEGRATION

Considerable progress in the study of grammatical units, variable in their sound composition, has been made by Chomsky & Halle (1968). One can only agree with Chomsky's statement that "phonology as a whole cannot be studied, without distortion, in total independence of higher level structure", and with his negative attitude toward the "absurd thesis of inseparability of phonology" from grammar. Quite naturally, the sense-discriminative function of distinctive features, as opposed to their sense-determinative role, involves no direct appeal to grammar. Around this necessary delimitation there unfortunately has

arisen a vacuous discussion of whether phonology is an "autonomous" discipline or not, as if "autonomy" were synonymous with "independence". In fact, the notion of autonomy is inseparably linked
with that of integration and thus long ago showed its incompatibility
with the abhorrent slogan of "total independence" or "isolationism"
(cf. RJ I: 314). The newly sharpened insight into the rules of alternations and into their morphological and syntactic prerequisites asks also
that greater attention be paid to the structure of nonalternating morphemes and of their groupings into higher grammatical units. On the
other hand, the expanding preoccupation with the grammatical use of
distinctive features calls for a new and deeper inquiry into their sense-
discriminative employment, their functional load, first brought to attention by Vilém Mathesius (1882–1945), and necessarily into their
own structure and interrelations. In connection with the structure of
the ultimate constituents of language, let us once more refer to Peirce,
specifically to his theory of groups: "How it possible for an undecom-
posable element to have any differences of structure? Of internal structure, it would be clearly impossible. But, as to the structure of its possible compounds, limited differences of structure are possible" (I: 289).

XVIII. UNIVERSALS

The set of distinctive oppositions existing in the languages of the
world, with certified selections of a group of oppositions capable of
coexisting in one and the same language, laws restricting such coexistence and laws governing the combinability of distinctive features in
their concurrent bundles (in particular implicational laws of irreversible solidarity), and the hierarchical relations both between and within
the different oppositions – all these aspects inherent in the network of
distinctive features are of the highest interest as the pivotal, utterly
structured totality of links between the *signans* and the *signatum*. The
system of distinctive features, the basic formal prerequisite for the
semiotic aims of language, is far from being, to use Cassirer's imagery,
"a mere mosaic, a mere aggregate of scattered sensations". A bare mechanical catalogue of features would lead us astray from a genuine insight into "the inner configuration of the sound system of a language,
the intuitive 'placing' of the sounds with reference to one another" (see
Sapir 1949: 35f.). The attentive inquiry into the gradual acquisition of
a first language by children in various linguistic areas is uncovering

common sets of ordered laws, or at least tendencies, similar to the rules which subtend the structure of languages throughout the world. These correspondences are particularly valuable when one takes into account the fact that the unfolding of sound laws begins in child language with the early, holophrastic stage, i.e. before the emergence of the first strictly grammatical (i.e. morphological and syntactic) rules.

The problem of two vitally interconnected linguistic aspects - universality and diversity - has been an age-old topic of philosophical discussions and has become an essential issue for the current science of language. The increasingly solvable questions and attainable prospectives of a linguistic typology uncover constant connections between fundamental properties in grammar and in the sound patterning of languages and bring us steadily nearer to an insight into linguistic universals without recourse to metaphysical speculations. The *a priori* and intuitively cognizable phenomenal unity of languages necessarily merges with the empirical data obtained from a continually greater number of the world's tongues. Unquestionably, discovering universal properties demands the greatest caution. Any parochial spirit, any universalizing statement based on one's own mother tongue (e.g., English) or academic language (such as Latin), is most hazardous. And a mere stock of assumed universals is, like any mechanical catalogue, an imperfect attainment: the place of these properties in the internal organization of languages should not be lost from view.

Pessimistic voices, despairing of knowing exactly the past, present, and future stages of the linguistic world, have been and will still be raised against the quest for universals: "Mais qui pourrait se vanter d'avoir fait un examen exhaustif de toutes les langues existantes ou attestées? Et que dire des langues disparues sans laisser de traces et celles qui apparaîtront demain sur la terre?" (Martinet 1955: 74). In short, where is the guarantee that the language contradicting some of the alleged universals will not be discovered in the jungles of Brazil or will not emerge somewhere in the fourth millennium A.D.? Actually, a few isolated tribal tongues have been found to be devoid of some property once assumed to be universal. As long as the Australian echidna and the Tasmanian duckbill platypus - both of which lay eggs - remained unknown to zoologists, viviparous reproduction was considered an essential property of all mammals. The discovery of oviparous mammals led to a new difinition of viviparousness as a property of the overwhelming majority of mammals and to a closer insight into the highly exceptional occurrences of oviparous mammals.

If in linguistics the properties assumed to be universal proved to be merely near-universal, and if among the over one thousand languages more or less familiar to the scholarly world a minute number of languages with a handful of speakers offered single deviations from the patterns used by the preponderance of languages and speakers, these rarissime exceptions would require a special investigation of the intrinsic and extrinsic conditions which engender such an "anomaly", and in addition they would ask us to seek the reasons for the near-universality of the property in question. In the search for universals, as in all linguistic operations, one has to deal not only with certainty, probability 1.0, but also with cases of probability less than but near to 1.0, whose overpowering majority must be taken into account. It is also notable that some of the rarest particularities are exhibited by languages with a highly limited radius of communication and number of speakers, especially by languages near extinction – in short, by languages of a lowered communicative load. In his introductory lecture of 1870 (see 1963: I: 57) Baudouin maintained that

> exceptions, subjected to an exact analysis, prove to depend on certain causes, certain forces which prevented the causes or forces underlying the given law from encompassing the apparent exceptions. Subsequently we will have to recognize that our generalized formulation of such a law was inadequate and that the *genus proximum* of the posited law has to be complemented by a limitative *differentia specifica*. Then the imaginary exception will become, strictly speaking, a clear confirmation of the general law.

The seminal distinction between 'context-sensitive' and 'context-free' languages finds a wide application in contemporary communication sciences and is eloquently exemplified by the large difference between the context-sensitive character proper to the "natural" languages and the context-free organization of various "formalized" languages. The firm interrelationship between invariance and contextual variants which characterizes any "natural" language on all its levels must be recognized and investigated also in the comparative analysis of languages with respect to their universal foundations; the diverse languages must be viewed as diverse contexts naturally offering contextual variations with underlying invariants. This view is the logical corollary to the recognition of linguistic universals.

If in a given language there is an opposition between a plain, unrounded consonant and a corresponding consonant with lip-rounding and if in another context, for instance before a certain class of vowels, the same plain consonant is opposed not to a rounded but to a pharyngealized consonant, we then must take into account the fact that the narrowing of the anterior, labial orifice and the narrowing of the posterior, pharyngeal orifice of the oral cavity give an equivalent lowering of the timbre; we thus consider the rounding and the pharyngealization as two contextual variants of one and the same distinctive feature (see below, pp. 116 ff.). Similarly, if certain consonants are distinguished in a language by the presence and absence of rounding and certain other consonants by the presence and absence of pharyngealization, then rounding and pharyngealization prove to be two contextual variants conditioned by a difference of concurrent features. The same method is to be used in the comparative analysis of different languages. If some of the languages oppose plain consonants to rounded ones while others oppose them to pharyngealized ones, both oppositions can only be interpreted as variants of one and the same distinctive feature, in agreement with Ockham's principle: *Entia non sunt multiplicanda praeter necessitatem*. The comparative study of the feature patterns of languages should pay attention both to the invariant essence of a given opposition and to its variable implementations, without confusing the latter with the former.

It is self-evident that such a comparative analysis should never be equated with an "instructional" textbook of pronunciation. Otherwise, one would we have to assign to diverse, separate features some ten or twelve variants of *a* classified in the manuals of phonetics as occurring in different languages. Trubetzkoy was precise in his statement of 1932 that

> many languages utilize in a sense-discriminative function *the difference between a lighter and a darker variety of consonants*. For that aim, quite different articulatory means can be used ⟨...⟩ The darker coloring may be achieved through rounding of the lips or through retracting the body of the tongue ('velarization') or through the combination of this retraction of the tongue with a pharyngeal shift (the 'emphatic sounds' of Semitic and African languages) or, especially for dentals, through the retraction of the tip of the tongue ('retroflexion'), etc. All these processes are articulatorily different and can be unified solely from an acoustic point of view. But for phonological purposes such a unification is very important. [1975: 461]

Trubetzkoy's observations proved to be applicable not just to the acoustic effect of the consonants cited. The common peculiarities of all these classes of consonants are actually apparent both on the acoustic level and in sound production; the lowering of the timbre is due both to a decrease in the opening of the orifice and to a subsidiary increase in the volume of the cavity itself (cf. below, pp. 97 f.).

The perusal of strict, exceptionless universals and near-universals in regard to the distinctive features reveals a system of rigid internal rules. The universal repertory of possibilities from which a given language makes a selection reflects the capability of the human mind to polarize certain sound elements for their efficient use as distinctive oppositions. The highly restricted number of distinctive features extant not only in a single language but also in the world's languages as a whole shows that in comparison with the great variety of acoustico-motor productions, only a very small number appear to be utilizable as discrete perceptional values. Among the multifarious physical minutiae which occur in an infant's babbling, there are elements which find no use at all in human speech or at least in its ideational, noninterjectional units. Thus both the voiced and voiceless varieties of the bilabial trill, spelled as *brrr* or *prrr* and frequent in babbling and in interjectional use, are not to be found in the world inventory of phonemes, as Jespersen noted (1931: § 16). His survey describes a sound intermediate between [p] and [t] or [b] and [d] or [m] and [n] formed through an occlusion of the tip of the tongue with the upper lip: "yet although it's one of the articulations which children particularly enjoy in their first years of life it hardly occurs in genuine language"; the author quotes this phonation as an expression of disgust in the Danish interjection which is usually written *ptoi* (§ 30). Even among those numerous varieties of sounds which the phoneticians are able to detect in our utterances, only a few are suitable for fulfilling the sense-discriminative function and thus for being exploited by distinctive features.

XIX. SPEECH PERCEPTION

The perceptual value of the distinctive features controls their physicomotor aspect and is directly linked with the acoustic level, which in speech is equally at the disposal of the speaker and of the addressee (see above, pp. 30 f.). "L'impression produite sur l'oreille", as Saussurre's still valid lesson stated, "est la base naturelle de toute théorie. La donnée acoustique existe déjà inconsciemment lorsqu'on aborde les unités phonologiques; c'est par l'oreille ques nous savons ce que c'est q'un *b*, un *t*, etc." (1916: 100; cf. Malmberg 1968). Through recent years, the question of motor feedback for the listener has been raised and followed with particular attention and insistence. Such feedback unquestionably reinforces the perceptual capability of the listener.

Moreover, the major importance of immediate auditory perception for the listener (cf. D. B. Fry's slogan "perception precedes production") may be corroborated by many convincing examples. In Hans-Lukas Teuber's (1916–1977) wording, "the case of the preverbal child, with his amazing ways of classifying speech sounds that he cannot yet articulate, certainly detracts from any idea that we pattern our perceptions of sound only *after* we have managed to adopt correctly the corresponding gestures of our vocal apparatus" (1976). Even before their first attempts at speaking, children show an ability to discern and to understand spoken language. Bruner refers to a well-attested game: in answer to their mother's requests to show the mouth, the eyes, the nose, etc., infants touch the corresponding parts of their own as well as their mother's heads (1977: 275); however, one should not exaggerate the auditory capabilities of the neonate by bringing forward in this connection fetal responses to the speech of the mother several weeks before birth (cf. Bernard & Sontag 1947; Cutting & Eimas 1974; Truby 1971). In the early stages of a child's acquisition of language, significant distinctions in adult speech are recognized by the child not yet able to produce these distinctions himself. The particularly salient trait of this period is the youngster's objections to attempts by adults to imitate his way of speaking by omitting those distinctive features which he has not yet developed in his own performance (see below, p. 162).

Another manifest instance of the significant features perceived and understood by the listener who is incapable of reproducing them in his own speech is observable in the experience of people who are accustomed to the speech of their alien surroundings and grasp all the minimal pairs presented to them in this language, but who themselves consistently omit these features in their own pronunciation. In this way, according to valuable information we owe to the Georgian linguist Thomas V. Gamkrelidze, several fundamental oppositions of the Georgian consonantal pattern are suppressed in Russian pronunciation: (1) the aspirated consonants change into their unmarked unaspirated opposites (/tʰ/ ~ /t/, /pʰ/ ~ /p/, /kʰ/ ~ /k/) – (tʰari 'musical instrument' ~ tari 'handle', pʰuri 'cow' ~puri 'bread', kʰari 'wind' ~ kari 'door'); (2) the glottalized (checked) affricate changes into the nonglottalized (/čʾ/ ~ /č/, /cʾ/ ~ /c/) – (čʾiri 'sorrow' ~čiri 'dried fruit', cʾeli 'year' ~ celi 'scythe'); (3) the post-velar glottalized consonant changes into a voiceless velar stop (qʾepʰa 'barking' ~ kepʰa 'back of the head'). As Gamkrelidze testifies, such modifications when used by Georgian native speakers are immediately noticed and objected to by Russians although they are themselves accustomed to marking these same substitutions.

The development of the child's ability to select the primary distinctive features from the stock of features he perceives in the speech addressed to him by adults cannot be interpreted as testimony to the gradual and slow growth of his articulatory skill. The prelinguistic, babbling phase of the infant's experience often shows the remarkable variety of his motor production, which subsequently gives way to a surprising scarcity of "functional sounds" in his early use of language. For instance, Natalie Waterson in her keen observations of her son's linguistic growth notes that the lateral [l], very common in his babbling, was for a while lacking in his early speech (1970: 6). A. N. Gvozdev, the observant pioneer of a systematic inquiry into children's language, noted that in their babbling children pronounce "sounds that bring to mind snapping, dripping, splottering, and the twitter of birds, sounds which not only are lacking in adults but which adults are sometimes even unable to produce. Later, during the acquisition of his native language, the child himself loses the ability to emit such sounds and clusters" (1961: 120). Those commentators who are inclined to derive the first verbal utterances of a child at the end of his infancy from his babbling activities disregard the relevant fact that babbling and the beginnings of verbal activities are as a rule clearly separated in children's behaviour either as two concurrent yet quite distinct forms of activity or rather as two temporally delimited stages – a shorter or longer interval of reticence or even silence often detaches the new, speech era from the earlier, babbling phase – and that the variety and opulence of the babbled sounds yield to a rigorous sparseness of speech sounds.

There is nothing puzzling in the fact that the child in his initial steps of language acquisition progressively chooses those sound oppositions which are the most salient for perception and reproduction, the most easily memorizable, and hence the most suitable as a stable and significant means of communications between speaker and listener in their interchangeable roles. The child's spontaneously selected system of distinctive features ensures close ties between the acoustic stimuli and the articulatory responses as a necessary prerequisite for his activities as an interlocutor in nuclear family dialogues.

Several strong pieces of empirical evidence for the primary role played by the auditory factor in speech perception have been offered for discussion by David S. Palermo (1975) and at least two of his arguments should be cited: speech perception develops prior to speech production and in pathological cases is possible without productive capacities, while "the reverse is never the case". The congenitally deaf child's incapacity to develop normal speech is the result of disabilities in the area of speech perception, and if deafness occurs after speech is acquired, speech production, no longer supported by perception, gradually disintegrates (p. 150 f.). Let us add that we possess innumerable eloquent illustrations from ancient times to the present concerning people who, as a result of illness, accident, or violence, lose some of their speech organs, such as part of the tongue or some of the teeth, and regain their ability to speak distinctly as long as their hearing remained unimpaired and thus renders possible the substitutive adaption of the speech apparatus (see below, pp. 99 f.). Palermo leaves open the question of how a motor (erroneously labeled "phonetic") theory could account for these facts, but in order to show that speech perception continues to precede speech production even at ages later than infancy, he notes that the learning of a second language requires a discriminative auditory perception before an appropriate sound production (p. 151).

The relation between the two levels of sound events reveals a substantial difference: one and the same acoustic result can be obtained by diverse means, whereas one and the same motor means cannot attain a diversity of acoustic results. Björn Lindblom et al. (1977) showed the striking ability of their examined subjects to compensate immediately for unnatural jaw openings and assumed the existence of a listener-oriented neural coding of vowels which guarantees an auditory invariance regardless of interfering articulatory impediments. The inquirers consider these outstanding compensatory abilities to be further testimony to the primacy of the perceptual stage, the sensory goal, of the speech event over its antecedent, motor stage.

XX. LIFE AND LANGUAGE

The nineteenth-century nativist mode of thought repeatedly hypothesized that the predisposition to 'role-switching' between speech emitter and receiver is a genetic endowment and that moreover there exists a universal, innate design of language with its system of fundamental rules and prohibitions facilitating and accelerating the infant's mastery of language. Yet the enormous stock of pertinent particularities prompted by the adult milieu from which the infant learns his primary language still must be accounted for. In this stock lies the specific contribution of the diversity of human languages, "Die Verschiedenheit des menschlichen Sprachbaus", as it was termed by the title of Humboldt's final work (1836: 6.1, 111–303). This diversity contributes a multitude of extraordinary intricacies to the pattern of sounds and grammatical categories and forms, and requires the particularly effective and persistent influence of the interaction between people of a different type and age.

If one shares the belief in the inborn fundamentals of language, it must be assumed that it is the universal sound patterning of speech, the lowest stratum of the linguistic system, which is the most enrooted in the psychobiological nature of humans. Of the two tasks of the distinctive features, their sense-discriminative utilization actually exhibits (as one could expect) the highest number of universal and near-universal laws compared to the much more regional rules regulating the sense-determinative application of the features. These rules naturally display a greater variety of local particularities.

The decisive import of the dyadic principle in the sound pattern as well as in the grammatical structure of language, and the consistently hierarchical relations within any dyad, between the given dyads (cf. below, pp. 92 f.), and apparently within the whole framework of language, advance the imperative question of isomorphisms between verbal coding and the central neural processes. In particular, the universal implicational laws in the patterning of distinctive features and the tempting question of their presumably biological foundations require careful and critical interdisciplinary research (see below, p. 72 f.). As the geneticist François Jacob wrote in his monumental account (1970), the two turning points in evolution are, first, the emergence of life and, some two billion years later, the evidently conjoint emergence of thought and language. Thus, perhaps, the biological comparison of these two widely separated evolutionary gains – life and language – made from the perspective of the earlier turning point, may be supplemented by a comparison made in the light of the later attainment, namely by a retrospective, viz. linguistic, interpretation. Jacob himself has convincingly ascribed to the linguistic model "an exceptional value for the molecular analysis of heredity" (1974).

At the first steps of biology in the sixteenth century, to which Jacob's *Logic of Life* refers, "the play of unknown forces was hidden behind that of language". But now a comparative view of the not-yet-unraveled natural and verbal mysteries may be of use to unbiased students of both disciplines, the rapidly advancing science of life and the millennially old science of language.

In the sciences of life and language - let us quote and supplement Jacob's thesis - "one can no longer separate a structure from its signification not only in the organism [and in language as well], but in all the sequence of events that have led the organism [as well as language] to become what it is". Both biologists and linguists have observed an impressive set of attributes common to life and language since the latter's consecutive emergence. These two information-carrying and goal-directed systems imply the presence of messages and of an underlying code. From the first appearance of a vital minimum, "the special status assigned to living organisms by their origin and purpose" consists of coded messages which specify the molecular structures and are transmitted as instructions from generation to generation. The respective makeups of the two codes - the genetic, discovered and deciphered in our time by molecular biology, and the verbal, scrutinized by several generations of linguists - have displayed a series of noticeable analogies.

Through a significant coincidence, the Prague Linguistic Circle and the geneticist Jacob have defined the object of their studies as "a system of systems". The principle of gradual integration governs the structure of the two codes. Both of them equally display a hierarchy of discontinuous units. As the biologist points out, each of these units, labeled "integron", is built by assembling integrons of the level below it and takes part in the construction of an integron of the level above. In a similar way the linguist Émile Benveniste (1902-1976) states that a unit of the verbal code may be conceived of as such only insofar as it appears identifiable within a higher unit (1966: 119 ff.). Among all the information-carrying systems, the genetic code is the only one which shares with the verbal code a sequential arrangement of discrete subunits - phonemes in language and nucleotides (or 'nucleic letter') in the genetic code - which by themselves are devoid of inherent meaning but serve to build minimal units endowed with their own, intrinsic meaning (cf. above, pp. 13 ff., 47).

In genetic information each of these meaningful units consists of three "letters" and is termed "code word" or "triplet". The equivalence between a triplet of nucleic letters and one of the twenty diverse protein units into which the given triplet is translated has permitted Jacob to emphasize that "a genetic code is like a language" and to refer in this connection to the relation between *signans* and *signatum,* the fa-

mous twofold delineation of verbal signs. The three triplets which find
no protein equivalents fulfill a syntactic, demarcative function: a sequence - sentence or gene - begins and ends with special "punctuation marks".

In accordance with the subdivision of phonemes into distinctive
features, two binary oppositions of polar properties underlie the four-
letter alphabet of the genetic code. This dichotomy allows the conversion of the abundant inventory of synonymous triplets into a set of ordered rules analogous to the linguistic operations with the sound structure of grammatical units. Of the four "nucleic letters", two *larger* ones,
namely purines - A(denine) and G(uanine) - are opposed to two
smaller ones, namely pyrimidines - T(hymine) and C(ytosine) - and
the "letters" within each of these two pairs display two polar orders between the donor and recipient.

In the final third of the triplet the difference between the two purines is always redundant, with two further specified exceptions. When
G is the medial component of the triplet, the difference between the final purines and pyrimidines is always redundant, whereas in triplets
with a medial T, such a difference is always significative. But when the
medial position belongs neither to G nor to T, the semantic status of
the final component is determined by the first component of the triplet. Then the initial G or C entails the redundancy of all four final components, while either T or A in the initial position endows the four final components with an autonomous reference to two distinct protein
units. Such a divergence between the treatment of the pairs G/C and
T/A is to be compared with the bifurcation of the four nucleic letters
into two indissoluble associations in both complementary fibers of the
linear sequence: "the symbols go in pairs", and one pair of conjoint associates is formed by G and C, the other by T and A. Some sets of four
synonyms with a G in the initial or medial position are supplemented
by two further synonyms with T or A as their initial component. The
two triplets devoid of synonyms have C in their final position.

The synonymy rules impose severe limitations upon the *semantic*
variety of the sixty-four different triplets by reducing their translation-
al equivalents to twenty distinct protein units. It is not the vocabulary
itself, but only the syntactic and suprasentential level of genetic messages that permits their broad diversification.

When proceeding from the simplest to more complex organisms,
Jacob makes it clear that in each of them the interaction of the constituent parts underlies "the organization of the whole" and that the inte-

gration confers upon the whole new structural properties. With the rise of cybernetics, such an interaction between the constituents of a living organism or between the organism and its surroundings, as well as between members of a human society, has been approached as a problem of communication, and language becomes a model example "of interaction between elements of an integrated whole". If the formation of a mammal or especially of a human being is written down in the genetic message and baffles the scientist's imagination as "a marvel of exactitude and precision", just the same may be said about human language as an extraordinary, faultless, and subtle device of both outer and inner communication. This device displays a context-sensitive structure, an array of supportive redundancies, a variety of creative transpositions, and above all a rich gamut of two-way transitions between explicitness and ellipsis. Finally it is a unique and universal system capable of generating jugdments and equational propositions.

Insofar as the "aptitude for language" is supposed to be the final genetic endowment in the rise of the human species, then presumably the fundamental plan of language, its indispensable design common to all verbal codes of the world, must belong to this endowment. The 'double articulation' of language (see below, p. 181) or, in other words, the composition of meaningful units from discrete subunits devoid of their own inherent meaning, is common solely to these two codes among all communication systems. The isomorphism displayed by the verbal and by the genetic codes proves to be deeply rooted in the entire model and mechanism of the two codes. Obviously we are not yet in a position to explain this salient correspondence, as long as for linguists the origin of language and, similarly, for geneticists the genesis of life remain unsolvable problems: "But then how did it all begin? ⟨...⟩ What is the origin of the genetic code? ⟨...⟩ Why does one nucleic-acid triplet 'mean' a certain subunit and not another? ⟨...⟩ Nothing indicates that the transition between the organic and the living can ever be analyzed". Moreover, "one does not yet know how acquired circuits are superimposed on the heredity network, nor how the innate and the acquired fit together".

Language, the primary vehicle of human society, was assessed by Sapir as "a great force of socialization, probably the greatest that exists". Another powerful socializer and individualizer in the history of the living world was the far earlier and "most important invention" of sex, whose role has been eloquently outlined in Jacob's book. As sexuality emerged and developed from a seemingly "superfluous gadget" to an obligatory method of reproduction, it gave rise to communication between individuals and to the process of integration on a higher level than the single organism. It created such novelties as choice of partners, radical reassortment of programs, and maximal individualization of progeny. Briefly, this "complication elaborated in the course of evolution" canceled the insipid prospect of "a rather boring universe without sex, ⟨...⟩ a universe peopled only by identical cells reproducing *ad infinitum*".

"As exchanges increase during evolution, there appear new systems of communication that no longer operate within the organism, but between organisms". Such is the line of development from the earlier innovation to the later one, from sexual intercourse to the wider radius of verbal intercourse, according to the Anglicism introduced by Saussure into French linguistic terminology. "Death imposed from within" as a compulsory, integral part of the sexualized system prompts us to recollect the conjoint imagery of love and death in world poetry and moreover suggests a comparison with the substantial part assigned to oblivion in the perpetual mobility of language.

The decisive evolutionary role played by "new systems of communication, just as much within the organism as between the organism and its surroundings", becomes, despite all incessant hesitations, ever clearer both to biologists and to linguists. Even the reference to random mutations based on chance, reproductional errors, accidental additions, omissions, and casual Spoonerisms in the genetic messages, finds a rectification in the reminder that the notion of an evolution resulting exclusively "from mutations, which occur each at random", proves to be "denied both by time and by arithmetic"; even on the microscopic level the simplest organisms "are built by a series of integrations".

Since "little is yet known" of the ways cells communicate with each other, since the differentiation of the living world, especially the development of its higher forms, is still waiting for elucidation, and since the danger of premature generalizations is never excluded, queries from other related fields of knowledge could hardly be out of place. In particular, students of linguistic evolution may ask whether the agglomeration of mistakes in the genetic messages which direct the multiplication of living systems happens by mere chance. To the older linguistic dogma of blind and fortuitous changes, which only afterwards might be followed by a reassortment, later studies of language are inclined to oppose the finality of "oriented lapses", as the topologist René Thom terms them. Such reiterative slips are deviations rather than simple mistakes. Whatever the answer to such tentative questions might be, the amiable and unprejudiced interdisciplinary dialogue demands to be continued and developed, particularly since the permanent "struggle between what was and what is to be, between the sameness of reproduction and the novelty of variation" is deeply implanted in the subject matter of the two kindred sciences.

XXI. ROLE OF LEARNING

There emerges from time to time the view of oral speech as a mere accidental human choice for verbal shape. This bias seems facetious when confronted with the genuine universality of spoken language. Oral speech rests upon universally elaborated acoustico-motor instrumentalities which are at the disposal of all sane human, and only human, offspring of the globe. This availability is inseparably tied to the necessity for all children of the world to follow an adult model in acquiring a language and to the fact that any extant language used by this model is masterable by the infant learner. The doubt sometimes intimated about the universal indispensability of learning and tutorship is based merely on a somewhat superficial, bureaucratic attitude toward the meaning of the words *tutor* and *learn*. Learning and imitation or more exactly, replication (cf. L. G. Jones 1967: 5), are widely creative phenomena, and tutorship frequently appears in a covert and latent form (cf. Whorf 1956: 70 ff., 88 ff., 105 ff.). The delicate and complex processes of children's gradual learning and of the continuing instruction by the older members of the nuclear family and of the environment still require an intense observation on the part of psycho- and socio-linguists and anthropologists. As Ben G. Blount rightly concluded (1972: 128) on the basis of adult-children conversations collected in Luo and Samoa, "the social enviroment is not a mere data-bank in the language acquisition process" and "the language models which serve the children cannot be dismissed as raw, undifferentiated linguistic information". The conventionalized 'baby-talk' initiated and taught by adults to children "until the baby has completely mastered the normal flow of language" is in Bengali used at least until the child's sixth year, and throughout the world it fulfills a substantial task in children's verbal development (see particularly Ferguson 1964 and Dil 1971). The total acquisition of the first language, far from being an avalanche-rush, proves to entail, as Carol Chomsky (1969) masterfully showed, a nearly decade-long process.

XXII. SPEECH AND VISUALIZED LANGUAGE

There is a substitutive system called 'sign language'. This label is deceptive since it obscures the fact that "natural" language likewise consists of signs (in this case verbal signs) and that in general language is a topic of the science of signs, alias semiotics. In any case, so-called 'sign language' is a humanly important and structurally attractive topic, but as William C. Stokoe noted (1975), "the proportion of native speakers to native signers is about ten thousand to one" and thus in the study of *universal* human speech this marginal system may be left aside.

Despite the enormous importance of reading and writing, we must take into account the omnipresent fact that these are but a secondary attainment in human life. Moreover, almost half the world's people are still totally illiterate and the actual use of reading and writing is the asset of a scarce minority. At the end of the sixties, according to official UNESCO data, the number of illiterates had risen by almost 60 million to about 800 million, out of a total adult population of 2,225,000,000. Since producers and receivers of written messages exclusively are exceptional, we must distinguish the speakers and listeners of mere oral messages from those who have recourse to reading and writing also. Between these two varieties of language users there are a number of characterological differences which have even led some investigators such as Goody & Watt (1963) to distinguish sociology, the science of man as a writing species, from social anthropology, the science of man as a merely talking animal.

It is true that a logographic script such as the Chinese one leads to a certain autonomization of the written word vs. speech (cf. Karlgren 1962), but even the reading of Chinese characters requires, to a high degree, their recoding into speech sounds. As experiments show, "the phonetic reading of visually presented nonphonetic symbols such as Chinese characters suggests that even if lexical readout may occur directly from visual input, speech recoding is still needed for the working memory stage" (Tzeng et al. 1977). It is interesting that in spite of evident graphic differences the reader's performance "was found to be impaired by the introduction of phonemic similarity into the test materials". But an alphabetic system necessarily prompts its user to associate it, to a high degree, with speech and to transpose the script into an oral performance. It is characteristic that the first stage of learning to read is reading out loud, and that the internalization of reading is a secondary, later process. An instructive and popular example is St. Augustine's account of his youthful surprise at finding his master reading a book silently and without moving his lips. In a recent comic strip, a youngster asks:

"Daddy, how can you read to yourself?"

"What do you mean?"

"I mean if you read to yourself, how do you know what it *says* if you don't *hear* anything?"

While the distinctive features and their combinations into phonemes differ from other linguistic constituents by the phenomenon of 'otherness' as the only or at least the main content of their *signatum*, the nature of letters is different. In general, the *signatum* of any given letter is a certain phoneme of the language in question. In diverse spelling systems there may be constraints such as homophonous letters or other limitative rules imposed upon the simple relation between letter and sound, but the essence of the relation between graph as *signans* and phone as *signatum* remains valid. In logographic script, a graphic entity is in turn endowed with a singleness of its *signatum*, but here the *signatum* consists of a lexical unit instead of a phonic one. It is indeed significant that of the two Japanese types of graphic symbols, the syllabic *(Kana)* and the logographic *(Kanji)*, only the former is impaired in aphasic disorders of the sound pattern (Sasanuma 1975). Thus the distinctive features of the speech sounds and their graphic rendering prove to be intimately associated with each other, and this association shows that aphasic impairments of speech sounds are intrinsically linguistic and not automatically motor or auditory losses.

Scholars insist on the autonomous and effective properties of written language on all levels, from the ultimate constituents up to the selection and organization of vocabulary, syntax, and even entire texts; the problems of alternating divergences and convergences between the two domains of communication demand a heightened and widened attention, as do the comparative characteristics of the varying social and cultural communalities and particularities of these two types of verbal activity (for emphasis on the study of written language, cf. Vachek 1976: 112–146 and Derrida 1967). The growing substitution of printed and typed messages for handwritten ones reduces the emotive and physiognomic roles of script; in this connection one could cite the traditional and still extant custom of writing intimate and ceremonial messages by hand.

Listening to speech is a sequential process dealing with just-vanished sounds, words, and sentences and involving the repetitive use of so-called 'simultaneous synthesis' (a transposition of a sequential event into a synchronous process) in the short-term memory of the perceiver. The question of the fading of the last word of the sentence as soon as the final sound of this word is uttered and the correlate problem of the reconstruction of the vanished sequence in the mind of the hearer thanks to his faculty to retain the right order of the evaporated strings and to remember the difference between such words as *nadī* and *dīna* or *rasa* and *sara* – all this was pervasively discussed in the Indic speculations on language (cf. Brough 1951; Ruegg 1959) and demands further exploration.

Carol Chomsky (1971) and C. Read (1971) have brought forward eloquent data on individual spelling reforms hazarded by unschooled children who were rigidly oriented toward a consistent endowment of English letters with the stable sense-discriminative value of the corresponding speech sounds. It is noteworthy that the expenditure of hours devoted in grade school to the acquisition of spelling is incomparably higher in English-speaking countries than, for instance, in Finland, Yugoslavia, or Czechoslovakia, where the orthographic system primarily reflects the sense-discriminative employment of the distinctive features and where, therefore, the percentage of spelling mistakes is correspondingly lower among average pupils and adults. In this connection, Luria's observations (1960) should be remembered: bilingual subjects suffering from agraphic disturbances undergo much more serious losses in the mastery of the spelling patterns of French and English than of Russian and German orthographic systems, which pay closer attention to the sense-discriminative elements.

Reading allows one to linger on single passages or even to turn back to preceding lines or pages. Reading and writing involve space while speech is an essentially temporal experience. The virtually lasting character of written communications is, both individually and socially, a most influential factor, which on the one hand secures the relative permanence, the testamental, memorial aspect of the written text, and which on the other hand diminishes the task of memorizing, as can be eloquently illustrated by the astounding memory of the illiterate reciters of thousands of epic verses. The natural, indispensable differences between written and oral style nonetheless allow deeper reciprocal influences of script on speech and vice versa and frequent occurences of spelling pronunciation. For a long time in the competition between oral and written communication, the latter seemed to be gained predominance in our culture, but at present the ever-expanding use of radio, TV, sound films, telephone, records, and tapes is effecting a number of changes in the mutual relation of the two rival systems.

The spelling and grammatical rules and the standardized vocabulary of written languages enjoy relative stability, prescriptibility, and uniformity of the code under the influence of school and various institutional interventions. Corresponding phenomena in spoken language, such as orthoepy in comparison with orthography, unquestionably play an appreciable role in the modern culture of spoken language, but in most cases to a lesser and less regularized degree than the requirement of norm and normalization imposed upon script.

XXIII. MULTIFORMITY AND CONFORMISM

Linguists, even when interested chiefly in oral speech, often unwittingly give way to the hypnosis of written language. It is peculiar that in discussing the order of some verbal units in a sequence they use the terms "left" and "right" instead of "before" and "after" and speak about the "left-hand" and "right-hand" environment of a speech sound. In their examples of linguistic ambiguities they quote sentences ambiguous merely in writing and perfectly distinguishable in their explicit oral form. It is perhaps under the influence of the higher uniformity proper to the code of written language that sometimes the idea of a rigorously monolithic code of language in general captures theoreticians and tempts them to believe in the puerile myth of a perfectly invariable speech community with equally competent speaker-hearers and to apply the delusive idea to concrete operations. However, "real individuals command a variety of related linguistic systems", a variety of styles of speech used in a range of social situations (as was succinctly noted by Chomsky & Walker 1976): "Individuals within a speech community may differ in these respects and speech communities sometimes may vary quite widely in the systems represented within what is popularly called a single language" (p. 21). Hence, any actual linguistic status contrasts strongly with the assumption of a grammar "uniformly represented as a single invariant system in the mind of each English speaker".

Witold Doroszewski (1899–1976), who was hostile to the idea of relational invariance in the sound structure of language, paid particular attention to the abundant diversity of variants in the everyday speech of Polish peasants which he recorded in his field work. These minute observations are particularly valuable because, contrary to the observer's anti-unitarian tenet, they bring to light the orderliness within the obvious variety. The several exponents of the Polish nasal ę used by all members of a rural Polish speech community near Plock were recorded and described in his French paper of 1935 (p. 28 ff.) and, with more detail, in a previous Polish report of 1934 (p. 249 ff.). The basic variants stand out against the marginal ones and the preponderant cases display competition and compromises between opposite tendencies: nearer vs. more distant in space or time, and either disappearing or developing; rural traits compete with urban influence; articulatory memory clashes with lexical borrowings preserving their sound shape. A closer interpretation of this eloquent "jeu des formes flottantes" could to a large degree find the key to this selection in the changeability of contexts and topics, momentary universe of discourse, difference of speech functions, and switching relations between speakers and hearers. According to Doroszewski's belief, the individual himself is completely passive and makes no deliberate choice between diverse possible solutions; he is influenced by opposite tendencies, whatever the difference between them: "les deux le travaillent, coexistent en lui". Doroszewski concluded that the system is a "Procustean bed", but his dialectal material is in fact an excellent *plaidoyer* for the pluralism of the verbal code both against the narrowly empirical denial of system and against the reductionist denial of multiform systems.

The expert observer William Labov (1964, 1970) exemplified the motivated and structured variability of sound forms in their interpersonal and personal usage and uncovered "a pattern of continuous and regular variation through different styles and contexts". He noted specific properties of speech "used in informal situations where no attention is directed to language" and in particular occurrences of spontaneous, excited speech "when the constraints of a formal situation are discharged". The science of language cannot but agree with Jacob's reference to the two apparently opposite properties of living beings – stability and variability – as "an inherent quality of the very nature of living systems". Any unbounded generalization of the stability and uniformity principle proves to be an impoverishing, stultifying "idealization" of the heterogeneous linguistic reality. "The association between structure and homogeneity is an illusion", as Weinreich et alii state, following in the footsteps of the Praguians; "the concept of a variable as a structural element makes it unnecessary to view fluctuations in use as external to the system, for control of such variation is a part of the linguistic competence of members of the speech community" (1968: 185–187).

Like any other social system, language is in continuous motion and self-generating development (cf. Lange 1962: 73 ff.). The verbal code and in particular the sound pattern of any language constantly undergo changes. In contradistinction to daylight savings time or to spelling reforms, which can be decreed and enter into common practice on a definite date, the start and finish of a sound change in spoken language go through a period of coexistence; they belong to two styles, two subcodes of the same language, and are actively used either by different speakers or by one speaker who oscillates between the "archaïsm" and the "modernism". Speakers and hearers may be aware of the time axis to which both items belong, and time itself thereby enters into the verbal system as a semiotic value. The belief earlier voiced among linguists that the process of linguistic change is never directly observed does not take into account the vital phenomenon of speakers' preoccupation with speech itself and their habitual metalinguistic talk about talking. There are frequent cases of a generational difference between interlocutors, the youngest of whom make use of the nascent innovations which the older ones understand but have not included in their speaker repertory. Similarly, the younger speakers comprehend the older ones although the younger no longer actively use the elements they deem "outdated". Besides such cases of manifest division between speakers and listeners, there obviously also occur frequent instances of mutual adaptation in intercommunication between people of different generations. Members of a speech community are competent to use both the start and the finish of the change, and the overall code of the given language must correspondingly be conceived of as convertible. Thus the two stages of a change in progress should be interpreted in terms of a dynamic synchrony. Concurrence and successivity are, therefore, interrelated both in single utterances and in the "overall code" of language (cf. Hockett 1958).

The tendency of Saussure's *Cours* to reduce the structure of any language system to concurrence (simultaneity) with disregard for successivity (temporal succession) - "l'axe des simultanéités, concernant les rapports entre choses coexistantes, d'où toute intervention du temps est exclue" (I: 177) - is as equally arbitrary and impoverishing a tendency as is the reverse attempt of the same *Cours* to discard concurrence from the structure of linguistic units and to confine them to a mere linearity - "caractère linéaire du signifiant" (Saussure I: 157; cf. LW 1976: 39 ff.).

With respect to the variable radius of communication from the nuclear family to interdialectal and even crosslingual verbal intercourse, the multiplicity of tasks again involves different subcodes adapted to changing interlocutors; herewith space enters into the overall code of the speech community and its members as a semiotic value. In both their temporal and spatial aspects the code and the circuit of messages exhibit a perpetual interplay between conformism and nonconformism. A spatial conformism, adaption to neighbors, usually implies a temporal nonconformism, in other words, a temporal discontinuity. On the other hand, there is normally a linkage between temporal conformism and discontinuity with the neighbor's pattern, alienation from it. The repeated assumption of an essential difference between the 'source' (Saussurian *foyer*) of a linguistic innovation and the area of its "contagion" and propagation clashes with the fact that any change is a phenomenon of propagation, from a slip of the tongue to its repetition and acceptance first by a narrow and then by a wide collective body; a change and its diffusion appear to be but two facets of one and the same ongoing "contagion". The plurality of subcodes and of the transitions from one subcode to another is an essential constituent of linguistic competence possessed by an individual and *mutatis mutandis* by his milieu. Doroszewski's records, discussed above, belong to a series of papers compiled by various field workers in order to prove that individual speakers do not use any integral system, since the texts recorded and published exhibit an extremely mixed character. If, however, one subjects these variables to an attentive analysis, then, may we repeat, all the supposedly conflicting textual peculiarities easily find a natural explanation in the alternation of thematic and stylistic factors and of addressees, and these variations display a complex integral system. The belief of the recorders in variability without integration is no less illusory than the belief of a theoretician in integral competence without inner variation. Also, in conditions of close contact between two dialects or two languages, people with bidialectal or bilingual competence can enjoy a prestigious position in their linguistic environment, and the partial merger of two neighboring codes which is typical of bilingual individuals or groups favors a wider expansion of certain particularities of one language, especially of its sound shape, to the adjacent tongue.

XXIV. INNER SPEECH

On the threshold of the transition from infancy (literally 'speechlessness') to language, a child starts his interpersonal communication by addressing one of the nearest adults, most usually his mother. Later, his one-to-one communication is complemented by a more-than-two person system with a plurality of participants and with a developing distinction between the true addressee of the child's messages and unaddressed auditors. On the other hand there arises a less-than-two person system – dialogues with an older interlocutor are complemented by the child's gradual mastery of a narrowed intrapersonal network of communication. Thus, the child's interlocutor becomes the child himself "as he will be a second after", according to Peirce's view of inner "dialogue between different phases of the ego" (4.6). Here arises a distinction between two kinds of communication, namely "the transmission of meaning by signs from mind to mind and from one state of mind to another" (Peirce: I.445). There emerges the so-called 'egocentric speech' of the youngster in the presence of others: the child's former interlocutor becomes a mere auditor while the child himself assumes the roles of both the addresser and the addressee. This "intermediate link between overt and inner speech" has been inspiringly sketched by Lev Vygotsky (1962). He pointed to the fact that structural peculiarities of inner speech and its functional differentiation from external speech increase with age; "the decrease of egocentric speech indicates no more than the diminution of one quality of this speech: its vocalization". Out-loud, half-dream, presleep soliloquies may follow as the next step in the absence of any possible human replier to the child but in the presence of such speechless addresses as a doll or a dog (cf. Weir 1962). Whispered, and then actually inner, silent speech are further steps in the internalization of language.

It is noteworthy that the sound shape preserves its motor traces in the unconscious movements of the tongue which usually, though to a lesser extent, accompany even the adult's inner speech. A. N. Sokolov's investigation of the relation between thought and inner speech shows how the latter "arises genetically on the basis of outer speech as its *interior projection* and constantly develops and improves under the direct influence of external speech. In spite of its elliptic and generalized character, inner speech does not possess any separate, idiosyncratic, logical and grammatical structure" (1959: 513; cf. his conclusive book of 1968). Inner speech is radically elliptic; the sound shape of words receives a merely fragmentary evocation in our mind, and frequently they totally lose their phonic makeup ("zero *signans*"). However, neither these losses nor the tendency to replace verbal signs by other semiotic units permit us to return to an assumption of wordless, or even signless, asemiotic thinking.

It would be a perverse castration to separate the cardinal idea of verbal communication from its vital and normally undetachable constituent, inner speech. In an authoritarian state, a scientist, asked by a police searcher what the Greek book on his desk was, answered, "Plato's Dialogues". - "Dialogues? But with whom?" - "With himself" was the alleged and intrinsically right answer. Both inner and uttered speech form a bridge between the person and his environment and both of these linguistic performances are rich in quoted speech and in verbal creativity; both exteriorized and interiorized speech carry the legacy of the past and the anticipation of the future.

It is an essential fact that the representation of the sound shape of the words which function elliptically in our internal speech remains in our thought, as was pointed out by the sagacious linguist F. F. Fortunatov (1848-1914). He realized that "in a certain respect, the phenomena of language themselves appertain to the phenomena of thought", and that "language as such, when our thoughts are expressed in speech, has its being precisely because it exists itself in our thinking" (1956: 111 ff.). It is difficult to pursue more consistently the idea of the inseverable ties between the sound shape and its semantic counterpart.

The structure of language underlies all of its manifestations, both patent and latent, and there can be no rupture between the structure and its purposes: an afunctional structure and a nonstructured function are both pointless and empty fictions. Our concepts are apprehended and delineated by the very fact of being named; this verbalizing activity endows them with permanence in time and continuity in space, and in this way secures and enhances our conservative ties with the past and creative connections with our future by securing and enforcing our intercourse with the environment. Our thought turns into an object of our naming and propositional activities, and our words and sentences in their interaction are converted into independent objects of our thought.

CHAPTER TWO

QUEST FOR THE ULTIMATE CONSTITUENTS

> The important thing about a trans-
> formation is what it doesn't
> transform, i.e. what it leaves
> invariant.
>> S.S. Stevens
>> *Mathematics, Measurement,*
>> *and Psychophysics*

> Tout est bilatéral dans le do-
> maine de la pensée. Les idées
> sont binaires. Janus est le mythe
> de la critique et le symbole du
> génie. Il n'y a que Dieu de
> triangulaire.
>> Honoré de Balzac
>> *Illusions perdues*

I. TO THE MEMORY OF PIERRE DELATTRE

Pierre Delattre, born in the French town of Roanne on the Loire in 1903, early in his career linked his scholarly activities with American universities–Michigan, Wayne State, Oklahoma, Pennsylvania, Colorado, and from 1964 the University of California at Santa Barbara. His rich and remarkable works in experimental phonetics gradually gained in precision and originality and by degrees moved toward the search for the ultimate constituents of language. Delattre's comprehensive address, "From Acoustic Cues to the Distinctive Features", delivered in a plenary session of the VIIth International Congress of Phonetic Sciences in September 1967 and published in a French version in the *Proceedings* of the Congress (1970a) and also in a slightly different, English version in *Phonetica* (1968a), marked a new stage in the creative work of this persevering, courageous seeker.

From their first, friendly meetings at the Ghent Congress of Phonetic Sciences in 1938, Delattre and RJ closely followed each other's research. When at the end of the VIIth Phonetic Congress Delattre airmailed to RJ the complete, original version of his paper, a close cooperation developed between them. In the summer of 1968 during RJ's three-day visit to the eminent phonetician, their discussions and tests "dans la tranquilité et l'intimité" of Delattre's house and of the magnificent laboratory he built up for the University of California at Santa Barbara matured into a plan for a joint, systematic outline of the psychoacoustic correlates of the system of distinctive features. An agreement arose on the need for a further and more consistent application of the slogan "economize and binarize," which Delattre advocated in the Prague debates, as he informed RJ in the coda of his letter of October 6, 1967.

Delattre came a long way from his early skeptical remarks about the apologists for "binarism and alleged distinctive features" to his final work guided by the motto cited above. To explain the development of his thinking, the scholar himself stated in the introduction to his Prague address that "the patient testing of numerous acoustic variables of speech for nearly twenty years has led us to a point where it is perhaps possible to assemble the pieces of the phonetic puzzle and look at the acoustic elements of a language as a system" (1968a: 198).

The original introduction to the Prague paper, inserted avowedly "pour détendre les esprits tendus" and almost entirely omitted in the drier printed texts of 1968a and 1970a, faithfully renders the author's scientific attitude and goals:

> In their endless quest for the Grail (la Queste del Graal), the Knights of the Round Table (les chevaliers de la Table Ronde) remind us of the phoneticians of today – they did not know what the Grail was, but they never gave up the hope of finding it. It was the mystery of the Grail that obsessed them, as it is the mystery of distinctive features that fascinates us today.
>
> In our quest for the Grail of phonemics, that is, for the Distinctive Features by means of which phonemic perception operates, there are good reasons for starting with acoustic correlates rather than with articulatory correlates.

A paragraph of resigned words closes Delattre's manuscript:

> So ends our quest for the Grail. And I dare not venture any further, because it is written in the second book of Perceval that when Galahad was finally able to contemplate the mystery of the Grail with his own eyes, he died instantly.

However, without superstitious fear, the mutual efforts to reach an ever-closer solution continued and developed, until in July 1969 the scheduled program of further personal meetings and the plan of collaboration and joint publication were abruptly cancelled by the tragic news of Delattre's sudden death. We venture to dedicate this chapter to his memory as our modest attempt to pursue this search in keeping with the late scholar's intentions.

One may note that it was at the Ghent Congress of 1938 that Delatt-re came into direct contact with phonology and with the Prague linguistic school for the first time, and it was on this occasion that he attended the first international discussion of the distinctive features (*"qualités différentielles"*) and their binary oppositions. The delivery of his lecture on distinctive features at the Prague Congress almost thirty years later was for Delattre, as he himself acknowledged, a symbolic turn toward the Prague phonological tradition. The final, printed text of his Prague paper (1968 a) begins by declaring:

> In our search for the distinctive features by means of which phonemic perception operates, there are good reasons for starting with acoustic correlates rather than with articulatory correlates. ⟨...⟩ The most objective approach to discovering the nature of distinctive features appears to be through their *acoustic* correlates. ⟨...⟩ We propose to look at the complete consonantal *acoustic structure* of a language and to extract from it the categories of acoustic cues which are relevant to linguistic perception, in isolation and in various combinations.

The paper concludes

> that if distinctive features are perceptual signals which can only be envisioned indirectly through their acoustic and articulatory correlates, and if the articulatory correlates can only be specified after the acoustic correlates have been isolated by synthetic manipulation and perceptual tests, there seems to be no better means of closing in on the distinctive features than by reaching a complete knowledge of what is distinctive in the acoustic signal.

Two basic concepts dating back to Delattre's fruitful cooperation with Haskins Laboratories and consistently applied in his Prague address were concisely defined by the speaker in its printed versions. In the *Proceedings* (see 1970 a) he describes 'formants' as "bandes étroites de son filtrés par la résonance sélective au tractus vocalique", and in the English version (1968 a: 201) in connection with his "locus theory" of consonantal distinctive features he defines 'locus' as "the frequency point toward which all the transitions that are related to the perception of the same consonantal distinctive feature converge, regardless of the vowel that precedes or follows".

Despite the clarity of Delattre's position and the cogency of his Prague-toned experimental attempt, the widespread reluctance to recognize his highly objective approach to the analysis of the ultimate constituents of language was sometimes quite stubborn. For instance in a detailed critical survey of 1974, Delattre's final lessons were totally disregarded and his earlier, still hesitant attitude was held up as a fore-cast for the future:

> It is quite possible that in the long run, Delattre's pessimism about the fea-sibility of finding an exclusively articulatory or exclusively acoustic set of correlates for distinctive features will turn out to be justified. [Lipski 1974: 428]

This surveyor (following Fudge 1967) cites the eloquent example of the four-member Mazatec vowel system of /i, e, o, a/ analyzed by Ni-da (1949: 31) as

	front	back
high	i	o
low	e	a

and warns against the danger of establishing patterns with no measur-able physical correlates and hence of positing "bizarre" and "arbitrar-ily constructed" correlations. The presumably random and abstract status of distinctive features is, however, due to a current confusion of void abstractness with purposeful relativity.

The distinctive features and the auditory cues for their recognition, far from constituting an "abstract framework" (cf. Fudge 1967), as-sume a concrete and detectable invariance of relation between the two opposite members within each pair. From time to time the tabulation of distinctive features meets with imaginary arguments which question the accuracy of measurements and the degree of descriptive precision. These objections are in most cases based on the substitution of a crude metrical attitude for a sane, relational, topological treatment. The op-position of /i/ to /e/ and correspondingly of /o/ to /a/ symmetrically confronts narrower vowels to wider ones (relatively diffuse vowels to relatively compact ones). The pair of advanced vowels /i/ and /e/ stands in an identical relation of acuteness to the gravity of the retract-ed vowels /o/ and /a/. This grave ~ acute opposition acquires a re-dundant enhancement by the parallel confrontation of a narrower ad-vanced vowel to a wider retracted vowel – /i/ to /o/ and /e/ to /a/. For further examples of the same type as the Mazatec vowel pattern, see Liljencrants & Lindblom 1972: 845 f., Four-Vowel Systems (a), (b). The imaginary deviations b', c, and d are actually due to the methodo-logical crudity of the schemes (Sedlak 1969: 32f.) they used as a source; Sedlak's diagrams also give the erroneous impression that only quasi-symmetrical vocalic patterns exist in higher numbered types of systems.

II. VOWEL ~ CONSONANT

In Morris Halle's evaluation (1976: 88 ff.), perhaps the chief question raised by the gradual discovery of distinctive features has been the consistent comparative analysis of vocalism and consonantism. The comparative investigation of this pair remained paralyzed for a long time by an unswerving abnegation of communalities between the two subsystems, and survivals of this abnegation "continue in wide use to this day" (Halle ibid.). Whatever definition for vowels and consonants could be considered the most precise, there is not the slightest doubt that this is the cardinal and most obvious bifurcation of speech sounds for linguists, for investigators of speech in its motor, acoustic, and perceptual aspects, for poets, and finally for the intuition of ordinary speakers. If the problem of the structural relationship between these two classes of speech sounds has become so involved and at times even controversial, it is because of the unique, most particular character of this relation as compared to the interrelations within each of these two classes (cf. RJ & LW 1979).

The main principle of intravocalic or intraconsonantal differentiation lies in the commutability of the members within each class. The essential function of such intravocalic and intraconsonantal distinctions rests upon their sense-discriminative role, beginning with the most elementary examples, such as *sheep~cheap, sip~tip, sheep~ship, sheep~shape, sheep~sheet, sip~sick.* Whereas the relations between the diverse members of the consonantal or likewise of the vocalic pattern are basically and chiefly paradigmatic, the mutual relation of vowels and consonants is built on their sequential interconnection. In agreement with the formulation made popular by Saussure's *Cours* (I: 282), "le rapport syntagmatique est *in praesentia;* il repose sur deux ou plusieurs termes également présents dans une série effective", in contradistinction to the relation which is now labeled 'paradigmatic' and which unites terms "*in absentia* dans une série mnémonique virtuelle". Any sequence is built of syllables; they are the fundamental divisions of any sequence, and in all languages they follow a clear-cut constructional model which consists of a nucleus (also called peak or crest) and margins (also called slopes or slants). Vowels function in languages as the only or at least as the most usual carriers of the syllabic nuclei, whereas the margins of syllables are occupied chiefly or solely by consonants.

As frequently occurs with the fundamental constituents of a province of knowledge, the strict definition of the paramount property which specifies the vowels on the one hand and the consonants on the other has proved to be perhaps the most entangled task in the multifaceted investigation of speech sounds. As stated by Kenneth Pike, "the most basic, characteristic, and universal division made in phonetic classification is that of consonant and vowel. Its delineation is one of the least satisfactory" (1943: 66). The phonetician Georges Straka's comprehensive survey of the attempts at an empirical delimitation of the two categories led him to favor the recognition of two opposite types of articulation: vowels as "mouth-openers" (*ouvreuses*) and consonants as "mouth-closers" (*fermeuses*) (1963: 72 ff.). And Nikolaj Žinkin's astute inquiry into the difference between these two competitive and alternating muscular activities led to his "pharyngeal conception of syllable formation" (1968: 287) and his illuminating inquiry into the mechanisms of speech. (For the history of the syllable concept, see particularly Laziczius 1961: 156–193.)

The traditional etymology of the Sanskrit name for consonant, *vyañjana*, as 'revelative' seems to carry the "suggestion that the consonants rather than the vowels are responsible for the differentiation of meanings" (Allen 1953: 81). And in fact the higher informativeness of consonants is a widespread phenomenon which finds expression in those alphabetic systems limited to signs for consonants only. In children's language the sense-discriminative role of consonants as a rule antedates that of vowels (i. e., oppositions within the consonantal system appear before those in the vocalic system). The primarily consonantal encoding of meanings, far from being confined to such extreme cases as the Caucasian Ubykh language with its two- or three-vowel phonemes and nearly eighty consonantal ones (see Vogt 1963: 13 ff.), shows up also in English. It is noteworthy that the authorities of acoustic laboratories in the United States were ready to disclose the images of vowels in the "visible speech experiment", whereas those of consonants were concealed until the end of World War II in order to hinder the deciphering of secret messages. Yet it is precisely the rich and semantically revealing class of consonants which still provokes complaints from acousticians because of the difficulty of determining the common essence of the consonantal feature. The attempt by Hugo Pipping (1864–1944) to define the common denominator of the consonantal phonemes still remains the most realistic. According to him, "all consonants carry a noise element. In fricatives it is inherent in the continuant noise, in nasal stops and laterals it is contained in the temporal contrast between sound segments with different excitation patterns along the basilar membrane. The sudden transition has the effect of a step excitation of the peripheral receptors which in turn is associated with a specific auditory quality." (See Pipping 1922; cf. Fant 1967.)

A thorough inquiry into the total sound systems of languages reveals the necessity of viewing the relation between vowels and consonants as two-faced. While consonants are opposed to vowels by the noise element, as Pipping noted, at the same time vowels are opposed to consonants through a clear-cut "sonority" *(Schallfülle)*, a concept enrooted in speech sound analysis since Edward Sievers (1850–1932) in his *Grundzüge* (see 1901[5]: § 528–535) and Jespersen in his *Lehrbuch* (see 1904: § 196 ff.) defended it. This problem has been dealt with in psychoacoustic studies from the point of view of the discriminable aspects of tones and particularly "tonal density" (see S. Stevens 1934 and Stevens & Davis 1938: 163 ff.). The combination of the two features – the consonantal and the vocalic – characterizes the liquids as concurrently consonantal and vocalic, and enables one to delineate the shifting class of sonorants.

III. SYLLABICITY

It is the mutual sequential contiguity of consonants and vowels which plays the main role in their interrelation within any given language. And it is the contiguity of the two contrastive functions within the syllable which contraposes both of its constituents – syllabics and nonsyllabics. Apparently, it has been precisely the predominant role played by the contiguity criterion as a *principium divisionis* that has caused some hesitations: it was difficult to decide whether the fundamental role in a paradigmatic classification of distinctive oppositions belongs to the duality of vowels and consonants or to that of syllabics and nonsyllabics. The recourse to syllabicity as a distinctive feature and even as the decisive one in the "coding tree" of features (cf. Fant 1973: 180) seems to be a rather arguable operation. Instead of following Chomsky & Halle's cogent appeal to make "use of the fact that the features have intrinsic content" (1968: 400), this operation employs a traditional, until recently favored distributionalist technique, the less recommendable since the roles of syllabics and nonsyllabics are as a rule automatically assigned in languages first and foremost to the vowels and consonants respectively.

Within those languages in which liquids and nasals can have a syllabic function, their primary, more diversified use remains nonsyllabic, and the syllabic variant of liquids is generally determined by strictly distributional rules (cf. Vachek 1976: 30). For example, Czech /r/ and /l/ are syllabic only when preceded by a consonant and not followed by a vowel within the same word; thus the liquid phoneme is here endowed with a syllabic contextual variant (cf. [lku] 'I weep' - (v̩lku] 'to the wolf', [jedl̩] 'he ate' - [jedla] 'she ate' - [jel] 'he rode'). In many languages syllabic liquids may function as stylistic variants: e.g., in certain styles of Russian speech the final, postconsonantal liquids and nasals are optionally used as syllabics and in other styles as nonsyllabics. In the latter case the liquid is devoiced after a voiceless consonant: e.g. [t'ígr̩] or [t'ígr] 'tiger' and [v'íxr̩'] or [v'íxr̩'] 'whirl-wind' (see Panov 1967: 269 f.). In Majakovskij's comedy *Klop* (*The Bedbug*), an ironically vulgar rhyme with a final syllabic nasal provides a telling example:

> šël ja vérxom, šël ja nízom [zəm]
> stróil móst v socialízm [izm̩],

while on the other hand, the same word *socializm* appears with a nonsyllabic final *m* in a lofty oxytonic line of the poet's solemn proclamation *Jubilejnoe (Celebrational)*:

> postróennyj v bojáx socialízm [izm].

The coadjacency of diverse segments of the sequence and particularly in the syllable as the cardinal constructive unit of the sequence confronts vowels and consonants as two fundamentally contrastive classes of phonemes. Yet it admits on the one hand transitional formations between pure vocalism and consonantism, and on the other hand extreme offshoots of consonantism such as obstruents, which differ from all other, sonorant types of speech sounds by the "direct" ("pluck") formant transitions and by turbulence and the absence of a "low link" (see Delattre 1968a: 212 ff.; Cutting & Rosner 1974, 1976; and RJ I: 496, 505). In such types of liquids as the Czech sibilant /ř/ and in geographically scattered lateral fricatives and affricates the turbulence is, if not eliminated, at least reduced, thanks to the freer flow of air either through lateral corridors or in the intervals proper to the intermittent variety of liquids - trills, flaps, or taps (cf. Trubetzkoy 1939a: 139 f. and Romportl 1973: 84 ff.).

The existence of a unitary genus 'liquid' cannot be doubted, despite the efforts of some critics to deny all propinquity between the various exponents of *r,* and also between those and *l.* Grammont underscores the distance between the uvular and the lingual *r* in French and states that from the expressive point of view their respective effects are to such a degree analogous that there is no reason for separating the two sounds from each other (1901: 276). Delattre cites the relation between 'dark' [ł] and pharyngeal [ʁ] as "an extreme example but a revealing one of how distant two speech sounds can appear to be at the articulatory level, yet how close they are at the acoustic level" (1968a: 223). The affinity between the two varieties of liquids, the intermittent [r] and the lateral [l], whatever their place and manner of articulation, finds manifold confirmations in the languages of the world. Besides a few languages devoid of liquids, such as, in particular, numerous North American Indian languages, there is, especially around the Pacific, an overwhelming number of systems with a single liquid phoneme which is either intermittent or lateral or which exhibits a contextual or stylistic variation of these two implementations. Among languages which discriminate between intermittent and lateral liquid phonemes, the two liquids often show a strong mutual constraint in their distribution within the word, e.g. only one of them is admissible at the beginning of the word and only the other at the end (cf. Benveniste 1939: 32ff.). The protracted substitution of one liquid for the other before the two are differentiated is a typical trait of children's language. The coexistence of two widely different articulatory variations of a liquid phoneme proves to be fully tolerated in many languages (e.g. rolled *r* and uvular *r* in French or Swedish; [ł] and [l] in many North Russian dialects).

One cannot but agree with Daniel Jones' statement (1962: 205f.) that "one of the most noteworthy cases" of the unity of the liquids is the so-called Japanese *r:*

> in the pronunciation of many if not most Japanese this 'sound' is very variable; they sometimes use a sound resembling an English fricative *r,* sometimes a lingual flap, sometimes a kind of retroflex *d,* sometimes a kind of *l,* and sometimes sounds intermediate between these. One and the same speaker will use all these forms indiscriminately ⟨...⟩ without being aware that his pronunciation varies. ⟨...⟩ In the absence of special training Japanese can neither hear the difference between these members nor make any of them at will. (One result of this is the well-known difficulty they have in hearing or making the difference between *r* and *l* when they speak European languages.)

Whereas all the paradigmatic sets within the consonantal and the vocalic classes are determined by a clear system of unambiguous oppositional features, the delimitative line between the consonantal and vocalic pattern and correspondingly between the nuclear and the marginal positions in the syllable remains naturally flexible. This flexibility can go as far as the *rarissime* case of those languages in which a syllable or even a disyllabic word may consist solely of obstruents with optional support by ultra-brief indeterminate glottal releases, the presence of which is denied by native speakers – for instance, such Korlak words as dissyllabic [ktkt] 'frozen snow crust' or [vtvt] 'leaf' or [qvqv] 'narrow', analyzed by the precise and observant linguist E. A. Krejnovič. (For examples of Bella Coola "words containing only nonsyllabic consonants" such as [k̓xɫc] 'I looked', see Newman 1947: 132 and Hockett 1955: 57 ff.) Similarly, in the Berber language Shilḥa, according to Applegate's analysis, "not only /l m n r/ but all consonants in certain environments have syllabic allophones" (1958: 13). Alan Bell's survey of syllabic consonants asserts that in languages "described as possessing syllables without vowels, such as Bella Coola, we always find that phonetically there is a release or transitional vocoid present. The question that must be asked is, 'how should such syllables be specified in phonetic representation?'" (Bell 1970: B 29). In this connection the delineation of the category 'syllabic' becomes an extremely intricate task (cf. Greenberg 1962: 78 ff.).

The contiguity of consonants and vowels in the speech sequence creates varied forms of interconnection between these two classes, in particular mutual assimilation and dissimilation. And the tendency toward the differentiation of the vocalic and consonantal roles in the verbal string requires at the same time an intrinsic identifiability of the systems of features which underlie each of the two patterns, vocalism and consonantism, a comparability which implies shared structural principles, but differing textures and interrelations. With respect to both vowels and consonants, binary oppositions remain the overwhelming, nearly exclusive form of organization. Hierarchical rules control the place of the diverse features within the system. And in turn the two opposite terms of each binary feature stand in the hierarchical interdependence of marked vs. unmarked with respect to each other.

IV. MARKEDNESS

In a letter of July 31, 1930, Trubetzkoy sketched his new reflections on the interconnection between correlative phonemes:

Statistics has nothing to do with it. And the essence lies in the so-to-speak 'intrinsic content'. of the correlation. Apparently any (or might it not be 'any'?) phonological correlation acquires in the linguistic consciousness the form of a contraposition of the presence of a certain mark to its absence (or of the maximum of a certain mark to its minimum). Thus, one of the terms of the correlation necessarily proves to be 'positive', 'active', and the other becomes 'negative', 'passive'. For instance, the tonality differences between correlative consonants are objectively confined to a 'maximally high tonality vs. maximally low tonality', but subjectively they are always transformed into an opposition 'heightened tonality vs. non-heightened tonality' (= 'maximally high vs. minimally high') or into an opposition 'unlowered vs. lowered tonality' (= 'minimally low vs. maximally low'): the former type is implemented for instance in the correlation 'palatalized vs. non-palatalized' consonant and the latter for instance in the North Caucasian correlation 'labialized vs. non-labialized' consonant (probably also in the Semitic correlation 'emphatic vs. non-emphatic' consonant). In both cases, only one of the terms of the correlation is conceived of as actively modified and positively endowed with a certain mark, while the other is merely conceived of as non-endowed with this mark and thus passively modified. [Trubetzkoy 1975: 162f.]

The addressee of this letter (RJ ibid.) answered:

I am coming increasingly to the conviction that your thought about correlation as a constant mutual connection between a marked and unmarked type is one of your most remarkable and fruitful ideas. It seems to me that it has a significance not only for linguistics but also for ethnology and the history of culture, and that such historico-cultural correlations as life ~ death, liberty ~ non-liberty, sin ~ virtue, holidays ~ working days, etc., are always confined to relations a ~ non-a, and that it is important to find out for any epoch, group, nation, etc., what the marked element is. For instance, Majakovskij viewed life as a marked element realizable only when motivated; for him not death but life required a motivation. Cf. the way the relation of life and death differs for the two heroes of Tolstoy's 'Master and Man'. Another example: the *Chekists* said that everyone is a man of the White Guard, and if not, it must be proved in every separate case. Here the Soviet allegiance is a marked element. At present in Soviet print there has emerged a slogan; they used to say that 'all those who are not against us are with us', but now they say 'all those who are not with us are against us'. That points to a shift of the elements, i. e. to a generalization of the Chekist standpoint. I'm convinced that many ethnographic phenomena, ideologies, etc. which at first glance seem to be identical, often differ only in the fact that what for one system is a marked term may be evaluated by the other precisely as the absence of a mark.

Trubetzkoy's discovery was first applied in the lecture on sound systems which he addressed to the International Phonological Congress held in Prague in December 1930 (see 1931a). In 1931 the first attempt to use the idea of markedness in the study of grammatical meanings was devoted to the structure of the Russian verb (RJ II: 3–15). In the search for general meanings of paired grammatical categories it was found that one category signals a certain grammatical concept which the other one leaves unsignaled. In French, with its grammatical distinction of the feminine and masculine genders, the marked feminine *lionne* 'lioness' specifies the female; the unmarked, called "masculine", *lion* 'lion' may include both the male and the female. Thus, the general meaning of *lion*, in contradistinction to that of *lionne*, implies no sexual specification, and only the "basic meaning" *(Grundbedeutung)* of *lion* prompted by informative contexts suggests a sexual specification: e. g. *lions et lionnes.*

There is an intrinsic communality between markedness on the level of grammatical categories and markedness on the level of distinctive features. This communality is, however, combined with the considerable difference between these two types of opposition, one based on the semantic level of *signatum*, the other on the sound level of *signans*. The constraining, focusing character of the marked term of any grammatical opposition is directed toward a more narrowly specified and delimited conceptual item. In the dyads of distinctive features the marked term is opposed to the unmarked one by its closer concentration on a certain, either positive or negative perceptual sound property polar to that of the unmarked term, and is accordingly characterized by a restriction of occurrence to specific sequential or concurrent contexts (cf. below, examples of such compulsory limitations, p. 136). The dyadic structures obligatory in the grammatical framework of language also widely permeate the field of lexical meanings and open new possibilities for the application of markedness concepts in lexis as well (see van Schooneveld 1978 and LW 1976b, 1977, & 1979c).

The linguistic couples of marked and unmarked terms belong to the dyadic forms with a preeminence of one of the two opposites. Such dyads are deeply enrooted in the cultural anthropology of the world. Their discussion, launched at the beginning of our century by Robert Hertz ([1909] 1973), has opened wide perspectives for the comparative analysis of ethnic structures. Linguists of the Prague Circle investigated the sound and the meaning problems of markedness and developed them further after the forced demise of the Circle itself (contrary to the apocryphal claims that the search for markedness was abandoned in the 1940s and 1950s), and this inquiry has now found a wider and more promising acceptance (cf. LW 1976: 89ff., 1978, 1979a & b; Greenberg

1966a & b; Chomsky & Halle 1968: 400ff.; Gamkrelidze et al. 1977: 98ff.; Melikišvili 1974 & 1976).

V. GRAVE ~ ACUTE

Among those features based on the tonal quality inherent in the speech sound – briefly, the tonality features grave ~ acute, sharp ~ nonsharp, flat ~ nonflat – the primary feature rests upon the opposition grave ~ acute. The question of the basic features common to vowels and consonants, particularly the obstruents, offers no difficulties as long as we adopt a strictly relational attitude toward the chief significant formants. The perceptual difference between grave and acute depends primarily on the interrelation between two formants, the third and second transitional formants for the consonants and the second and first formants for the vowels – as shown especially by Plomp's analysis (1970, 1975) of the variance between the spectra of different vowels; also, in the spectra of the vowels the first and second formants, in Delattre's formulation, "always comprise the most intense harmonics and suffice to characterize the timbre of the oral vowels" (1966: 237). This strictly relational approach eradicates such supposed dissimilarities as the one pointed out by Pavle Ivić: "compact vowels are marked by a convergence of F1 and F2, whereas in the transitions of the compact consonants the coverging formants are F2 and F3" (1965: 59).

Thus, to use the determinant formants, for the vowels the second formant is the Superior one and the first the Inferior one, whereas for the consonants the third formant is the Superior and the second the Inferior. (A more precise appraisal of the Superior Formant for the vowels could be taken over from present-day acoustics, which for this purpose makes use of the symbol F'_2 in referring to "an estimated perceptual mean of F_2 and higher formants" [see e.g. Fant 1973: 194f.].) Thus, instead of the absolute values of the first, second, and third formants, it is the binary relation between the Superior and Inferior Determinant Formants which should be used as the classificatory criterion within each of the two patterns:

Determinant Formants

	Superior (SF)	Inferior (IF)
Vowels (V)	2 (F'_2)	1
Consonants (C)	3	2

The equivalence in the relation between these two fundamental criteria of division becomes quite obvious if, instead of using the absolute figures for the first, second, and third formants, we turn to the relational invariant which underlies both the system of vowels and that of consonants.

In applying the dyad SF ~ IF one unfailingly obtains an identical formula for the grave ~ acute distinction in both vocalism and consonantism. The high locus of the Superior Formant (F'_2 in vowels, F_3 in consonants) opposes an acute phoneme to the corresponding grave one:

$$\left.\begin{array}{c} V \\ C \end{array}\right\} \; SF \qquad \begin{array}{l} \text{acute} \\ \text{high} \end{array} \qquad \begin{array}{l} \text{grave} \\ \text{low} \end{array}$$

Delattre's Prague paper (1968a) includes "a structural chart of the spectrographic patterns of French consonants based on acoustic features alone": see Figure 3. (Delattre's [ʃ], [ʒ], and [ɲ] correspond to [š], [ž], and [ň] in our transcription.) If we compare the first column depicting all the labial consonants with the second column displaying the corresponding dentals, we clearly see the invariant property of all the labials, as opposed to that of all the dentals: the downward direction of the Superior Formant (i.e. F_3 in the consonants) of the labial, grave consonants vs. the upward direction of the same formant in the dental, acute consonants. It is to this difference that the perception of the lower tonality of grave phonemes vs. the higher tonality of acute phonemes proves to be closely tied.

In languages in which velar consonants are paired with palatal consonants, all other things being equal – /k/ with /tˇ/ and /x/ with /š/ (e.g. in Czech [see Romportl 1973: 104], Slowak [see Pauliny 1961 and Isačenko 1968], and Hungarian [see Tompa 1968]) – the Superior Formant shows the same relation: a downward direction in the grave velars and an upward direction in the acute palatals. The high-frequency components of the consonantal bursts displayed by the acute obstruents contribute to their distinction from the grave obstruents endowed with low-frequency components in their specific bursts. This complementary phenomenon becomes decisive in certain contexts, chiefly when the obstruents are not adjacent to vowels and are thus deprived of perceptible formant transitions to neighboring vowels. Cf. for instance the Czech stops in such usual initial clusters as /tk, tx, tr, tř, pt, px, ps, pš, pr, př, bd, bz, bž, br, bř, kt, kp, ks, kš, kx, kf, kr, kř, db, dž, dr, dř, gd, gb, gz, gž, gr, gř/ and such Czech words as *pstruh* 'trout' and *pštros* 'ostrich', both of which can be accompanied by the preposition *k*

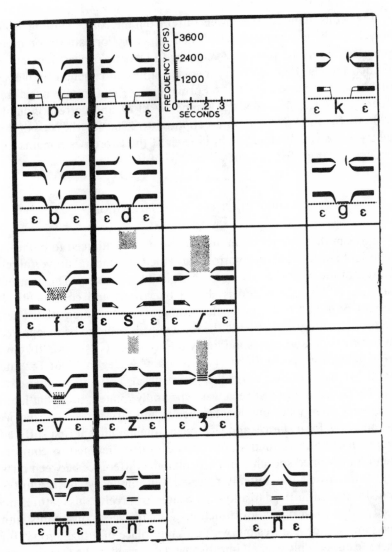

Figure 3.
P. Delattre's chart of the spectrographic pattern of French consonants,
in *Phonetica* 1968, p. 199.

'to' (cf. *k pštrosu* 'to the ostrich'). The discriminability of all the components is maintained: the identification of stops distant from a vocalic
environment depends primarily on their specific bursts, although even
in some of these cases the role of transitions is not totally discarded (cf.
Malécot & Chermak 1966).

Like consonants, grave vowels differ from the corresponding acute vowels by the lower frequency of their Superior Formant (F_2 or, more precisely, F'_2 in the vowels). According to Delattre's measurements of French vowels (1968c: 53), for a voice with a fundamental frequency of 120 cps the Superior Vocalic Formant of the /u/ in *loup* has a frequency of 750 cps vs. 2250 cps for the /i/ of *lit*, and correspondingly 800 cps for the /o/ of *l'eau* as opposed to 2200 for the /e/ of *les*, whereas the vocalic Inferior F_1 in each of the two cases remains unchanged, 250 cps for /u/ and /i/ and 375 for /o/ and /e/.

VI. PRODUCTION AND DECODING

The truism that "we speak in order to be heard and need to be heard in order to be understood" corroborates the fundamental universal relevance of the opposition between high and low tonality. The acoustic salience of this opposition is shared by vowels and consonants. It should be noted that during the temporary inactivation of the left hemisphere discussed above, "the front vowels begin to be recognized as back vowels and correspondingly the consonants /t/ and /d/ tend to be taken for /p/ and /b/" (see Balonov & Deglin 1976: 142 and Table 14). Barry Blesser's (1972) experiments also offer instructive data for comparison. When speech was "spectrally rotated, such that high-frequency energy became low-frequency and vice versa", spoken *we* became *you*, for instance, and vice versa. Intelligibility at first suffered from such a transformation, but "some subjects learned to comprehend transformed speech". In particular, the difference between back and front vowels was initially reversed, but minimal exposure to the transformation sufficed to allow the hearer to perceive this feature correctly. "The most difficult distinctions were between consonants with the same source features but with different place of articulation"; for these features "only a small improvement occurred in the first few sessions". /t/ followed by a back vowel was most often perceived as /p/, while before a front vowel the hearer's perception of it oscillated between /p/ and /t/.

Halle is right in asserting the common foundations of the vocalic and consonantal patterns (1976). The existence of differences between the articulation of vowels and consonants is self-evident. One must remember, however, that it is not the position of the tongue which is the self-sufficient and decisive factor in speech production and in the formation of purposely discriminative speech sounds (see above, chap. 1). We must maintain a thoroughly realistic attitude and correlate the role of the tongue with the other articulators and with the whole of the speech apparatus, as well as with the auditory and speech-discriminatory goal achieved by the total complex of the motor devices, both the surface and the deep ones such as the pharynx and the larynx. In particular, tongue-height-fronting, as Delattre insists, "has very little relation to the acoustic result, that is, to formant frequency-intensity-time display", whereas the place and narrowness of constriction and especially the shape and volume of cavities correlate best with the acoustic and perceptual result (1967: 22 f.). The study of speech sounds has often suffered from a kind of tongue-fetishism, supported perhaps by the metonymic closeness of the vocables for 'anatomic tongue' (*langue, jazyk*) and 'tongue = language' (*langue, jazyk*).

For the delineation of the articulatory employments of the tongue, the age-old attention to substitutions made in the pathological cases of tongueless speakers has provided quite instructive material. Many testimonies have been collected and cited to show that the amputation of a large portion of the tongue is not necessarily incompatible with the power of speech: reports of the fifth century about African confessors who preserved the gift of speech although their tongues had allegedly been cut out; or, later, such publications as Belebar's description of 1630 "d'une bouche sans langue quelle parle"; or the Amsterdam surgical report of 1652 about a *mutus loquens;* or Jussien's memoir "sur la fille sans langue" of 1718; or a physiological account in the Philosophical Transactions of the Royal Society in 1742 of the case of Margaret Cutting, "who speaks distinctly though she has lost the apex and body of her tongue"; or various documents of the last century with titles like "The Tongue Not Essential to Speech" (Twistleton); or finally the May 12, 1944 *New York Times* communication that at the Annual Meeting of the Medical Society of the State of New York, the Medical Director of the National Hospital for Speech Disorders, Dr. James S. Green, demonstrated a seventy-seven-year-old patient whose tongue had been removed because of cancer but who nevertheless was able to speak distinctly and even to recite Lincoln's Gettysburg address and who thus, in the Director's opinion, "refuted the age-old idea that the tongue is the principal organ of speech" (cf. Heffner 1964: 90).

The common denominator in the production of a grave consonant or vowel, all other things being equal, is the use of a larger and less compartmented mouth cavity in comparison with the smaller and

more divided cavity needed for the corresponding acute sound, as was
first formulated some four decades ago (cf. RJ I: 274, 281f. [= 1939])
and later elaborated and confirmed by precise measurements. An
acoustically important and ever-present factor attested by numerous
measurements is the considerable dilation of the pharyngeal orifice of
the mouth resonator for the acute consonants and vowels, and conversely its contraction for the vocalic and consonantal grave phonemes. Thus for instance, X-ray pictures, skillfully produced and mea-
sured by Polland & Hála (1926; cf. RJ et al.: 30) show how the cross
section of the pharyngeal cavity for the two classes of Czech vowels
and consonants deviated from its width in silence (13.3 mm), dilating
for the acute and contracting for the grave phonemes:

Grave		Acute	
/u/	−3.8	/i/	+15.2
/o/	−5.5	/e/	+ 4.0
/f/	−4.7	/s/	+ 6.3
/x/	−3.8	/š/	+ 1.7
/p/	−2.5	/t/	+ 0.5
/k/	−2.6	/t̆/	+12.7
/m/	−2.5	/n/	+ 8.9

If we compare the distance of the *os hyoïdeum* (hyoid bone) from
the wall of the throat at rest with its distance for the articulation of
Czech obstruents, we observe the consistent bifurcation of consonants
into the class of grave labials and velars and the class of acute dentals
and palatals; the former class displays a widening and the latter a narrowing from the position at rest (Polland & Hála 1926: 35):

Grave		Acute	
/f/	+0.5	/s/	−4.0
/x/	+1.5	/š/	−0.5
/p/	+1.0	/t/	−1.0
/k/	+3.0	/t̆/	−3.0

One can cite characteristic examples of assimilative changes of grave
into acute consonants under the influence of subsequent acute vowels:
the Eastern Czech shift of labials into dentals in examples such as [tīvo]
from [pīvo] 'beer', [četice] from [čepice] 'cap, headgear', [niň] from
[miň] 'less'; the Rumanian dialectal change of all labials into corresponding dentals before *z;* and the widespread appearance of palatal
substitutes for velars before front vowels.

VII. COMPACT ~ DIFFUSE

The opposition of higher and lower tonality is a universal which in most languages is shared by the consonantal and the vocalic patterns and which in all other languages appears in one or the other of these patterns; languages without such an opposition are unknown. Also universal is the feature of compactness and diffuseness, to use the terms proposed by S.S.Stevens, an expert in psychoacoustic questions of hearing. *Mutatis mutandis,* this feature is common to vowels and consonants, and takes part in the vocalic and/or consonantal patterns of all languages of the world. It was Gunnar Fant's pilot studies (1949: 38 ff. & figure 19; 1950; 1952) on the transmission properties of the vocal tract which first threw light on the dimensions separating /k/ from /p/ and /t/, which advanced, as Georg von Békésy (1899-1972) conveyed in his oral comments, the question of consonantal compactness, and which furthered collective steps toward the *Preliminaries to Speech Analysis* (Jakobson, Fant, & Halle 1952).

In compact vowels, as opposed to diffuse ones, the Inferior Formant (F_1) is drawn in the direction of the Superior Formant and "the onset is characterized by a concentration of a larger part of the spectral energy to a single formant" (Fant 1973: 67). As exemplified by Delattre's measurements (1968 c) of the French vowel pattern, the Inferior Formant in the tense and lax varieties of the compact /a/ has the highest frequency, 750 cps versus 250 cps for /i/, /u/, und /ü/. In the diffuse vowels, the Superior Formant (F'_2) is more distanced from the Inferior Formant in the acute vowels, and is weakened in the grave vowels.

In the compact consonants, the Inferior Formant (F_2) is drawn in the direction of the Superior Formant (F_3), and/or the sound is reinforced by a turbulence in the concentration area. In the diffuse consonants the Inferior Formant is at a greater distance from the Superior Formant and/or the sound is weakened by a reduction of energy at the head of the Inferior Formant.

Briefly, in compact phonemes the strong concentration of energy in a more central region of the spectrum is achieved through the nearing of the Inferior Formant to the Superior Formant and (particularly in the consonants) through the reinforcement of turbulence in the concentration area; in the diffuse phonemes the drop in concentration of spectral energy is achieved through a distancing of the Inferior Formant from the Superior Formant and (particularly in the consonants) through a reduction of energy at the head of the Inferior Formant. In compactness the net effect is a concentration of energy in the mid-frequency region of the spectrum, as opposed to the spread of energy over a wider frequency region in diffuseness.

The bursts and their relative duration and energy play a great role in the identification and distinction of stops, especially when the stops are not adjacent to vowels, and it is chiefly the compact /k/ and /g/ which, whether contiguous to vowels or not, require a burst for their identification. Thus even in contexts containing /p, t, k/ between /s/'s "a negative transition in the first /s/ – vice versa in the second – is a powerful place cue for /p/ and the positive transition in the first /s/ – vice versa in the second – is a powerful place cue for /t/", even though the burst is weak, whereas "to be intelligible, /k/ in the same context requires an appropriate [strong] burst" (Malécot & Chermak 1966). According to the results of a set of experiments, "bursts and transitions tended to be reciprocally related: where the perceptual weight of one increased the weight of the other declined. They were thus shown to be functionally equivalent, context-dependent cues" (Dorman et al. 1976). Correspondingly, the complementarity of bursts and transitions engenders the need for treating them as constituents of one and the same burst-plus-transition stimulus (see also Fant 1973: 67; and Stevens & Blumstein 1976; cf. Cole & Scott's argument [1974] for the necessity of an integral exploration of the transitional and invariant cues which contribute to the perception of consonants).

In such controversial cases as the supposed difference between the (English or French) syllables /gɛ/ and /go/, the same strategy enables us to discover the acoustic invariance of the consonant: the concentration of spectral energy in contradistinction to its spread in diffuseness. The variables, which are due to the appearance of the same phoneme /g/ before two different vowels, exhibit an equally observable difference on the acoustic as on the motor level: the velar articulation of /g/ before /o/ is distinct from the palatovelar character of /g/ before /ɛ/. Thus, in languages in which a velar stop and a palatal stop are not matched as two distinctive means, there is no strict separation between velarity and palatality, and contextual or stylistic variants of velars easily expand into the palatal domain. Delattre's question as to whether in such a case the articulatory correlates of a distinctive feature are "more invariant than its acoustic correlates" (1967) is firmly answered in the negative by a newer, joint investigation of bursts and transitions, which corroborates the emphasis in his Prague paper on "the acoustic elements of a language as a system".

Blumstein & Stevens' comprehensive scrutiny (1977) of the invariant acoustic properties evidenced by consonantal compactness ~ diffuseness has clearly shown that "there is a diffuse spread of spectral energy for labials and alveolars. The spectrum slope is either flat or tilted toward lower frequencies in the case of labials, and is tilted toward high frequencies for alveolars. Spectral energy is concentrated in a prominent mid-frequency peak for the velars." (See Figure 4.) In particular, the burst characteristics at offset proved to be similar to those at onset and clearly suggested "that there are invariant acoustic properties for place of articulation in stop consonants in both initial and fi-

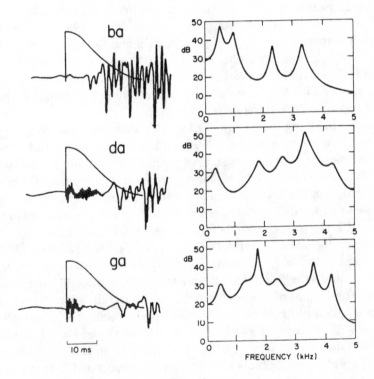

Figure 4.

Spectrograms of American English *ba, da,* and *ga.* S. Blumstein & K. Stevens' slide illustrating their paper at the annual meeting of the Acoustical Society of America, December 1977. "These spectra illustrate the basic properties for the three consonantal classes. There is a diffuse spread of spectral energy for labials and alveolars. The spectrum slope is either flat or tilted toward lower frequencies in the case of labials and is tilted toward high frequencies for alveolars. Spectral energy is concentrated in a prominent mid-frequency peak for the velars."

nal positions", and confirmed the phenomenon of unifying acoustic properties "across phonetic contexts and among different sound classes". The capacity of all speakers to perceive the distinctive features of consonants "across different vowels produced in different environments by different speakers" has been totally confirmed.

The difference between compactness and diffuseness of both vowels and consonants is manifested in more than one way. Velar and palatal stops are more powerful than labials and dentals and display a "stronger concentration of explosion" (Fischer-Jørgensen 1954: 59), while compact vowels are more powerful than diffuse ones. Compact phonemes display a higher intra-oral air pressure, according to Malécot's measurement of American English stops, which show a higher peak pressure in /k, g/ than in /p, b/ and /t, d/ (1966a: 72) and a higher amplitude for /k, g/ in preaccentual and final positions (1968: 98). Similarly, a shows the highest and u, i the lowest vocalic amplitude (see Hála 1941: 233, and earlier testimonies about the higher audibility, discriminability, and resistability of compact sounds in relation to their diffuse opposites referred to in RJ I: 385f.).

All other things being equal, compact phonemes evidence a longer natural duration, both for vowels and for consonants. The Czech sound pattern, with its consistent opposition of velar and palatal stops to the corresponding labials and dentals, reveals a regular arithmetic regression in the average duration of the compact stops, nasals, and vowels vs. their diffuse partners. According to the measurements of average Czech vowels referred to by Hála & Sovák (1947[2]), the optimally compact /ā/ takes 24 centi-seconds vs. 18 for /ū/ and 17 for /ī/ (20 for /ō/ and 19 for /ē/), and correspondingly short /a/ takes 12 csec vs. 9 for /u/ and 8 for /i/ (10 for /o/ and 9 for /e/). It is notable that in Slovak, with its pair of compact vowels, the natural duration of both the grave /a/ and the acute /æ/ significantly exceeds that of the other vowels (cf. Isačenko 1968: 139f.). The consistency of Hála & Sovák's (1947[2]) data for the total duration of stop and nasal consonants is particularly eloquent, because the question of compact and diffuse consonants was a problem alien to these experimenters:

k	tˇ	g	dˇ	ŋ	ň
19	17	14	12	13	11
p	t	b	d	m	n
18	16	13	11	12	10

Thus, the length of the compacts exceeds by 0.01 of a second that of their diffuse correspondents. The voiceless are 0.05 sec longer than their voiced counterparts. Graves are 0.02 sec longer than the corresponding acutes. The voiced stops are 0.01 sec longer than the corresponding nasals. Eli Fischer-Jørgensen's (1954: 46) acoustic perusal of Danish stops shows that the duration of /k/ and /g/ and especially of their explosion is consistently longer than that of the corresponding labials and dentals.

An analogous difference was revealed by Fant's (1973: 64) measurements of the average duration of the Swedish stop burst in msec "from the leading edge of the explosion wave-front to the onset of voicing in the following vowel":

k	t	p	g	d	b
60	50	40	20	12	8

According to these measurements, the duration of the /k, g/ transients – the voice onset time (VOT) – is longer than for any other stops. In /k, g/ spectral energy is concentrated, whereas in /t, d/ and /p, b/ it is spread, with an emphasis on lower frequencies in /p, b/ and on higher frequencies in /t, d/. Fant's production theory (see 1973: chap. 7) provides a basis for an explanation of the difference between the concentration and spread of the spectral energy: "the main formant of the /k, g/ sound derives from the cavity in front of the tongue constriction", while the "diffuse spectra of the /p/ and /b/ release originates from the lack of any front cavity" and "at release the dispersion effect is pronounced". The /k, g/ "have a free pole before release. In the critical segment after release, this pole cannot display very rapid movements. The /t/ and /d/ have a small and narrow front channel, behind the source, which is associated with a high-pass sound filtering." All these data support the conclusion "as to k, g being compact, p, b being diffuse and grave and t, d being diffuse and acute" (Fant 1973: 114 ff., 135 ff.). (See Figure 5.)

With all the modifications which the articulation of vowels requires compared to that of consonants, the separation of phonemes into the classes of compact and diffuse offers such rich and equivalent criteria for acoustic products of the vocalic and consonantal motor activities that is becomes necessary to search out the most efficient sources creating this conspicuous and cardinal acoustic and perceptual divi-

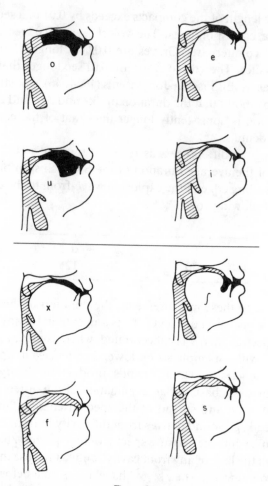

Figure 5.

X-ray photographs of Czech vowels and consonants. Adapted from S. B. Polland & B. Hála (1926) and Hála (1956), as reproduced in the *Preliminaries to Speech Analysis,* p. 49. Horizontal pairs illustrate the articulatory correlates of the opposition grave vs. acute. In the articulation of the grave member of the opposition (left), the front cavity (black area) is larger while the pharynx and lips are more contracted than in the corresponding acute (right). Vertical pairs illustrate the articulatory correlates of the opposition compact vs. diffuse. In the production of the compact phonemes (above) the ratio of the volume of the front cavity (black area) to that of the back cavity (shaded area) is higher than in the corresponding diffuse (below).

sion within both consonants and vowels. Primary attention must be paid to those configurations of our motor apparatus which are the most effective for attaining the physical and perceptual dichotomy in question. The results would be erratic if one focused on the various details of tongue movements without concern for the acoustic and perceptual effects intended, and without regard for the evident parallelism between the vocalic and consonantal dichotomy. Fant was right in stating that "the front cavity to the back cavity volume ratio is equally well applicable" both to vocalism and to consonantism (1970[2]: 218), and that, as he himself pointed out, the front cavity appears to be a significant determinant of formants for the compact phonemes. A synthetic approach focusing on the relational invariant and recognizing the different aspects this invariant assumes within the vocalic and consonantal subsystems is scientifically preferable to a mechanical absolutization and isolationist treatment of the back ~ front classification of consonants and the wide ~ narrow, low ~ high one of vowels.

The relational invariance of the opposition compact ~ diffuse, which is one of the two cardinal oppositions underlying the sound pattern of language, naturally displays a variability in its productional means due to the difference in the concurrent features, vocalic in the one case and consonantal in the other. It is appropriate to repeat here the reminder voiced nearly one century ago by M. Trautmann, an outstanding forerunner of acoustic phonetics: "What most frequently has harmed the strivings in the study of consonants is the insufficient regard for the sound itself and the opinion that everything could be obtained with the indication of the mouth configurations, which, however, are a mere means to a goal ⟨...⟩ but the sound as such always remains the main thing" (1884: 103).

Attempts to call into question the multifold evidence for the parallelism in the distinction of compact ~ diffuse with respect to both the vocalic and the consonantal patterns have resorted to deadly artificial contrivances, even based at times, as strange as it may seem, on mistakenly quoted examples. For instance, McCawley (1967/1972) was prompt to oppose "high vowels and velar and palatal consonants [which he labeled " + high"] to mid and low vowels and alveolar, dental, and labial consonants" [which he labelled "− high"] on the basis of "an unambiguously assimilative effect on a consonant or vowel respectively" within each of these two classes. A "crude empiricism", to use Karl Brugmann's cutting term, rendered the scholar deaf to the intrinsic value of the distinctive features, to their role in the network of language, and to the need for their "cross-linguistic" study. Arguments for relational invariance in the perception of a feature as such are replaced in McCawley's study by incidental and odd references. Instead of opposing the forward-flanged phonemes (low vowels and velar or palatal consonants) to the backward-flanged phonemes (high vowels and labial or dental consonants) as compact to diffuse, McCawley tried to make the reverse match of velar and palatal consonants with high vowels and labials and dentialveolars with low vowels, and claimed to "have been able to find" three pieces of relevant evidence for the superiority of his premise.

First McCawley cited the Sanskrit backing of /s/ after [i], [u], [r] and [k], "since Sanskrit [r] has palatal place of articulation" and thus was one of the phonemes which allegedly assimilated the sibilant (however, cf. Andersen's 1968 contrary view based on the analysis of the compact ~ diffuse opposition). Yet McCawley did not bear in mind that this change had taken place in Indo-Iranian, in Slavic, and in Baltic, and that there are no indications whatever for palatal [r] in these linguistic areas. His second piece of "evidence" for the universal law of a match between the diffuse consonants and compact vowels was a quite free rendition from memory of a confusing statement by Sarah Gudschinsky about "the vocalic allophony of the consonants" in Maxacalí, spoken by some 300 Amerindians in Brazil. (For the association of the compact /k/ with the compact /a/, see the much more persuasive experiment by A. M. Liberman et al. 1952.)

Finally, McCawley crowned his case with his third proof, namely data allegedly taken over from Žirmunskij's *Deutsche Mundartkunde* (1962) (going back to his *Nemeckaja Dialektologija*, 1956) which exemplify the change of dentals into velars after high vowels in the Ripuarian dialect group as "an assimilation of highness", i.e. "[huŋk] 'dog', [kiŋk] 'child', [lūk] 'people', [tˢik] 'time' corresponding to standard German *Hund, Kind, Leute, Zeit*". Yet on the contrary, Žirmunskij himself, in both the German and the Russian versions of his exhaustive treatise, points to the parallelism of two phenomena – a vowel-widening (vowel-lowering) and a change of dentals into velars – and among innumerable examples of parallel changes lists [hoŋk], [keŋk], [lök], and [tˢek]! Žirmunskij discusses mutations such as [t] to [k] after long [ī, ū, ü] which themselves lower to [e, o, ø]: [krok] 'Kraut' (MHG [krūt]), [šneg.ə] 'schneiden' (MHG [snīden]), [rēg.ə] 'reiten' (MHG [rīten]), [lōg.ə] 'to weep' (MHG [lūten]), and also [lȫg.ə] 'läuten' (MHG) [liuten]): "the change into velars takes place there where the vowels are widened into [e, o, ø]". This strange case of consistent misreading found its way into various manuals which assure the reader that "strong arguments have been advanced for a new feature 'high'" and that "it has been observed by McCawley that in the Ripuarian dialects dentals are replaced by velars after high vowels". And thus, this peculiar misobservation has become a typical instance of an annoying phenomenon labeled "errant errors" by the philosopher L. P. Karsavin.

Even the principle underlying McCawley's dubious examples, his insistent appeal to the catchall of assimilation, is false: in language the phenomenon of dissimilation is just as strong. Thus, in the East Caucasian language Artshi, rounded consonants appear in contact with all vowels except before and/or after rounded ones (Trubetzkoy 1931b: 44). The Ukrainian and Bulgarian palatalized consonants, with their maximally high formant transitions, lost their palatalization precisely before the old /e/ and /i/ (both advanced and unrounded). Let us mention in passing that various qualitative shifts of vowels adjacent to velarized and/or pharyngealized consonants show, counter to McCawley's emphatic affirmation, no substantive difference from those vocalic shifts which have been observed in adjacency to rounded consonants, and his attached descriptive data (McCawley 1967/1972: 524) regrettably do not correspond to the phonetic data we possess on languages endowed with the features in question (cf. e.g. Obrecht 1968).

The striking parallelism between the two perpendicular axes of the vocalic and consonantal patterns - high ~ low tonality and concentration ~ spread of spectral energy - was acknowledged as early as in the Sanskrit writings on speech sounds. As Allen notes (1953: 61), in the later phonetic treatises of ancient India, /a/ is grouped with the velar series "under the term *kaṇṭhya* ['glottal guttural'], thus adding considerably to the symmetry of the *varṇa-samāmnāya* ['sound system']". In his early book, rich in far-sighted intuitions, Jac. van Ginneken (1877-1945) remarked that "the consonantal differences in the place of articulation create different degrees of timbre" and that in particular "the labials, the dentals, and the velars for the most part correspond to the set of vowels *u, i, a*" (1907: 384).

At present one could refer to the fruitful ideas in Hüssein Yilmaz's psychophysical theory of speech perception (1967 & 1968). As an "implementation of the theory of invariance into devices for speech and pattern recognition" he posited a vocalic and subsequently a consonantal circle based on the spectral correspondence of consonants and vowels. In proceeding from the perceptual organizations and transformations which are exhibited by the consonants, in particular by their specific bursts, he finds correspondences with "vowel space and color space". Hence he posits a joint circle of vowels and consonants based on their spectral similarity and endowed with two perpendicular diameters: the proximities *p-u* and *t̃-œ* form the end-points of the first diameter and the proximities *t-i* and *k-a* function as the end-points of the second one. In Balonov & Deglin's study (1976) of the relative resistability of speech sounds to the inactivation of the left hemisphere (see above, p. 36 f.), it is noted that "the most powerful and most stable differential cue for the discrimination of vowels is the frequency of the first formant" (p. 194); thus /a/ appears to be the most tenacious among the vowels and its recognition remains the least impeded (p. 132). Correspondingly, /k/ proves to be the most resistant consonant, and the most readily distinguishable from /p/ and /t/ (Balonov & Deglin: Table 14).

When we return to Delattre's chart (cf. Figure 3), we see that all the phonemes of the last three columns - the palatoalveolar, hushing consonants š (*chat*), ž (*joue*), the palatal ň (*gnon*), and the k, both velar (*cou*) and palatovelar (*qui*), as well as g, both velar (*gout*) and palatovelar (*guide*) - despite their articulatory and acoustic diversity have in common an upward direction or reinforcement of the Inferior (transitional) Formant or at least a turbulence reinforcement at its head. The palatoalveolars š and ž are separated from the velars k and g by the distinctive feature opposing the continuousness of the former to the abruptness (occlusion) of the latter. The palatal ň is separated from the stops k, g and continuants š, ž by the distinctive feature which opposes the presence of nasality to its absence. The two oppositions continuant ~ abrupt and nasal ~ nonnasal are features shared, as Delattre's chart indicates, by the compact and the diffuse consonants. On the other hand, the distinctive feature opposing the grave consonants to their acute counterparts and proper to all five pairs of diffuse consonants (p, b, f, v, m versus t, d, s, z, n) is a mere redundancy in the compact consonants, because none of those consonants evidence the distinction grave ~ acute, all other distinctive features being equal. (There is no would-be acute /t̃/ to oppose /k/, no would-be grave /x/ to oppose /š/, and no would-be grave /ŋ/ to oppose /ň/, at least in the native vocabulary of standard French.)

The lack of the distinctive opposition grave ~ acute in the compact consonants engenders the free, stylistic substitution of the velar [ŋ] for the palatal [ň] (as phoneticians beginning with Sweet have repeatedly noted in colloquial French), as well as the tendency pointed out by Marguerite Durand toward a palatal articulation of k and g in Parisian speech. The redundant difference between palatoalveolar and velar articulation, used here to reinforce the distinctive opposition of the abrupt /k, g/ and the continuant /š, ž/, finds a parallel in the reinforcement of the distinctive opposition between the abrupts and continuants with the help of a redundant difference in place of articulation: the bilabial [p], [b] vs. the labiodental [f], [v], and the apical [t], [d] vs. the alveolar [s], [z]. In Common Slavic (as in various other languages), differences such as that between [g] and [ž] are conditioned by the position before a grave and an acute vowel respectively (e.g., *bogŭ* 'God' in the nom. becomes *bože* in the voc.). Cf. the analogous change of [t] to [s] before [i] in the Nasioi language of New Guinea where there is no distinctive opposition of continuants and abrupts (see Hurd & Hurd 1971).

Thus, to remove the redundant features from Delattre's chart of French consonants and to focus on the distinctive features, we may replace the three right-hand columns by unifying the five compact sounds into one single column symmetrical to the first two columns:

	grave diffuse	acute diffuse	compact
abrupts	p	t	k
	b	d	g
continuants	f	s	š
	v	z	ž
nasals	m	n	ň

As Delattre agreed (in personal communication), the maximum deployment of formants is wider in consonants than in vowels, while the minimum deployment of formants is narrower in vowels than in consonants. Hence, the optimal and correspondingly unmarked vowel is the pole of compactness, whereas the optimal and correspondingly unmarked consonants are the maximally diffuse ones. The attenuation of diffuseness, viz. the relative compactness in the consonants, brings them closer to vowels and functions as a mark in the consonantal opposition of compact ~ diffuse. On the other hand, the attenuation of compactness in vowels gives rise to their relative diffuseness, brings them closer to consonants, and functions as the mark in the vocalic opposition diffuse ~ compact. Jacob Grimm (1785-1863) viewed the compact /k/ as the fullest consonant, and the compact /a/ as the fullest vowel, "pure, firm, and opposed to /i/ and /u/, one high, the other deep, and both fluid and capable of consonantization". It is evident that the unmarked compact vowel /a/ is the earliest vowel to become established in infants' language and that the marked, compact consonant /k/ is among the latest acquisitions in the repertory of children's stops. In this connection one may note the results of Malécot's (1970) psychophysical tests: dorsovelar articulations (k, g, š, ž) are felt by American English "naïve subjects" to be "more difficult" than labials or dentialveolars (p, b, f, v, t, d, s, z). Malécot's tests proved that in accordance with the impression of articulatory difficulty, Frenchmen find the velar stops, whatever the mode of their articulation, to be the "strongest" of all the consonants (1977: 31).

The vocalic and the consonantal patterns show a few striking symmetrical traits: in each pattern the division into grave and acute opposites is much more frequent, even nearly universal, within the set of diffuse consonants and vowels than within the compact ones. Thus, the triangular scheme is widespread both in vocalism and in consonantism; cf. the parallelism between

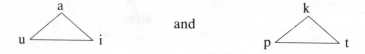

with two perpendicular axes: grave ~ acute on the horizontal and compact ~ diffuse on the vertical. Particularly noteworthy is the fact that neither the system of vowels nor the system of consonants (especially of stops) ever displays in the languages of the world an 'inverted triangle', namely a system in which the grave ~ acute opposition is lacking among diffuse phonemes but is present among compact phonemes. The phenomenon underlying this universal is quite natural: the concentration of spectral energy hampers the development of low ~ high frequency opposites, whereas the dispersal of spectral energy furthers such an opposition. As was already clear to Stumpf (1926: 339), we know no language which has the /u/ ~ /i/ distinction in vowels without the /u-i/ ~ /a/ distinction.

There are no languages without the opposition diffuse ~ compact. Whether among those North Caucasian languages which contain the minimal vocalic pattern in the linguistic world there occur unique languages such as Kabardian and Abaza which supposedly have no vocalic oppositions and are confined to one single vowel phoneme remains a controversial question (cf. Allen 1965; Genko 1955; Halle 1970; Kuipers 1960; Kumaxov 1973; Lomtatidze 1967; and Szemerényi 1964 and 1977: 356). But in those Caucasian languages whose vowel pattern is at least bivocalic, the systems consist of an optimally compact /a/ and its diffuse, marked opposite /ə/, implemented through diverse contextual variants (Vogt 1963: 22). Thus in general, insofar as a language contains a vocalic opposition, it is that of compact ∼ diffuse. Three-vowel patterns most usually display the widespread triangular combination of the two oppositions compactness ∼ diffuseness, the latter in its two tonality poles:

In the common four-vowel quadrilateral system each of the two features is displayed twice:

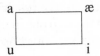

VIII. SHARPNESS AND FLATNESS

The terms grave ∼ acute, as applied to the tonality feature, were widespread in French and German psychoacoustic studies on language and were adopted and popularized by the Prague-inspired phonological literature. Although condemned occasionally for being merely "impressionistic", they exactly render perceptual attributes which underlie both auditory and generally sensual contrasts, and each finds its confirmation in the intuition of ordinary speakers (Fischer-Jørgensen 1967; cf. below, p. 119 f.). This opposition is engendered by a salient difference in the size and shape of the mouth resonator: a stricture, or a maximal narrowing, in the velar or labial region of the mouth creates a more ample and less compartmented resonator with a narrowed pharyngeal orifice for the production of labial and velar consonants and of the retracted vowels (vélaires in French terminology) vs. a resonator of smaller size, greater compartmentalization (stricture in the medial-dental or palatal region) and widened pharyngeal orifice used for dentialveolar and palatal consonants and for the advanced vowels (*voyelles palatales*). Since the main stricture or narrowing takes place nearer to the ends of the buccal channel in the case of grave phonemes and farther from the ends for the acute phonemes, the former may, in their motor facet, be labeled peripheral and the latter medial.

In the consonatal pattern this grave ~ acute opposition is the fundamental feature; the secondary tonality features, which are common in consonants and enjoy a wide geographical diffusion, are known under labels borrowed from musical nomenclature: sharp ~ nonsharp and flat ~ nonflat (RJ et al. 1952). Fant repeatedly subjected to careful investigation the sharpness of Russian consonants effected by the reduction of the oral cavity through the raising of part of the tongue against the palate and through the dilation of the pharyngeal passage (its greater widening for acute consonants and lesser narrowing for grave consonants). His spectrographic measurements of sharp consonants in the connected speech of males and females led him to the conclusion that the Inferior Formant (F_2) is as a rule higher for a sharp consonant than for a corresponding nonsharp one in the same context, and that in addition a heightening of the Superior Formant (F_3) contributes to the distinction and in certain contexts plays an important auxiliary role. This higher spectral level characterizes at least one of the consonantal phases, including its transitions to the preceding or following vowel. (Cf. Shupljakov et al. 1969; Derkach et al. 1970; Fant 1969b & 1970[2]; cf. RJ I: 242f. on the geographical extension of this feature; for the contextual variations of the sharpness feature in Russian, see Zinder et al. 1964.)

The comparison of the two consonantal features – acuteness and sharpness – shows that the raising effect in acuteness is displayed chiefly and solely by the Superior Formant and in sharpness mainly by the Inferior Formant with a characteristic tendency toward the analogous heightening of the Superior Formant as well. Experiments indicate that the main cues for sharpness are chiefly noticeable at the end of the consonant and those for acuteness at its start. Yet it would be unjust to assign the sole role in the distinctive perception of sharp consonants to the prevocalic transitional formants. For instance, a Russian clearly distinguishes sharp consonants from nonsharp ones when no vowel follows or precedes: cf, *vožd'*/vôšt'/ 'leader' ~ *košt*/kôšt/ 'expenses', *vskol'z'*/fskól's'/ 'casually' ~ *val's*/vál's/ 'waltz'.

The consonants particularly susceptible to being split into sharp and nonsharp opposites are the diffuse acutes (dentialveolars); they thus display a tendency toward a maximalization of the opposition grave ~ acute. Moreover, it is characteristic that, like the feature grave ~acute, this secondary tonality feature lends itself more to the diffuse than to the compact consonants. In particular, it remains alien to the palatals, which are a marked, acute variety of the marked, compact consonants. In its early stages children's language often acquires dental consonants in their sharp palatalized variety, even in words where this feature is unknown to adult speech, and even in languages which are not endowed with the opposition at issue (cf. RJ I: 383). Languages supplied with this feature are prone to use sharp dentals in customary baby-talk, as in such traditional Russian consonantal reduplications as [t'át'ə] 'Daddy', [d'ád'ə] 'Uncle', [t'708't'ə] 'Auntie', [n'án'ə] 'Nanny', [t'ut'ú] 'look for!', [n'ún'ə] 'cry baby', [z'úz'ə] 'wet', [s'ús'u] 'pee-pee', [s'ís'ə] 'nursing breast'.

The flatness feature, as opposed to sharpness, involves predominantly the lowering of the Inferior Formant, accompanied by a decrease in the mean frequency of the spectrum, or as Fant defines it, "a shift down in the frequency location of formants retaining the general shape of the spectrum" (1973: 148 ff.). The flat (narrowed-slit) vs. nonflat (wider-slit) phonemes are produced through a decreased front (or back) orifice of the mouth resonator and a concomitant velarization, which expands the mouth resonator itself. A letter from Delattre commenting on his spectrograms and X-ray pictures of the Russian syllables *pa* and *ta* with and without palatalization states that the pharynx is held wide before the passage of /p'/ and /t'/ to /a/ and that the spectrograms show that the locus of the transitions of the second and third formants is distinctly higher than for /p/ and /t/, whereas similar records of the so-called 'emphatic' (pharyngealized) and nonpharyngealized stops in Arabic indicate that "l'emphatique est exactement le contraire de la palatalization. Pour le *ta* emphatique la langue se porte immédiatement vers le pharynx, rendant la constriction pharyngale plus étroite pendant le passage de /t'/ à /a/. Sur les spectrogrammes cela abaisse le locus des transitions du 2e et 3e formants" (cf. also Obrecht 1968).

Various supplementary constrictions at the posterior end of the buccal channel lead to essentially kindred acoustic and audio-perceptual results of flatness. There remains, despite all the possible shades and gradations, a common nuclear effect, whether the emissive process involves chiefly either a pharyngeal constriction or a velar tightening, as opposed to dilation or loosening. Usually the production of pharyngealized buccal consonants is accompanied by a velarization (cf. Marçais 1948: 27). The Serer (West African) postvelar /q/, apparently devoid of the usual uvular stridency and opposed to the postpalatal /k/, seems to be an example of the joint effect of pharyngealization and velarization, a display of the flatness feature with its typically lower position of the transitional formants (see Ladefoged 1964: 21f.; cf. Chomsky & Halle 1968: 305).

The choice between velarization or pharyngealization for the primary role occurs partly as a free, stylistic variation and partly as a contextual variation depending on sequential and concurrent distinctive features. As Ladefoged observes, "no language uses a contrast" between velarization and pharyngealization, "the former being associated with the raising of the back of the tongue, and the latter with its retraction. ⟨...⟩ In Berber languages the distinction between emphatic and non-emphatic consonants is largely that the former are velarized or pharyngealized, whereas the latter are not." (Ladefoged 1971a: 63f.) A few other facets of the backing processes aiming at a downward shift in the frequency location of formants are, because of the common function they fulfill, viewed as manifestations of the same generic feature in all these cases. This natural recognition of the common genus could hardly be attacked as fallacious, especially since the delineation of the genus by no means precludes the systematizer's supplementary attention to the diverse species. But of course the depiction of motor species must imply due concern for the entire physico- and psycho-acoustic genus.

A number of salient clues always exist which reveal why in the oppositions sharp ~ nonsharp or flat ~ nonflat it is sharpness or flatness which serves as the marked opposite. There are always constraints both in the sequential contexts and in the context of other features pertaining to the same phoneme; there are also contraints in the frequency with which one of the two opposites occurs in the lexical code and in the corpus of utterances. Such constraints point to the marked term of the opposition at issue. In this respect the Russian consonantal pattern offers an intricate example. In contradistinction to the sharp, palatalized Russian consonants the nonsharp ones are always velarized, unless they are followed by a palatalized consonant, in which case they either undergo an assimilative palatalization or at least avoid velarization. A Westerner learning Russian has to adopt the processes not only of palatalization but also of velarization, and correspondingly such variations of the preconsonantal /e/ as [p'ǽtʲ l'i] 'whether sung', [p'ét' l'i] 'whether to sing', [p'ɛtl'i] 'knots'. It is worth nothing that Arabs, when listening to a Russian, tend to associate his nonsharp consonants with their native pharyngealization. The question has thus arisen as to which of the two contrary differences – sharp ~ nonsharp or flat ~ nonflat – is independently significant in Russian. It is evident that the two contrasts reinforce each other. The use of these two merged distinctions is confined in Russian to the diffuse consonants (if we abstract from the single exceptional instance of palatalized /k'/ – [tk'om] 'we weave'). In the set of (diffuse & acute) dentals, a weak velarization is contraposed to a strong palatalization, whereas in the set of (diffuse & grave) labials, a strong velarization is matched by a weak palatalization. (See Baranovskaja 1970.) Systematic constraints on the appearance of distinctively palatalized consonants and on the modification of the vowels in the neighborhood of palatalized consonants are among the Russian clues for the marked character of sharpness and for the effective redundancy of the velarization (flatness) proper to all nonsharp consonants of this language (cf. Bondarko & Verbickaja 1965).

An articulatory modification of the acute consonants which leads to the distinctive opposition flat ~ nonflat is implemented in a few geographically scattered languages by the contraposition of flat alveolars to dentals (including the dentialveolar variant of the latter). The relative widening of the cavity in front of the alveolars as compared to its narrowing in front of the dentals gives rise, according to Malmberg's observations (1971: 78 f.), to "a considerable acoustic difference between the dental and alveolar type. The latter has a much lower formant than the dental one, in a few cases used as a distinctive means." Here belong, for instance, Temne and Isoko (cf. Ladefoged 1971a: 38 f., and 1964: 19 f.), the Dravidian language Malayalam (cf. Ladefoged 1971a: 38 f.; cf. also Soubramanian 1962: 104; and Gendron 1970), the Araucan language of Chile (cf. Echeverría & Contreras 1965; and Malmberg 1971: 79), and a few Australian languages (cf. Wurm 1972: 53). Fant in turn asserts that the alveolars, by the lower frequency of their main formant, are opposed to the dentals "in terms of the flatness feature" (1973: 145; cf. p. 38). Ladefoged (1971a: 39) prudently insists on the pertinence of this difference between dentals and alveolars: the concomitant "apical-laminal distinctions" remain irrelevant "at the systematic phonemic level" (1971a: 39).

A division similar to the one between the dentals and the alveolars is achieved by splitting the compact subset of acute consonants into the distinctly lower-pitched retroflex postalveolars and the palatals. (The relatively flat effect of the retroflex consonants brought out by Trubetzkoy [1939a: 133f.] has found its acoustic confirmation in the work of Fant 1973: 38 and 138f.; Ladefoged 1971a: 39f.; and Stevens & Blumstein 1975.) The set of stop phonemes in Araucan offers a clear example of the parallel division of the acute consonants, in both their diffuse and their compact varieties, into flat and nonflat, with the diffuse variety represented by a nonflat dental and a flat alveolar, and the compact one by a nonflat palatal and a flat retroflex. The two latter phonemes exhibit a tendency toward affrication (see Echeverría & Contreras 1965: 133). For the parallel oppositions, alveolar ~ dental and retroflex ~ palatal, cf. also the Tamil "inventory of phonemes (Pillai 1960: 28). In languages in which the compact acute subset is represented merely by retroflex consonants without palatal partners, the retroflex phonemes apparently function simply as the compact acute consonants of the given language, e.g. in Ewe (cf. Ladefoged 1964: 20 and plate 8A; 1971a: 39), in Burushaski, and in a number of languages in Central Asia (cf. Toporov 1970). In these languages the retroflex stops are opposed to the diffuse ones in much the same way as compact, hushing continuants stand in opposition to their diffuse, hissing counterparts. (For a survey of the geographical spread of the retroflex consonants see the preliminary draft by Bhat 1973.)

It has been noted that foreigners unfamiliar with pharyngealized consonants, for instance Bantus and Uzbeks, are inclined to imitate the Arabic 'emphatic' articulations by rounded consonants (see Polivanov 1928: 109; and RJ I: 512): instead of the back passage the front orifice of the buccal channel is contracted. As both spectrograms and perceptual tests have disclosed, the difference in the place of contraction does not prevent an essential communality in the acoustic effect, which for flatness consists of a downward shift and for sharpness of an upward shift of the Inferior Formant with a concomitant shift of all formants whereby the general shape of the spectrum is retained (cf. above, chaps. 1 and 2). Nevertheless, McCawley concludes "that even if there are no languages in which rounding and pharyngealization function as an independent opposition, a theory which treats them as separate must still be held superior to a theory which subsumes them under a single feature" (1967/1972: 524). When a physico- and psycho-acoustically homogeneous phenomenon implemented at both ends of the oral cavity in a similar manner (particularly in regard to an increase in its length) is counterfactually treated as two unrelated processes instead of being seen as a variance in the implementation of one and the same constant, doesn't this indicate the desertion of the search for constants in cross-language comparative analysis and a confinement of this analysis to superficial implementations which disregard the cardinal scientific problem of invariance?

Such an attitude is particularly spurious in view of the usual combination of rounding and velarization. Specialists in African and Caucasian languages, where the feature in question is most frequent, tend to use the term 'labiovelarization', because labialization "is not confined to the rounding of the lips but inflicts upon the whole sound also a raising of the back part of the tongue" (Jušmanov 1937: 28). The relative restriction of the pharyngeal passage at the emission of labiovelarized consonants (its stronger constriction in grave consonants and restrained dilation in acute consonants) limits the acoustic distance between labiovelarized consonants and strictly pharyngealized ones (cf. Ladefoged 1971a). The stylistic fluctuation between velarization and rounding has been mentioned frequently in linguistic literature; for instance, a few decades ago the female style of colloquial Moscow usage tended, and in fact, still tends, to round the velarized consonants. (See Westermann & Ward on this in the Suto-Chuana group of African languages, 1933: 102ff., with a figure of a labialized and simultaneously velarized [sʲ].)

IX. INTERRELATION OF TONALITY FEATURES

A very high number, perhaps the majority, of languages are endowed in their consonantal patterns with only one tonality opposition: grave ~ acute. Within the diffuse class of consonants, the grave (labials) occur less frequently in the code and in the corpus of utterances, in comparison with the usually more frequent appearance of their acute (dental) correspondents. This telling fact points to the markedness of the former, grave subclass of diffuse consonants in contradistinction to their unmarked acute opposites. Cf. for instance the much more usual presence of the unmarked, acute /s/ compared to the marked, grave /f/ in the consonantal patterns of the languages of the world. Inversely, the compact class of consonants seems to show a greater tendency toward using the grave (velar) phonemes than the acute palatal class, and if there is no distinctive opposition of velar and palatal consonants in a given language, this class is represented by a velar consonant (/k/); thus, for the compact consonants an opposite direction may be assumed: unmarked graves vs. marked acutes.

To sum up, besides the nearly universally extant grave ~ acute opposition (cf. below p. 128) chiefly concerned with the downward ~ upward shift of the Superior Formant, consonantal patterns offer two polar kinds of tonality features, each dealing with the predominant shift of the Inferior Formant and the concomitant shift of the Superior Formant, without a change in the general shape of the spectrum as a whole. The first kind is represented by the solely consonantal opposition sharp ~ nonsharp; the other one, flat ~ nonflat, is implemented by different emissive devices. Only two of the tonality features function in the vocalic pattern, namely grave ~ acute and flat ~ nonflat, and the second is always effected first and foremost by the distinction of rounded and unrounded vowels.

Both the total repertory of tonality features and their interrelation are different in vowels as compared to consonants. The unmarked, compact /a/ is strikingly distinguished from the other vowels of this system by its nonparticipation in their tonality opposition and shares neither (marked) flatness with /u/ and /o/ nor (marked) acuteness with /i/ and /e/. The syncretism of the two tonality features is the fundamental form of the vocalic system and is especially common in the diffuse vowels: flat grave vowels are distinctively opposed to their corresponding nonflat acute counterparts. In a large number of languages the syncretism of both tonality oppositions is indissoluble. But certain patterns allow the abolition of one of the two features in certain contexts. For instance, in Russian the rounded vowels change into advanced (fronted) vowels under the influence of adjacent palatalized consonants, particularly when they fall directly between two of them; in this way the opposition grave ~ acute becomes effaced and only the feature flat ~ nonflat remains valid. On the other hand, there are languages, such as Japanese (see Trubetzkoy 1939a: 101), in which in some contexts the rounded retracted vowels lose their rounding, so that only the grave ~ acute opposition remains irremovable. However, even in those cases in which only one of the features is unwaveringly significant, the other one remains as a redundancy. In a language with a vocalic tonality feature, there is always at hand at least one pair consisting of a rounded back vowel and an unrounded front vowel in a distinctive or at least in a merely redundant function.

The split of the vocalic opposition flat grave ~ nonflat acute gives rise to two autonomously significant distinctions. A most frequent phenomenon in this respect is the set of acute flat (front rounded) vowels, which always implies the copresence of the two, according to the French phonetic nomenclature, "primary" sets: nonflat acute and flat grave. The *série secondaire* combines two conflicting effects: "when the orifice decreases the tone descends; when the cavity decreases the tone ascends" (see Millet 1938: 63 f.). Apparently F'_2, with its formants above the Superior one, has a noticeable influence on the recognition of the identity of such "secondary" vowels of this series as /ü/ and /ø/ and especially on their distinction from the nonflat /i/ and /e/ (see Carlson, Granström, & Fant 1970; cf. Joos 1948: 95). The dependence of the split of the acute vowels into flat and nonflat on their diffuse character was stated by Trubetzkoy (1939 a: 111 f.).

In addition to the two basic combinations (flat grave ~ nonflat acute), the reverse combination of gravity and nonflatness occurs in many vocalic patterns and builds diffuse counterparts to the compact /a/, which otherwise in most languages appears as the apex of the vocalic triangle and is devoid of a direct diffuse counterpart. Less frequent are the patterns which oppose to the two basic combinations the two additional partnerships of flatness with acuteness and nonflatness with gravity, combinations readily joined with vowel harmony (see below). Thus, the concurrence of vocalic acuteness and flatness (e.g., /ü/) is marked in contraposition to the unmarked combination of acuteness with nonflatness (e.g., /i/). Similarily, vocalic gravity with no concurrent flatness (e.g., /ɯ/) is marked in contraposition to the unmarked combination of gravity and concurrent flatness (e.g., /u/). The syncretic tonality opposition of grave flat vowels such as /u/ and their acute nonflat counterparts such as /i/ proves to be equipollent, viz. there is no mutual markedness relation between these two syncretic opposites.

In all those vocalic systems which exhibit a triangular structure and counterpose one single (unmarked) compactness apex to the tonality oppositions of the other rows of the pattern, this apex, the unrounded and unadvanced /a/, is contraposed to the two polar attributes of the tonality pairs by the absence of flatness on the one hand and by the absence of acuteness on the other. As Trubetzkoy (1939 a: 99 f.) pointed out, in languages with a tonality couple for the compact vowels, either the retracted one is rounded (/å/), as in some dialects of Polish, or neither member of the couple is rounded, and the opposition grave ~

acute ($/æ/ \sim /ɑ/$) remains the constant one, as has been observed in some Serbian dialects of Montenegro. The syncretism of both oppositions is consistently applied in the Uzbek dialect of Tashkent, where the vocalic phonemes are divided into a 'maximally dark' /å/ (grave flat) and a 'maximally light' /æ/ (acute nonflat); thus, the compact vowels here follow the same fundamental principle as does the total vocalic pattern.

The coappearance of the four simultaneous combinations – grave flat, grave nonflat, acute flat, acute nonflat – is comparable to the rarer copresence of four tonality types in consonantal patterns. The hierarchic distribution in the latter differs, however, from the vocalic "quadruplets" outlined above: in consonants the grave $\sim$ acute opposition is primary while the flat $\sim$ nonflat and sharp $\sim$ nonsharp oppositions are secondary. Thus the combined absence of either flatness or sharpness is the simplest case in consonantal systems in relation to the presence of flatness or of sharpness, whereas the combination of these two strictly conflicting tonality effects offers the most complex variety. Trubetzkoy claimed to have discovered all four possible bundles of these features built upon the oppositions flat $\sim$ nonflat and sharp $\sim$ nonsharp (e.g. [t], [t'], [tˤ], [tˤ']) in the Dungan dialect of Northern Chinese (1939b) and pointed to a similar phenomenon in an Abkhazian dialect which divides the hushing sibilants into "four tonality classes: neutral, simple-palatalized, simple-labialized, and ü-colored = palatalized-rounded" (1939a: 133). Georg Morgenstierne brought to light analogous "quadruplets" in Kashmiri (1941: 88f.; cf. however, Zaxar'in 1975: 146ff.). Spectrographic records of the four tonality classes in question were made by the Rumanian linguist Emil Petrovići from his native dialect and were later analyzed by Halle. The peculiar sharp flat variety shows a lowering of all formants due to rounding, accompanied by a rising transition of the Inferior, i.e. second, Formant in the adjacent back vowel. (See RJ I: 661f.) It should be noted that for all these languages there have emerged linguistic discussions on the interpretation of the quadruplet series either as single consonantal phonemes or as consonants absorbing a latent vowel [ə, i, u, ü] (cf. Avram 1976).

The connections between the secondary tonality features and other consonantal features show close interrelations. The sharpness opposition in Russian (as already mentioned, p. 114) is spread only over the diffuse, ergo unmarked, consonants, especially over their acute (dental) class, which is unmarked in its turn, whereas the marked compact consonants make no use of this opposition except in totally isolated velar examples. Gaelic uses this feature only in the unmarked sets of the diffuse acute dentals and the compact grave velars (cf. Ternes 1973). In Dungan (cf. Trubetzkoy 1939b: 24) only consonants of the unmarked, diffuse class can be sharp, whereas consonants of the marked, compact class can display only the flatness feature, never sharpness. Among the diffuse consonants only the acute (unmarked) ones, not the grave (marked) ones, are endowed with the flatness feature.

X. AND WHAT NOW?

This chapter has been devoted chiefly to the examination of two kinds of distinctive oppositions - tonality features and the feature compact ~ diffuse. Both of these kinds are, to the best of our knowledge, universally present in the consonantal and/or vocalic patterns of the world's languages (see below). Here we have further developed our preliminary assumptions, approved by Pierre Delattre, about those two features which underlie all five columns in his "structural chart" of the French true consonants: compact ~ diffuse and grave ~ acute. Our inquiry into both oppositions and their further ramifications has remained, as we hope, faithful to the Prague watchword of the French-American seeker for the Grail of the distinctive features: "economize and binarize". Yet a simple, orderly enumeration and discussion of the delineated couples will hardly suffice, and there may emerge critics prone (if they read poetry) to take up the hesitating lines of a recent poet and linguist, Jack Spicer (1925-1965):

> I have forgotten why the grail was important
> Why somebody wants to reach it like a window you
>   throw open. Thrown open
> What would it mean?

But the window thrown open means a way cleared to a venturesome contemplation of the inner laws which govern the overall texture of these elementary relational units, and any further inquiry promises an ever deeper insight into the hierarchical cohesion of the ultimate constituents within their entire network.

CHAPTER THREE

THE NETWORK OF DISTINCTIVE FEATURES

> 'Stay,' said Hanbury, 'what is
> structural unity?'
> Gerard Manley Hopkins, 1865
> *On the Origin of Beauty*

I. SIGNIFICANCE OF THE DISTINCTIVE FEATURES

All those who try to separate the physiological or the physical questions of the distinctive features from the inquiry into their linguistic functions will find a foresighted reply made by Peirce in 1905: "We may classify objects accordingly to their matter: as wooden things, iron things, silver things, etc. But classification according to *structure* is generally more important" (8.213).

Through the last decades the significance of the concept of distinctive features has become increasingly apparent, both through perceptual experiments and through linguistic debates (cf. A. S. Liberman 1974). Neurolinguistic investigations strikingly corroborate the perceptual reality of the distinctive features: "It becomes evident that as a rule the left hemisphere brings about the classification of phonemes on the basis of their distinctive features and supports the hierarchy of these features ensuring the stability of the phonological system of language" (Balonov & Deglin 1976: 182). As demonstrated by Blumstein (1974), "features are independently extracted during the speech perception process" (p. 140), and "single feature contrasts [are] easier to identify than double feature contrasts" (p. 344; and cf. Blumstein & Cooper 1972). The specification of aphasic disorders and of their typical feature disturbances in connection with cortical lesions of certain posterior and anterior parts of the 'speech areas' showing deteriorations of the paradigmatic and syntagmatic organization respectively has gradually brought appreciable results (see Luria 1973, 1976; Vinarskaja 1971; Lecours & Rouillon 1976; RJ 1971). As Hans-Lukas Teuber said, "the 'distinctive features' would be more than a universal schema for classifying phonemes, in all their diversity across languages; the features would be 'real', in the sense of being universal neuronal mechanisms for producing *and* for perceiving sounds of speech" (1976).

The clever intricacy of the networks which the distinctive features underlie can give the superficial impression of being hocus-pocus, contrived by the investigator, yet it is in fact language itself which surprises the student with its intricate, one could even say hocus-pocus, tricks.

The indisputable universality of buccal sound production in all speech communities renders untenable the assumption that the choice of sound matter would be fortuitous rather than organic, even though such an assumption has repeatedly emerged in the linguistic literature, from the reluctance expressed by William Dwight Whitney (1827–1894) to admit any "peculiar connection between thought and articulate utterance" (1875) to the question left open by Chomsky of "whether the sound part is crucial" (1967: 85). The severe restriction of audio-motor elements called to serve for sense discrimination in the languages of the world reveals a significantly smaller set than the articulatory and auditory capacities of human beings could allow. The principles of this ordered selection disclose a psychobiological regard for the optimal framework of communication. Moreover, the selection exhibits a considerable number of underlying rules which render certain of these elements incompatible within one and the same system of language and rules which make use of a given element dependent on the copresence of a certain other component within the same system. These two types of implicational rules, one excluding the coexistence and the other implying the solidarity of components, substantially restrict the variety of systems. Rules, some compulsory, some optional, determine the hierarchical interrelation of distinctive features and reduce the diversity of usual and even of possible types of systems.

Here linguistic science faces the responsible task of discovering the typology of languages with respect to their sound systems. This problem encompasses the entire variety of phonic constituents employed by languages to serve sense discrimination and other aims. Such a typology of sound systems, envisaged and approached in various ways by generations of inquirers, has to take into account the distinctive features, their simultaneous and/or sequential (in Gamkrelidze's terminology, "vertical" and "horizontal") combinability, their hierarchical interrelationship in the system, and finally their stability and mutability in space and time. It must step by step reveal both the diversity and the invariance of structures, as has been foreseen at different stages in the international development of linguistic thought. For instance, during the epoch of rationalism, the philosopher and linguist Jan Amos Komenský (Comenius, 1592–1670) in his anticipatory work clearly discerned *lingua* and *sermo* (Saussure's *langue* and *parole*) and acutely viewed two levels of givens: on the one hand the diverse *linguae* with their *structurae* and in a higher, general aspect *lingua* and its *structura* (*Panglottia*: chap.3 [1966]). The question of the sound pattern pertained to the widely recognized scientific program of that century; to quote one example, the *Theses Grammaticae in Collegio Harvardiano* for the commencement of 1653 included the topic "Bene Grammaticari est vocum Proprietates et structuram interpretari" (Morrison: p.590).

It should be remembered that *structura* (both the concept and the term) as applied to language, to its sounds and their properties, is centuries older than the present-day emphatic slogans around this label and than the new endeavor for a deeper mastery of the same idea. The questions of universal convergences and local divergences in the sound shape of language are inseparable and one must take into account the fact that multifarious mutability – variability both in space and time as well as essential variability in an individual's use of language, in his personal performance and competence – is perhaps the most striking invariant throughout the linguistic world. Whichever of the two fundamentally indissoluble aspects we focus on – language already acquired and utilized or the process of its acquisition and utilization – the entire network displays a systematic hierarchical arrangement.

If, in accordance with Sapir, we do justice to a "certain innate striving for formal elaboration and expression and to an unconscious patterning of sets of related elements of experience" (Sapir 1949: 156), and if, correspondingly, we concentrate our attention on the "relative innateness of the acquisitions and on the apparent limits of their modifiability" (Teuber 1976), we realize that the templates of the whole sound structure are anything but scattered and disordered particulars. They are rather purely relational 'counters', and in the buildup of the cohesive system of all the other linguistic constituents the neuropsychological foundations of sensually determined structural units (viz. the *signantia*) with their rigorous rules of interrelation show the most reliable pathway to the innate inheritance. The framework of universal laws and implicational universals (Holenstein 1976a: 1255ff.), observable in the sound shape of languages even more clearly than in the meanings and organization of the grammatical categories, justifies the earlier surmise of Teuber that certain universal devices of human language, especially "such as the patterning of phonemes in terms of distinctive features, are innate" (1967: 206). Even if a student of language finds the typological vistas sketched above insufficiently attractive or even boring, and if he prefers to concentrate on other areas of our extensive science, such a subjective preference still does not justify claims that the vast field in question has been exhausted and is not worth exploring (cf. e.g. Chomsky 1977). Obviously some observers, skeptical of biological explanations, may attribute the structuration of distinctive features primarily to the institutional character and wide scale of interchange of verbal patterns, especially since such an interchange stays to a high degree outside conscious control. Actually, given such a supposition, the inner logic of these constraints can be most instructive not only for linguistics but also for the social sciences in general.

II. THE TWO AXES

The further that research on the distinctive features progresses, the clearer it becomes that any single opposition makes up part of a complex and coherent whole whose parts may be adequately explained only if the intimate interconnection between the total structural unity and its subsystems – down to the single constituents – is taken into consideration. None of the questions involved may be considered exhausted. The separation of speech sounds into vowels and consonants, with the peculiar superiority of contiguity over similarity in their interrelation (see above, pp. 87 f.), requires an ever stricter delimitation of the two classes and an ever greater attention both to the communalities and to the differences of the features proper to each of them.

The oppositions compact ~ diffuse and grave ~ acute are, let us repeat, the only two features which belong to vocalism and/or consonantism in all languages of the world; but in the whole ensemble of the world's languages, with a small handful of exceptions, these oppositions usually pertain *both* to the vocalic *and* to the consonantal systems.

If the vocalic pattern is reduced to one single opposition, it is the diffuse ~ compact feature, as has been observed in a few Caucasian languages (cf. pp. 112 f. above, the controversial question of one-vowel and two-vowel systems). While in children's language three-vocalic triangles (a ~ u ~ i) compete with linear patterns a ~ o ~ u (see Kania

1972: 126), in the world's languages the presence of the second feature, the tonality opposition, is nearly universal in three-vowel systems, and is fully universal in languages with a higher number of vowel phonemes. (Cf. the first charting of the vocalic triangular pattern in the 1781 doctoral dissertation of Christopher Friedrich Hellwag [1754–1835]: see Figures 6 and 7.)

Nearly universal is the participation of the two features grave ~ acute and compact ~ diffuse in the consonantal pattern. A few languages with an uncommonly scarce inventory of consonants limit the

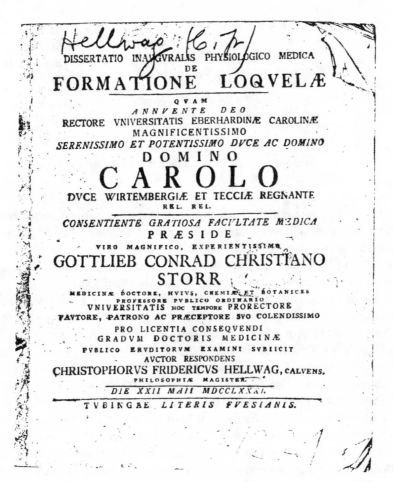

Figure 6.
Title page of C. F. Hellwag's dissertation of 1781.

§ 57.

Princeps vocalium, reliquarum bafis, vel in fcala pofitarum centrum eft *a*: ex hac duplex afcendit fcala, in gradus extremos *i* & *u* terminata: gradibus his extremis & homologis inferioribus termini interjacent intermedii. Graduum & terminorum intermediorum ad bafin relatio fub hoc fchemate concinno poteft repræfentari:

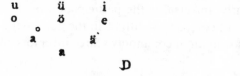

Vocalis *o* medium tenet inter *u* & $\overset{o}{a}$, $\overset{o}{a}$ inter *o* & *a*; fimiliter *e* inter *i* & *ä*, *ä* inter *e* & *a*; per *ü* fit tranfitus ex *u* ad *i*, per *ö* ex *o* ad *e*: exprimi poteft terminus, per quem ex $\overset{o}{a}$ ad *ä* tranfitur. Gradibus hifce fcriptione defignatis infiniti alii poffunt interpolari, quos gentes linguis & linguarum varietatibus differentes inter loquendum conftanter exprimunt, Nonne fic omnes, quas unquam edidit humana lingua, vocales ac diphthongi quafi mathematice fecundum gradus poterunt determinari?

Figure 7.
The vowel triangle in C. F. Hellwag's dissertation *De Formatione Loquelae*, 1781, pp. 25–26.

validity of this statement. The compact and diffuse opposition of consonants is common to all languages of the world, with isolated exceptions such as Tahitian, which is devoid of compact consonants (Tryon 1970), and Kasimov Tatar, which has replaced all the velar stops, fricatives, and nasals by a glottal catch (Polivanov 1928: 85f.).

As to the tonality feature, there exist as singular exceptions languages devoid either of acute (dental) or of grave (labial) stops. Labial stops are lacking in a few North American Indian languages, some of which, however, exhibit labial ~ dental pairs among the nasals, as does, for instance, Cherokee (see Bender & Harris), or there emerges a 'labialized' (flat) velar /k°/, as in Tlingit (see Swanton 1911: 195; and Krauss 1964). A few Iroquoian languages, such as Seneca (Chafe 1967: 5), lack labials, and probably in at least a few of these languages the absence of labials was caused by the former tradition of wearing labrets. In Africa, where this habit is confined to females, the lack of labials distinguishes women's from men's speech. The consonantism of Oneida, known to us through Lounsbury's masterful description (1953), offers a unique pattern. In this language the oppositions grave

~ acute and compact ~ diffuse merge with each other: the indissolubly grave-compact /k/ is opposed to the acute-diffuse /t/, whereas in
the vowel pattern the oppositions acute ~ grave and diffuse ~ compact are mutually independent *(i ~ o, e ~ a; i ~ e, o ~ a)*. Each of the
other few consonantal phonemes appears here endowed with one single distinctive feature: /s/ is the only continuant, /n/ the only nasal,
/l/ the only liquid (= consonant with a simultaneous vocalic mark).

There occur in the Austronesian stock single languages which have
recently replaced, or which tend to replace, the dental by the velar
stop. Such is the situation in Standard Hawaiian; in other dialectal
variants of Hawaiian, especially Niihau, the /t/ is still preserved, while
the place of the velar has remained vacant following the general Hawaiian change of the velar stop into a glottal catch. Hawaiian speakers
belong to different transitional types; some of them use [t] and [k] alter-
nately, sometimes dissimilating the two stops within a word, or em-
ploying the acute [t] only after an acute vowel, or distinguishing the
two variants depending on the initial, medial, or final position of the
consonant in the word or in the phrase. Lastly, [t] may prevail in chants
(cf. Pukui & Elbert 1965; and Newbrand 1951). Even in the standard
consonantal pattern of Hawaiian, the opposition grave ~ acute has
not been lost but is carried by the nasals /m/ ~/n/, whereas the stops
/p/ ~/k/ evidence the opposition of diffuse ~ compact. In Leuangiua, whose consonantism is reduced to a minimum - /p/ and /k/
stops and /m/ and /ŋ/ nasals - the grave ~ acute opposition seems to
be carried by the continuants /v/ and /s/. (See Lanyon-Orgill 1944: 8).

The substitution of /k/ for /t/ and of /ŋ/ for /n/ in Samoan was,
as Gabelentz observed, a limited dialectism in 1863 and three decades
later appeared "all over the group; ⟨...⟩ it is difficult to say how this
change commenced but its spread has been noted and every attempt
has been made to arrest it, but without effect. Many of the people now
seem unconscious of the difference" (1891: 201). The innovation still
remained a mere provincialism at the beginning of our century (Neffgen 1903: 2), but has now widely expanded, at least in the colloquial
language (Arakin 1973: 14; cf. Churchward 1926: 16), whereas formal
Samoan speech preserves the voiceless apicodental stop and the apicodental nasal (Pawley 1960: 48). The acute opposites to the grave stop
and nasal are carried by the archaic, still valid variants /t/ and /n/.

Two prominent psychologists, Carl Stumpf (1848–1936), who was
the first to say that one cannot assess psychological problems without
approaching the question of the search for structural laws (1907:

61 ff.), and his great inspirer in psychoacoustics, Wolfgang Köhler (1887-1967), renowned particularly for his synthetic Gestaltist work (cf. 1929), revealed the role played in the vocalic system by these two axes - the "U-I process" and the "A-process" (in Stumpf's terms). Both scholars invoked "a phenomenological, adequate coordination" of these two dimensions with the corresponding dimensions within other sensory domains and particularly within the system of colors (see Köhler 1910-1915; and Stumpf 1926, especially his insightful chapter "Psychophysics of speech sounds"). The profound reflections of these two pioneering investigators subsequently proved to be relevant not only because of the positive results they obtained, but also because of the questions they daringly raised.

The further development of the acoustic inquiry into sound shape and of its linguistic interpretation has permitted the expansion of the idea of the two axes onto the whole framework of language, as well as the comparison of their treatment in the vocalic and consonantal sub-systems, a comparison taking into account both convergences and divergences (*Struktureigentümlichkeiten*) in these two opposite subsystems (cf. RJ I: 378 ff.). Also, the solution to the problem of "intersensorial correspondences" is advancing, particularly in the question of the parallelisms between the structuration of speech sounds and that of colors. When Köhler advocated the traditional German labels *hell* and *dunkel,* 'light' and 'dark', corresponding to the terms 'acute' and 'grave' current in present-day linguistics, he stated that for him these names were *never* mere metaphors based on distant associations: "If optical examples emerge, then tone and image are not attached to each other through a senseless habit but a light tone appears to be similar to a light optic image. Anything which I'm accustomed to name 'light' on the optical level faces me, even if through mere similarity, in the acoustic field as well" (Köhler 1915: 181 f.; cf. Stumpf 1926: 320).

In the vocalic triangle, the pronounced sonority, according to the linguistic term - or, to use the corresponding visual term, the pregnant chromaticity - of the compact vowels stands in opposition to the attenuated sonority - or, correspondingly, attenuated chromaticity - of the diffuse vowels (acute and grave), with their extreme contrast, both auditory and visual, of light and dark. Likewise, the consonantal lack of distinct sonority - or, correspondingly, the lack of pregnant chromaticity - underlies the intense *chiaroscuro* of the light, acute consonants in contrast to the dark, grave ones, and opposes these two polar species to the attenuated nonsonority - viz. attenuated achromaticity - of the 'greyish' compact consonants (cf. Hurvich & Jameson on the "balanced equilibrium condition associated with neutral 'grey' sensation" [1957: 386]). In Dora Vallier's promisingly sketched formulation, "within the achromatic (consonantal) ensemble, unmarked in itself, one proceeds from the attenuated achromaticity of the grey which is marked to the unmarked achromaticity of black and white" (1975: 290ff., cf.§ 27; cf. also RJ I: 324). The linguistic tonality oppositions such as u ∼ i and p ∼ t find their close correspondents in the blue ∼ yellow and black ∼ white paired system of the "opponent-process theory" of color vision (see below, p. 194).

The question which was raised by Köhler concerning the "central physiological and perceptual correlates" to the two axes (1915: 182f.) does not warrant any suspicion of a disparity between the psychological unity of the speech sounds and the duality of the underlying cerebral processes (see Stumpf 1926: 334). This problem has now been cancelled through the dissolution of the supposedly indivisible phoneme into distinctive features and through the recent findings supporting the relation between the brain and the speech sound pattern (see above pp. 37, 98, 109f., and 125).

The closer connection of the diffuse ∼ compact feature with vocalism and of the tonality feature with consonantism is reflected in the noticeable differences in the structuring of these features within the vocalic and the consonantal patterns. The feature diffuse ∼ compact, clearly dyadic in the consonants and dyadic also in the vocalism of numerous languages, shows, nonetheless, a greater complexity in multifarious instances of vocalic organization, namely the occurrence of middle terms in addition to the two extremes of the compact and of the diffuse vowels. It is necessary to take into account the particular frequency of five-vowel triangles such as the Czech system of short vowels:

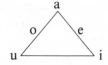

Here the /a/ does not participate in the tonality oppositions characterizing /i, e/ (acuteness) and /o, u/ (flatness). Though these triads have repeatedly been used as an argument against the generality of binary oppositions in the structure of distinctive features, we are, actually, clearly faced in these cases with the bifurcation of the binary opposition diffuse ~ compact into a pair of binary oppositions noncompact ~ compact and nondiffuse ~ diffuse. Such bifurcation appears natural when one acknowledges the diffuse ~ compact relation as the fundamental axis of the vocalic system, whereas the accessory character of the same axis in respect to the consonantal system universally inhibits any subdivisions analogous to the vocalic ones. It must be remembered, for instance, that the existence of the geometric mean /e/, which is noncompact in relation to the compact /æ/ and nondiffuse in relation to the diffuse /i/, is paralleled by the results of psychological experiments in which /e/ was obtained through the mixture of /æ/ and /i/. Analogous experiments in mixing vowels situated on the tonality axis show that grave and acute vowels when sounded simultaneously are not perceivable as a single intermediary vowel (see Huber 1934; and RJ I: 500). The treatment of colors located on the two corresponding axes seems to yield equivalent results.

The question of the copresence of two binary oppositions compact ~ noncompact and diffuse ~ nondiffuse does not present particular difficulties in analysis as long as one uses a consistently relational approach. The question of whether there exist sets of four vowels along the diffuse ~ compact axis requires further investigation. In particular, the four-term system assumed for the Danish vowel pattern may still be revised, as Eli Fischer-Jørgensen hints (1972a: 199f.), with respect to the possible role of the lax ~ tense feature (see below, pp. 138f.). The closer connection of the tonality axis with consonantism, obviously explainable by the larger display of the tonality phenomena in the optimally diffuse (minimally chromatic) part of the sound system, finds its expression in the differing organization of the tonality features within the consonantal and vocalic frameworks respectively. The autonomous opposition of acutes and graves (Köhler's *hell* and *dunkel*) among consonants and the use of two subsidiary but likewise autonomous oppositions - sharp ~ nonsharp and flat ~ nonflat - contrast with the widespread vocalic syncretism of the acute ~ grave and flat ~ nonflat oppositions and also with various examples of the subordination of one of these two oppositions to the other.

III. NASALITY

The distinctive copresence of vowels and consonants is the fundamental universal in the sound pattern of languages. Besides the tonality feature, which in one of its cardinal manifestations universally operates in at least one of the two subsystems, consonantism and vocalism, and the compact ~ diffuse feature, which is comparably ubiquitous, the nasality opposition is a near universal in the consonantal pattern of language. (See Ferguson 1974 and 1975; Crothers 1975; and Ruhlen's preliminary draft, 1973, for a survey of nasalization.) A few languages of the Northwest Coast of North America are devoid of nasal consonants and the expansion of this deficit seems to have been the result of areal diffusion (cf. Hockett 1955: 119; Haas 1969: 112; Thompson & Thompson 1972; and Ferguson 1974). In some of these cases nasal consonants have been changed into voiced stops. Among the languages of this area, the Puget Sound dialects make use of nasal consonants as a special affective means only. Nasals appear solely in the common word, diminutive in its lexical meaning, /miˀmaˀd/ or /miˀmaˀn/ 'minute, small'; in the special case of certain diminutives in baby-talk where a voiced stop is replaced by a directly homorganic nasal; and in ritual sayings, songs, and myths where "certain characters customarily speak with a regular conversion of voiced stops to nasals" (Thompson & Thompson 1972: 448; cf. below, p. 210).

The consonantal opposition nasal ~ nonnasal is one of the earliest features to be acquired by children and is frequently even *the* earliest (RJ I: 538 ff.). Rarer by far is the occurrence of the distinctive feature nasal ~ nonnasal in the vocalic pattern. It is typical for the relation between the marked nasals and correlative phonemes without nasality that the number of different nasal consonants is not superior to but is usually inferior to that of oral consonants. The West African language Igbira, quoted as an exception, apparently opposes not only its labial, dental, palatal, and velar nasals to the corresponding four voiceless ~ voiced pairs of stops but also a labiovelar nasal /ŋʷ/ to a labiovelar 'approximant' (cf. Ladefoged 1964: 24, 58). In turn, the number of nasal vowels in those languages endowed with them is usually lower than or equal to that of oral vowels, but never higher. For instance, Cuicateco in Mexico has nasals corresponding to all six of its oral vowels /a, ɛ, o, e, u, i/ (see Needham & Davis: p. 139).

If the number of nasal phonemes is inferior to that of the corresponding nonnasals, it is the unmarked variety of the compact ~ diffuse system which is always supplied with a pair or pairs of nasal ~ nonnasal oppositions. Besides exceptional cases of systems with a single /n/ or /m/ (see Crothers 1975: 155 f.; and Foley 1975: 219 ff.), there are a great many languages with one single pair of nasal consonants – /n/ and /m/ – in the unmarked, diffuse set of consonants but without a velar and/or a palatal nasal in the marked, compact set of the consonantal system (see Ferguson 1963: 56). Thus, languages with an opposition of graves and acutes in the set of diffuse as well as of compact consonants (/p/ ~/t/ ~/k/ ~/t́/) have an /m/ ~/n/ couple in the diffuse set of nasals but no compact nasals (neither /ŋ/ nor /ň/) – for instance Cham (see Blood). Often, languages with a distinction between velars and palatals among compact nonnasal consonants have only one corresponding compact nasal: usually it is velar /ŋ/, "somewhat more common" than palatal /ň/ (Crothers 1975: 156, 161), since among compact consonants the graves are unmarked and the palatals marked. In many languages which possess a velar or palatal nasal consonant, it occupies a much more marginal place and plays a much more limited role than /m/ and /n/. But there are no languages which have solely /ň/ and /ŋ/ and lack /m/ and /n/. In turn, systems endowed with nasal vowels always have a compact and thus un-marked nasal /ã/ (Ferguson 1974: 11; cf. Meinhold 1970). To sum up, the nasality feature is primarily most compatible with the unmarked members of the compact ~ diffuse opposition, i.e. with diffuseness in consonants and with compactness in vowels. It is one of the many ex-amples of the tendency to avoid the accumulation of marks within phonemes.

Both in its motor and in its acoustic facet the nasality feature exhib-its a common essence, along with certain differing particularities. On the motor level, the common trait is the "opening of the velic passage which connects the nasal cavities with the oral one, with a certain dif-ference in the production of this opening" (see Delattre 1968c: 72). The substantive communality between the nasal vowels and conso-nants on their acoustic level seems to become clearer as soon as rela-tive definitions are substituted for absolute statements. Fant's evidence that nasal consonants are "characterized by a spectrum in which F_2 is weak or absent" actually refers to the Inferior Formant of the two de-terminative formant transitions. Delattre surmises that in the nasal vowels, as compared with oral ones, the F_1 loses much of its intensity in favor of the F_2 (1968c: 64f., and 1970b). In other, relational terms, the Inferior of the two distinctive vocalic formants proves to be weak-ened, like the Inferior Formant of the nasal consonants. Hence, the na-sal characteristics find their place in the lowest regions of the vocalic and consonantal spectra. In the consonants, the 'nasal murmur' pro-duced during the occlusion finds its expression in a narrow and rela-tively weak nasal formant (F_n), according to Delattre "à une fréquence fixe de quelque 250 cps" for French. This formant is engendered by the total pharyngeobuccal cavity behind the buccal occlusion, a cavity variable in its form rather than in its overall volume (Delattre 1968 b: 71 f.). As Malécot has observed, the nasal resonances clearly differentiate the nasals from the orals, and moreover together with the formant transitions participate in the distinction between single nasal consonants (1956).

The interplay of the nasal murmur and formant transitions splits the opposition grave ~ acute into two relatively autonomous features, grave ~ nongrave and acute ~ nonacute. The formant of the murmur effected in the pharyngeobuccal cavity behind the occlusion is somewhat lower when this occlusion is made in the anterior part of the mouth cavity than when the occlusion is made in its posterior part. The two pitches due to the nasal formant F_n and to the formant transitions are grave in /m/ and acute in /ň/, whereas in the dental and velar nasals this opposition may be neutralized by the discrepancy between the gravity and acuteness of the two pitches (murmur and transition or vice versa). Thus, in languages such as Czech, Slovak, Serbo-Croatian, or Hungarian with the three nasal phonemes /m/, /ň/, and /n/, the velar [ŋ] functions as a contextual variant of /n/ (cf. Fischer-Jørgensen 1958: 491); as Malécot's experimental study confirms, the [m] resonances are strikingly different from [ŋ] and [n], whereas the two latter nasals "are rather similar, often indeed indistinguishable" (Malécot 1956: 281). Such a split of the feature grave ~ acute in nasal consonants is here favored by the lesser discernibility of the compact ~ diffuse feature in them as a result of the weakening of the Inferior Formant. In a few languages where [n], [ŋ], and [ň] act as mere contextual variants of one and the same phoneme, this phoneme is opposed to the purely grave timbre of /m/ by a greater or smaller admixture of acuteness.

The question of whether the lower formant of 250 cps proper to nasal vowels could be identified with the F_n of the nasal consonants was presented by Delattre as an item "qui sera très difficile à vérifier" (1966: 246). One may add that the acoustics of the nasalized vowels still remains one of the least clarified and most controversial questions, along with the linguistic delimitation of vowels with a nasal feature from combinations of vowel and nasal consonant (cf. the contributions to this discussion by Schane 1968 and Tranel 1974 for French; Avram 1972 for Portuguese; Elizarenkova 1961: 26 f. for Hindi; Vertogradova 1967: 19 f. for Prakrit Māhārāshtrī; and Lunt 1973 for Guaraní). Re-

iterated attempts (prompted by the traditional spelling pattern) to interpret the French nasal vowels as a mere implementation of a sequence –
oral vowels + nasal consonant – meet with a number of obstacles, as is
indicated particularly by Tranel 1974, Klausenberger 1974, and by
Halle's (1972: 189f.) reference to the different treatment of cases such
as *rien à faire* [rjēnafɛr], with a sequence of a nasal vowel and nasal
consonant, vs. *bon ami* [bɔnami], with an oral vowel followed by a nasal consonant, and *bon à manger* [bō a māže], with the absence of the
nasal consonant.

IV. VOICED ~ VOICELESS AND TENSE ~ LAX

Any vowel system has at its disposal two properties which bring the
vowels into relief in their role as syllabics, in contrast to the nonsyllabic
consonants, which in their pattern are endowed with two opposite
properties. Primarily, optimal vowel phonemes are voiced, in contradistinction to the optimal, voiceless consonants; secondarily, optimal
vowel phonemes are tense and therefore particularly distinct, in contrast to the optimal, lax consonants. There are a relatively limited number of languages in which, as Greenberg assumes, "a phonemic contrast between voiced and voiceless vowels exists, namely the Keresan
languages of Santa Ana and Santa Domingo, the Shoshonean languages Comanche and Ute, Mayan Chontal and Galla, and Teso and
Bagirmi in Africa" (1969: 156; see especially Canonge 1957 for Comanche). In Greenberg's evaluation, in no language with voiceless
vowels does their number exceed that of the voiced ones. In most of
these languages all the voiced and the voiceless vowels match each
other in quality, but none of the languages with fewer voiceless than
voiced vowels lacks diffuse voiceless vowels (1969: 162f.).

Besides the rare opposition of marked voiceless and unmarked
voiced vowels there exists the quite common opposition of marked lax
and unmarked tense vowels. Significant steps have been made toward
a portrayal of the relation between tense and lax vowels; in particular,
tracings of X-rayed vowel articulations from numerous languages and
X-ray motion films of English, Egyptian, Swedish, and Eskimo phonations

> reveal consistent differences of both degree of constriction and of pharyn-
> geal volume between tense and lax vowels. In addition, there are also dif-
> ferences of lip position (less rounded, sometimes less spread, for lax vow-

els) and larynx position (deeper for tense vowels, especially for rounded vowels). The articulatory gestures involved appear to be much the same irrespective of the language, which points to a universal physiological and biological basis for the acoustical contrasts founded on this difference. [Wood 1975: 111; cf. Halle 1977b: 611f.]

While voiceless vowels distinctively opposite voiced ones are a rare occurrence in the world of languages, the opposition of tense and lax vowels exists in a wide number of languages and plays a considerable role in their sound systems - cf. such lax ~ tense pairs in French as *patte ~ pâte, sotte ~ saute, tette ~ tête, taie ~ thé, jeune ~ jeûne* (RJ et al. 1952: 36ff.) and in American English as *pull ~ pool, ship ~ sheep, let late,* etc. In German such differences as length and shortness of vowels, or the two persistently discussed forms of *Anschluss* ('contact', the intrasyllabic variety of the prosodic length feature), appear to be secondary manifestations of the systematic opposition of tense and lax vowels (see Larson).

Still, in spite of numerous observations (cf. RJ I: 550ff.) and the suggestive comparison of the lax ~ tense opposition with the difference between the twofold system of open and covered singing techniques, the latter with "a shift of the vowels toward the middle of the vocalic triangle" (Stumpf 1926: 258ff.), an exact formulation of the motor and acoustic essence of the lax ~ tense feature has remained somewhat indefinitive. Investigators refer to extant uncertainties, unsolved problems, and allegedly insurmountable difficulties in reliably measuring such phenomena as the force of articulation, the degrees of organic pressure in the supraglottal and subglottal cavities, and the relative stiffness of the walls (cf. Kent & Moll 1969). On the other hand, the simple intuition of ordinary speakers and listeners clearly points to the manifest difference between tenseness and laxness (both of vowels and of consonants) and to the greater general effort in the production of the tenseness effect, notwithstanding the varying subtleties of the motor procedures (cf. Fischer-Jørgensen 1972b; and de Groot's confrontation of the Dutch vocalic and consonantal patterns, 1929: 549f.; also RJ I: 550ff.). The main difference between the production of the tense ~ lax pairs in the two patterns, vocalic and consonantal, seems, according to Perkell's cineradiographic studies of speech (1965), to depend on the articulatory effort produced by the extrinsic muscles for vowels and by the intrinsic muscles for consonants.

As we noted above, the optimal consonants are either voiceless, in contradistinction to the natural, optimal voicing of the vowels, or lax, in contrast to the tenseness of the optimal vowels; what is specific to consonants is that they can combine the distinctive properties of voice-lessness and laxness. On the other hand, there are languages, for instance Finnish and Estonian and the prevailing type of Australian languages (Wurm 1972), which in the consonantal pattern are devoid of these two oppositions. The attribution of the universal validity of a sense-discriminative role to one of these two features is totally unfounded. If one of the two consonantal oppositions - voiced ~ voiceless and tense ~ lax - functions in a language, then two possibilities occur. In consonantal systems such as the Slavic ones with the active opposition voiced ~ voiceless, it is the presence of voice which is marked, and the laxness of voiced consonants is merely redundant, whereas in languages which assign the autonomous role to the tense ~ lax feature, the mark belongs to tenseness.

Tenseness may be implemented in two diverse ways, characterized by Fischer-Jørgensen (1968) as a difference between the prevalent use of articulatory force in one case and of a stronger air flow (with aspiration) in the other. Such an aspiration may be limited to special contexts, as it is for the initial stops in American English, or it can have wider implementation. Thus, for instance, in English the relative force of the tense consonants, independently of any position favoring or excluding aspiration, finds a clear manifestation in their relative length and their abbreviating influence on the preceding vowel, if there is one (cf. Raphael 1972). According to Malécot's recent contribution to the study of force of articulation in French, native speakers feel that the tense consonants are stronger than their lax homologues. His experiments show that, of the three parameters of inter-oral air pressure, which all vary significantly with the manner of articulation of the obstruents, air pressure pulse (French 'impulsion') is the most efficient criterion. The glottis closes for the 'voiced' consonants and opens for the 'voiceless', "whether there is voicing or not". The duration of the vowel decreases with a rise in the articulatory force of the following consonant, and the duration of the retention of the consonant itself is relatively longer for the tense consonants and shorter for the lax ones (Malécot 1977: 31 ff.). In spite of the rich and fruitful results of investigations carried out on tense and lax consonants in different languages, Fischer-Jørgensen's conclusion of her recent paper (1976: 197) remains valid: "much more research needs to be done before we can give a sufficiently well-documented description of stop production" with respect to this cardinal opposition.

In the French consonantal system the articulatory and acoustic properties of the tense and lax consonants are usually accompanied by the absence and presence of voice respectively, but in contexts requiring the assimilation of voiced to subsequent voiceless consonants, e. g. *vous la jetez* with voiceless lax [ž] vs. *vous l'achetez* with the voiceless tense [š], the tenseness remains in force and the tense ~ lax opposition appears to be the valid one (as was underlined by Malmberg 1962). Voicing may be completely absent, as it is in Swiss German dialects, or else, as a redundant element, may constantly or optionally accompany laxness. Thus, laxness tends to be attached to voicing, and voicelessness to tenseness. If each of the two features is simultaneously used in a distinctive function, then the doubly unmarked voiceless lax stops occur in opposition to a markedly voiced counterpart on the one hand and to a markedly tense (aspirated) one on the other hand: /t/ in relation to /d/ and to /t^h/. Finally, in even rarer cases, there occurs an accumulation of both marks: a voiced and tense stop /d^h/, and at least in some of these cases actually a murmured one, /d^h/ (for Igbo see Ladefoged et al. 1976; for Pali, Elizarenkova & Toporov 1965: 45; and for the Prakrit languages, Vertogradova 1967: 64f.).

The recent attempts to characterize "voice-onset time (VOT), defined for word-initial stop consonants as the interval between the onset of the release burst of the consonant and the onset of laryngeal pulsing" (Cooper 1975: 25; cf. Lisker & Abramson 1964, 1971), are quite informative, but they can hardly be utilized as a rational classificatory criterion for the features discussed. Frequent doubts as to which partner of the couple is the marked one are due to the confusion of the two oppositions - voiced ~ voiceless and tense ~ lax. And some of the solutions proposed are unfortunately only partial ones, for they share with a few of the recent phonetic studies a neglect of consonants other than stops.

It is appropriate to state here that ingenious and promising efforts made by the Georgian linguists Thomas Gamkrelidze (1975) and Irina Melikišvili (1970, 1974, 1976) have inaugurated the systematic analysis of the gaps in the paradigmatic patterns of phonemes of highly diverse languages. Such prevalently "empty slots" are corroborated by statistical data from those few languages in which these gaps are filled, but the fillers are phonemes of low frequency in the lexicon and/or in the corpus of texts. This research offers very valuable, sometimes surprising evidence as to the manifest tendency to avoid certain concurrences of distinctive features. Such discoveries open new vistas to the hierarchical interrelation of the different features and to the interplay of their marks. Laws of negative implication, which cancel or limit the coexistence of certain features, are receiving an ever-closer explanation and are powerfully contributing to the world typology of sound systems as well as to the search for universals. In addition, the task of scholars involved with the reconstruction of older and prehistoric linguistic patterns is becoming more exact and comprehensive (cf. Gamkrelidze & Ivanov 1973).

Of the interconnections brought to light in the studies at issue one may cite a few examples. The comparison of labials (diffuse grave), dentals (diffuse acute), and velars (compact) shows that the dentals adhere the most to the opposition voiced ~ voiceless (/d/ ~/t/), whereas labial and velar sets easily lack either the voiceless /p/-/f/ or the voiced /g/-/ɣ/ respectively, in contradistinction to the presence of the voiced labials and voiceless velars. The laxness proper to voiced consonants conflicts with the force of the compacts (see Malécot 1968) and therefore /g/ and /ɣ/ are easily omitted from the system; also, children's preference for the *voiceless* representatives of the velars, as pointed out by Ferguson & Farwell (1975: 435), obtains a clear explanation. Apparently the low frequency of the sound energy in the grave consonants attracts the 'voice bar' and thus threatens the individuality of a voiceless labial.

V. STRIDENT ~ MELLOW

In contraposition to vowels, characterized by *sonority,* consonants display an increased damping of sound and, on the other hand, a closer approximation to noise (see above, p. 88 f.). The optimal damping is achieved by the abrupt obstruents (i.e., stops), opposed by their closure to the continuant obstruents; the optimal noisiness, achieved by a supplementary obstacle in the way of the airstream and a consequent intensified turbulence, opposes the strident obstruents to the nonstrident (mellow) ones.

Since many misunderstandings have arisen around the strident ~ mellow feature, it seems useful to recall the concise paragraph (§ 2.322) devoted in the *Preliminaries to Speech Analysis* (RJ et al. 1952) to its production:

> Strident phonemes are primarily characterized by a noise which is due to turbulence at the point of articulation. This strong turbulence, in its turn, is a consequence of a more complex impediment which distinguishes the stri-

dent from the corresponding mellow continuants: the labio-dentals from the bilabials, the hissing and hushing sibilants from the non-sibilant dentals and palatals respectively, and the uvulars from the velars proper. A supplementary barrier that offers greater resistance to the air stream is necessary in the case of the stridents. Thus besides the lips, which constitute the sole impediment employed in the production of the bilabials, the labio-dentals involve also the teeth. In addition to the obstacles utilized in the corresponding mellow consonants, the sibilants employ the lower teeth and the uvulars, the uvula. The rush of air against such a supplementary barrier following the release of the strident stops yields the characteristic fricative effect that distinguishes these from other stops. [See also § 2.324 and RJ I: 277.]

In languages in which the mellow consonants of the compact set are represented only by velars (grave) and not by palatals (acute), the strident counterpart may be either uvular or alveopalatal ("hushing"), thus using either the uvula or the lower teeth as the supplementary barrier.

The interpretation of strident consonants as the counterparts of the mellow ones, and of the mellow stops in particular, troubled some phoneticians, in view of a constant difference in the point of articulation between the two alleged correspondents. Yet this is precisely the characteristic difference between an articulation creating a supplementary obstacle and one without such an obstacle.

The optimal, unmarked stops are mellow; the optimal, unmarked stridents are continuant. Thus the combination of abruptness with mellowness is unmarked, as is the combination of stridency with continuancy. Of the two opposites – abruptness and continuancy – the latter is marked; the closure of the buccal channel in the stops vs. its openness in the vowels is the most elementary and palpable manifestation of the polarity between consonants and vowels. Diverse languages of Africa, Oceania, and South America (see Schmidt 1926: 287), deprived of the opposition between abrupt and continuant consonants, as a rule use obstruents under the form of stops; where this opposition does exist, the number of different continuant phonemes is usually lower than that of abrupt ones. The general preponderance of the hissing (e.g., s, z) over the hushing ($š$, $ž$) continuants (see Melikišvili 1976: 153f.) – and, let us add, over any other variety of continuants – shows a tendency to avoid the accumulation of marks: since continuants are marked in opposition to abrupts, it is the unmarkedly diffuse acute continuants which are preferred. Mellow continuants, as compared to the strident ones, are marked concurrences of features and appear in languages more rarely and, if they do occur, then in a more restricted number. The most frequent of the mellow continuants, the interdental θ, ð, are characterized, in comparison with sibilants, by a weak intensity of friction (cf. Delattre 1966: 264). Likewise, the affricates, which combine abruptness and stridency, are marked concurrences of features, in contradistinction both to the strident continuants and to the mellow abrupts, and therefore the affricates occur more rarely and in a more limited repertory (cf. RJ & LW 1979).

Strident turbulence has been viewed as an indispensable property of affricates – even their name alludes to their strong friction. Baudouin de Courtenay's definition of affricates as "fricative stops" remains persuasive (see the comprehensive treatment of this definition in Dłuska's monograph of 1937; cf. also Ladefoged 1971a: 107). However, McCawley thought he had found in the vast world of languages an exception to the traditional view: in his declarative article of 1967, he referrred to Chipewyan, "which has a three-way contrast between [t, t^θ, t^s]" (p. 523). Fang-Kuei Li gathered material on this language at Fort Chipewyan, Alberta, Canada in 1928 (cf. Sapir 1949: 79) and in his transcription, he distinguished: /d/ ("a voiceless unaspirated stop with a soft articulation"), /t/ ("very strongly aspirated with a guttural spirantal glide"), and both /t^θ/ and /t^s/ ("also strongly aspirated but without the guttural spirantal glide"); each of these latter two has a corresponding voiceless lenis /d^t/ and /d^z/ (1933a: 431; 1933b: 122; 1946: 398). Mary Haas in her meticulous notes (1968) on another (Yellowknife) Chipewyan dialect, "virtually identical with the dialect recorded by Li", notes however "one striking difference". The phoneme transcribed singly as *t* by Li was consistently replaced by [k] in Yellowknife. Li's [tθatiłi] 'needle' and [tɛlk'ałi] 'weasel' are matched in Haas' records by [tθakįł] and [kɛlk'ali], etc. The Chipewyan dialect of Fort Resolution, characterized by Rice (1978) as "in most respects the same as that reported by Li in Fort Chipewyan, Alberta", has replaced the latter's velarized *t* by *k*, but consistently displays *t* in place of Li's t^θ. The merger of a strongly velarized dental with the velar has received an adequate phonetic explanation by Mary Haas (p. 166f.) and by Harry Hoijer (1942). Briefly, the difference between Li's *t* and t^θ implies first and foremost an opposition between the presence and absence of velarization (flatness), and the transcription t^θ must have rendered a distinctly and purely homorganic release of an occlusive obstruent manifestly deprived both of the velarization ("guttural spirantal glide") proper to his /t/ and of the strident sibilant voice proper to the actual affricate t^s. Thus, one would substitute for the transcriptional symbols applied by Li the international signs: [ƚ] = Li's [t], [t] = Li's pseudo-affricate [$t^θ$]; no distinctive features are to be added to stridency and to flatness (implemented by velarization) in order to account for the sense-discriminative means of Chipewyan. The role of velarization has been confirmed in the letter we received from the specialist Michael Kraus, professor at the University of Alaska. The [$t^θ$] which for instance in Ponopean is "a 'free variant' with fricative release" of the phoneme /t/ (see Garvin 1971: 56) seems to be the sole implementation of this phoneme in the Chipewyan dialect recorded by Li. Finally, the latest observations by Ronald Scollon (1978) point to the actual vagueness of the Chipewyan entity cited as "$t^θ$" and to the need for a revision and limitation of the whole pattern in question.

However, even if there should actually be found one tiny isolated exception to the indisputable stridency of all known affricates from thousands of languages, how could one sacrifice the relevant common denominator of the world's affricates to a *hapax legomenon* ('a single occurrence') in Chipewyan and in a minor number of other Athapaskan languages (cf. Hoijer et al. 1963; Krauss 1964, 1973; and Haas 1968)? For the mere sake of the solitary and even doubtful "affricate" [$t^θ$] McCawley made a perverse attempt to abolish the perceptually, acoustically, and articulatorily conspicuous distinction between the presence and absence of consonantal stridency and put in force two *ad hoc* invented oppositions with no perceptual, acoustic, or motor substantiation: (1) "abrupt release" to separate [t] from both [$t^θ$] and [t^s], and (2) "proximal" to distinguish [t^s] from [$t^θ$]. Thus, reflections on Li's solitary [$t^θ$] burgeoned into a series of "*ad hoc* cover features", to apply Anderson's pointed expression (1974: 302).

VI. CONSONANTAL CORRESPONDENCES TO THE PROSODIC FEATURES

In order to answer the question of what corresponds in the vocalic pattern to the interconnected consonantal oppositions strident ~ mellow and continuant ~ abrupt, we need to assess the difference between the inherent and prosodic features. Adolf Noreen (1854–1925) explained the separation of those features he termed "prosodic" from the rest of the distinctive features, "qualitative" in his terminology, but later labeled "inherent", as the difference between the direct dependence of the prosodic features on the temporal sound sequence and the possibility of defining the inherent features without reference to this sequence. (See Noreen I: § 48 and II: § 30.) This division remained unclear even to some adherents of the great Swedish linguist; they objected that any sound feature depends on its place in the string. Yet Noreen is right. The inherent features in their implementation may depend on the context, but their definition depends only on the relation between the two poles of the opposition independently of the appearance of these two polar terms in a given utterance and independently of the variations due to the contextual implementation of the opposites in question, whereas a prosodic feature cannot be defined without regard for the occurrence of the two opposites in the same utterance. Thus, a higher tone is recognizable as such only in relation to the co-occurrence of the lower one in the same sequence; the identification of a long vowel requires a comparison with the copresent short vowels of the same string, etc.

As was emphasized by Pavle Ivić, the determination of such units "involves the element of time. The central role is played by relations between points at a certain time distance, as a rule within the same utterance; whereas inherent oppositions involve a simple (paradigmatic) comparison (cf. English pit↔bit), prosodic oppositions imply first syntagmatic comparisons within the spoken chain and only then paradigmatic comparisons with other words" (1972: 118). As to such cases in which prosodic opposites are lacking, their recognition is facilitated by redundant cues or by the familiarity of the listener with the speech habits of the speaker, his normal speed and voice register. The prosodic oppositions are those properties which bind the phoneme as such to the time axis (RJ I: 308 f.; cf. Fischer-Jørgensen 1957: § 8.9). Notwithstanding the manifold implementation of prosodic features, investigation discloses their distinctly binary foundation (see e. g. Posti 1965; Mahnken 1967; Wang 1967; Vanderslice & Ladefoged 1972).

Characteristically enough, the prosodic features are a property of phonemes when functioning as syllabics and thus are primarily a property of vowels. In contradistinction to the relatively transient consonantal phonemes, vowels have been repeatedly delineated as relatively sustained, stationary units, prone to extension in time (cf. Andersen 1972). Therefore they prove to be suitable for a set of prosodic features which are based on a contrastive comparison of a given vocalic phoneme with the vocalic phonemes of the surrounding syllables – stressed phonemes with unstressed ones, higher pitch with lower pitch, greater length with shorter length – or on the contrastive comparison of the beginning and the end in the temporal course of the syllable through the use of level and deflected tones in their different rising or falling modulations (cf. Halle's challenge for the discussion of stationary and nonstationary tones, 1972: 190ff.; and earlier assessments by Trubetzkoy 1939a: 194ff., and RJ 1968: 598f.). Since consonants are oriented toward noise and since on the other hand the prosodic features are closely linked with vowels as the chief exponents of sonority, which despite the pertinent role of whispering is normally and primarily tied to the varied participation of voice, there is a certain correspondence between the feature high-pitch ~ low-pitch (or, in languages with expiratory stress, heightened ~ reduced loudness) and the consonantal inherent feature stridency ~ mellowness. The heightening of the pitch or of the loudness and the strengthening of the turbulence are contrastive expressions of the optimally vocalic and optimally consonantal character respectively.

We have mentioned the rare existence of a marked set of vowels opposed by the absence of voice to the usual voiced vowels as a reverse analogue to the widespread, quite usual opposition of marked voiced ~ unmarked voiceless consonants. Besides two correspondences - the first one between the vocalic high-pitch ~ low-pitch feature and the consonantal stridency ~ mellowness feature, and the second one between the vocalic and consonantal voiced ~ voiceless features - one runs into a third, surprising correspondence between the vocalic high-pitch ~ low-pitch feature and the consonantal opposition of voicelessness and voicing. The study of Chinese dialects has shown that a connection of high-pitched vowels with voiceless consonants and of lower-pitched vowels with voiced consonants used to exist in Chinese (see Karlgren 1915: chaps. 14-16). An interrelation between the prosodic opposition of the first and second register vowels and the inherent opposition of the antecedent tense and lax consonants has been observed in different Mon-Khmer languages (Huffman 1976). A complex system of interaction between prosodic tones and the types of antecedent consonants - voiced ~ voiceless, tense ~ lax, checked ~ unchecked (see below, p. 153) - was assessed in Haudricourt's insightful essay (1961).

As Malmberg (1969: 189f.) pointed out, one variety of deflected tone in opposition to level tone is the Danish 'stød' and similar examples of so-called 'broken' pitch - an abrupt decrease of intensity and fundamental frequency, as opposed to a more even movement: "the popular Danish designation of the lack of 'stød' is 'flydende tone'

(= 'flowing tone'). It indicates that interruption is the essential characteristic of the opposite term." 'Stød' is a modified form of the falling intonation opposed to the even or rising one. A close parallel to the opposition of deflected and level pitch, and especially of the stød-variety of this distinction, is the opposition of abrupt and continuant consonants. In consonants the lack of abruptness, as noted above, is marked; in vowels the mark belongs inversely to the abruptness or more generally to the deflection vs. levelness.

The widespread prosodic opposition between the unmarked, short, unprolongable vowels and the marked category of long, prolongable ones is one of the natural expressions of the essentially sustained nature of vocalic phonemes (cf. Trubetzkoy 1936) and has no directly symmetrical correspondence in consonantism. Swadesh (1937) rightly acknowledged that he had found no case in which length is the autonomously differentiating feature of consonantal phonemes: their length is dependent on "differences of voicing, of force of articulation, of aspiration," and most usually long consonants function as biphonemic clusters.

While vowels are easily subject to a dilation of their energy into length, consonants find their marked opposites in the higher rate of energy discharged within a reduced interval of time vs. a lower rate of discharge within a longer interval. The marked term of this feature is obtained by the different varieties of extrapulmonic consonants. The merely contextual difference between two of these varieties – ejectives and implosives – has been confirmed by Greenberg on rich material (1970: cf. also Haudricourt 1950). Moreover, clicks should be treated merely as a different contextual, partly geographically conditioned implementation of one and the same distinctive feature, checked ~ unchecked, with due recognition of the retouches to be made in the delimitation of these three subspecies outlined by RJ on the basis of older, sometimes incomplete, phonetic contributions to the study of clicks in South African languages (RJ I: 720ff.; cf. Lanham 1969). Thus, the consonantal abbreviation feature is, in relation to the vocalic prolongation feature, one of the striking examples of the mirror symmetry relating the consonantal and the vocalic subsystems to each other. Yet apparently the shortening of the checked consonants finds its counterpart in prolongation as a typical particularity of the tense consonants in their opposition to the unmarked, lax ones. The frequent co-occurrence of three corresponding consonants – tense, lax, and checked – speaks in favor of this interpretation.

VII. VOWEL HARMONY

We have completed our cursory survey of all those features which build the vowels and are seconded by closer or more distant correspondences in the structure of consonants. All inherent vocalic features and some of the prosodic ones take part in diverse forms of a constructive device called 'vowel harmony' or 'synharmonism' which is used in and plays a relevant configurative role in the organization of sound and word systems by numerous and various languages widespread throughout the world. This device serves, according to Baudouin de Courtenay's metaphoric expression, to "cement" the unity of words (cf. Shaumyan 1965: 91): the feature displaying vowel harmony in a given language can be represented only by one of two opposite terms throughout all the vowels of a group of morphemes or of a whole word. The makeup of such an integral unit is subject to a considerable variety of rules within different languages. The process of vocalic unification throughout the word may go, depending on the structure of the given language, in a progressive or regressive way from syllable to syllable or from morpheme to morpheme and, in the latter case, from the root to the affix or vice versa, as in Uigur (see Nadžip 1960: 37; Kajbarov 1966: 369f.; cf. Reformatskij 1955: 105f.). Such a unification may be complete or may admit certain superpositions and limiting rules. (Cf. the discussions of 'harmony' by Reformatskij 1966; Aoki 1968; Ultan 1973; and especially by Kiparsky 1973: §§ 1.5 & 3.3.)

The comparative study of vowel harmony in different languages lays bare the binary structure of all vocalic constituents and displays their operational autonomy and intuitive foundation with utmost clarity (RJ I: 635). Thus, the vowels of a word must be either all diffuse or all compact in the Manchu-Tungus languages, in the adjacent Chukchee-Koryak group, and in the Lhasa dialect of Tibetan (cf. Aoki 1968; Širokov; Sprigg; and R. Miller). In his shrewd examination of Chukchee vowel harmony, O.S. Širokov divides the morphemes of this language into "marked" and "unmarked". The "marked" ones (*o, a, e*) are characterized by constant relative compactness and differ from each other in the following way: *o* from *a* through flatness, *e* from *a* through acuteness, and *a* from *o* and *e* through its optimum compactness. The corresponding vowels of the "unmarked" morphemes are relatively diffuse: *u, e, i* (see Bogoraz's description, 1934: 14). In words or, more exactly, in incorporating units containing some "marked" morphemes, the vowels of the "unmarked" morphemes change into their compact counterparts. Thus, the relatively diffuse opposites to *o* and *e* are *u* and *i* respectively. Some students were puzzled (cf. Kiparsky 1973: 50f.) by the fact that the diffuse counterpart to the compact *a* proves to be a vowel either near to *e*, but somewhat retracted and lower and laxer in articulation (Širokov 1973: 592), or even homophonous with *e* in some dialects. However, thest two *e*'s cannot occur in similar contexts and the sound which in "marked" morphemes functions as the compact counterpart to *i* plays in "unmarked" morphemes the role of the diffuse counterpart to *a*. Thus, the system of vowels outlined takes the form of:

The vowels of the word unit are either all grave or all acute in many Finno-Ugric languages, in most of the Turkic languages (see Bogorodickij 1933), and in the Northern Mongolian languages (cf. Poppe) and Korean (see Xolodovič), and are mostly accompanied by diverse forms of the autonomous use of the flat ~ nonflat opposition in an interplay with the opposition diffuse ~ compact. In such languages as Kirghiz, all three oppositions of the root morpheme automatically determine the features of the affixal vowels (cf. Batmanov). Most of the Turkic languages show an interconnection between the flatness and compactness features; usually the assimilative flatness (rounding) is confined to the diffuse vowels of the affixes, whereas the affixal compact vowels do not undergo flattening (Baskakov 1966a). But in the Altai language the distribution involves the difference between the compactness and diffuseness of the vowel in the initial syllable: if this vowel is compact, the succeeding ones when compact must be flattened, but if it is diffuse, the use of flatness is limited or even optional; if the rounded (flat) vowel of the initial syllable is diffuse, then the further vowels if likewise diffuse must be flattened, but if, however, they are compact, they do not undergo flattening (Baskakov 1966b: 508).

Among Finno-Ugric vowel systems displaying a tonality harmony, such languages as Finnish and Karelian (Makarov 1966: 63) evidence the peculiar phenomenon of applying the grave ~ acute harmony only to those vocalic pairs in which a grave vowel is matched by an acute one when the two correspondents are either both rounded (flat) or

both unrounded (nonflat). Cf. Karelian pairs ü/u and ø/o as well as
æ/a and at the same time the neutral position in the system, i.e. the
nonparticipation in the vowel harmony, of the vowels /i/ and /e/. (On
additional specifics of Finnish synharmonism see Kiparsky 1973: 36ff.
and 114ff.; cf. Ringen 1976.) The naturalness and vitality of the recourse to the grave ~ acute variety of vowel harmony is confirmed by
its spontaneous generation in children's language (see Ross 1937). To
exemplify Turkic vocalism and to show its dichotomous structure Lotz
used a cubic model (see Figure 8), which illustrates vowel harmony in
its different facets (Lotz 1962: 344f.; cf. Mel'nikov 1966). Cornelis H.
van Schooneveld (1978) widely developed this model in application to
the analysis of cardinal semantic structures.

The cases of the copresence of the diffuse ~ compact opposition
with the opposition flat ~ nonflat can be supplemented by examples
of a copresent flatness attraction in those Southern Manchu-Tungus
languages with diffuse ~ compact harmony, such as Ulch (Sunik
1968a: 152), Udege (Sunik 1968b: 214), and Orok (Petrova 1968: 173).

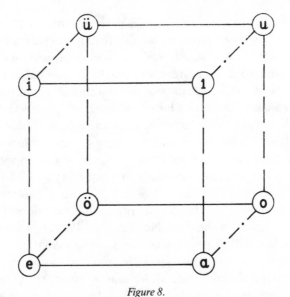

Figure 8.
The Turkish vowels represented as a cubic graph by J. Lotz in 1942 (reproduced in 1962: *American Studies on Altaic Linguistics* 13, Figure 1).

Oppositions:

————————	front ~ back
— — —	high ~ low
— · — · —	rounded ~ unrounded

The West African area builds its vowel harmony on the tense ~ lax feature. The latest and most exact description of these phenomena has been given by Colin Painter, who in his study on the Twi language of Ghana refers to the tense ~ lax opposition at the level of competence and to pharynx width at the level of articulatory configuration as "the most useful way of characterizing vowel harmony in Twi": within any vowel pair in question, "the tense vowel has a wider pharynx than the lax one" (Painter 1971 & 1973; cf. the evasive considerations of Stewart 1967; see also the earlier testimonies on Bari by Westermann & Ward 1933: 128, and on Maasai by Tucker & Tompo Ole Mpaayei 1955).

According to Henry Hoenigswald, in Hindustani, particularly in colloquial Urdu, "a vowel or sequence of vowels within a word is either entirely oral or entirely nasalized ⟨...⟩ If one oral and one nasalized sequence come together (regardless in which order) the entire resulting sequence is nasalized" (1948: 143 f.). Cf. Kaye's observations (1971) on nasal harmony in the Desano language of the North-West Amazon Basin.

One should also mention instances of the occurrence of consonantal harmony based on secondary tonality features, in particular the fact that "in Moroccan Arabic, emphatics cannot occur with non-emphatics in the same word" (see Greenberg 1963 b: 37) and the change in the dialect of North-West Karaïtes of the traditional Turkic vowel harmony into a consonantal one based on the sharp ~ nonsharp opposition (see Kowalski 1929). Actually, the basic type of Turkic harmony encompasses both the vowels and consonants of the whole word. It is a 'syllabic synharmonism', combining the acute ~ grave opposition of vowels with that of sharp and nonsharp consonants (see Šaraf 1927; Jakovlev 1928: 60 f.; Polivanov 1929: 536; Kjazimov 1954: 94). An instructive example of a syllabic synharmonism is the opposition of flat and nonflat words in the Aramaic dialect of Persian Azerbaijan described by the skillful phonetician Ira Garbell (1965: 33 f.): in 'flat' words both vowels and consonants are "more or less pharyngealized, according to individual speakers". Moreover, vowels are retracted, and labial consonants are produced with a hightened protrusion and rounding of the lips. This dialect exemplifies a merger of different implementations of flatness - pharyngealization, velarization, and labialization - and a fusion of flatness and gravity in vowels (cf. above, pp. 115 ff.). Smith quotes a characteristic example of consonant/vowel harmony in child language which requires the occurrence of labial (grave) stops only with back (grave) vowels and of alveolar (acute) stops most frequently with front (acute) vowels: e. g. *bugu:* 'broken', *di-di:* "little' (N. V. Smith 1973: 163).

To the various types of vowel harmony which are based on the inherent vocalic features we must add vowel harmony based on the prosodic opposition of high and low pitches recorded in the Austronesian Jabêm language of New Guinea. In any morpheme where the vowels are low-toned, all obstruents are voiced, whereas in words with high-toned vowels all obstruents are unvoiced (Dempwolff 1939; Milke 1965; Greenberg & Kaschube 1976: 335).

The instances of the extension of a harmony between successive morphemes of the same stem to a harmony between successive words as observed by Stewart (1967: 190) find an interesting correspondence in Kalmyk folklore, which extends the monopoly of grave or acute vowels to a whole verse line (see Pestovskij 1925). Such extension is telling proof of the actual creative vitality and productivity of vowel harmony and of the distinctive features underlying it, in particular the feature tense ~ lax, which belongs, to use Sapir's expression, to "the functionally and aesthetically determining shapes" (Sapir 1949: 48) of our linguistic experience, notwithstanding the intricacies of their articulatory and acoustic implementations.

VIII. GLIDES

According to Sweet's statement, "synthesis introduces us to a special class of elements, called 'glides' or transitional sounds" (1906[3]: § 113). The term 'glide', used in linguistic literature with somewhat divergent meanings, may be applied to phonemes restricted to a minimum of features or even to a single feature. André Martinet, when interpreting the aspiration of Danish consonants as the main cue of the force of articulation and as a mark of their opposition to the unaspirated tenues (lax) consonants, had the fortunate idea of associating with this correlation the opposition between the initial aspirate *h* and the mere *initiale vocalique*. He reinforced this generalization by indicating the full parallelism between the conditions of occurrence of this *h* and the aspirated consonants (1937: 31 ff.). Such an opposition between the aspiration in the one-feature glide *h* and the absence of aspiration (zero phoneme) lays bare the common denominator unifying the pairs of aspirated and nonaspirated consonants and points to their common tense ~ lax feature. The presence of the phoneme *h* in languages makes particularly clear the fact that the valid feature is not voiced ~ voiceless but rather tense ~ lax (with a marked tenseness).

In German, the unmarked counterpart to *h* is the glottal catch (= abrupt onset), which stands in the same position and is optionally omissible (see Krech 1970). Such an omission, and therewith the substitution of a zero phoneme for the lax one, is even more frequent in English, where the more explicit variety shows a tendency for the glottal catch implementation. Yiddish dialects subject to Slavic influence substituted the voiced ~ voiceless feature for the tense ~ lax one, and this change was paralleled by the loss of *h*.

In Arabic the marked glottal glide *h* carries the tense mark, in opposition to the corresponding lax phoneme labeled 'hamza' by Arabic grammarians and implemented by a glottal catch in free variation with zero or simply by a zero, similarly to the couple *spiritus asper* and *spiritus lenis* of Ancient Greek. But in Arabic the tense ~ lax opposition appears, not only in consonantal phonemes but also in the extra-buccal glides, to be superposed by a tonality opposition: namely, both glottal glides possess their flat, pharyngealized *(ayned)* counterparts, one strong and voiceless (tense), and the other weaker and voiced (lax) (cf. RJ I: 518 f.).

Standard French has two peculiar entities known as *h aspiré* and *e muet*. The first of these has been treated as a phoneme by Robert Hall (1948) and described by him as a "slight faucal constriction, with renewed syllable onset and optional glottal stop" (p. 10). According to Dell (1973 b: 256), *h aspiré* is implemented as a glottal catch when preceded within a phrase by a word with a final consonant - e.g. *il hache* [ilᵖaš]; for certain speakers such use is obligatory, for others it is optional. The final vowel or the final consonant of the preceding constituent of the same phrase or of the same compound is treated by the *h aspiré* in a similar way as it would be by a consonant in the same position. Flydal's (1974) magnificent study on the place of the *e muet* with all its stylistic variations from the most elliptic high-speed slang to the maximally explicit pattern of French pronunciation - the classical norm of French verse and, even more, of French song - shows that the *e muet* can be characterized as an optionally pronounced syllabic with differing degrees of omissibility according to position and style (cf. Pulgram 1961). When pronounced, "the mute-e has much less individuality than any other French vowel" (Malécot & Chollet: p. 26 f.): it has a low force of articulation and low intelligibility and is both quantitatively and qualitatively indefinite. In his essay on the contextual and expressive variants of this indefinite unit, Pierre Léon (1971: 67) revives Paul Valéry's whimsical characterization of "L'E muet qui tantôt existe, tantôt ne se fait presque sentir qu'il ne s'efface entièrement et qui procure tant d'effets subtils de silences élémentaires et qui termine et prolonge tant de mots par une sorte d'ombre ..." (Valéry: p.623 f.).

These two more or less indefinite sound units in latency appear to be in complementary distribution: *h aspiré* occurs only in an initial prevocalic position, *e muet* in all positions except the initial and prevocalic one. This notion of latency, first developed by Mathesius (1911, see 1964), Sapir (1933, see 1949), Martinet (1933, but cf. 1972), and Hjelmslev (1961²), remains an essential concept in linguistics. Both *h aspiré* and *e muet* may be viewed as contextual variants of one and the same phoneme, a latent glide in opposition with a compulsory zero: *il hait* with an optional glottal catch vs. *il est* without a glottal catch, or *ferais* with an optional schwa vs. *frais* with no schwa permitted. When the two contextual variants – *e muet* and *h aspiré* – follow each other, only the first is materialized and this implementation is obligatory: *je haïs*. If one were right in interpreting the difference between the opposition of a potentially omissible *h aspiré* or *e muet*, on the one hand, and a compulsory zero, on the other hand, as the difference between greater strength and absence of effort, then the opposition in question could be identified with the tense ~ lax opposition which functions both in the vocalic and in the consonantal subsystems of French (see above pp. 139 ff.).

Sounds conventionally characterized as 'semi-vowels' are endowed with unlike roles in the different sound patterns of languages. Thus, in many languages they function as mere contextual variants of the diffuse vowel phonemes (cf. Swadesh 1947; Andersen 1972). In diverse European countries where the Latin alphabet was used for native languages, no separate letters were needed in order for ancient and medieval scribes and readers to separate nonsyllabic from syllabic *u*'s or *i*'s. This fact illustrates the mere complementary distribution of these vowels and semi-vowels. There are languages in which the nonsyllabic variants [y], [ɥ], [w] of [i], [ü], and [u] respectively obtain in rare situations a sense-discriminative value, as do the French [i]/[y] – *Ay/ail, abbaye/abeille, pays/paye* – which apparently implement the opposition of a tense /i/ and its lax counterpart and thus seem to belong to the same series of pairs as e/ɛ, o/ɔ, ɑ/a, etc. (see the spectrograms of *Ay/*

ail taken from F. de Saussure's grandson: in *Preliminaries*, p. 46; cf. Martinet 1933 and Ščerba 1915: 72 f.).

In particular cases, certain semi-vowels may assume the role of glides, for instance in Russian, which supplements the pairs of sharp ~ nonsharp consonants by the opposition yod ~ zero (cf. such pairs as [r'at] 'row'/[rat] 'glad' and [jat] 'poison'/[at] 'hell'). It is noteworthy that before /e/, where only the marked member of the opposition sharp ~ nonsharp is admitted, the palatalizable consonants are obligatorily palatalized and, in the absence of a consonant, yod is obligatory (cf. *t'el-d'el-p'el-b'el-m'el-jel*). Initial /e/ occurs only in words which retain their foreign sound shape (/el'f/ 'elf', /éra/ 'era'), in interjections (/ex/, /ej/), and in deictic morphemes of interjectional origin and tinge (/ét'i/ 'these', /étak/ 'in this way, so'); likewise, non-sharp consonants followed by /e/ occur only in loanwords retaining their foreignism (/sép'ija/ 'sepia', /ser/ 'sir').

IX. THE NASCENT SOUND SHAPE

The analysis of any given language uncovers the existence of rules which govern the interrelationship between the different distinctive features within a linguistic system, their co-occurrence, and their combinability into simultaneous bundles and successive strings. The comparison of such sets of rules acting in the manifold languages of the world enables the inquirer step by step to find out which of these regularities remain valid for most of, or even for all of, the languages investigated. A typology of linguistic structures which is being developed on the basis of such interconnections helps us to approach the fundamental problem of linguistic universals. The typology of languages lays bare both the extant variations and the universal and nearly universal invariants which underlie them. We are looking for the structural laws, either prohibitive or merely preferential (cf. RJ 1968: 600), which rule over the linguistic systems of the world, and this search must be complemented, corroborated, and enhanced by a similar inquiry into a fundamental ontogenetic domain: the development of children's language and especially the elicitation of the successive order in the build-up of its sound pattern.

On the eve of World War II (1937), a book by the French-Belgian linguist Antoine Grégoire (1892–1961) heralded the beginning of what he later called "la renaissance scientifique de la linguistique enfantine"

(1950). Grégoire's diary offers an exhaustive, minute picture of the verbal life of his two young sons, with a continuous, careful concentration on each developmental moment. Every new attainment of the children is thoroughly observed and described. Grégoire's two-volume monograph (1937, 1947), along with the farsighted Russian studies by N. Gvozdev (1892–1961) which appeared in various publications from the twenties on and were later collected in his volume of 1961, and with the volumes of painstaking observations (1939–49) made by Werner Leopold, the relentless German-American investigator of the language of his two bilingual daughters – all of these could be best compared with motion pictures. By their rich linguistic and environmental data and by their precise and explicit evidence, these studies surpass the increasingly common "snapshots" of a child's verbal behavior and of his linguistic repertory at a given instant. Such snapshots are made by visiting the child during a few months at weekly or longer intervals for half an hour with a tape recorder or even by limiting the acquaintance with the infant to a single 100-minute recording session. These rare and cursory meetings between the child and an actual stranger fragmentize, mechanize, and distort the total dynamic image since the mutative processes and their order remain hidden and the innermost dynamic circumstances of the gradual buildup cannot be detected (cf. RJ 1977).

The first drafts of linguistic ontogeny were outlined in the years of World War II (see RJ I: 317ff. and 328ff., and the synopsis by Ferguson & Garnica 1975: 162–168). These *Drafts* attempted a structural analysis of the infant's growing language ("la langue en devenir") with respect to the emergence and treatment of distinctive features and to their "lois générales, ou tendant à être générales, si l'on préfère être plus prudent" (RJ I: 317). The comparative scrutiny of a vast amount of material brought up the question of irreversible solidarity between certain distinctive features successively gained by the child and subsequently also the question of striking communalities in the stratificational order among children not only of one and the same language but also of quite different linguistic realms. For certain acquisitions of distinctive features and their concurrent and successive combinations the relative temporal order proved to be the same, no matter where and no matter when. Such laws of irreversible solidarity point to a layered constitution of language, homogeneous in many respects. The "highly likely" hypothesis, defended in Björn Lindblom's notable research, that "not only perceptual but also articulatory, physiological criteria may guide the child in its search for its first contrastive signals" (1972: 79) actually stands in agreement with the attitude of the *Drafts*.

The appearance of several special studies on the successive order of children's acquisitions proved to be an important checkup and validation of the main implicational laws proposed in the ontogenetic *Drafts* (see Rūķe-Draviņa 1977). Harry V. Velten's rich and astute essay (1943) based on a record of his daughter's speech from her eleventh to her thirty-sixth month opened these studies about the growth of phonemic and lexical patterns in infant language. Let us quote some further contributions with abundant reinforcing testimonies from diverse languages: S. Nakazima's (Part IV, 1972) comparative study of the speech development of Japanese and American English in childhood; Arne Vanvik's (1971) description of the "phonetic-phonemic development" of a Norwegian child from his first to his eighth year, with the inference that the main theses of the *Drafts* about the order of the development of phonemes and phoneme sequences are confirmed by the Norwegian data (cf. H. Abrahams 1955); and Andrew Kerek's (1975) conclusion that Hungarian studies on children's acquisition of this language likewise support the drafted scale of implications (cf. also Meggyes 1972). The concise essay (1968: 337 ff.) of the Spanish linguist Emilio Alarcos Llorach led to parallel and further encouraging conclusions, as did the Dutch testimonies of Anne Marie Schaerlaekens (1977). As Marlis Macken, a research participant in the Child Phonology Project at Stanford University, recently pointed out, the general claims of the *Drafts* with regard to the universal order of consonantal acquisition fit the pattern revealed in the latest studies of Mexican children's Spanish and confirm "a set of substitutions predicted" by the *Drafts* (1977: 31).

Particularly rich and corroborative has been the postwar series of monographs by observant Czech and Polish linguists on the whole process of language acquisition by their own children. For Czech we possess the penetrating studies by Jaroslava Pačesová (1968, 1970), who especially points out the priority of the unmarked terms of oppositions in relation to the marked ones. Karel Ohnesorg's two Czech volumes (1948, 1959; see also Bartoš 1959) are filled with valuable material. Ohnesorg sees the immediate task of international research on child language as confirming and enriching "la liste des constatations" of the early *Drafts* (1970: 698). The order of the unfolding of children's sound pattern has been the main focus of this linguist; he has become an active contributor "à la pédophonétique comparée" and maintains that a broad comparison enables us to discern many resemblances and coincidences in the sound evolution of children's language in the most diverse linguistic environments, as, for instance, is already known from a comparison of French, Latvian, Polish, Russian, Slovenian, Czech, German, English, Italian, and Rumanian data (Ohnesorg 1972: 186). Closely cognate *mutatis mutandis* with these Czech inquiries are the Polish investigations of Leon Kaczmarek (1953) and later of Maria Zarębina (1965) and Józef Kania (1972). In his *Introduction to Modern Linguistics,* Manfred Bierwisch in turn states that "within the universal inventory a certain hierarchy emerges" (1971: 25) and corresponds to the order in which a child develops his ability to distinguish between sounds and which on the other hand underlies aphasic losses.

According to Charles Ferguson, who for the last two decades has led the American linguistic research into children's learning of speech and who organized the Stanford University Child Phonology Project, the hypothesis of a universal order of acquisitions first advanced in the *Drafts* "has proved to be stimulating and fruitful, ⟨...⟩ the most detailed, explicit and suggestive one available" (Ferguson & Farwell 1975: 434). These two authors state that the respective linguistic developments of three children under their care were quite similar, and that they corroborated many of the proposed suggestions: priority of "labial and alveolar stops with nasals and glides in these positions developing later, and fricatives even later ⟨...⟩, labial nasals before others ⟨...⟩, velar consonants begin development much later than those of other areas" (Ferguson & Farwell: 435). The claim that between certain distinctive oppositions there reigns a uniform order of development is indeed supported by numerous correspondences. One must remember, however, that the relative chronology does not encompass all the constituents of the system. For instance, if the place of semi-vowels or of /h/ was not determined in the ordered rules of the *Drafts,* it was not for "lack of appropriate attention", but simply because the data available had not yet permitted the assignment of a definite position in the developmental scale of acquisitions to these items; it is characteristic that even between the three children cited by Ferguson & Farwell there are divergences in this respect (cf. also the discussion above, pp. 153 ff., on the different functions of *h* and semi-vowels).

The *Drafts* were never meant to become dogma and they deliberately called for a checkup of working hypotheses and for further, more precise formulations, corrections, and additions. Moreover, even where the claim of universality appears to be overstated and the al-

leged universal is demoted to the status of a near-universal, the importance of rules with probability near 1.0 remains highly relevant for the
question of general linguistic laws (cf. above, pp. 61 f.). At the pilot
conference on language universals (Dobbs Ferry, New York, April
1961) the promoter of psycholinguistics, Charles Osgood, advocated
the view that "it is the non-universal statistical universals that are the
most interesting", since the exceptions reflect interactions among a
whole set of functional laws (Osgood 1963: 302).

The particular value of Irina Melikišvili's pioneering inquiry (1970)
into the universal regularities *(Gesetzmäßigkeiten)* in the system of distinctive features lies in her careful explanation of the supposed exceptions through the use of more specified rules based on a wider scope of
interacting features. Thus, for instance, the position of affricates in the
world's language systems and in the linguistic development of children
receives a far more exact formulation; supposed exceptions disappear
as soon as inner factors, namely the compact ~ diffuse, grave ~ acute,
and voiced ~ voiceless oppositions, with their mutual hierarchy and
distribution of marks, are taken into account and as soon as the role
played in the buildup of the affricates by the two competing pairs, continuant ~ abrupt and strident ~ mellow, is adequately interpreted.
Melikišvili (pp. 67 f.) ascertains not only a set of near-universals, but also universals with probability 1.0, for instance the fact that the existence of affricates implies the copresence of a diffuse acute continuant
in the same system, and in particular that the occurrence of [c] implies
the co-occurrence of [s]. Such a progressive and careful improvement
of the formulations brings us ever closer to the wide network of strict
implicational laws which actually underlie and determine the sound
structure of the world's languages and which regulate the order of children's linguistic acquisitions.

Moreover, the same laws of irreversible solidarity receive ever new
confirmations in the mirror symmetry of children's gains and aphasic
losses (cf. Holmes 1978). Growing clinical evidence shows that "it is always in relation to the system and its principles of organization that
the phonological dissolution of speech can be characterized". Sheila
Blumstein's manifold evidence for this conclusion (1973: 75) and her
linguistic study of patients' errors demonstrate that the marked members of oppositions tend to disappear earlier than the unmarked ones
(pp. 53 & 60; cf. RJ II: 312). This basic uniformity cannot be disregarded or viewed as invalidated by pointing to inaccuracies, whether
true or imaginary, found in the first attempts to draft the universal

framework. The urgency of further examining and elaborating the vast connections posited was insisted upon in David McNeil's psychological treatise on the acquisition of language (1970a).

If the original *Drafts* left no room for a consideration of the nature of individual oscillations in sound development or for a "highly detailed analysis of the idiosyncratic paths which particular children follow in learning to pronounce their languages" (Ferguson & Farwell 1975: 438; cf. 434f.), this one-sided orientation was conditioned by the central topic of research, which focused on the elicitation of the invariants from the fluctuating variations. These variations neither cancel out nor even hide the manifest invariance, and even if the "description and explanation of such differences" are of great interest to linguists and have "relevance for therapy and education", such variants cannot be thoroughly understood without an extraction and explanation of the invariants hidden behind them. In Stanley S. Stevens' terms (1951: 21), it is "not that variability is ever banished from empirical science, but successive expansion of the domain of invariance can reduce the dominion of variance to tractable proportions".

Neither in individual children nor in any speech community are changes effected with abrupt and instantaneous generality (cf. above, p. 80, and below, pp. 172ff.). A period of diffusion from word to words, from speech style to speech styles (cf. Labov 1970), and from speaker to speakers fills the interval between the start and the finish of a development. The process of acquisition has been repeatedly observed and portrayed. Ohnesorg (1959: 29) recalls both Roussey's image of a dayslong "va et vient du son quitté au son nouveau" (1899–1900) and the note in Saussure's *Cours* on "beaucoup de tâtonnements, d'essais, et de rectifications" in the child's gradual mastery of sounds. Arne Vanvik recounts how a newly acquired sound becomes a favorite one: "we again witness a swing of the pendulum from absence of a sound to the exaggerated use of it" (Vanvik 1971: 306). Ferguson & Farwell add to these observations (1975: 433, 436) a new and valuable note on the lexical selectivity of the child in picking words which contain his favorite sound and avoiding words with sounds as yet unfamiliar to him. However, none of the circumstances which accompany the enrichment of the child's system of distinctive features obscures or disturbs the temporal order of his gains, notwithstanding the frequent diversity between his styles of speech, for example the child's playful reversions to earlier verbal infantilisms with the omission of certain distinctions (see Ohnesorg 1948: 52f.). A child may initially use a lately acquired distinction only when addressing adults: thus a Polish girl employed the newly mastered continuants [v] and [f] in talking with her parents, pronouncing *krewka* 'blood' as [klefka], but still repeated to herself [kepka] in her former fashion (Zerębina 1965: 25).

The youngster's attention to the distinctive features is remarkable indeed; even before he actively possesses them, their recognition may be perfectly attained. As Pačesová observes,

> the phoneme /r/ was one of the consonants which appeared in the child among the last phonemes in the developmental series. In the meantime, he replaced this phoneme mostly by /l/. Neither in production nor in acoustic impression was there any difference between items such as *vlásky - vrásky, Ilenka - Irenka*. The child, nevertheless, readily commented on our incorrect interpretation and demanded the distinguishing of the two liquids in our speech though he himself was content with the realization of one of them. Similar data may be found with regard to other consonants, cf. for example *uvař - uvaž* (both the items had the identical form [uvaš], *koníček - Toníček* (both realized as [toni:ček]), thus indicating that the mastering of the correct phonetic realization is not simultaneous with the identifying of the distinctive features in phonemes: the latter, evidently, precedes the former in appearance [1968: 230f.]

(Cf. RJ I: 715f., and Berko & Brown 1960: 531 - "Not fis, fis!" instead of *fish*.) MacKay (1970b: 320) cites the dialogue of a mother with her child, who months earlier had been able to produce [f] and [p] in his babbling and now asked her to "give me my pork" (meaning *fork*); when she handed him his fork, saying in his style "Here's your pork", she received the answer: "No, no! Pork! Pork!"

The consciousness of or at least subliminal set *(Einstellung)* upon sound features does not, however, justify the experiment performed and reported by Graham & House (1971) in which they presented thirty girls ranging in age from three to four and one-half years with the task of discriminating between any two given consonants selected from the ensemble of test sounds by making judgments of "same" and "different". This experiment was done to determine whether children still in the process of learning the sound pattern of their language discriminate in terms of distinctive features and to evaluate the "hypothesis of the sequential development of phonological oppositions". The abstract question of sameness and difference, when disconnected from the sense-discriminative task of the features, is aprioristic and lies outside the ordinary cognitive processes, competence, and spontaneous use not only of beginners but also of mature speakers, and the question of sameness is a most ambiguous one (cf. above, p. 53f.).

In fact, no artificial experiments are needed for the recognition of, for example, the fact that in the relatively numerous minority of languages devoid of the continuant ~ abrupt opposition, the obstruents are universally represented by stops as the only or at least as the basic implementation (cf. RJ I: 360) and that correspondingly in the evolving systems of children, stops are firmly established before the introduction and stabilization of the continuants, which then become the marked term of the newborn opposition continuant ~ abrupt.

If from the omnipresence of stops one proceeds to the rare participants in the sound patterns of the world's languages, these rarities prove to belong to the last acquisitions made by children (cf. Ferguson 1973; Ingram 1978), and one may expect that with further expansion of the inquiry into the most diverse geographical varieties of nascent language the late emergence of such constituents will turn out to be general. All types of extrapulmonic consonants are relatively infrequent among the speech communities of the world, and in those communities which make use of them, they belong to the late acquisitions of native youngsters, as has been repeatedly stated by observers of Caucasian and American-Indian languages endowed with ejectives. According to a personal communication from Franz Boas, Indians with such languages are accustomed to replacing these consonants by plain stops when telling stories to those children who have not yet assimilated this kind of phoneme. L. W. Lanham recounts the results from a new investigation of Zulu child language: "clicks are among the last consonants to be acquired", and before their acquisition, simple obstruents are substituted for them (1969: 159).

The currency of a single liquid among the sense-discriminative elements in the world's languages (see above, p. 91) is paralleled by the fact that, as has been observed repeatedly, in the experience of children the second liquid, usually some kind of [r], belongs to their last acquisitions (cf. Avram 1962: 246f.); for instance, the emergence of the r ~ l distinction in Polish children is assigned by observers to the period between the third and sixth years (Zarębina 1965: 31; Kaczmarek 1953: 55). As to the Czech sibilant vibrant /ř/, one of the most unusual appearances in the world of languages, all inquirers affirm it to be the last of the phonemes attained by native children (e. g. Ohnesorg 1959: 40f.; Bartoš 1959: 8; Pačesová 1968: 178f.). The relative rarity of nasal vowels as compared to the near-universality of nasal consonants and the substantial delay in children's use of the former as opposed to the latter are generally known facts which find constant confirmations in the Polish, French, and Portuguese linguistic literature, and one is surprised that an inattentive reader of the basic sources may mistakenly report lack of evidence (see Olmsted 1971: 108 f.).

The occasional oversight of the relevant difference between the two consonantal oppositions - voiced ~ voiceless and tense ~ lax (see above, pp. 138 ff.; cf. Jakobson & Halle 1968: 441) - has clouded the discussion about the role of voicing in children's gradual acquisition of language. There is a significant developmental difference between children learning a language with a voiced ~ voiceless feature and those acquiring a language with a tense ~ lax feature as the sense-discriminative means. Slavic children who face the former type of system begin with voiceless stops before attaining the next step, viz. the establishment of voiced stops as the marked counterpart. At the onset of this stage, the voiced character of /b/ and /d/ "remains unstable, thus revealing that the distinction of voice is not yet fully acknowledged"; this shows up especially in the frequent fluctuation of the voiced and voiceless phonemes, the former replaced by the latter in most cases and for most children (Pačesová 1970: 11 f.). During this intermedium the set of voiced consonants is sometimes implemented by Czech children with "weakened voicing" (Ohnesorg 1959: 53).

It is likewise voiceless consonants that usually represent the initial stage in the speech of children faced in their environment with the tense ~ lax opposition (see for instance Alf Sommerfelt's remarks about the unaspirated voiceless stops used first by Norwegian children - 1929: 273; cf. also Leopold 1974: 119 f., and Preston). The next, seemingly strange, change (see Ferguson & Farwell: pp. 432 f.), namely the urge to replace voiceless stops by voiced ones, *papa* by *baba,* [pɪti] (pretty) by [bɪdi], etc., is easily explainable as a transition from the voiceless, unmarked term of the potential voiced ~ voiceless distinction to the lax, unmarked term of the anticipated tense ~ lax opposition. This second stage, sometimes introduced by the use of voiced and voiceless consonants as mere contextual variants (cf. Velten 1943: 283), either follows the first one (cf. Durand 1954: 89) or in rarer cases immediately starts the development prompted by the adult's distinction of tense and lax consonants (cf. Leopold). The distinction between both classes, at least in English, becomes fixed quite late.

The pertinent role played in the sound system of language by the compact ~ diffuse opposition is exemplified by the delayed appearance of the compact consonants, especially velar stops, as compared to the diffuse ones, a phenomenon paralleled by the sound pattern of a few languages of the world (see above, pp. 129 f.). The observation of Quintilianus on children's customary substitution of dentals for velars - "et cum C ac similiter G non valuerunt, in T ac D emolliuntur" - finds confirmation in the enduring (sometimes years-long) lack of velars in children's language, as was observed already in the seventeenth century by Jan Amos Komenský in the speech of children who substitute not only *l* for *r*, and *z* for the *ř*, but also *t* for *k: toláč* for *koláč* 'bun' (*Informatorium:* cap. 8, p. 554) and has been ascertained by some thirty investigators listed in Ohnesorg (1959: 25, and 1972: 188) and by numerous other observers throughout the world.

The delay in the emergence of velar stops, sometimes prolonged for years, as the primary school reports of various countries assert, and a dramatic portrayal of an adolescent boy still replacing velars by dentals, entered into world literature through Sholom Aleichem's short story *Di Fon* 'The Flag' (1900). Here a penniless wretch is given the mocking nickname Topele Tutaritu and is ridiculed by both children and adults for his inability to pronounce with a *k* his name *Kopele* ('Jacob') and the rooster's call *kukariku*; his misfortune is aggravated because he is surrounded by people with the inaccessible velars in their names, such as his mother Gitl, his father Kalmen, and his school teacher Gershen Gorgl von Galaganovka! Children's final hard-won attainment of the velars frequently provokes their stubborn, hypercorrect use of these consonants. The daily greeting "Guten Tag, Herr Doktor", which first sounded like "Duten Ta, Herr Dotta", may finally change into "Guken Gag, Herr Gokka" (Nadoleczny 1926: 61).

The alleged individual exceptions to the mass scale of proofs for the emergence of compact (velar) stops after and not before the diffuse (dental) ones cannot be reinforced by examples of individual children who utter a few words containing both kinds of stops, because between the emergence of the two classes there may in some cases be a prolonged and in other cases a merely minute interval. "The relative chronology is the same although the absolute time-scale varies considerably" (Velten 1943: 282). It should be added that the fragmentary data presented by observers often do not reveal the entire "longitudinal cut" (cf. Menn); even if there did occur an exception from the pretendedly "elegant schema" - "no compact stops established before the diffuse ones" - such a minimally possible aberration might diminish the universal probability 1.0 by only a hundredth or even a thousandth. Through this minute lessening, the developmental schema under discussion might perhaps be said to lose some of its alleged "ele-

gance" but not its relevance, because, far from being "over-simplifi-
ed", it still gives an insight into the structuration of language, in particular of its sound shape. It must also be added that some of the words
picked up by the little learners from mature speakers first tend to preserve the adult pronunciation before the integration of these borrowings into the child's own pattern, as happened with Leopold's daughter, who began with a nearly perfect reproduction of the phonetic form
of 'pretty' before shifting over to the assimilated form [pɪti] (cf. Ferguson & Farwell: p. 432). This case resembles the habit of borrowing foreign words of endearment and evaluation with an only temporary
preservation of their sound shape.

A monograph by Thelma E. Weeks (1974) devoted to the slow
speech development of a bright child was based on visits to the little
girl of an hour or longer once a week except during vacation periods.
The first five holophrases (or 'monoremes') noted at the end of the infant's first year were *dada* 'Daddy', *momo* 'Mommy', *gogo* 'doggie',
baba 'pattycake', and fifth example, *gaga,* which should be singled out
as a purely affective element with no notional reference (cf. Vendryes
1953: 27) for it "seems to serve as an expression of happiness," an expression "always uttered in a quite high pitch different from the others" and abandoned a little later (Ferguson et al. 1973: 40). It remains
unknown whether the labials as designations for the parents emerged
before the velar monoreme for the dog or after it. Moreover, one must
add that the course of acquisitions of this child through her first four
years shows so many anomalies and aberrations from the usual linguistic development that the case must be interpreted as obviously abnormal, notwithstanding her (intellectual) sanity and her later apparent recovery from her verbal inabilities.

It is worthy of note that even in the unique case of a girl who first
came in contact with human language as a teenager (see above, p. 51),
her initial acquisition of speech involved a regular substitution of /t/
for /k/, /n/, and /s/ in all word positions (Fromkin et al. 1974: 89).

Universal propensities may be traced in the growth of children's
language from its earliest beginnings. It becomes increasingly evident
that the production and recognition of contoural features such as intonation which impart an emotional coloring, in particular an expression of displeasure or pleasure, to a sentence, or rather to an entire utterance, and which signal the end of an utterance, appear universally
"as the first of the true language periods, following the stages of crying,
cooing, and babbling" (Weir 1966: 156 ff.; cf. Tonkova-Yampol'skaya

1969; Crystal 1970 and 1973; and Fónagy 1972). As Pačesová observed, "the priority of melody in language acquisition is once again confirmed. The child reproduced easily the intonation contours given to him for imitation. Furthermore, the pitch variation performed a certain function from the very beginning." In the first developmental stage of language, intonation provides "the main means of the child's expressing approval, protest, demand, astonishment, surprise, regret, etc." (1968: 18).

It is indeed characteristic that, in contradistinction to the later linguistic gains of the child, "the right hemisphere is directly involved in the processing of intonation contours" (Blumstein & Cooper 1974: 156; cf. above, pp. 48 ff.), although a clear-cut separation of linguistic roles assigned to the two hemispheres seems to crystallize only toward age four or five. An interesting parallel to the place of the contoural features in children's verbal achievements is the fact indicated by Böller & Green that "some aphasics unable to distinguish the semiotic content of the words in the sentence know when they are being given a command, a question, a declarative sentence". In this regard one would rather and with more right speak about utterances than sentences, because the division of an utterance into sentences is a later accomplishment in the infant's progression and an earlier disturbance in aphasic deterioration.

The intonational contour enables the beginner in speech learning on the one hand and the aphasic loser of language on the other to discriminate both in perception and in production between utterances full of and those devoid of evocative power, and among the former to distinguish those of feeling (emotive) and of appeal (conative), to discern and hence to specify emotion and volition. Such a child is already, and such an aphasic is still, competent to make a distinction between an appeal to action (imperative utterance) and an appeal to answer (interrogative utterance). The interrogative intonation combines a cadence with a semicadence – the intonation of the end and that of the continuation: the utterance is finished but requires the response-utterance of the interlocutor. Julia Kristeva is right in assigning to these phenomena a "pre-syntactic function", in contradistinction to the subsequent "digital" constituents of language and to the cognitive strategies exhibited by syntax (1977: 437 ff.). As Dwight Bolinger adduced, sentential intonation displays its invariant core notwithstanding manifold regional variations: a dichotomy of tension and relaxation lies behind fluctuations in fundamental pitch; the universality of this phenomenon rests on our psychophysical makeup (1964: 843); and patterns of intonation are "the first linguistic subsystem that a child learns to use" (1977: 18).

The innermost reason for the over-cautious attitude sometimes taken toward the *Drafts* under discussion hardly lies in the squabbling over controversial details but rather in some readers' inattention to or their distrust of the nuclear thesis: "it does not suffice to expose the regularity of the superposition of values but their hierarchy has to be explained by disclosing its *necessity"* (RJ I: 322ff.). Two incompatible attitudes have clashed with each other: the search for interconnected laws and their inner elucidation (cf. RJ I: 325) collides with the belief in the assumed "absence of any linguistically motivated ordering principle" (see Ferguson & Farwell: p.430).

X. DYNAMIC SYNCHRONY

Linguistic facts and linguistic theory imply each other, and are equally indispensable for a clear insight into the buildup of child language and of its sound shape. A lack of theory is the most hazardous and most speculative theory. The idea of language as a structured, coherent system of devices from the smallest to the highest units has for ages been enrooted in sciences striving against the superstitious and lifeless image of a fortuitous aggregate of scattered particulars. Wilhelm von Humboldt, great heir to a centuries-old tradition of philosophical grammar and precursor of present-day linguistic views, insistently claimed that "nothing in language stands by itself but each of its elements acts as a part of a whole" (IV: 14); he contended "dass in der Sprache Alles durch Jedes und Jedes durch Alles bestimmt wird" (V: 394; cf. Telegdi 1970). The designation of language as a system "où tout se tient" has entered into the primers of French and international linguistics.

Language remains a coherent system both in its being and in its becoming (cf. Shaumyan 1977). Children's nascent language is but a particular case of language in becoming, and must be viewed as a developing system. Such a consideration is fully valid also with respect to the sound shape. The universal rules and tendencies disclose the intimate conjunction between the constituents of the pattern and the implicational order of these relations in the structuration of language as well as in the successive manifestations of this order in the child's linguistic maturation. It is necessary to see the forest and not just the trees, and in the given case to see the whole network of distinctive features and their simultaneous and sequential interconnections and not just an apparent mosaic of unrelated acquisitions. In present-day scientific thought, according to the terse formulation of Oskar Lange (1904–1965), "*system* is taken to mean a set of elements together with the set of relations between the elements; the set of such relations (and of all their isomorphic transformations) is called the *structure* of the system".

The notion of structure is inseparable from that of 'transformation' (transmutation) and, as Lange points out, "wholes can never remain in a changeless state, they must change constantly" (Lange 1962: 1 & 17; cf. Ashby 1956: 83, and Thom's theory of catastrophes [1974a, b]). In this respect, language is not an exception among systems, and the frequent question "why do all languages keep changing all the time?" loses its edge. In linguistics, the incessant attempts to disconnect the concept of system and of its structure from that of change lead to an unrealistic view of language and an oversimplistic conception of its network. These attempts inhibit the explanation of changes through a reluctance to see them as necessary components of the system.

Between the changes in children's language during its acquisition and the changes in extant languages of entire speech communities there are appreciable differences. The task of the former development is to construct language, while the latter process is aimed at the partial restructuration of language. However, in children's process of constructing their language, the restructuration of the adult model is vitally involved. In any case, there is a set of essential correspondences between both kinds of changes. Any change involving distinctive features exhibits a temporal distance between its initiation and conclusion (cf. above, pp. 161 f.). The interval between these two boundary markers is frequently characterized by students as a temporary disorganization – chaos, heterogeneity, mixture, an irregular state of 'unstructuredness' – whereas in fact the coexistence of entities which were compulsory before a change began with those which presumably will have monopoly after its completion does not mean a disruption of orderliness. If some of the members of the same speech community, in particular the senior ones, use solely the older forms, while the others, especially the junior ones, have constant recourse to the innovations, a new rule is added to the linguistic code of the whole community, concerning a difference in the forms employed by speakers and listeners of diverse ages. Another limiting variation of basically one and the same linguistic status would be a preference for the older form by the younger generation when addressing older people and a corresponding concession by the older speakers to the younger listeners.

If, however, free choice between both kinds of forms characterizes the same speakers independently of the addressees' age (and this seems to be a quite frequent case), the freedom of this variation is subject to significant restraints: the selection of older and newer forms depends on the style of speech – more or less hurried, slipshod, elliptic, informal, expressive, or the opposite of each of these modes. The elliptic origin of many sound changes is indisputable, for instance the developing loss of the vocalic lax ~ tense feature in contemporary French (cf. Martinet 1945). Often the sound shapes of diverse words undergo the same change with different speed, a discrepancy which is closely tied to their different stylistic coloring. Thus we must for a given moment in the course of a certain sound change distinguish between the different subcodes which belong to the multilayered overall code of the whole community or of certain of its subgroups. An observer's heightened attention to such subgroups and their subcodes is necessary in order to avoid the myth of temporary disintegration.

As noted above (pp. 80 f.), any change is a gradual diffusion of one of the variables among diverse speech uses and diverse speech users, with a gradual widening of the radius of intercommunication. As long as they co-occur for diverse communicational purposes, the older and newer shapes must be viewed as synchronically coexistent. They are part of the code of the same collective body even if they are felt to pertain to temporally diversified layers of the overall code. Since the competing phases of the change prove to be copresent, the change in progress constitutes a part of one and the same synchronous cut (Saussure's *section transversale*). It is encompassed in a dynamic synchrony (cf. the stimulating contributions by Fónagy 1956 and Wang 1969 to the still insufficiently examined questions of "competition between coexisting rivals").

The neogrammarian division of sound changes into 'spontaneous' vs. 'conditioned' has undergone a double modification, and most of the alleged 'spontaneous' changes in fact appear to be 'conditioned' ones. Firstly, a change constrained by the surrounding sequential context was formerly the only type to be labeled 'conditioned', whereas the change of a feature constrained by the concurrent, simultaneous features was not conceived of as 'conditioned' but was treated as if it were 'spontaneous'. Secondly, it was not seen that the confinement of a given change to a single verbal style means a specific context through which the change is 'conditioned'. At present ever greater attention is being paid to the stylistic context of changes, regarded as the "embedding problem" (Weinreich et al. 1968: 185) and defined as the "location of the change within the linguistic and social matrix which governs its development" (Labov 1972: 114). One may add that those factors of changes which had been envisaged as external now demand a revised interpretation. Take, for instance, the prestige pattern, which furthers the diffusion of features from dialect to dialect or from language to language. Whatever the reason for the privileged position of the sound pattern or vocabulary or grammatical structure of a given dialect or language with respect to others, this position becomes an intrinsic attribute assigned to one linguistic system in relation to some other one and hence requires an inner, strictly linguistic interpretation.

The neogrammarian belief, tenacious in historical linguistics, that grammatical constraints on a sound change are to be viewed as posterior to the completion of the change itself proves to be in disagreement with the observed facts and gives way to the recognition of (at least) an initial confinement of a sound change to some certain class of morphemes (cf. van Coetsem et al. 1979). The wider the scope of 'conditioned' changes becomes, the more obsolete the rubric of 'sporadic exceptions' to a sound law appears to be. They can be "better accounted for in terms of internal factors of the implementation of sound change" (Chen 1972: 494). The state of a change in progress appears to Hans Vogt "as a more or less free variation between forms of expression equally admissible within the system" (1954: 367). This observer is right when he accents the limiting "more or less": the image of "free variants" equally admissible within a system pushes us to investigate the supposed "freedom" and "equality", which actually depend on an interplay of internal factors.

Scholars have been accustomed to assigning the accomplishment of a sound change to the moment when the fluctuations of the earlier stages have disappeared and no residual forms remain, so that the action of the sound law appears to be achieved. If these conditions were not fulfilled, one was supposed to state that the change "has come to a premature end" (cf. Chen: p.493) and consequently remained unsuccessful (cf. Wang 1969: 16). However, if the grammatical and/or stylistic constraints are an inseparable part of the sound law in question, the "unsuccessfulness" becomes a subjective characterization imputed by the detached onlooker who has been accustomed to the *ausnahmslose Gesetze* of the Leipzig tradition. As it was densely formulated in Osthoff & Brugmann's declaration of 1878: "Any sound change in its mechanical progression is affected according to exceptionless laws, viz. the direction of the sound alteration is for all the partakers of a speech community except the case that dialectal scission enters, always the same, and all words in which the sound undergoing alteration appears under the same conditions are subject without exception to the change" (p. XIII).

Several supposedly controversial questions thus seem to lose their edge. One of these concerns the duration of the change and in particular the notion of "changes that continue in the same direction over several generations" and perhaps even span centuries (cf. Weinreich et al. 1968: 146; and Chen 1972: 492). If the phenomena discussed overstep the limits of synchrony and the generations involved actually do not coexist in time, then we are dealing with a train of successive changes, each of which is witnessed by a speech community at one of its consecutive historical stages. Each of these synchronously experienced changes has its own particular traits with regard to the other changes of the same historical chain, although the tendencies of the whole set of changes may show a homogeneous direction, especially in view of the continuous overlap of generations. The historical comparison of these successive changes and of the temporal variables as well as static invariants in the evolution of the given linguistic systems is the task of diachronic investigation.

Notwithstanding protracted discussions, there is no real contradiction between the view of gradual change and change *per saltum* (cf. Wang 1969: 14). The mutative, abrupt character of a change does not mean a sudden disappearance of old forms for the sake of the new one in the overall code of the speaker or of the speech community. It means on the one hand the newborn possibility of abandoning the old form and of accepting the new one in one of the individual or communal subcodes, and on the other hand the irreversible loss of the old form and the emergent monopoly of the new one.

One of the facets attributed to the idea of "gradual changes" is the "route by which one state of the language passes into another" (Labov 1972: 114): "intermediate" articulations between the original sound form and the concluding one have been claimed to be improbable. According to Labov's report, instrumental studies on the location of the first formant have allowed him to delineate the transitional stages of a Martha's Vineyard dialectal change, namely the centralization of [aw] (1972: 126 ff.); cf. observations on the optional weakening of rounding in the pretonic /o/ on its way to a merger with /a/ in the dialects in the northern proximity of Moscow (see RJ I: 587 f.). The distinction of the two pretonic vowels becomes a feature of lesser importance for those speakers under the influence of neighboring, "prestige" dialects and according to the style of speech is either totally abandoned or at least readily lessened. Transitional implementations are possible but not compulsory in certain sound changes while they are improbable in other instances (cf. Chen 1972: 494). The most relevant and general aspect of gradualness is the interplay of styles, which is sometimes imprecisely labeled 'overlapping' and which furthers the expansion of a sound change from one speech style to another.

Attempts to explain linguistic shifts, and sound changes in particular, by the discontinuity between the parent's and the child's models of language keep cropping up and have been discussed since the threshold of this century (see e.g. Delacroix 1924: 179 ff.; Jespersen 1922 b; RJ I: 332 f.; Halle 1962; and Weinreich et al. 1968: 144 ff.). These surmises leave several questions unanswered and unanswerable: Why would the restructuration of the elders' model show a sameness in all the children of the speech community? Why should we assume that the spatial continuity between the coevals of the speech community is stronger than the temporal continuity between parent and child? And finally, if there should exist in the speech community an inner demand for just such a change, and if we take into account the inner dynamics of certain linguistic styles and the collision between the different styles within an individual linguistic framework and within a dialogue of any given interlocutors, would these conditions not suffice for the urge toward innovation and restructuration and for its accomplishment and its diffusion? Briefly, a parent-child linguistic tension may occur as a factor furthering some given changes but can scarcely be viewed as a necessary or adequate reason for change. The chief thing is that any linguistic system, both individual and collective at any moment of its life, necessarily implies the coaction of two forces, stability and mutability, so that the need for change is constantly inherent in any verbal code, with its permanent switching between subcodes. Thus the ongoing sound changes invariably belong to the proper essence of any living system: permanent variability in space and time and in speech praxis is the main universal of language.

Featural changes of different kinds – mergers, splits, transfers (cf. Moulton 1967) – display a goal-directed character in regard to the sound system which undergoes them. Such a character, one could add, implies not only goal attainment but also goal failure.

The once-popular concept of "blind changes" has, not only in linguistics but also in all studies of human activities and of living systems in general, yielded to a patent or at least latent recognition of a means-ends relation and to a search for the inner motivation of changes. Besides changes with an equilibratory, prophylactic, and stabilizing role for the language system, those with a reverse, disequilibratory aim attract the ever-closer attention of the explorer; he has to take into account the interaction of verbal styles, in particular those styles which imply a disautomatization of linguistic constituents and a collision with the static order of things and which in this way favor structural changes. The purposefulness of the change merges with that of the system which undergoes the change (cf. Shaumyan 1977).

The question of purpose is sometimes obscured by its submission to the involved discussion of the speaker's awareness, although the inner logic of language is evident independently of the oscillation of verbal activities between the unconscious and consciousness. Moreover, one should not forget that metalinguistic operations, which prove to be one of the cardinal functions of language, ensure a high-level awareness of both the stability and the mutability of the linguistic system (cf. RJ 1979). The constituents of the linguistic network and of its ongoing changes are, whether consciously or subliminally, perceived and recognized as functional both by the adult and by the child (cf. Waterson 1971 b).

Even during the earliest stages of language acquisition the child evidences the presence of subcodes in his linguistic stock. The difference between the addresser's and the addressee's competence is manifest in children (see above, pp. 162 ff.). Various kinds of conformism and nonconformism play a great part in the gradual changes of children's language. Natalie Waterson's son at 1 year 6 months was "capable of producing a clearer version of his form, i. e. a form closer to the adult's, when his first effort was not understood. This suggests that he had some idea of certain features of the adult form that he did not normally use and that were redundant for him at this stage" (1970: 3). As this careful observer of children's speech noticed, they frequently recognize their recent linguistic increments as innovations, but on the other hand they preserve their memory of and feeling for the "archaïsms" of their earlier verbal experience and use them on occasion in utterances of a retrospective tinge. A telling example is given by Waterson: at 1 year 8 months her child's form for *pudding* is [pʊpən], but the old form, [pʊpʊ], reappears "under emotional stress, an urgent request: [bɪˀɪ dzæm pʊpʊ] 'a bit of jam for my pudding'. This indicates that the form which was last used by the child two months previously was still in his competence" (1970: 14).

In discussing the diffusion of a sound change within and between speech communities, we can extend this notion also to cases of the convergence of similar but independent changes in different local sources (Saussure's *foyers d'innovation*), because both processes complement each other: a convergent anticipation of the change-to-occur is a furthering condition for a "successful" diffusion. In an analogous way, the submission of the little tutee to his language tutor is furthered by the former's anticipation of the structural rules to be mastered, an anticipation due to the antecedent stages of his linguistic training and to his inherent abilities and predispositions for the adoption of language design and especially for the featural network.

The particularities of the child's gradual acquisition of new words with new sound features bring up the question of whether for him the primacy lies on the lexical or on the phonic level, and Ferguson's discovery of a child's patent avoidance of words with those sound features which he has not yet mastered and his penchant for words with those features which have just entered into his repertory (see above, pp. 164 f.) clearly shows how entangled the question of such primacy is. We are faced with a similar problem when turning from children's language to so-called "lexical diffusion" (Wang 1969) in the world's languages. Matthew Chen points out rightfully that a "much more detailed and better controlled study of the child's acquisition of phonology in the context of lexical diffusion would shed precious light on the implementation of sound change" (1972: 492 f.) and he cites H.-I. Hsieh's valuable account (1971) of the acquisition by a five-year-old Taiwanese child of the initial velar stops over a period of ten weeks. The child's first approximations were either [t] or [tʰ]. Only gradually did the velars accrue to the learner's inventory, and in that stage the velar variety tends to prevail when conditioned by a favorable phonic environment; otherwise, the original velars of the adult model either continue to be reproduced by a dental or else in certain words show an allegedly "free" variation between the still prevailing earlier dental substitute and the newly acquired velar. The difference between lexical

examples with a regularly conservative treatment and those with alternating [t] and [k] requires further investigation of the different place of
these words in the child's vocabulary and its stylistic development.

XI. VISTAS

The child's gradual acquisition of distinctive features sheds an ever-
brighter light on the fundamental conception of *opposition* as the innermost constructive principle of the whole of language. As long as the
unfortunate confusion of opposition and contingency has not completely disappeared from linguistic theory, it is important to recall the
still timely elucidation of the concept in question by Hendrik Pos
(1898–1955):

> Opposition is not an isolated fact, it is a principle of structure. It always
> unites two things which are distinct but at the same time bound to each oth-
> er in such a way that one cannot be thought of without a co-presence of the
> other. The unity of opposites is always formed by a concept which implicit-
> ly contains both opposites in it, and is bifurcated into an explicit opposition
> when it is applied to concrete reality. ⟨...⟩ Opposition in givens is not a
> schema which science introduces in order to master the givens and which
> would remain extrinsic with respect to them. Its importance exceeds epis-
> temological order: when linguistic thought orders givens according to the
> principles of opposition and of system, it meets that thought which creates
> these very givens. [Pos 1938: 245; see also Pos 1939; cf. above p. 24]

Henri Wallon's (1879–1962) classic work on children's minds
should be comprehensively quoted as a seminal guide to the vital role
of binary oppositions in the development of children's thought and
language:

> What can be asserted at the start is the existence of coupled elements. The
> prime of thought is just this binary structure and not the constituent ele-
> ments. Duality has come before unity. The couple, or the pair, is anterior to
> the isolated element. Any term, identifiable by thought, and thinkable, re-
> quires a complementary term from which it is differentiated and to which it
> can be opposed. What is true e. g. for the distinction between colors, which
> according to Koffka can be first recognized by contrast solely, is valid also
> for intellectual notions. Without the initial relation offered by the couple
> the whole succeeding edifice of relations would be impossible. [Wallon
> 1945: 41]
>
> ⟨...⟩ As a general rule any expression, any notion is intimately tied to its
> opposite so that one cannot be thought of without the other. It is from the
> latter that the former gets its raison d'être, viz. its primary meaning, its most

elementary specification, the grossest but the most essential one, for there is neither thought nor language without delimitation between the imagined or claimed object and the rest. The simplest and the most gripping delimitation is opposition ⟨...⟩ The bond becomes nearly automatic between yes-no, white-black, father-mother, so that sometimes they seem to come to one's lips at the same time and as if one would have to make a choice and repress that one of the two terms which doesn't fit. [p. 67]

⟨...⟩ The contrasts *clair-obscur, lourd-léger, grand-petit* are elementary structures underlain by the perceptual differentiation. They mark the instant when something becomes distinct in the impressions undergone. [p. 129]

It was in French linguistics that the question was raised of why the successive dichotomies in the child's gradual acquisition of the system of distinctive features would "necessarily affect the functioning of the adult's system" (Martinet 1955[2]: 74), but Wallon's decisive answer was given beforehand:

Bien que l'existence des couples ne nous soit apparente que dans la pensée de l'enfant, il se pourrait qu'ils soient encore utilisés comme tels par celle de l'adulte pour des raisons de plus grande facilité, d'économie soit d'effort soit de temps, tant qu'ils sont du moins d'une précision suffisante et sous le contrôle des buts, des exigences les plus évoluées de l'intelligence. [p. 42]

The notion of linguistic oppositions and especially of distinctive features became particularly vital and relevant for further research as soon as the question of features was increasingly subjected to an analysis made from the point of view of the interrelation of features and their place in the whole - whether consonantal or vocalic - sound system of language. It is this orientation toward the interrelation between parts and wholes and between the diverse parts of one and the same whole which on the one hand led to a wider comprehension and application of the difference in the 'functional load' of the various features of the same system (cf. Mathesius 1931 and the recent survey of this question by Szeremény 1977) and on the other hand brought into the foreground and classified the notion of the inequality between the terms of any opposition, namely the fruitful idea of the correlation between markedness and the absence of mark. The decisive role of the dichotomous principle in the structure of language and the consistently hierarchical (marked ~ unmarked) relation within any dyad and within the whole linguistic framework, especially the sound system, advance the imperative question of isomorphisms between verbal coding - down to the ultimate constituents - and the central neural processes. The universal and near-universal implicational laws in the sound patterning of language and the tempting question of their possible biological foundations require careful and critical interdisciplinary research.

The ongoing investigation of the interconnection between language and the brain pointed to above (pp. 32 ff.) already indicates the cerebral substructure of the distinctive features and permits us to discriminate the roles of the left and right hemispheres in their control of language. The more and more palpable regularities which children's buildup of language reveals to us in the systems of distinctive features and of grammatical categories promise to be particularly instructive for such an interdisciplinary exploration. In particular, the linguistic syndromes of aphasic deficits disclose connections with the character and topography of brain lesions. These syndromes point especially to a difference between the basic sections of the 'speech areas' of the cortex, in particular between the anterior and posterior parts of these areas.

In discussing givens "of the utmost importance for further linguistic research", Alexander Luria (1902–1977), world expert in the study of the brain and of language disorders, concluded that:

> lesions of the *anterior* parts of the major hemisphere result in a marked deterioration of *syntagmatical* organization of verbal communication while the *paradigmatical* organization of linguistic codes remains relatively preserved. In contradistinction, lesions of the *posterior* cortical areas of the major hemisphere result in a breakdown of the *paradigmatic* organization of linguistic structures at different levels (phonemic level in lesions of the posterior parts of the left temporal lobe, articulatory systems in lesions of the lower part of the left post-cortical zone, semantic- or logicogrammatical level in lesions of the posterior tertiary zones), while the *syntagmatic* organization of the fluent speech remains preserved. [1974: 12; 1976; and especially 1977; cf. Goodglass 1978; and RJ II: 289–333]

There may still be heard puzzling assurances that "classifications based on linguistic criteria cannot fit with the physiology of aphasia since language mechanisms do not develop according to linguistic rules"! (See Lhermitte & Gautier 1969: 98.) But since 1947 Luria understood the decisive role which the new linguistics, with its stress on the sound/meaning relation, had to play in the analysis of speech disorders, and the future belongs to his final conclusion that "a new branch of science arises – NEUROLINGUISTICS" (1973: 57) – as a significant link between the science of language and the exploration of the brain, a link equally important both for linguistics and for neurology. The prospects of a rising and mutually harmonious cooperation between the science of language and aphasiology is still underestimated, even in the outline by Hécaen & Albert (1978), who apparently are unfamiliar with the last, most productive stage of Luria's contributions to neurolinguistic discoveries (1973–1977). A realistic picture of the situation today "would show the development of communication among the several disciplines concerned with the study of aphasia", as Ruth Lesser has underscored in her timely survey of the current linguistic contributions to the delineation and classification of the diverse aphasic syndromes (1978: 22); the occurrence of divergent approaches to certain modalities of aphasic disintegrations and regressions furthers the interest in joint interdisciplinary research.

CHAPTER FOUR

THE SPELL OF SPEECH SOUNDS

que tels sons signifient ceci
Stéphane Mallarmé
Fragments

I. SOUND SYMBOLISM

The autonomization of minimal formal units, a characteristic procedure of the arts and sciences around World War I, was saliently manifested in the growing inquiry into the sound shape of language, especially into its sense-discriminative constituents. The question of double
articulation, revived in modern Russian and then in Western linguistics, may be traced back at least to the medieval doctrine *de modis significandi* and its clear-cut idea of a discriminated and interconnected
articulatio prima et secunda. This idea seems to have emerged under
Greek incentives and means that one of the two articulations turns the
sound matter *(vocis articulatio)* into words, while the other employs
words to generate sentences (cf. RJ 1975: 292). The doctrine in question clearly implied that *vocis articulatio* obtains its signification *ex humana institutione* or, in Plato's terminology, *thései* (by convention) and
that the task of the speech sounds, which have no autonomous meaning themselves, is to differentiate word meanings.

The pervasive trait of linguistic science from the trailblazing efforts
of the 1870s through the last hundred years, and during the interwar
period in particular, has been the increasingly precise and systematic
inquiry into the patent differentiating role of speech sounds as their
paramount task. On the other hand, linguists began to turn their attention toward the immediate and autonomous significance of the constituents of the verbal sound shape in the life of language. This significance was supposed to be prompted directly by their nature, *phýsei*, according to Plato's dialogue *Kratylos* dramatizing the contest between
the two permanent linguistic forces – convention and nature.

One cannot but agree with Coseriu (1969) when he acclaims Georg
von der Gabelentz (1840–1893) as a "precursor of present-day linguistics" and especially as a promoter of "fruitful ideas on sound symbolism". Let us mention here that the widespread use in linguistics, poet-

ics, and psychology of the term 'symbolism' for the figurative relation
- *phýsei* - is at variance with the semiotic terminology introduced by
Peirce, who called those signs built *phýsei*, 'icons', in contradistinction
to those based *thései*, which he labeled 'symbols'. However, the term
'sound symbolism', designating an inmost, natural similarity association between sound and meaning (*signans* and *signatum*), is so deeply
enrooted in the protracted scholarly debates on this problem that our
survey of this discussion will keep to the locution 'sound symbolism'.

In the comprehensive critical scrutiny of linguistic "tasks, methods,
and achievements" which concluded Gabelentz's research (1891), he
repeatedly raised the question of the proper expressive values inherent
in the sounds of language. He detected such values in the creative process of children's linguistic growth and cited, for instance, the case of a
little German boy who used the root *m-m* for anything round. This
child named the bright moon and a white plate *mem*, a large round pan
mom or *mum*, and the little white stars *mim-mim-mim-mim-mim*, using
a symbolic repetition. In his lexicon, a regular chair was *lakeil*, a little
doll's chair *likill*, and grandpa's armchair *lukul*. His father when
wrapped up in a heavy fur coat changed from *papa* to *pupu* (p. 65).

Gabelentz's theory of creative *Lautsymbolik* (1891), first supported
by the omniscient Hugo Schuchardt (1842-1927), staunchly asserts in
the paragraphs entitled "The sound-symbolic feeling" (pp. 217-223)
that sound and meaning prove to be - not *thései* but *phýsei* - inalien-
ably interconnected for the naïve members of any extant speech community. In defiance of the scholastic slogan claiming the arbitrariness
of verbal signs, a native German is prone to believe at heart that
Frenchmen are silly when they name "ein Pferd Schewall" (p. 217). As
learned in etymology as Germans may be, in their perception words
like *Blitz* 'lightning' and *Donner* 'thunder' or *spitz* 'pointed' and *rund*
'round' nevertheless merge with their imagery in such a natural way
that in none of these pairs would an exchange of meanings be conceivable. *Blitz* evokes a sudden flash, whereas the French *foudre* according
to Gabelentz depicts a crushing blow. He quotes similar emotional
reactions to the sound shape of *Blitz* from earlier authors - Schottel
1641: "erschreckende Schnelligkeit"; Herder 1770: "das Urplötz-
lichschnelle" (see Wandruszka 1952: 223).

As we gradually acquire our mother tongue, "our feeling etymolo-
gizes, so to speak, without any regard to historical linguistics" (Gabelentz 1891: 218). According to the ingenious comparisons advanced in
1879 by Mikołaj Kruszewski, "grammatical analogy" and so-called

"popular etymology" are two varieties – one morphological and the other lexical – of one and the same "integrating power" in the life of language: both of them display a mutual adjustment between competing paradigmatic items. Gabelentz, followed by Schuchardt, detected "a fruitful concept" in these historically "false" but synchronously valid etymologies, which are based on mass agreement within a given speech community. Words linked together by both sound and meaning manifest "elective affinities" *(Wahlverwandtschaften)*, able to modify the shape and the content of the vocables involved. The sound affinity may be provided by the similarity of initial and/or final sounds and clusters. The verb *stehen* 'stand' is felt to be related to the alliterative forms *steif* 'stiff', *starr* 'staring', *Stock* 'stick', *Stamm* 'stalk', *steil* 'steep', *stopfen* 'stuff', *stauen* 'stow away', *Stab* 'staff', *stützen* 'stay, sustain', *stemmen* 'stem', "whatever they have to do with the root **sthā*". There is a simultaneous concord in rhyme and sense between *stemmen* and *hemmen* 'hem' or *klemmen* 'squeeze' (p. 219).

In his masterful observations on "Die Tonmalerei der Sprache und die Sinnensymbolik des Worts" Albert Wellek (1931 a: 250) calls to mind Goethe's jesting lines from the *Walpurgis Night:*

> Nicht G*rei*sen! G*rei*fen! – Niemand hört es *ger*n,
> Dass man ihn *Greis* nennt. Jedem Worte klingt
> Der Ursprung nach, wo es sich her bedingt:
> *Grau, grämlich, griesgram, greulich, Gräber, grimmig,*
> Etymologisch *g*leicherweise stimmig,
> Verstimmen uns. –

For Gabelentz, monosyllables with the same "deep" ('dark') vowel, such as the *u* of curses like *Schuft, Hund, Lump,* etc., impart an identical mood. If, conversely, the sound difference is confined to the inner vowels of words similar in all other respects, the vocalic discrepancy in question persistently looks for a semantic motivation (p. 363). In this connection, Gabelentz quotes the three Batta verbs *džarar* 'creep' (in general), *džirir* 'creep' (up to small beings), *džurur* 'creep' (up to big and frightful animals). A casual remark prompted by some Quechua examples and assuming a possible similarity common to the sound-symbolic pattern of quite different languages (p. 218) awaits a systematic verification.

A decade later the French explorer Maurice Grammont (1866–1946) also overcame the attitude of an external onlooker, distant in time and/or space, and announced a strictly synchronic view of "expressive" or "impressive" phonetics, according to his varying terms. In

Grammont's studies (from 1901 to 1913 and 1933) the same close interplay between sound and meaning underwent a careful examination in
terms of the syntagmatic (sequential) axis: chief attention was focused
on the order of alternating phonemes in reduplicated or triplicated
word forms and upon reiterated phonemes within syntactic groups. In
his programmatic paper "Onomatopées et mots expressifs" (1901),
Grammont persuasively declared that "the domain of onomatopoeia is
much vaster than it seems to have been generally believed; the scope of
expressive words, which are to be added, is not less considerable; and
between the two fields there is no clear-cut boundary" (p.319).

This experienced French phonetician was primarily concerned with
the evocative value of vowels. For him their latent effectiveness was an
objective, universal fact. But their significance actually manifests itself
only when it is prompted by the meaning of the text or when it at least
does not stand in contradiction to the latter; the degree of this significance depends, moreover, on the subjectivity of speakers and listeners,
as well as on situations (p.289). Affective speech and, even more, poetry were seen by Grammont as the most favorable contexts for a thorough realization or a full display of the hidden values of vowels. He
concluded his paper with the following statement: "The values of a
sound from the expressive point of view result uniquely from its nature
and we have no right to attribute to the sound some value which would
disagree with its nature. ⟨...⟩ All that we are empowered to do is to feel
or not to feel in a given case the expressive value which is possessed by
such a phoneme in *potentia*. The subjective component of these questions terminates herewith" (p.321).

The peculiar "onomatopoeic apophony" (1901: 292), reduplication
with a vocalic change in the repeated constituents, attracted Grammont's unflagging attention. There seems to emerge a universal or at
least a round-the-world attested law in their construction. Triple
groups generally are based on the relation [i] – [a] (sometimes [å] or [æ])
– [u] – e. g. *pif-paf-puf* – and double formations on [i] – [a] (or more rarely, [u] – [a]) – e. g. *pif-paf* (or, for instance in German, *puf-paf*: cf. Spitzer
1927: 215). The persistent emergence of [i] as the first member of such
groups contrasted with the following [a] led Grammont and some later
examiners to speculate about the specific value of this vowel.

One must acknowledge that in setting the question of the proper se-
manticity of [i] Grammont did not confine the problem to the relation
between front and back vowels, but realized the specific significance of
the difference between the high front vowels, termed by him an "acute

species" *(espèce aiguë)*, within a wider category of front vowels = "clear vowels" *(voyelles claires)* and contraposed to the back vowels generically termed *voyelles graves* and in turn divided into two species: higher vowels, labeled "dark" *(sombres)*, and lower vowels, called "bright" *(éclatantes)* (see e.g. 1933: "Valeurs impressives des voyelles": 383 ff.). In his classification of vocalic values, Grammont specified nasal vowels as "damped" *(voilées)*. He described for example the "clear vowels" as particularly able - in contradistinction to the heaviness of the grave vowels - to express "fineness, slightness, mildness, softness, and the correlated ideas" (1913: 248 ff.); "d'une manière générale les voyelles claires peuvent peindre à l'oreille tout objet tenu, petit, léger, mignon" (p. 251; cf. 269). As one of the illustrations, he quoted the following lines by Victor Hugo:

> Quand la demoiselle dorée
> S'envole au départ des hivers,
> Souvent sa robe diaprée,
> Souvent son aile est déchirée
> Aux mille dards des buissons verts.
> Ainsi, jeunesse vive et frêle,
> Qui, t'égarant de tous côtés,
> Voles où ton instinct t'appelle,
> Souvent tu déchires ton aile,
> Aux épines des voluptés.

In his classification of vocalic figurative capacities, Grammont, far ahead of the later inquirers into this field, added to the analysis of the front ~ back distinction also that of high and low vowels, but left unanswered the question of the interplay of two other pairs of properties: rounded ~ unrounded and lax ~ tense. One may note immediately that most of the difficulties which investigators of "impressive phonetics" met were due to the search for the proper value of entire phonemes and not of their distinctive features. Since the entire phoneme as a bundle of features contains a diversity of elementary properties - for instance, /ü/ is opposed to /i/ in one respect and to /u/ in a quite different way - the oversimplified assignment of the phoneme /ü/ together with /i/ to the "clear vowels" hampers the search for the *chiaroscuro* imagery hidden in the vowels. Thus, languages like French with its separate phonemes /i, ü, u/ differ from languages in which [ü] is a mere contextual variant of /u/ or /i/. Most objections to the search for the inner significance of speech sounds arose because the latter were not dissected into their ultimate constituents.

The problems approached by Gabelentz and Grammont particularly attracted two other outstanding international linguists, Otto Jespersen (1860–1943) and Edward Sapir. Not only did each of them publish a series of pioneering contributions to this intricate field of investigation but they also wrote each other on this subject during the decade 1918–1928. Sapir "apparently sent his correspondent a large collection of raw data", and Yakov Malkiel (1978) is right in suggesting that it would be worthwhile to "salvage and publish this transatlantic exchange of letters". In a Danish essay of 1918 Jespersen acclaimed the coaction of the factors *phýsei* and *thései* in human languages, and in a discussion of the Danish *men* 'but' broached the question of "sound gestures" nesting in vocabulary, a topic already touched upon in Schuchardt's remarks on the *Lautgebärde* (1897) and inherent both in Grammont's comparison of articulatory movements, grimaces, and gestures (1901: 316f.) and in his concept of "articulatory gesture". The American English example of *nope* and *yep* discussed by Jespersen in this connection later was conclusively interpreted by Dwight Bolinger (1946).

Jespersen reviewed Saussure's *Cours* soon after its publication and criticized the Genevan for overexaggerating the role of arbitrariness in language and for minimizing the role of onomatopoeias and of sound symbolism (see 1933: 144). Later, the Danish linguist devoted three closely interconnected outlines directly to sound symbolism. In the first outline, published in the *Nordisk Tidskrift,* Jespersen mentions his cooperation with Sapir, "one of the best connoisseurs of American Indian Languages" (1922a: 128).

Jespersen's first English argument for the wide import of "Sound Symbolism" - chapter 20 of the book *Language* - concluded with a vehement attack against the narrow antiquarianism of those linguistic tenets which still concentrated on merely historical etymologies, disregarding the etymological creativity of the living speech community, and assigning the creation and use of echoic and symbolic words solely, if at all, to former ages. In fact, the natural correspondence between sound and sense is a constantly renewable and vital process, whereby, as Jespersen believed, "languages in the course of time grow richer and richer in symbolic words" and develop progressively "towards a greater number of easy and adequate expressions - expressions in which sound and sense are united in a marriage-union closer than was ever known to our remote ancestors" (1922b: chap.20, § 12). This remarkable chapter discusses the direct imitation of the audible phenomena

by sound production and the use of speech sounds, their groups, reduplications, lengthenings, and omissions, to designate, metonymically
or metaphorically, sound producers, movements, things and appearances, states of mind, sizes and distances. The suggestiveness of sound
imagery makes some words "more fit to survive".

Most of the masterfully collected data exemplifying the widespread
and productive "Symbolic Value of the Vowel *i*" are concentrated in
the 1922 essay of this title (see now 1933). In the initial paragraph, after
positing that "sound symbolism plays a greater role in the development of languages than is admitted by most linguists", Jespersen announced his "attempt to show that the vowel [i], high front unrounded,
especially in its narrow or thin form serves very often to indicate what
is small, slight, insignificant or weak" (p. 283). The survey detects this
vowel in numerous words for little, for the child or young animal, for
small things, as well as in diminutive suffixes, verbs meaning 'to make
or to become small', etc. The associability of [i] with smallness and
lightness first noted by Socrates, according to Plato's dialogue, has
been repeatedly confirmed. For example, the feeling for the expression
of relative smallness and bigness was documented by Swift's Gulliver,
who called the land of dwarfs *Lilliput* and that of giants *Brobdingnag*,
while Gulliver himself in the latter country was reduced to *Grildrig:*
"the word imports what the Latins call *nanunculus*" (a very small
dwarf) (Jespersen 1933: 284). Gulliver's neutral human size found its
opposites in the phonetically expressed dwarfness of the Lilliputians
and on the other hand in the again phonetically expressed superhuman bulk of the giants.

Children's language is particularly rich in constructed pairs of
sound symbolic /i/ and /u/ words, as was illustrated by Alf Sommerfelt (1892-1965) in a note on his three-year-old daughter, who cut two
grotesque images out of a magazine: one was "Shadow" ("somber"
and "heavy-jowled") and the other "Light" ("gay" and "radiant").
They were called *Mump* and *Mippe* respectively by the girl, and she
never confused their names (1928: 30). In an experiment Maxime
Chastaing (1965a: 41) asked fifty children between five and six to use
[pim] and [pum] as names for two cardboard human figures; 76 percent
chose *pim* for the smaller one and *pum* for the bigger one.

The ready associability of [i] with small things is explained by the
high pitch of the vowel. Jespersen adds that the perception of the small
lip-aperture "may have also its share in the rise of the idea" (pp. 284f.),
but shies away from the later, often whimsical endeavors to find the ex-

planation for sound symbolism in the speaker's articulatory configurations. Jespersen recounts that during the great drought at Fredriksstad (Norway) the following words were posted in a W.C.: "Don't pull the string for *bimmelim,* only for *bummelum.*" These instructions were immediately understood (p. 284) – obviously in view of the opposite size associations between the high sound of [i] and the deep sound of [u] (cf. the nursery references to *little business* and *big business*). In English a similar relation remains between the diffuse consonants and vowels of *peepee* and the compact ones of *kaka;* however, an association with the difference between the anterior and posterior parts of the body referred to seems to be farfetched (cf. Wescott 1971: 421 f.).

Sapir, who in his early manual was even inclined to see "a real psychological connection between symbolism and such significant alternations as *drink/drank/drunk*" (1921: chap. 6), continuously thought that "the sounds and sound processes of speech can not be properly understood in ⟨...⟩ simple mechanical terms" of "sensorimotor habits" (see 1949: 33). At the beginning of his "Study in Phonetic Symbolism", Sapir pointed out the phonetic difference between the emphatically diminutive *ee* of *teeny* and the normal *i* of *tiny;* for him this divergence was "directly expressive of the difference of meaning", and as early as 1929 (see 1949: 61ff.) he called this type of relation "latent expressive symbolism". Two years before (1927), in a weighty essay on "Language as a Form of Human Behavior", unfortunately omitted from his *Selected Writings,* Sapir proclaimed: "If anyone is inclined to doubt the reality of such symbolisms in speech, let him try the following experiment which I have myself tried a number of times with practically 100% success" (p. 429). Listeners were asked to use the imaginary words *la, law, li* to name three tables of different size; they chose *li* to symbolize the small table, *law* the big one, and *la* a middle-sized table, a table *par excellence.* His subsequent experiments in this direction went far in demonstrating the reality of such unconsciously cogent feelings for the "magnitude-symbolism" of certain differences in vowels and consonants. According to Sapir, "to put it roughly, certain vowels and certain consonants 'sound bigger' than others" (p. 69). The relevance of Sapir's research greatly contributed to Jespersen's observations. Undoubtedly this inquiry would have been even more conclusive if the questions had concerned the symbolic relations within any single pair of phonemes and if the magnitude test had been complemented by tests involving a few other semantic pairs of associations as well.

Sapir's experiments in sound symbolism were further developed by his disciple Stanley Newman, who attempted to outline a symbolic magnitude scale of the entire American English vowel pattern. He subjected every pair of vowels to questions of their "small-to-large" or "dark vs. bright" symbolism. For all the respondents, all the vowels proved to be rigidly and similarly patterned on a symbolic scale, and this led to the conclusion that "the basis of phonetic symbolism is fundamentally objective" (1933: 75). The interpretation of consonants brought likewise interesting but less elaborated results. The judgments of small to large for *t-p-k* showed a consistent correspondence to the vocalic scale *i-u-a*, and permitted a clear inference to the equivalent structure of both the vocalic and the consonantal triangles (see above, p. 112) and to the constant order of the sequence *pif-paf-puf*. Newman's inspiring experimentation would have been even more conclusive if the question of binary relations had guided his mapping of sound symbolism and if his careful regard for symbolic value had overcome his bias toward determinant "mechanical factors". To what risky speculations such a bias can lead may be illustrated by Peterfalvi's complementary note (1970: 63; cf. Genette 1976: 409) about Newman's evidence that the acute vowels seem to us "the lightest": Peterfalvi alleges that the acute vowels articulated toward the exterior of our bodies are judged to be "light", whereas those articulated toward our interior are imagined to be "dark", because "the further you penetrate into the body, the darker it is there"! A collection of fanciful explanations of the light ~ dark sound symbolism was meticulously brought together by Fónagy (1963: 60 ff.).

In any case, Sapir's and Newman's scrutiny eloquently shows how rapid and fruitful, both for linguistics and for psychology (cf. Bentley & Varon 1933), this new stage of inquiry into sound symbolism was, as compared with the meagerness of Debrunner's earlier historical survey (1926). Questions about how far the actual lexical and morphological stock of language reflects the symbolic value discovered in the sound pattern by Sapir and Newman led to several studies (by Orr 1944 & 1945; Thorndike 1945; Wandruszka 1952, etc.) and brought to light especially the phenomenon of "antiphony, i.e. the opposition of vowel sounds in words relating to, roughly, the same psychological field: e.g. *tip* and *top*, *slit* and *slot*, *strip*, *strap*, and *strop*" (Orr 1945).

The question of the congruity between the purport of speech sound sequences and abstract graphic figures was posed by the Georgian psychologist D. Usnadze (1924) and taken up again by Köhler (1929), but the longest series of experiments was devoted to the question of whether, and if so, to what degree, lexical oppositions in meaning bear any consistent lawful relation to the symbolic properties of sounds or, as Hornbostel (1927a) termed them, *Lautsinn* ('sound sense'). (See in particular Tsuru & Frics 1933; Brown et al. 1955; Maltzmann et al. 1956; Brackbill & Little 1957; Wertheimer 1958; Brown & Nuttall 1959; Miron 1961; Taylor & Taylor 1962 & 1965; Taylor 1963; Oyama & Haga 1963; Weiss 1963a & b, 1964a & b, 1966; Johnson et al. 1964; Atzet & Gerard 1965; Ertel 1969; Roper et al. 1976.) One of the chief means used was asking the experimental subjects to guess at the correlation between two antonyms in a language unknown to them and the corresponding pair of antonyms in their native language. A few of these and similar experiments produced correct responses, which were viewed as mere chance by distrustful critics; some other cases gave rather negative results.

In these deciphering efforts too many complex factors were involved to permit less uncertain conclusions. Roger Brown et alii went so far as to affirm that their "investigations, using three lists of English words and six foreign languages, have shown superior to chance agreement and accuracy in the translation of unfamiliar tongues" and that such an "accuracy can be explained by the assumption of some universal phonetic symbolism in which speech may have originated or toward which speech may be evolving". In any case, "some kind of imitative or physiognomic linkage of sounds and meanings" seemed evident to the investigators (1955: 393). However, the desired solution to the question of whether there exists a universal sound symbolism still requires a preliminary crosslinguistic comparison of the framework of distinctive features and their groupings in the languages confronted. Nonetheless, it becomes ever clearer that when the diversity of the systems brought together is taken into account, a general pattern of sound-symbolic values stands out and we face two urgent and responsible problems – the sound-symbolic typology of languages, and the sound-symbolic universals ensuing from such a typology – as a counterpart and superstructure to the equally important, likewise typological and universalist questions bearing on the structuration of distinctive features. Cf. Peterfalvi's critical survey of the studies and tasks involved (1970: chap. 5).

The symbolism of French vowels found an assiduous observer in Maxime Chastaing. His main essays treat in particular the vowel /i/ and its associations with acuteness and smallness, and are accompanied by excurses on lightness, rapidity, and closeness (1958), as well as the light ~ dark opposition of front and back vowels (1962), and by his concluding research on the vocalic symbolism of smallness (1965a). In the latter work there are germane remarks on the role of this symbolism in the distribution of vowels between the various strata of French vocabulary, but Chastaing leaves open the question of to what degree such symbolism dictates the selective changes and selective conservation of vocabulary and to what degree the lexical stock itself furthers sound symbolism. A few casual notes by this inquirer assess the symbolic values of consonantal oppositions, and from this point of view examine the opposition of tense and lax consonants in French (1964). He was inclined to assign "hardness" to the stops, as opposed to the "soft" continuants (1965b), and noted that his students felt /r/ to be "very rough, strong, violent, heavy, pungent, hard, near-by, and bitter" in contrast to /l/, which seemed "light-weighted, debonair, clear, smooth, weak, sweet, and distant" (1966: 502f.).

Most instructive are the tests carried out by Fónagy (1963) with groups of Hungarian children and adults. The comparison of /i/ and /u/ gave the following impressive results: /i/ was "quicker" than /u/ for 94 percent, "smaller" for 88 percent, "prettier" for 83 percent, "friendlier" for 82 percent, "harder" for 71 percent, whereas /u/ was "thicker" for 98 percent, "hollower" and "darker" for 97 percent, "sadder" and "blunter" for 92 percent, "bitterer" for 86 percent, and "stronger" for 80 percent (pp. 42ff. & 120f.); equally iluminating are the responses of the subjects concerning the symbolic relation on the one hand between /r/ and /l/ (the former was "wild, pugnacious, manly, rolling, and harder" for the overwhelming majority), and on the other hand between the Hungarian dentals (diffuse acute) and palatals (compact acute): the latter were sensed to be "more humid" than the former.

II. SYNESTHESIA

Such evaluations, universal insofar as they find support in the sound systems of the given languages, are obviously far from being accidental. It should be remembered that such contrasts as light ~ dark, light ~ heavy, and small ~ big belong to the "elementary structures required by perceptual differentiation" (see Wallon 1945: 129), and it is no wonder that they build constant (or near-constant) and universal linkages with the elementary features underlying the languages of the world. Peterfalvi, in his exemplary monograph on sound symbolism (1970), refers (pp.44f.) to P.Guillaume's *Psychologie de la forme* (1937), which pointed to the multivalued symbolism contained in speech sounds as universal synesthetic givens; on these premises Peterfalvi foresaw the progressive access of science to the biopsychological universals which underlie the ubiquitous and everlasting systematics of the distinctive features and of their symbolic capabilities (pp.156f.).

The intricate questions of the phenomenal interconnection between the different senses – briefly, the problem of synesthesia – came to light once again through the many-sided development of the linguistic and psychological preoccupation with sound symbolism in its various aspects. "Les Synesthésies" is the subtitle of Chastaing's paper inviting the readers to give their personal responses to one of the most striking and entangled facets of synesthetic questions, namely *audition colorée* ('colored hearing'), an old term which he revived (1960). In the course of two months Chastaing received 133 replies. Despite the variability of the answers, the inquirer did not overlook the manifest attractions between certain colors and phonemes, nor did he make a concession to the hasty assumption that "each person sees the vowels in his own way". The coherencies emerging between the color and sound patterns were too palpable to be denied (1961: 359ff.). Thus, for instance, the unambiguous tendency to feel that the back vowels are "darker" and the front vowels are "lighter" finds further support in the assignment of darker colors to back vowels and light colors to front vowels by diverse kinds of observers.

The chief difficulty in answering the question of what colors one associates with each of the vowels of one's language lies in the double operation with a plurality of two kinds of things, vowels and colors. The task becomes much more concrete and feasible when the respondent has to deal with the binary relations between any two given vowels and any two given colors. The sagacious Clark University psychologist, Heinz Werner (1890–1964), recommended to experimenters that they present a subject with successive pairs of vowel sounds along with diverse successive pairs of colors and then ask him which pairs of speech sounds and colors he feels to be closest. Through such a series of steps one comes to grasp the fundamental polarities which tie together the colors and the distinctive features of language (cf. Karwoski et al. 1942: 216).

One cannot but agree with E.H.Gombrich (1961[2]: 370f.) that the problem of synesthetic equivalences will cease to look embarrassingly arbitrary and subjective if, hereto, we fix our attention not on likeness of elements but on structural relationships within a scale or matrix. When we say that *i* is brighter than *u*, we find a surprising degree of general consent. If we are more careful still and say the step from *u* to *i* is more like an upward step than a downward step, I think the majority will agree, whatever explanation each of us may be inclined to offer.

This expert in the language of pictorial representation expresses his belief "that once again the research of linguists offers us the best chance to make this much discussed problem a little more manageable". To try out the linguistic suggestion that synesthesia concerns relationships he uses a 'party game':

> It consists of creating the simplest imaginable medium in which relationships can still be expressed, a language of two words only - let me call them *ping* and *pong*. If these were all we had and we had to name an elephant and a cat, which would be *ping* and which *pong?* I think that answer is clear. Or hot soup and ice cream? To me, at least, ice cream is *ping* and soup *pong*. Or a Rembrandt and Watteau? Surely in that case, Rembrandt would be *pong* and Watteau *ping*. I don't maintain that it always works, that two blocks are sufficient to categorize all relations. We find people differing about day and night and male and female, but perhaps these different answers could be reduced to unanimity if the questions were differently framed: pretty girls are *ping* and matrons *pong*, it may depend on which aspect of womanhood the person has in mind.

The consistent application of binary oppositions for the vowels' symbolic values - brighter ~ darker, bigger ~ smaller, thinner ~ thicker, harder ~ softer, lighter ~ heavier - furthered the stimulating experiments by Eli Fischer-Jørgensen on the reactions of Danish students to the perceptual systematics of Danish vocalism; however, she found that presenting vowels *en bloc* "in alphabetic order" without dividing them into successive oppositive pairs led to "not very clear results" (1967).

The advancement of a general vowel theory brought into relation with principal adjacent fields of human experience was charted by Wolfgang Köhler (see above, pp. 132 f.), whose conception had been aptly anticipated in the early nineteenth century by the English scientist Robert Willis (1800–1875). According to the latter's treatise published in 1830 by the Cambridge Philosophical Society: "the generality of writers who have treated on the vowel sound appear never to have looked beyond the vocal organs for their origin ⟨...⟩ considering the vowels in fact more in the light of physiological functions of the human body than as a branch of acoustics" (p. 231). Willis decided to lay down a different plan of operation; namely, neglecting entirely the organs of speech to determine, if possible, by experiments among the usual acoustic instruments, what forms of cavities or other conditions, are essential to the production of these sounds, after which, by comparing this with the various positions of the human organs, it might be possible, not only to deduce the explanation and reason of their various positions, but to separate those parts and notions which are destined for the performance of their other functions from those which are immediately peculiar to speech (if such exist). In repeating experiments of this kind, it must always be kept in mind that the difference between the vowels, depends entirely upon contrast. [pp. 233 f.]

Willis's program, independently resumed and widely advanced by Köhler (cf. his note 1910a: 288f.), grew into an inspiring demonstration of the original character and consistent structuration proper to the human vocalic framework (cf. Köhler 1915, commented upon by Stumpf 1926: 320ff.).

The fundamental role of the light ~ dark opposition in the structure of both the vocalic and the consonantal patterns was first outlined by Köhler. Let us now repeat and underscore that for him, lightness and darkness as names for this phenomenon were far from being "mere metaphors", but were rather designations of actual "intersensorial analogies", phenomenological correspondences pointing to a "central physiological perceptual correlate" (1915). The analogy with the arrangements of different sense domains is evident here and leads to the unprejudiced conclusion that the vowel system displays "almost the same fundamental properties [Systemeigenschaften] as the chromatic colors" (p. 192). The hypothesis that light ~ dark is a universal attribute of all senses is constantly being tested in new domains. More and more the continuing inquiries into the inner organization and grouping of colors reveal a concrete coherence between speech sounds and colors and give rise to the thesis that sensation should be described in terms of polar oppositions (Hartshorne 1934: 134). In particular, we refer to Hering's opponent-process theory of color vision being developed by Leo Hurvich & Dorothea Jameson, which treats these processes as a model of neural organization (see especially 1957, 1974): the two members of each pair, such as white ~ black and yellow ~ blue, "are opponent, both in terms of the opposite nature of the assumed physiological process and in terms of the mutually exclusive sensory qualities" (1957: 385).

Proceeding from the evolving analysis of colors and from their assessment in recent anthropological literature (such as Berlin & Kay

1969, and Turner 1967), Marshall Sahlins (1976) has approached the discrimination of lightness and darkness as the most rudimentary distinction, "perhaps universally significant" and semantically motivated for any given culture; he considers the second stage "in the evolution of basic categories" to be the opposition of red, which "has the most color" and which "is to the human eye the most salient of color experiences", and the black ~ white achromaticity. This "triad of red-white-black" as "the substantive perceptual result of the crossing of the basic dark/light dualism by a second contrast in hue/neutrality" (Sahlins: 14) significantly corresponds with the primary triangle *a-p-t* of child language (see above, pp.111f.; cf. Turner 1967: 60, on the tripartite classification which relates to the colors white, red, and black in African rituals). The binary light ~ dark oppositions, which underlie the pairs of achromatic white and black, of attenuatedly chromatic yellow and blue, and finally of optimally chromatic colors, are noticeably correlated with the grave ~ acute oppositions which underlie the pairs of diffuse (achromatic) consonants and of diffuse (attenuatedly chromatic) and compact (optimally chromatic) vowels (cf. Vallier 1978).

We could continue our comparative survey of the striking correspondences between the respective organizations of the hue-coding system and the network of distinctive features (cf. above, p. 132f.), but let us merely conclude, along with Hurvich & Jameson (1974: 101), that "the opponent-process concept, used as a guiding principle in analyzing specific aspects of particular psychological phenomena, may continue to provide the most useful key to the behavior of the nervous system, as it has already proved to do in the analysis of particular visual [and, let us add, speech sound] phenomena".

The role of sound symbolism in our mental life found an original and penetrating interpreter in Benjamin Lee Whorf (1897–1941). In a paper (see 1956: 267f.) written shortly before his untimely death he pointed out:

> in the psychological experiments human subjects seem to associate the experiences of bright, cold, sharp, hard, high, light (in weight), quick, high-pitched, narrow, and so on in a long series, with each other; and conversely, the experiences of dark, warm, yielding, soft, blunt, low, heavy, slow, low-pitched, wide, etc. in another long series. This occurs whether the **words** for such associated experiences resemble them or not, but the ordinary person is likely to **notice** a relation to words only when it is a relation of likeness to such a series in the vowels and consonants of words.

Whorf notes that "the vowels *a* (as in 'father'), *o, u* are associated in the laboratory tests with the dark-warm-soft series, and *e* (English *a* in 'date'), *i* (English *e* in 'be') with the bright-cold-sharp set. Consonants also are associated about us as one might expect from ordinary naive feeling in the matter." He considers particularly significant the fact that

> language, through lexation, has made the speaker more acutely conscious of certain dim psychic sensations; it has actually produced awareness on lower planes than its own: a power of the nature of magic. There is a logic mastery in the power of language to remain independent of lower-psyche facts, to override them, now point them up, now toss them out of the picture, to mold the nuances of words to its own rule, whether the psychic ring of the sounds fits or not. If the sounds fit, the psychic quality of the sounds is increased, and this can be noticed by the layman. If the sounds do not fit, the psychic quality changes to accord with the linguistic meaning, no matter how incongruous with the sound, and this is not noticed by the layman.

It would be difficult to present more pointedly the link and competition between the mere building-block use of the phonemes and the universal feeling-content, "basically alike for all persons".

The relation of, let us say, /i/ and /u/ as *signantia* to such *signata* as smaller ~ bigger, quicker ~ slower, more ~ less pretty, more ~less friendly, bitterer ~ sweeter, is much more likely to be noticed by the layman than is the correspondence between the constituents of two homologous sensory patterns of *signantia,* the spatial pattern of colors and the temporal one of speech sounds. The main reason for the lower uniformity and greater vacillations in the layman's direct ascription of colors to the vowels probably lies here. Hornbostel recollects having seen "mother and daughter arguing furiously: – *E* is red! No, yellow! – But to both it seemed bright, clear, and sharp" (1927b: 85). Nonetheless, as has been repeatedly noticed, the polarity of light and dark vowels enhances the visual contrast between the Latin *dies* and *nox* or between the Czech *den* and *noc* as compared to the French pair *jour* [žur] and *nuit* [nɥi] repudiated by Mallarmé because of its nonconformity to the usual correspondence (cf. R.-G. Cohn 1977). Among the polar semantic associations which, according to Whorf's summary (cited above) are tieable to the vowels /i/ and /u/, the Frenchman Lévi-Strauss (1976/1978) unconsciously chooses the vocalic and semantic correspondence between *jour* ~ *nuit* and the experiences of slower ~ quicker: "JOUR has a durative aspect, congruent with vocalic gravity, NUIT a perfective aspect, congruent with vocalic acuteness; *ce qui, à sa manière, fait une petite mythologie.*"

Albert Wellek, an expert in synesthesia (1931b: 330f.) and in the

history of its investigation, was astounded by one of the earliest communications in this field, John Locke's Essay III, 4: "A studious blind
man, who had mightily beat his head about visible objects and made
use of the explanations of his books and friends, to understand those
names of light and colours, which often came in his way, brayed one
day, that he now understood what *scarlet* signified. Upon which, his
friend demanding what scarlet was? the blind man answered, it was
like the sound of a trumpet." And in Ernst Jünger's *Lob der Vokale*
(1934: 32) it is written that "die Farbe, die wir für das A wählen
würden, müsste das Purpur sein". The apparent connection between
an optimally chromatic color such as scarlet and the optimally chromatic trumpet-ring and the summits of vocalic (/a/) and consonantal
(/k/) chromaticity in the color name scarlet ([skarlət]) is indeed spec-
tacular and evoked multiple responses in the writings of Anthony Ash-
ley Cooper (third Earl of Shaftesbury), Henry Fielding, Adam Smith,
and Erasmus Darwin. A man with a sharp feeling for "a congruity, a
harmony, something like a logical relation" between speech sounds
and colors, and especially between the vowel *a* and the color red, acknowledged that, if he had to underline words in a text with an *a,* he
would use a red pencil, feeling that it was the right color, but would use
other colors for words with other vowels (Beaunis & Binet 1892: 450).

Saussure's colleague, the Genevan psychologist Edouard Claparède (1873-1940), observed that the capability for comparison between
colors and speech sounds seems to exist in each individual in at least
an elementary stage (1900: 517), and in fact in this respect children
manifest much more readiness to respond, a higher certainty in analogies between the two experiences, and less disagreement among themselves (see Reichard et al. 1949: 224). In Hornbostel's words: "what we
knew as children, we now must grope for", because "sight and sound
have fallen apart" (1927b: 89). Yet even in the responses of adults
there are fundamental attractions between the two patterns, despite all
their variability in detail; the prevalent redness of /a/, yellowness and
whitishness of /e/ and /i/, and darkness of /o/ and /u/ clearly stand
out (cf. Argelander 1927: chap.5; Reichard 1945: 226, 231ff.; RJ I:
386ff.; Masson 1952: 40). Of course, what must be avoided is the mixture of these usual ways of translating from the speech sound to the col-
or level with literary declarations often strained and deliberately made
à rebours. Rimbaud's backwards proclamation - "*A,* noir corset velu
des mouches éclatantes" - prompted skeptical attitudes toward the
idea of 'colored hearing', attitudes which, let us add, still make use of

the acoustico-visual view of /a/ propounded by this poet (see Clavière 1898: 163 f.).

It is true that various factors, in particular the lesser separability of consonants in our actual verbal experience, and their more or less achromatic greyish character, hamper the exact determination of consonantal links with colors: consonants "have no patent colors *[couleurs franches]*, they are all more or less greyish" (Beaunis & Binet 1892: 456). Nonetheless, the fundamental consonantal categories such as, in particular, grave ~ acute are easily recognized by the respondent as parallels to the dark ~ light pairs of opponent colors.

III. WORD AFFINITIES

In some cases to a wider, and in many others to a lesser extent, most languages of the world show a marginal set of vocables which are semantically fluid, more expressive than cognitive, and which open broader possibilities for sound symbolism. At present, these lexical strata, which until recently were considered to lie beyond the bounds of language proper, are beginning to attract a greater attention from linguists, as William Samarin has particularly emphasized in his study about inventory and choice in expressive language (1970). Here he deals in particular with words termed "ideophonic" in the Africanistic terminology. The author claims that for some of these languages, for instance Gbeya, he has a file of about five thousand ideophonic adverbs, which he compares with the Korean "impressionistic" adverbs (or "mimetics") examined by Samuel Martin (1962) and with analogous phenomena in Turkic, Malayan, American Indian, and some other languages. Analogous formations in Japanese were termed "sound gestures" by Evgenij Polivanov (1891–1938) and in 1916 were subjected by him to a minute analysis (reproduced in 1968). Closer attention to the extent and display of the *Lautsinn* (see above, p. 190) in these varied types of ideophones is a timely pursuit for the science of language.

One manifold class of constructions which directly and patently connects sound and meaning is so-called 'reduplication'. Sapir's *Language* (1921: chap. 4), in portraying grammatical processes, clearly delineates the typical traits of reduplication, the tight repetition of entire words or of all or part of their radical elements: "Words of these types are all but universal." This process exhibits tremendous semantic vari-

ety and is "generally employed, with self-evident symbolism, to indicate such concepts as distribution, plurality, repetition, customary activity, increase of size, added intensity, continuance." In short, we are
dealing with an "exuberantly developed" variation of one and the
same quantitatively or qualitatively augmentative meaning, a meaning
of effected continuous or discontinuous repetition, as Sapir's (1921)
collection of examples (complemented especially by Gonda 1950; cf.
H. Key's brief overview 1965) conclusively illustrates. Thus, the iconicity relation between the reduplicated form incorporating the more-
than-one appearance of the word with itself and the idea of more-than-
one in the semantic content of these words (e.g., Somali *fen-fen* 'to
gnaw at on all sides' from *fen* 'to gnaw at') is the principle connecting
the "process" and the "concept" of reduplication. Moreover, the diversity of variables is reinforced by the emotive, emphatic character
usually inherent in reduplication.

The affective and in part directly genetic connection between reduplication and nursery vocabulary furthers the often childish style and
playful character of this construction. Yet there is a clear-cut difference
between total or partial repetition of existing words and the repetition
of syllables which do not exist in the lexicon outside of such binomials.
In the latter, the reiterative tinge of meaning is not necessarily implied,
and such reduplication of syllables common in children's vocabulary
and in infant-adult nursery language fulfills a different function. By
the repetition of the same syllable, children signal that their phonation
is not babbling but a verbal message to their adult interlocutor, and
through reduplication the child recognizes a message addressed to him
and is helped by the repetition to decode it. The process of reduplication is similar here to the iteration of verbal and other acoustic signals
in long-distance navigational communication. As noted by Lévi-
Strauss (1964: 345 f.), such a reduplication "a pour fonction de signifier la signification". A large number of units used only in reduplications are either onomatopoeic imitations of natural and instrumental
sounds or metonymic designations for the originators or activities concomitant with these sounds (cf. the comprehensive review of such lexemes by Gonda 1940), and in its semantic function this type of iteration distinctly differs from the reduplicated forms built from simple,
independently existing units.

The relation between the functions of reduplicative words and between such words and other lexical strata, the place of reduplicated
forms in the different styles of language, and the geographical distribu-

tion of the various relations – all these questions are only beginning to be examined with sufficient precision, and we need thorough monographic studies on the position and character of these peculiar types of words within diverse languages. Nils Thun's industrious dissertation (1963), *Reduplicative Words in English,* based on a collection of about two thousand samples of (1) "identical reduplication", (2) reduplication with change of initial consonant, and (3) reduplication "with change of stem vowel", confronts us with numerous unsolved problems. In particular this raises the question of the functional distribution of these three types of reduplication, both in English and in other languages of the world, and points out the necessity of searching for the structural rules of consonantal and vocalic alternations both in English and in any language where such alternations exist.

Words undergoing reduplication are augmented both in their form and in their meaning. They are "italicized". The dissimilation of the initial consonants renders the iterative reinforcements more sharply discernible and in Russian, for instance, impart to the reduplication a somewhat playful, "advertising" touch, and at times an ironical, disparaging, inflated character. Thus *zakón* means 'law', *zakón-makón* 'a frivolous, disrespectable kind of law', and *sífilis-pífilis* 'such a nothing as syphilis'. The extensive role of reduplication, with the change of identical consonants in Russian and a few other Slavic languages, is based upon the Turkic model; and in the Slavic as well as in the Turkic area the dissimilation of consonants is subject to a set of strict rules which make the juxtaposition of paired words particularly conspicuous. In Russian pairs of alternating initials, the leading role belongs to labial (grave diffuse) consonants, especially to the nasal /m/. The two alternating consonants cannot be both acute (dental), both grave (labial), or both compact (velopalatal); thus, the three summits of the consonantal triangle underlie the dissimilation, with exceptional combinations of nasal and nonnasal labials: e.g. *barán-marán* 'a good-for-nothing ram' (cf. RJ V: 343 f.). The basic ordering principle of vocalic alternation in languages where it is used in reduplicative words is (cf. above, p. 184) the progression from a diffuse vowel, especially /i/, to a compact one. (Cf. the overwhelming predominance of *i* as the first of the vocalic alternants in English [e.g. Thun 1963: 220] and on the other hand the rare occurrences cited by Gonda, such as Javanese *djas-djis* 'worthless' and *ʈar-ʈir* 'run up against ...' [1940: 189].)

The English reduplicative *flip-flap* (or *flip-flop*), with its two regularly alternating vowels, one diffuse and the other compact, is actually

composed of two forms (either verbal or nominal) which are different
and yet related, thanks to their common consonantal frame and to the
mutual proximity of meanings. These two factors suffice to reveal the
relationship of these same words even when used separately. Within
one and the same language many words disclose arresting similarities
both in sound and in meaning, and whether these verbal ties go back to
a genetic kinship or not, the outer and inner affinity between such vocables is intuitively felt by the ordinary members of the speech community: "the tendency of forms to mold themselves on other forms
with like meanings, and meanings to mold themselves on other meanings, conveyed by like words, is universal", as was convincingly accented by Dwight Bolinger, the expert in the revelation and interpretation of these "verbal affinities" based on "the grouping of similar
meanings about similar sounds".

Three centuries after the initial efforts of John Wallis (1653) it was
Bolinger who made momentous achievements in such an interpretation of the English lexicon (a series of studies summed up in his book
of 1965). Both *flap* and *flip* belong, in Bolinger's view (1965: 245f.), to
two "constellations of words": "the family of *slap, clap, rap, tap, flap,*
and *lap* denotes actions that strike and then glide off," while "a lighter,
or sharper blow or its result is suggested by the group *nip, clip, tip, sip,*
dip, grip, pip, quip, yip (contrast *yap*), *flip* (contrast *flop* [and *flap*]), *drip*
(contrast *droop* and *drop*)". The postvocalic labial stop at the end of
the monosyllable is sensed to be like a 'blow', and the /i/ vs. /æ/ opposition seems to suggest a briefer focus upon the action. Both *flap*
(flop) and *flip* belong to the family of initial *fl-* clusters, which has repeatedly attracted Bolinger's attention (pp. 198, 207, 217) and which
Jespersen (*Language,* 1922b: chap. 20) earlier had singled out as expressive of movement; he quoted *flow, flap, flake, flutter, flicker, fling,*
flit, flurry, flirt (sect. 5; cf. Marchand 1959: 154, 266f.).

Bolinger drafted the principles of a *sui generis* synchronic etymology. Collocations of phonemes common to a set of words and suggestive of a stronger or vaguer semantic interconnection were extracted in
his verbal analysis as "submorphemic differentials"; these were also
labeled "psychomorphs" by Markell & Hamp (1960–61: 1), while
Householder (1946: 83) made use of the term "phonestheme" and
maintained that about 15 percent of standard English monosyllables
with a stress on /ʌ/ belong to phonesthemes or at least are tied with
them by secondary associations. In the discussion of Householder's
conclusions, Giuliano Bonfante pointed out that in Latin and in Indo-

European, short /ă/ "is found almost entirely in words of a special kind, referring to diseases and physical defects, or infantile expressions" and that in all German words, except perhaps *Deutsch,* the sound /č/ "is clearly expressive" (1939: 84). Thanks to the expressiveness of the sound groups involved and to the ostensibility of such "submorphemes," this class (as observers note) also possibly attracts new members by borrowing or by neology and at the same time furthers the survival of the class' older members; thus, it may achieve a higher semantic cohesiveness. There truly exists an interplay between the fact which Bolinger has called "sound suggestiveness" and "the creation of counters or tools which in essence are not suggestive but manipulable" (1965: 192f.). Whatever it may be, the patent or latent role played by the "intrinsic value", *videlicet* by the spell of the speech sounds, is undeniable.

Not only does Bolinger consider continuous and discontinuous clusters, e.g. the set /str-p/ which in *strip, strap, strope, stripe* refers to a "line having breadth" or the set /sp-t/ which in *spit, spate, spout* refers to a "rush of liquid" (p. 224), as submorphemic differentials, but he notes also that in certain positions single phonemes appear to be treated in similar terms, e.g. the tense /u/ in words which "suggest foolishness" – *rube, boob, galoot, loon,* the verb *moon, nincompoop, stooge, coocoo, goof, spoof,* etc. (p. 200). It may be added that such submorphemic differentials occur both within lexical and within grammatical morphemes, namely within affixes. Thus, as discussed above (p. 59), among Russian declensional desinences only the endings of two 'marginal cases', instrumental and dative, may include the phoneme /m/, while the Polish desinences of the instrumental go even further in assigning a compulsory character to a submorphemic differential and in reducing its size to a subphonemic, featural level. Any desinence of the Polish instrumental must contain the nasal feature, represented in a one-vowel ending by vocalic nasality and carried elsewhere by the phoneme /m/ (RJ II: 181).

Hans Marchand, who devoted a detailed study to "phonetic symbolism in English word-formation," declares that he split roots into their components: in his opinion roots are not indivisible units, but are composites, as, for example, *fl-ash, fl-ick,* with a modification of the vowels or the consonants (1959: 153). He divides the extracted components into initial and final symbols, consisting of alliterative sounds or clusters in the first group and of "their rhyming counterparts" in the latter class (pp. 155ff., 264ff.), and he assigns to both classes of such various sound symbols the capacity of creating actual word affinities. Nevertheless, he himself asserts "the impossibility so far to find out what the symbolism is based upon". In his earlier study (1957: 56), Marchand posited that "the symbolism underlying ablaut variation is that of polarity which may assume various semantic aspects". Likewise, Morton Bloomfield (1953: 160f.) insisted on the importance of "semantic-sound parallelism" which "probably moves on a subconscious level".

Sometimes, in describing languages of a remote structure, the idea of segmenting roots into smaller significant units with their own sound-symbolic value suggests itself. Diffloth, in his essay on the "very large word-class" of "expressives" (or "ideophones") in Semai, an Austroasiatic language, countered the evidence that neither expressives nor certain verbs and nouns related to them are subject to the condition of "lexical discreteness". There arose the obvious question of whether one should not be prepared "to discard the conventional notions of root and morphology" (1976: 261). Perhaps the most impressive attempt to disclose the sound-symbolic components of grammatically indissoluble units was the tentative paper by Gladys Reichard about "Composition and Symbolism of Coeur d'Alene Verb Stems" (1945). In addition to a vocalic symbolism discernible within a few verbal categories, the study detects a consonantal symbolism which displays a similar specifying effect on the meaning of the stem, no matter whether the consonant's position is initial or final. In Reichard's opinion, "the suggestions offered by such an analysis are fascinating and ⟨...⟩ rewarding, especially when compared with similar attempts at breaking down the phonetic structure of stems so as to relate the sounds to meanings, as has been done with other languages, English for example, chiefly with negative results" (p. 53).

IV. SOUND-SYMBOLIC ABLAUT

The morphological utilization of the substitution of features in certain consonants or vowels within the root of a word and sometimes also within its affixes is a particular example of the use of single sound differences in the direct service of grammatical meanings. This sound-symbolic ablaut has its widest spread in America, especially in the northwest, where the investigation of these phenomena has disclosed various diffusional strata and directions (cf. e.g. Nichols 1971: 837ff., and Haas 1970). While in America it is mainly the inherent features of consonants or less frequently of vowels which undergo such shifts, in Africa the main alternations of this type are chiefly in prosodic features. Cf. Westermann's references 1927 and 1937 to the opposition of low tone vs. high tone in Yoruba to designate the difference between large and voluminous vs. small and slender, with various metaphorical modifications of meanings, e.g. *bìrì* 'to be large', *bírí* 'to be small', *šùrù* 'to be big', *šúrú* 'to be little', *gbòrò* 'to be wide', *gbóró* 'to be narrow', *kìbìtì* 'of big size', *kíbítí* 'of small size'; see also Westermann's similar examples for Ewe (1927: 323; 1937: 193) and Wescott's observations on Bini (Nigeria) "tonal icons", uniformly high-tone adverbs for "tall, thin, tight" vs. low-tone adverbs for "short, thick, loose" (1973). There is, moreover, an analogous utilization in Ewe of the qualitative differences between dark and light vowels (Westermann 1927: 324 ff.; 1937: 171). In Avatime, lax consonants correspond to large objects, and tense consonants to small ones: *tótò* 'with small opening' – *dódò* 'with large opening', *kpókpò* 'thin' – *gbógbò* 'thick' (cf. in Ewe *kpóvíó kplé gbòvìò* 'here and there [near and far]'), "with a parallelism of high tone and tense consonant, of low tone and lax consonant" in the two languages (p. 327). Particularly illuminating are Westermann's remarks on compact consonants (1937: 205): "In Ewe 'sound images' [*Lautbilder*, later named 'ideophones'], it's the energetic character of an explosive back sound which determines the essence of *g*. The acoustic impression is decisively harsher than that of *b*. Hence *g* assigns a strength to the meaning of something bent, resistant, violent, primarily before *a*" (cf. above, pp. 102 f.), and *x* in turn receives a similar semantic evaluation (1937: 208). A rare example of a European use of a productive sound-symbolic ablaut is the Basque formation of diminutives by the sharpening (palatalizing) of dentals and sometimes velars (Lafitte 1962: 147).

Johanna Nichols' detailed survey of consonantal alternations in Western North American languages (1971) is a valuable contribution to the future systematic analysis of this peculiar and complex set of sound shifts and offers an ordered collection of previously scattered linguistic observations on Amerindian languages. Nevertheless, there is still need for a more systematic analysis of the sound changes undergone and of their semantic import, and for a clearer view of the various stages in the continuously productive or merely residual character of the ablaut rules. It must be repeated, however, that in finding a more exact answer to all these questions the classifier is hampered by the many serious gaps in the available materials.

In regard to the semantic scope of the two directions of gradation (diminutive, augmentative), Nichols notes that the meanings conveyed by diminutive shifts "may symbolize only the large/small contrast, or may involve extensions of this semantic domain such as bright/dark, light/heavy, quick/slow, near/far, and the endearing and pejorative senses" (p. 828). The chief topic of Nichols' outline is the "diminutive consonantal symbolism"; this is the natural first step, because the diminutive meaning in its various nuances and metaphoric and metonymic extensions proves to be the most widely spread of the shifts under discussion. The opposite function of such sound alternations is the buildup of augmentative forms, but in languages with merely two terms of sound-symbolic gradation, either the opposition is confined to the diminutive vs. a neutral meaning, or else the neutral meaning is opposed to one 'marked' category, labeled "affective" by Nichols (p. 827) and "comprising both diminutive and augmentative". Thus all languages with an augmentative category also possess a diminutive one: "an augmentative shift presupposes a diminutive shift" (p. 827). Also, in languages which besides the neutral category possess the diminutive and the augmentative, the diminutive is usually represented by a higher number of lexical examples than the augmentative.

Particularly helpful for the comprehension of the sound-symbolic ablaut in single languages are detailed and careful descriptions like the one compiled for Dakota by Franz Boas in cooperation with Ella Deloria, a sensitive indigenous research worker intimately familiar with the all-embracing symbolism of her native language and culture. According to Boas & Deloria, "the vocabulary of Dakota shows clear evidence of an ancient sound symbolism. It is not a live process but it may be illustrated by many examples" of words which change their hushing (acute compact) continuants into hissing (acute diffuse) continuants to proceed from a neutral level of designated intensity to a low, diminutive grade; similarly the change of hushing (acute compact) continuants into corresponding velar (grave compact) continuants suggests the highest, augmentative grade of intensity (1941: 1, 16 f.): diminutive *suza* 'it has a slight bruise' - neutral *šuža* 'it it badly bruised' - augmentative *xuya* 'it is fractured'. There occur forms with the analogous vocalic alternations of a diffuse *i* diminutively oriented vs. the neutral acute compact ɛ, and a grave compact *a* augmentatively graded: *kpi, kpɛ, kpa*, "which mean in order a **light** crackling, the noise of stick striking stick, and a **sharp** noise like that of a firecracker" (p. 1). The coauthor of Boas' *Memoir*, Ella Deloria, categorically associated these three vowels with colors: /i/ with white, /ɛ/ with yellow, and /a/ with red (Reichard et al. 1949: 231). "The importance of the acoustic sense expressed in Dakota appears particularly in the various forms of sound symbolism" (Boas & Deloria 1941: 1) and in "the particular kind of synesthesia between sound, sight, and touch" (Boas 1938: 132, and Boas & Deloria 1941: 1), an interrelation which also finds eloquent expression in the parallel Dakota alternation between colors and the consonants used in naming them: zi 'it is yellow' - ži 'it is tawny' - ɣi 'it is brown' (1941: 18).

G. H. Matthews' interesting remarks (1970: 102 ff.) on sound symbolism in the Siouan languages supplement Boas & Deloria's data: "What we see here exhibited is a rather direct correspondence between sound and meaning, i. e., the occurrence in a stem of a dental, palatoalveolar, or velar obstruent continuant corresponds to an aspect of the meaning of the stem which might be characterized as diminutive, normal, and augmentative respectively" (cf. his Dakota examples ptúza 'bent', ptúža 'pieces cracked but not broken off', ptúɣa 'pieces broken off'). "This sound symbolism is what might be called semi-productive in Dakota, i. e. many speakers are aware of it and may produce new stems on analogy with existing stems and the sound symbolism. However, these newly created stems are used for the most part in jokes and puns, and do not normally become a part of the language." Matthews refers to some other Siouan languages in which "the sound symbolism is in no way productive, although there are a number of pairs and a few triples of stems in these languages which clearly exhibit it". Whereas in the subfamily, Mississippi Valley Siouan, the sound symbolism possibly "has a certain degree of productiveness."

In his discussion of sound symbolism, Boas (1938: 132) maintained that "it is not by any means certain that the same impressions are conveyed in all languages, but similar phenomena are not rare". Furthermore, Sapir (1911: 645 f.) and Nichols (1971: 838) disclosed an important principle: the presence of a conventional grammatical alternation in a given language seems to preclude the occurrence of an identical sound-symbolic ablaut in that same language and in this way to limit the repertory of such ablauts. In the American sound-symbolic ablaut it is the alternation of obstruents which plays the primary role, although vocalic alternations between vowels and between liquid and nasal sonorants also occur. In the diverse types of consonantal ablaut, strident consonants alternate either with each other or with nonstrident, mellow ones. Such is, for instance, the interchange of the uvular affricate [q] and the velar [k] (Tillamook *waqaq* 'frog' – *wūwekek* 'tiny frog') and the widespread alternation of [*l*] with the lateral affricate [λ]. In the diminutive consonantal ablaut, no interchanges are permitted between grave and acute consonants, and in grave consonantism, no exchange between diffuse and compact. The only alternating features proper to the abrupt consonants (stops and affricates) are the oppositions tense ~ lax and checked ~ unchecked (cf. above, pp. 147 ff.). Thus, the only axial oppositions used are almost always those between acute diffuse and acute compact. The mutable compact consonants always imply the diffuse character of their counterpart in the ablaut. In turn, the diffuse consonants in such ablauts imply the compact character of their counterpart, with the exception of the alternation [s] ~ [c] attested, according to Nichols (p. 828), by a very few and rather uncertain examples in Northern Paiute, Nez Perce, and Wishram. In addition, rare cases of strident laterals in an ablaut with sibilants are also noted.

The direction of sound change from the neutral to the diminutive form can oscillate, and reverse tendencies in the distribution of alternants are observable in various American languages which utilize sound-symbolic ablauts. However, the favored and most frequent patterns help to reveal the general factors underlying the assignment of the alternatives. For instance, the favored diminutive function of the diffuse consonants in opposition to the neutral function of the compact ones finds a clear and persuasive interpretation on the auditory, perceptual level and herewith gives new proof for Nichols' conviction that a motor, "kinesthetic basis for symbolism is not needed" (p. 834). The inversions of choice between sounds with diminutive and opposite function can be compared with the relations observed by Lévi-Strauss concerning American masks: "Like myths which are reversed in proceeding from one population to another, the plastic aspects of those masks which carry one and the same message are also reversed" (1975 II: 89; cf. on markedness reversals LW 1979 a and above pp. 194 f.). The semantic difference observed by Margaret Langdon (1971) between tense (voiceless) and lax (voiced) laterals as "large" and "small" respectively in the sound symbolism of Ipai and other Yuman languages finds an adequate explanation in the greater force and duration of the tense consonants (see above, pp. 139 f.). The question of the suitability of checked, noticeably shortened consonants (see above, p. 148) for diminutive symbolism has been rightly pointed out by Dell Hymes' private communication to Langdon (1. c. 172).

V. SPEECH SOUNDS IN MYTHOPOEIC USAGE

In comparison with the various forms of sound-symbolic ablaut briefly outlined in our survey, further, more radical devices which break the regular hierarchic scale in the relationship between sound and meaning may be elicited in "abnormal types of speech", according to the term of Sapir, who as early as 1915 devoted a revealing study to this complex of questions (reproduced in 1949: 179-196). He presented his data after five years of ethnological and linguistic research mainly among the Nootka Indians, and his intent was "to indicate the general class of linguistic phenomena ⟨...⟩ to render these latter less glaringly bizarre by providing them with parallels of a more general character" (p. 180). His remark that "consonantal play to express modalities of attitude is doubtless a fruitful field for investigation in American linguistics and should receive more attention than has hitherto been accorded it" (p. 186) still remains relevant.

Sapir's central theme is the Nootka custom of implying "in speech some physical characteristic of the person addressed or spoken of, partly by means of 'consonantal play' ⟨...⟩ [which] consists either in altering certain consonants of a word, in this case sibilants, to other consonants that are phonetically related to them, or in inserting meaningless consonants or consonant clusters in the body of the word." When speaking to or about a child, it is customary to add "the regular diminutive suffix -'is to verb or other forms, even though the word so effected connotes nothing intrinsically diminutive ⟨...⟩ In talking to or about fat people or people of unusual size, the suffixed element -aqʰ is used in a manner analogous to the diminutive -'is" (pp. 180f.): acute diffuse vowels and consonants serve to pinpoint the diminutive suffix, and grave compacts the augmentative one. The same diminutive suffix is used in addition to some consonantal modification of the words to characterize beings with visible blemishes. People who are abnormally small (e. g., dwarfs) are spoken of with (in addition to the suffix) a palatalization (sharpening) of all hissing and hushing sibilants.

An approximative analogue to this kind of word-building with a suffix and with a sound change could perhaps be seen in the German treatment of the diminutive suffix -chen which, as Leonard Bloomfield brought to light in 1930, also involves an unusual consonantal alternation. But German, in contradistinction to Nootka, manifests the alternation in the suffix itself. At the beginning to this diminutive suffix there appears a palatal continuant different from the corresponding velar continuant occurring in the same sound sequence elsewhere: thus, only this sound difference discriminates two words: *Kuhchen* 'little cow' has a palatal continuant at the beginning of the diminutive suffix *-chen* added to the root *Kuh* 'cow', while *Kuchen* 'cake' has a ve- lar continuant (see the previous discussion of this question summed up by O. Werner 1972: 48).

As Sapir points out, in Nootka those with some defect of the eye (the cross-eyed, those who squint, and those with some other defect of the eye, but not the blind) are spoken of or even addressed with the conversion of all sibilants into the corresponding voiceless laterals; thus "the diminutive -*'is* itself becomes -*'ił*". Talk about or even direct- ed to hunchbacks transforms the ordinary sibilants by pronouncing them with a protrusion of the lower jaw. People with some deformity in their extremities are spoken about with a special, at least partly hushing sibilant used as an infix. The exact position of the infix within the word "apparently depends on the whim of the speaker", while for left-handed people and for circumcised males and for greedy, grasp- ing, gluttonous people (i.e. long-handed or long-beaked beings), the infix is inserted after the first syllable of the word. In the last case (the only one listed with no literal distortion of the body involved) there is no diminutive suffix. The same substitutions of sibilants and sibilant infixes are used when alluding to such animals as the Deer, Mink, Ra- ven, Sparrow, Wren, especially when they appear in mythological narra- tives, and similar kinds of "consonant plays as a device in mythology" are used in application to supernatural characters. Sapir quotes Boas' materials on the Mink of the Kwakiutl, "a trickster who regularly transforms all anterior palatals to corresponding sibilants" (p. 187). Frachtenberg's commentary (1920) on the Nootka study concludes that the cited forms of unusual speech "apply only to persons physi- cally abnormal and to mythological beings or animals" (p. 296). It is worth mentioning that the mythological connections of the physical deviations, whether unwanted or wanted, do not include cases of total infirmities, such as blindness, deafness, lack of feet, etc.

Sapir's reference to "the well-known American habit of comparing one that is marked by some peculiarity of temper or habit with a favor- ite mythological character" (p. 192) and to "the clownish episodes of rituals which are so characteristic of America" is a suitable key for un- derstanding the links between the similar consonantal plays applied to "myth character forms," as well as to animals either magical or tradi- tionally associated with mythology, and to the abnormal, unusual persons closely dependent upon and guarded by the upper forces. The peculiar sound plays noted above reveal an etiquette of significant, inseparable combinations made up of a satirizing and at the same time reverential attitude toward the supernatural world. People spoken of or to with the use of a deliberately strange sound-means are "set apart by nature as falling short in some respect of the normal type of individual", and are simultaneously "stamped as inferior" (p. 185) and as connected with the superior forces of nature. Sapir intuitively grasped that the opposite modalities of attitude expressed by consonantal changes and increments concurrently involve such various feelings as contempt, affection, and respect (p. 186).

Sapir also saw "that quite analogous processes are found employed as literary devices in American myths and songs". He points out that

the phenomenon of consonantal and vocalic play is also well illustrated in Indian songs. Song diction is an extremely important, though rather neglected, field of primitive lore ⟨...⟩ Song texts often represent a mutilated form of the language, but study of the peculiarities of song forms generally shows that the normal forms of speech are modified according to stylistic conventions, which may vary for different types of songs. Sometimes sounds are found in songs which do not otherwise occur in the language. [149: 188]

Sapir refers to special song sounds such as certain sonorants – laterals and nasals – which under ordinary circumstances outside of songs are difficult for the Indians to articulate. On the basis of his comprehensive field word, George Herzog found that in the songs of the Pima (Arizona), voiceless vowels of ordinary speech become voiced, vowels are inserted, stops and affricates are frequently changed into the corresponding nasals, one of which, the palatal [ň], is "unique in poetry, being nonexistent in ordinary speech" (1946). (For the Peyote songs, cf. Nettl 1953, and for the insertion of initial prevocalic yod or [χ], widespread in Russian folk songs, see Bogatyrëv 1962 and RJ IV: 533 f.)

The use of wide consonantal shifts is, in some languages, for instance certain Sahaptin dialects (south-central Washington), confined to the "rhetoric myth narration, distinguishing it from normal speech" (see Jacobs 1931). The highlighting of mythological characters through conventional sound shifts is particularly salient when it introduces speech sounds foreign to the usual pattern of the given language. According to Frachtenberg (p. 297), in the North-West American Quileute language, words used when speaking of the mythological Deer replace all sibilants with laterals, and the pronouncements of the Raven's wife change [d] and [l] to [n], and [b] to [m]: "these abnormal forms are the only instances in Quileute where the nasal *m, n* occur", for these two nasals are always represented by /b/ and /d/ respectively. Cf. an analogous mythological conversion of voiced stops to nasals in Puget Sound dialects (see above, p. 135).

Consonantal insertions or changes in the speech of (or about) mythical animals are observed in diverse Amerindian languages, e.g. in Takelma by Sapir (1922: 8), and in Nez Perce and Coeur d'Alene by Aoki (1970: 7f.; 1975: 190). Particularly notable are Margaret Langdon's reflections on "animal talk in Cocopa" (1978), from which she is able to infer that "animal characters in Cocopa folklore and mythology have their own distinctive speech manner, each animal being associated with its own favorite consonant", and hence she raises the question of whether such consonantal modifications in the speech of, to, or about these sacred animals existed throughout the Yuman family of languages (p. 13).

VI. VERBAL TABOO

The far-reaching questions of the modification and truncation of word shapes caused by verbal taboo are in fact closely associated with the problems of the lexical alterations which American Indian languages undergo when used to speak to or about certain beings and forces. On the one hand, such transmutations camouflage the subject meant or addressed; on the other hand, these conventional contrivances, as compared to ordinary forms, highlight and in a certain way specify the character designated. As the noted specialist in Indo-European etymologies Joseph Vendryes (1875–1960) pinpointed, religiously motivated interdictions against certain nouns were

> far from purging the vocabulary of the words judged to be evil. They could be preserved on the condition of being modified in their form, for instance reversed in their sound sequence, in order to become inoffensive [cf. Fónagy 1956: 239]. Herewith is explained a number of accidents in the structure of certain words, notably names of animals (especially wild animals undergoing a hunters' taboo), names of body parts or of physical blemishes, and finally religious terms designating ritual notions or acts. [1924: 383]

Wilhelm Havers (1879–1961) devoted a large part (pp. 117ff.) of his detailed monograph on verbal taboo to substitutive devices and especially to sound changes, the insertion of sounds or sound groups, metathesis, alternation or deletion of initial, internal, or final sounds or clusters.

The distance between the tabooed word form and its substitute is one aspect of the relationship between the two sound shapes. As long as the link between the prohibited form and its replacement is sensed by the speakers, there are rules, or at least dispositions, against surpassing a certain phonic remoteness between the two shapes. Thus for instance, Czech utilizes several substitutes for the tabooed ecclesiastical terms *sakra* and *sakrament* (Latin *sacra* and *sacrament*), whereby the voiceless /s/ and /k/ are given solely voiceless substitutes, still sibilant for /s/ and still grave for the Czech velar /k/, and the sonorants /r/ and /m/ are replaced by the liquid /l/ and the 'semi-sonorant' /v/: *safra, cakra* (with an initial dental affricate), *sakva, saprment* (with a syllabic [r̩]), *cakrment, sakvament*, and *sakulent*. Among the numerous American English exclamations collected by E. C. Hills (1924), there is a distinct tendency for stops replaced by stops to maintain their original laxness or tenseness and for sonorants to replace sonorants. Thus, *God* becomes *dod, dog, dig; Christ* appears as *crimp, cripes; damn* changes into *darn, garn, ding, durn, dang, deen, been.*

One may add that as long as speakers feel the link between the prohibited form and its substitute, the replacement of a tabooed word by its modified form is a conscious or subliminal expression of a fear of attracting danger, bad luck, or ill will through the direct, explicit evocation of a supernatural or ill-omened, ill-intentioned power or through the direct naming of a potential victim, prey, or target of such a power. Fr. Specht appraises word taboo as a characteristic manifestation of verbal magic (*Sprachzauber* 1940: 112ff.; 1944: 395), frequently combined with a playful touch (cf. Havers 1946: 127). Such "abnormal types" of speech-sound uses as the American Indian symbolic ablauts concern the speaker's potential addressee; they always have in mind a second person, either present and spoken to, or absent and spoken about. The abnormal sound changes in the word taboo have as their aim to hide the tabooed noun from its carrier or from the supposedly undesirable listener.

The "male and female forms of speech" in their turn assign to speech sounds a task quite different from a mere sense-discriminative one. In languages which differentiate the sound patterns used by females and males, women identify themselves as women by avoiding the forms of speech and the repertory of speech sounds proper to the men's pattern. In certain languages, analogous means of self-identification are used by males, but this phenomenon is less general; and there are languages, for instance Yana (North California), in which the specifically male pattern is confined to men dealing with men, whereas when either the addresser or the addressee is a woman, the female pattern is employed. The spread and character of sex discriminations in the languages of the world require a much more detailed and systematic study. Differences between the more ceremonial and the more reduced character of speech on its various levels have been pointed out in several descriptions, and attempts at a sociological explanation have been made, but in fact in some of these cases, such as Yana, the more reduced forms characterize the female (Sapir 1949: 211f.), while in some other languages they characterize the male variety of speech, as observed in Chukchee dialects (Bogoraz 1922: 665) or in Caraya (Ehrenreich 1894: 23).

Also, the degrees of taboo interdictions against a recourse to the language of the other sex are uneven. In Yana "a female uses the male forms without hesitation when she quotes the words of a male speaking to a male, as in relating a myth in which one male character speaks to another" (Sapir 1949: 207). On the other hand, in the USSR, when schools with Chukchee as the language of teaching were first opened, "little girls blushed and refused to read words containing an *r*-sound", because "the use of men's pronunciation was accounted indecent for women, accustomed to replace *r* and *č* phonemes by the hushing *š*". At the same time, it is to be noted that the pronunciation of speech sounds usually confined to the male pattern is, here again, familiar to females and is used when they quote male speech, especially in relating men's tales (see Bogoraz 1922: 665, and I. Diakonoff's convincing comparison of two Sumerian dialects, the men's and women's: 1974: 113).

From the scattered data we have at our disposal, it is difficult to extract common principles of sound differentiation in the sexually bifurcated languages known to us. A number of these bifurcations in some way involve sonorants and affricates. For instance, one may cite the female's replacement of final stops by nasals which Boas observed in some Eskimo tribes (1911: 79), the substitution of a sibilant affricate for liquids in the female Chukchee (Bouda 1953: 33) and Koryak (Stebnickij 1934: 58), the supplanting of all *l*'s and of the palatalized *r* by yod in the speech of Russian women in Northeast Siberia (Bogoraz 1901: 5ff.), and the loss of velarization by the women's *l* in scattered Russian and Ukrainian dialects (Šerech 1952). Among the Gros Ventres in Montana women's velar stops correspond to men's sibilant affricates, as Regina Flannery noted (1946).

A peculiar sound feature distinguishing men's and women's speech has been observed in Gogo-Yimidjir (Australia). Here the language has no sense-discriminative opposition of tense and lax (or of voiceless and voiced) stops, but women use a tense (concomitantly voiceless) variant, whereas men correspondingly employ the lax (concomitantly voiced) variant (de Zwaan 1969: 26 f.). This situation is similar to the female variety of Yana with its devoiced and reduced final vowel of polysyllabic forms and a tense antecedent stop, e. g. male: [siga:ga], female: [siga:kʰª] 'quail' (Sapir 1949: 208; Sapir and Swadesh 1960: 3). A significant instance of a direct connection between taboo and a female sound pattern was pointed out by Dmitrij Zelenin (1878–1954) in his fundamental treatise on verbal taboo (1929–30: 142): Kazakh women were prohibited from calling their in-laws by their true names and either had to use words which resemble the original in sound shape or had to modify directly the phonic makeup of the interdicted name. In various ways both the verbal taboo and the sexual bifurcation of language display certain changes in distance – either estrangement or rapprochement – between the sayer and the real or imaginary sayee.

VII. GLOSSOLALIA

One use of speech sounds totally deprived of a sense-discriminative role throughout an entire pronouncement, but nonetheless destined for a certain kind of communication and aimed at an actual human audience or intended to be received and apprehended by a divine spirit, pertains to a special kind of verbal or quasi-verbal creative activity labeled *glossolalia*. The coalescence of two functions is a characteristic trait of glossolalic pronouncements: they connect the human and divine worlds on the one hand as prayers from the former to the latter and on the other hand as messages transmitted from the divine power to the assembled human body in order to inspire, unify, and emotionally exalt it (cf. Samarin 1972b). Different forms of glossolalia are widely spread in various countries, epochs, and beliefs (cf. May's 1956 survey of glossolalia in non-Christian religions, also Jaquith 1967; and with a special concentration on Christian glossolalia, Lombard 1910, Cutten 1927, and Samarin 1972a & b). Its lack of resemblance to any actual language of the present or of the past leads to glossolalia's designation as a language of spirits. The chapter 2 passage of the Acts of the Apostles on the Pentecost miracle, which gave believers the "gift of tongues" for a direct verbal communion with heaven ("and they were all filled with the Holy Ghost, and began to speak with other tongues, as the Spirit gave them utterance"), provides the background for the multiform rise and reappearance of a "speaking in tongues", glossolalic movement.

Only a few of the diverse glossolalic pronouncements within the different varieties of Pentecostal trends are available in written or taped records for an analysis of their form, although such an analysis promises to yield significant results. William Samarin, the devoted examiner of Christian glossolalia, surmises with confidence that "glossas from different parts of the world will have striking similarities, perhaps even more similarities among themselves than each does to its source language" (1972 a: 77).

Suggestive data may be derived from the Khlysty, apparently the oldest Russian mystical sect, with a firm glossolalic tradition (cf. especially Konovalov 1908: 227–252: "Peculiarities in the pronunciation and combination of sounds, words, and sentences of ecstatic speech"). Archives of a special Moscow Committee which investigated sectarian activities throughout the middle of the eighteenth century preserved examples of glossolalia recorded from three Khlysty prophets (see Nečaev 1889: 179; cf. RJ IV: 641 f.). They considered whirling to be a second, supreme baptism, because the Holy Ghost descends on the whirling people (see Nečaev: 140).

The St. Petersburg preceptor of the Khlysty, Ivan Čurkin, taught a woman who worked for him to say, while whirling: *Kindra fendra kiraveca*. It is easy to observe the rigorous selectiveness and recurrence of the sounds used. All four odd syllables of this sequence contain an unrounded front vowel, while the vowel of all four even syllables is an apparently unstressed *a*. All three internal *a*'s of this formula, which build the second syllable of its three members, are introduced by *r*, and the first two *ra*'s are preceded by one and the same cluster, *nd*. Of the four odd front vowels, the first and third are *i*'s with an antecedent *k*, while the second and forth are *e*'s with a preceding labial continuant: first *fe*, then *ve*. *Rentre fente*, the first two "words" of an invocation written down in 1747 from a Moscow prophet of the Khlysty, the trader Sergej Osipov, correspond to the *kindra fendra* of Čurkin's text in the number of syllables (2 + 2), the similar clusters, and the identical consonants, differing only by the voicelessness of the dental stop and the lack of *k*. In the glossolalia of a monk from the Moscow Čudov monastery, Varlaam Šiškov, interrogated and tortured in 1748, several analogues appear; in particular, the exclamation *natrufuntru*, translated by this esoteric preacher as 'be fearful, man, before praying', coincides entirely with the consonantal makeup of Osipov's quoted passage. The sectarians' designation for the gift of tongues – *govorenie inostrannymi jazykami* 'speaking in foreign languages' – finds justification in the use of such prevalently alien traits as the consonant *f* and the clusters of *ndr* or *ntr* by all three performers. Of the three words of Čurkin's precept, one begins with *f* and two finish with *ndra*. In Osipov's 18-syllable pronouncement, the *f*, repeated four times, is the only continuant obstruent, and the cluster *ntr* occurs four times, as does *nt*. Šiškov's 94 syllables contain ten *f*'s, seven *ntr* and *ndr* clusters, and four *nt*'s. Šiškov, ordered to translate his glossolalia into Russian, made a "translation" based consistently on similar sound-associations (na*sontos* – *sna*, *lesontos* – voz*lej*, furt*lis* – vrazum*is'*, etc.), but devoid of any *nt* or *nd* combinations and of any etymological *f*.

A capable and eccentric peasant, a skilled craftsman and alleged sectarian, once lived in the village of Zaxarovka, Belëv district, Tula province. There RJ, invited by a schoolfriend, Vladimir Žebrovskij, met him. In early 1914, Vladimir's sister Ol'ga, looking for the craftsman, entered his hut and saw him sitting on the floor, intently stroking a cat on its back. She asked, "What are you doing?" and was told, *"Kýndru po féndre gláźu"* ("I'm stroking the *kýndra* along the *féndra*"). RJ (see his IV: 641 f.), who at that time was studying the Khlysty's glossolalia, had Čurkin's invocation still fresh in his memory and asked Ol'ga to question the man as to what a *kiraveca* was. "*Kiraveca* is an old word, a wise word," was his reply. "And what does it mean?" – "Well, don't you know the proverb? Women's hair is long and reason short. Thus, it is beyond your reason *[Ne tvoego uma]*." Similarly, the whirling prophets used to state, according to Nečaev's survey, that they spoke 'beyond their own reason' *(ne ot svoego uma)*.

The 'strange tongue' *(strannyj jazyk)* of the ecstatic prophecies revealed not only salient, tangible uniformities, but also curious similarities with the abstruse vocables of children's 'game preludes' and of charms, in particular the same penchant for unusual phonemes like *f* and clusters such as *n + t* or *d*, alone or followed by *r*. We can also compare the Khlysty texts of the eighteenth century with the American Pentecostal glossolalia of our time. In the prayer of a Presbyterian minister which consists of 28 "sentences" or "breath-groups" (Samarin

1972a: 77f.), we observe 40 *ndr* and 30 *ntr* clusters, plus 11 *nd* and *nt;* it begins with the sentence or breath-group *kupóy shăndré filé sundruku-mă shăndré lása hóya tăkí,* and is built up of similar groups. Two brief samples of neo-Pentecostal glossolalic discourse, one of 43 and the other of 38 seconds (Samarin 1972b: 129), comprise 15 *nd* combinations each. Both of F. Goodman's (1969) short examples of glossolalic texts abound with *nd* and *nt* phonations (cf. also Samarin 1972a: 115f.). This international inclination toward combinations of *n* with *d* or *t,* which perhaps can be interpreted as prenasalized stops (cf. Ladefoged 1971a: 33f., and Trubetzkoy, 1939a/1969: 169), is astonishing indeed.

Before allowing some generalized inferences, such examples of cross-cultural correspondences in glossolalic, one might add "supra-conscious", verbal art, demand a comprehensive international and interdenominational collection of records of glossolalia in the widest sense of this Greek term. Here again, one must remember the simultaneously reassuring and warning legacy of Boas about the frequency and relative inconstancy of similar properties in different languages (cf. above, p. 206). The dependence of glossolalic texts on the sound pattern of the emitter's native language as well as on individual variations in the makeup and distribution of repetitive sound groups concurs with the common ubiquitous principles of structuring a half-improvised and half-traditional esoteric composition of quasi-words.

The same conjunction of convergent and divergent factors may be, perhaps with a stronger emphasis on tradition than on improvisation, observed in the widespread subclass of incantations composed of nonsensical words designed to keep the inscrutable mythical beings to whom the message is addressed at a distance from the addresser and to safeguard the latter. We may cite an example of a magical Russian formula filled with cryptic, imaginary words and chanted for protection against mermaids (RJ IV: 639f.):

Au Au	šixAr*dA* k*A*vd*A*
šivdA v*nozA*	mittA *mino*gAm
k*A*l*A*ndi indi	jAkut*AšmA* bi*tA*š
o*kuto*mi *mi*	nuffAn zi*dimA*

This charm displays a tenacity with its 18 *A*'s (here capitalized) and its twice or thrice hypnotically reiterated sound sequences (here italicized), and again we come across the same cluster: *kalandi indi.*

The awakening and growth of interest in subliminal impulses and products of verbal creativity were manifest in the scientific – especially linguistic, psychological, medical – and literary worlds toward the end of the last century. Individual cases of glossolalia of entranced persons also attracted international attention. In a French Swiss case of somnambulism with glossolalia, a young Genevan lady, Catherine-Élise Muller (known in the international scholarly literature under the pseudonym Hélène Smith), believed that in her trances she communicated in one language with Martians and in another with people of ancient India. She was carefully observed by psychologists, in particular by the popular Geneva professor Théodore Flournoy (1854–1920), who devoted to her case two monographs (1900, 1902), which evoked lively interest within the international intellectual milieu.

Flournoy's Genevan colleague, Ferdinand de Saussure, grew interested in the analysis of her supposedly Sanskrit discourses, examined the records he received, and after transcribing her frenzied utterances, wrote down his detailed remarks. They were reproduced by Flournoy (1900) and were succeeded by a circumstantial critical account on Mlle Muller/Smith's glossolalia by the Paris linguist Victor Henry, whose book *Antinomies linguistiques* (1896) inspired, to note *à propos,* some concepts of the Saussurian *Cours.* The conclusions of both linguists remained surprisingly indecisive. In spite of the evidence that in her rational life the somnambulist knew no Sanskrit and was neither an impostor nor a .publicity-seeker, amidst a *"mêli-mêlo* of syllables" Saussure detected a few incontestable traces of Sanskrit, and among the unintelligible syllables he found no elements "en opposition avec la figure générale des mots sanskrits" (Flournoy 1900: 303; cf. Lepschy 1974; and Todorov 1977: 323–338). No matter what the results of the joint work of linguists and psychologists were in this case, it should be seen as a stimulus for further interdisciplinary steps, and in particular for a bilateral structural analysis of glossolalia also in its individual, delirious manifestations.

VIII. SOUND AS THE BASIS OF VERSE

We have touched upon several types of verbal manifestations in which speech sounds have an immediate relation to meaning or where they function as direct carriers of a latent, concealed imaginary meaning, but notwithstanding their frequency, all the phenomena surveyed are optional in space and time. There is, however, one kind of verbal activity which is omnipresent and necessarily characterized by the greater or lesser self-determination of speech sounds. This is 'poetic language'. In its nuclear meaning, this term is applied to the verse-form of language, and this statement must not lead, as sometimes happens, to misunderstandings. It does not mean that the role of poetry is conceived of as reduced to the sound-form or that the meaning loses its import. Rather, the notion of verse implies the indispensable presence of a certain specific, *ad hoc* organization of the verbal sound matter. Against the generality of this principle one may cite diverse ways of damping or deleting certain metrical conventions in different forms of 'free verse'. However, on the one hand, any vers libre in order to be sensed as verse must, despite its relative freedom, display certain formal constants, or at least nearly constant tendencies, especially in the prosodic organization of syntactic groups and their intonations. On the other hand, free verse is an attenuated form of verse, a compromise between poetic and ordinary language, and presupposes the copresence of stricter verse forms in any given speech community.

The essential fact is the universal coexistence of two poles of language: verse and ordinary prose. The essential mark of the former pole, namely incontrovertible evidence that in verse "equivalence is promoted to the constitutive device of the sequence" (see RJ 1960: 358), has been sufficiently discussed for years and does not need a long exposition: if a syllable is treated as a pertinent constituent of a verse-line, then one syllable is equated with any other syllable of the same sequence, whereas speakers do not measure the number of syllables in their ordinary speech. In a similar way, in certain verse-systems word-stress is assumed to equal word-stress, as unstress equals unstress, and word-stress becomes herewith a spontaneous unit of measure. Likewise, a metrical grading of stresses creates an equality within each grade and a scale of gradation between the different subunits. Correspondingly, prosodic long is matched with long, and short with short, word boundary equals word boundary, absence of boundary equals absence of boundary. Syntactic pause equals syntactic pause, absence of pause equals absence of pause. Briefly, the verse pattern makes a choice of prosodic elements utilized by the meter, and following such a choice, syllables are converted into units of measure, as are stresses and 'morae' (the minimal quantitative units in a language with an opposition of longs and shorts).

All the elements of verse, whether obligatory, or optional, or finally autonomous in a given system, demand an exact linguistic analysis with respect to the sound system of the given language. Sound correspondences become evaluated with regard to the closeness or remoteness of meaning between the morphemes and higher entities to which these sounds belong. Rhyme and alliteration, as well as metrical parallelism, offer manifold examples. Multiform wordplays by themselves are a striking manifestation of the poetic function even outside of poetry. But, notwithstanding varied proofs of speakers' and listeners' thorough attention to speech sounds, the pattern of ordinary language refrains from the promotion of their equivalence to the constitutive device of the sequence.

IX. CHILDREN'S VERBAL ART

The universal existence of poetry and demand for poetry find a powerful corroboration in studies of children's language. In his renowned book *From Two to Five,* the Russian writer Kornej Čukovskij (1882-1969), one of the most experienced specialists in child language, conclusively defended the thesis of the infant's parallel acquisition of language and penetration into poetic rudiments and claimed that "any rhyme gives a child particular joy" and that "rhyme-making at two years of age is a regular stage of our linguistic development. Those children who don't go through such linguistic exercises are abnormal or sick" (pp. 293, 301). Children either string rhyming words together – *bánja-Mánja* 'bathhouse-Mary' – or invent words to rhyme with existing ones – for instance, *cygán* 'gypsy' obtains an invented rhyme-fellow *mygán* – or they constantly chain a set of rhyming nonsense vocables together, like the two-year-old girl observed daily by Čukovskij (p. 301) –

> Kunda, munda, karamunda,
> Dunda, bunda, paramun –

with six instances of the same *nd* clusters we noted in glossolalia (see above, pp. 215 f.).

Anna Kern, who was a friend of Puškin, recollects in her memoirs how a seven-year-old boy invented and, in the poet's presence, recited the following couplet –

> Indijanda, Indijanda, Indija!
> Indijadi, Indijadi, Indija! –

and how Puškin kissed the child and surnamed him "Romanticist." Those two verses again display eight *nd* clusters, common also in such

meaningless trochaic lines as those which children sing dancing in a
ring:

Èndendíne, betetón!
Èndendíne, betetón!
(Čukovskij: p. 308).

As Mary Sanches and Barbara Kirschenblatt-Gimblett point out in
their perspicacious study "Children's Traditional Speech Play and
Child Language" (1976), it has been "found that for young children
and feeble-minded persons, as contrasted to normal adults, the conditioned responses tended to generalize to words whose similarity to the
original stimulus word was determined by features of *sound* rather
than by grammatical and semantic features ⟨...⟩ That children enjoy
playing with sound for its own sake has long been recognized as a
prominent feature of child speech" (p. 78). A typical instance quoted in
the same study is a skillful tongue twister in which eleven otherwise
similar monosyllables alternate their prevocalic velar stop with a dental one and their final velar with a labial:

A skunk sat on a stump.
The stump said, "the skunk stunk."
The skunk said, "the stump stunk."
Which one stunk, the stump or the skunk?

Among the numerous examples of "the child's play with sound"
brought by Ruth Hirsch Weir (1926-1966) in her superb monograph
(1962), she cites a paragraph from the half-dream soliloquy of her two-
year-old son, with a symmetrical distribution of labials and velars:

Like a piggy bank	k p g	b ŋ k
Like a piggy bank	k p g	b ŋ k
Had a pink sheet on		p ŋ̩ k
The grey pig out.	g p g	

(The end of this paragraph reminds us of the 'counting-out' formulas.) Particularly clear-cut in their construction are jocular concatena-
tions of words, alternating their distinctive features one after the other,
such as in an example of Czech children's play quoted by Ohnesorg
(1966): "*Dípa - kípa - títa - bádu - dábu - mábu.*" The directive role of
sounds, their alliterations and assonances in children's argumentation
is beautifully exemplified by H. Wallon (1945: 57):

"La foudre c'est de la poudre."
"Où roule-t-il le soleil? Dans le ciel." [sɔlɛj – sjɛl]
"Comment est fait le ciel? C'est du feu."
"Comment peut-il rouler dans le feu?"
"Enfer ... le soleil est en feu."

The specific kind of children's folklore widespread in the world and known as 'counting-out rhymes', French comptines, Russian sčitalki, Polish wyliczanki, offers in various languages striking examples of the pronouncement which French students term glossolalie ludique. These are ritualized 'game preludes', casting lots for the participants of a game or deciding who will be "it." These 'ludic' performances combine a predilection for strange and alien vocables (cf. Pisarkowa 1975) and the magical intent of incantations with a playful attitude (cf. Bolton 1888; Ferdière 1947; Baucomont et alii 1961; Gump 1965; as well as G. Vinogradov's astute approach to the miniature play-myths of Russian folk children's counting-out formulas [1930]). From a book of wide and unexpected outlooks – Speech Play (1976) – we draw Sanches & Kirschenblatt-Gimblett's example of what they term "gibberish", where "only the phonological rules are observed: the phonological sequences neither form units which have grammatical function nor lexemes with semantic reference" (pp. 92 f.):

> Inty, ninty tibbety fig
> Deema dima doma nig
> Howchy powchy domi nowday
> Hom tom tout
> Olligo bolligo boo
> Out goes you.

One could say that the avoidance of a rational lexis and grammar permits, nevertheless, a rigorous structuration of the whole sextet with its initial three lines of four downbeats per line and subsequent three lines of three downbeats each; the middle line of the latter tercet opposes two disyllabic intervals to the zero intervals of the marginal lines. Only the first and last pairs of lines rhyme, and each line except the final, the only meaningful one, is interwoven by similar and contrastive vowels and consonants.

Child poetry is, without doubt, an imposing creative tradition, and Sanches & Kirschenblatt-Gimblett thoroughly understood its significant difference "from adult verbal art". They noted certain peculiar features in the productions of young children, particularly "the relatively greater importance of phonological structure" and a "greater in-

cidence of nonsense"; but the insistence on alleged "striking irregulari-
ties" and on a child's supposed inability "to conceptualize the whole
form at once" still prevents the detached adult from estimating at its
true worth the organization of a totality such as the magnificent jump-
rope rhyme cited by Sanches & Kirschenblatt-Gimblett from Roger
D. Abrahams' collection (1969: 23), in turn taken over from Norman
Douglas' *London Street Games* of 1916. Jump-rope rhymes are, as Abrahams points out, connected both with counting-out and with divina-
tion (IX):

> ₁Caroline Pink, she fell down the sink,
> ₂She caught the Scarlet Fever,
> ₃Her husband had to leave her,
> ₄She called in Doctor Blue,
> ₅And he caught it too –
> ₆Caroline Pink from China Town.

This six-line spell against a miss in jump-rope, dramatized as the
story of an unlucky jump, is firmly integrated. It is built of two couplets, each with plain rhymes, one feminine *(Fever - leave her),* the other masculine *(Blue - too).* These couplets are embraced by the two marginal lines, the first and the sixth, which are mutually connected by the
rhyme *down - Town,* and by the repetition of the heroine's double
name. The first line is tied together by the inner rhyme *Pink - sink.* The
role of ternary correspondences is striking and they may be associated
with the "triple-skip" of the game (cf. Abrahams: § 15). The triple velars of ₁*Caroline,* ₂*caught* and *Scarlet* reappear in reversed order (mirror symmetry) at the end of the poem – ₄*called,* ₅*caught,* ₆*Caroline.* The
pronoun *she* is repeated thrice. A triple alliteration binds the first two
lines with the last – ₁*fell* – ₂*Fever* – ₆*from* – and ties together the third
line – ₃*her husband had.* The sixth line is bound by three diphthongs
followed by [n]: *Caroline* [ayn] – *China* [ayn] – *Town* [awn]. The name
Caroline is associated with *Scarlet* by a bright paronomasia; and three
different binomials are semantically linked by color associations: *Pink
- Scarlet - Blue.* These three colors as well as the three vowels of their
designations form a triangle: the light *Pink* with its [ɪ], the chromatic
Scarlet with its chromatic (compact) [a] (cf. above, p. 197), and the dark
Blue with its [u]. Thus, the wordplay with colors proves to permeate the
whole piece and the Pink of the beginning returns in the Pink of the
end.

X. SAUSSURE'S *POÉTIQUE PHONISANTE* SEEN FROM TODAY

It is difficult to find in history a cultural epoch of as numerous and patent contradictions, not only within a society but also within any single thinker typical of that time, as the decades bordering the last and the present centuries. The question of antinomies was a favorite topic of authoritative representatives of the epoch such as Ferdinand de Saussure, but even this great linguist's treatment of these internal contradictions remained inherently discordant. One of the general principles of his *Cours* – "caractère linéaire du signifiant" – is at variance with the only work of the same period which he planned and prepared for publication, namely his voluminous inquiry into the paratexts of Latin, Greek, and Vedic poetry. These writings are imprecisely called *Anagrammes,* although the work was to cover a much wider complex of problems. Besides being linearly employed as sense-discriminating elements in the service of higher, grammatical units, speech sounds are invested with their own, plenipotentiary task as verse components. For instance, a vowel in Saturnian verse demands the copresence of an equivalent in some other place within the verse. There is in turn a corresponding and no less strict law for the consonants. All of these constituents are exactly coupled, reiterated in even numbers; hence Saussure adduced his slogan: NUMERO DEUS PARI GAUDET (see Starobinski 1971: 21–23, 33). He underlined that this principle is not confined "to a juxtaposition in a sequence but may act irrespective of any linear order" (p. 47).

A further factor reducing the principle of linearity was Saussure's discovery, recorded by him in a letter of 14 July 1906 – "J'ai pu vous annoncer que je tiens maintenant la victoire sur toute la ligne" (see Starobinski: p. 20) – and acclaimed by Antoine Meillet's declaration "qu'on aura peine à nier la doctrine en son ensemble" (Starobinski: p. 158): most of the ancient poems analyzed by Saussure seemed to reveal to him manifold anagrams alluding to the names of people involved in the plots of these poems; thus these sounds functioned simultaneously in the text proper and in the paratext, and thereby endowed the latter with "une seconde façon d'être, factice, ajoutée pour ainsi dire à l'original du mot" (quoted by Starobinski: p. 31). If Saussure's manuscripts of this massive work had not been spurned for many decades as supposedly "futile digressions", the international struggle for a science of poetics would have received beneficial incentives (cf. Benveniste 1964: 109–114).

Such pages in the creative biography of the Geneva teacher as his concentrated interest in somnambulic glossolalia and his profound passion for the analysis of verse and for poetic anagrams are among the many proofs of his personal and scientific complexity and one of the telling signals which presaged the powerful expansion of vital themes and multiform standpoints facing linguistics now and in the future.

Poetic language has forcefully entered into the field of linguistic research, and notwithstanding the objections, as multiple as they are vapid, of some literary critics shockingly unfamiliar with the new vistas and even with the primary principles of the science of language, linguists are assessing more and more systematically the manifold and intertwined problems of poetic sound shape and grammar, as well as of tropes, figures, and composition. Since both aspects of language, the ordinary and the poetic, are two copresent and coacting universals familiar to the human being from his first linguistic steps, one could with equal right and equal one-sidedness speak about poetry and its 'ungrammaticality' or on the contrary assail ordinary language for its casual, crude, and retrograde grammatical organization and character.

Poetry, whether written or oral, whether the production of experienced professionals or of children, and whether oriented toward or against ordinary language, displays its own peculiar sound shape and grammatical structuration. In particular, the passive prosaic submission of sounds to superposed, grammatical units can never exhaust the task of a poetic work, notwithstanding its epoch, literary school, and the temporarily ruling slogans. The sounds of poetry indispensably carry a distinctly more autonomous task, and their bonds with poetic semantics are not reducible to the ordinary role required from them within these conventional units by the humdrum use of language. In poetry speech sounds spontaneously and immediately display their proper semantic function.

XI. INFERENCES FROM A CUMMINGS POEM

E.E.Cummings' (1894–1962) work has provoked reproaches for being "a kind of baby-talk" and occasioned hostile or perplexed questions, which are ironically echoed in Irene R.Fairley's studies on this poet (1968: 105; 1975: 1): "How is it that he includes so much grammatical irregularity without losing the reader? How can we *explain* the ungrammaticality we find in his poems?" He himself said about his poems: "Everywhere tints childrening, innocent, spontaneous, true" (*Complete Poems:* p. 462). An attentive parsing of one of the fifty texts issued in 1950 (see 1972: 530) demonstrates the poet's "ineluctable pre-occupation with The Verb" (p. 223):

I   ₁love is more thicker than forget
     ₂more thinner than recall
     ₃more seldom than a wave is wet
     ₄more frequent than to fail

II   ₁it is most mad and moonly
     ₂and less it shall unbe
     ₃than all the sea which only
     ₄is deeper than the sea

III   ₁love is less always than to win
     ₂less never than alive
     ₃less bigger than the least begin
     ₄less littler than forgive

IV   ₁it is most sane and sunly
     ₂and more it cannot die
     ₃than all the sky which only
     ₄is higher than the sky

This iambic poem is divided into four stanzas, each of which builds a clear-cut syntactic whole. The beginning of each stanza is signaled by *is* on the first downbeat, preceded either by the subject *love,* which opens the first and third stanzas, or by the anaphoric *it* at the beginning of the second and fourth stanzas.

Each of the four stanzas is divided into four lines. The two odd lines of each quatrain display a closer metrical correspondence with each other than with the even lines; the latter are more similar to each other than to the odd lines. Correspondingly, the lines of each quatrain are connected by alternate rhymes.

All lines of the odd quatrains end with consonants, while all lines of the even quatrains end with vowels. In contrast to the consonantal closes of the preceding, odd quatrains, the vocalic closes indicate the more conclusive character of the even quatrains.

In every odd quatrain the odd lines and in every even quatrain the even lines are bound with each other by regular rhymes (I ₁*forget* – ₃*wet*, III ₁*win* – ₃*begin*, II ₂*unbe* – ₄*sea*, IV ₂*die* – ₄*sky*), whereas the even lines of the odd quatrains, as well as the odd lines of the even quatrains, make use of semi-rhymes which confine the correspondence in terminal sounds to those which follow after the accented vowel (I $_2$re-call - $_4$fail, III $_2$alive - $_4$forgive, II $_1$moonly - $_3$only, IV $_1$sunly - $_3$only). This distribution shows a certain correspondence between the opposition odd ~ even in lines and in quatrains.

All the odd lines contain a larger number of syllables than the even lines. All even lines of the poem are trimeters with masculine endings and thus consist of six syllables. The odd lines of the odd quatrains are tetrameters with masculine endings and thus contain eight syllables each. The odd lines of the even quatrains are trimeters with feminine endings and thus are composed of seven syllables. Hence, the odd lines of the odd quatrains are the only tetrameters of the poem and the odd lines of the even quatrains are the only feminine ones. The shorter length of the even lines contributes to their conclusive character as compared to the preceding odd lines. The four odd lines of the even quatrains have the only feminine closes and all four are bound by the same semi-rhyme -nly.

The phrasing of the lines exhibits an equivalent structure in both odd quatrains, and differs from that of the even quatrains, which in turn are similar to each other. The place of the break falls regularly after an upbeat in the odd quatrains (after I $_1$thicker, $_2$thinner, $_3$seldom, $_4$frequent; III $_1$always, $_2$never, $_3$bigger, $_4$littler), but the even quatrains have their break after the downbeat in the first three lines and after the upbeat only in the final line (II $_1$mad, $_2$less, $_3$sea; IV $_1$sane, $_2$more, $_3$sky; but II $_4$deeper, IV $_4$higher). This difference highlights the final line of the even quatrains and in this way furthers the division of the poem into two octets, each opened by the noun love, the only substantive devoid of article in the poem. Moreover, as a result of this particular phrasing of the final lines in the even quatrains, these lines share their rhythmical profile with the end lines of the odd quatrains: I $_4$more frequent / than to fail, II $_4$is deeper / than the sea; III $_4$less littler / than forgive, IV $_4$is higher / than the sky.

The whole poem reveals a severe selective simplification in the network of grammatical categories and a striking originality in their syntactic exploitation. Only nine "formal" ("grammatical") verbs - all of them finite - occur in the poem: the copula is once in each couplet, with the exception of the sixth, and one modal verb in the second line of each even quatrain - II $_2$it shall unbe - IV $_2$it cannot die. The infinitives of the "lexical" verbs appear only at the end of the line: once in each even quatrain and three times in each of the odd ones.

The poem contains eight nouns, two in each quatrain, but in the odd quatrains they are divided between all four odd lines (I $_1$*love*, $_3$*a wave;* III $_1$*love*, $_3$*the least*), whereas in the even quatrains each line of the even couplets is endowed with one twice-repeated noun, each accompanied in both quatrains by accessory words (II $_3$*all the sea which,* $_4$*the sea;* IV $_3$*all the sky which,* $_4$*the sky*).

The limit between adjectives and adverbs is obliterated. Lexical adjectives never appear in the poem as attributes. All of them are predicatives and function as adjectives or adverbial terms of grading: either superlatives (II $_1$*it is most mad and moonly;* IV $_1$*it is most sane and sunly*) or comparatives, the latter in twelve "*than*-constructions" (cf. Strang 1968: 134 f.). These constructions cover all the lines of the poem except the two mentioned lines with the four analytic superlative forms. The only case of a *than* followed by a clause – I $_3$*more seldom than a wave is wet* – presents us with the sole adjective in the so-called "positive degree of comparison". *Than* occurs four times in the four lines of each odd quatrain, and two *than*'s appear in the even couplets of the even quatrains.

Cummings' poem shares its dominant theme with Edward Sapir's monograph *Grading*, which, like the poem, was composed in the late 1930s. As the latter of these two experts in the mysteries of verbal work and art contended at the beginning of his "Study in Semantics": "Judgments 'more than' and 'less than' may be said to be based on perceptions of envelopment" (1949: 122). The grading gamut deployed along the poem is at the same time subtly intricate and diaphanous. The text begins with a chain of four comparative *more*'s (I_{1-4}) and a superlative *most* (II_1) and at the end returns to the sequence of *most* and *more* in the opposite order ($IV_{1, 2}$); a set of five *less*'s comes between these two *most*'s, and each *less* takes care of two adjectives.

An elaborate system of mirror symmetry underlies the relation between the two odd quatrains. The eight *than*-constructions offer four comparatives with *more* in the first quatrain and, correspondingly, four with *less* in the third one. The initial two comparatives of the first quatrain and the last two of the third one blend analytic and inflectional forms of comparison; moreover they have a spatial denotation (I $_1$*more thicker*, $_2$*more thinner,* etc.). The final two comparatives of the first quatrain and the initial two of the third offer purely analytic comparatives with a temporal denotation (three of which are adverbs: I $_3$*more seldom,* III $_1$*less always,* etc.). All four of the spatial comparatives have their root vowel /ı/ in common, and moreover, the first two have a common initial /θ/. By virtue of the above-mentioned blend, the two polar couplets of the odd quatrains are whimsically underscored: I $_1$*more thicker than forget,* $_2$*more thinner than recall* and III $_3$*less bigger than the least begin,* $_4$*less littler than forgive.* The etymological figure *less littler* is confronted with the substantivized superlative *least* and with the colorful paronomasia *bigger - begin,* which is akin to children's folklore (see above, pp. 221 ff.) and supported by the sequence /gɪ/ of *forgive.* Also, both quatrains help to build a mirror symmetry in their hemistichs. Thus, I $_1$*forget* and III $_4$*forgive* correspond to each other both in sound ([f..g]) and meaning *(forget and forgive),* and the initial couplet of the first quatrain and the final couplet of the third end with disyllabic verb forms (I $_1$*forget,* $_2$*recall;* III $_3$*begin,* $_4$*forgive).* The final line of the first couplet and the initial line of the third end with monosyllabic infinitives introduced by *to,* and I$_3$ and III$_2$ are the only lines in these quatrains with a nonverbal ending *(wet - alive).* The antonymy I $_4$*to fail* - III $_1$*to win* strengthens the mirror symmetry between the two odd quatrains.

The *than*-constructions in the even quatrains, two in each, differ from those of the odd quatrains: each of the even quatrains includes a pair of *than*-constructions in which the second is subordinated to the first. Unlike those in the odd quatrains, these subordinating constructions contain neither an adjective nor an adverb superposed to the *less* of the second quatrain or to the *more* of the fourth: II $_2$*and less it shall unbe* $_3$*than all the sea* or IV $_2$*and more it cannot die* $_3$*than all the sky.* Conversely, the final subordinated *than*-construction of each of the even quatrains makes use of inflectional comparatives and, in contradistinction to those in the odd quatrains, does not resort to the *less* or *more:* II $_4$*is deeper than the sea* and IV $_4$*is higher than the sky.*

Each of the even quatrains is endowed with a sequence of a temporal and a spatial *than*-construction. The three concluding lines of the second quatrain (II$_{2-4}$) suggest that the extinction of love is a less imaginable event than the disappearance of *all the sea* which excels any sea in depth, and four words with identical vowels underscore the imagery: II $_2$*unbe* - $_3$*sea* - $_4$*deeper* - $_4$*sea.* The three-line finale of the poem varies and reinforces the same motif: the death of love is more inconceivable than that of the firmament which surpasses the height of the skies; here four identical diphthongs underscore the imagery: IV $_2$*die* - $_3$*sky* - $_4$*higher* - $_4$*sky.*

A pivotal task in the structuration of the poem is achieved by sound figures which permeate and embrace the whole. Among word-initial consonants, two sonorants – /m/ and /l/, each occurring nine times – play the leading alliterative role in the poem. The nasal /m/ is centered around the upward terms *more* and *most;* the liquid /l/ is centered around the downward *less* and *least* and moreover heads the principal noun of the whole work, *love,* which out of all the nouns of the poem is the only one to appear as the first syllable of verse lines. Except in the first line of the poem *(love is more thicker),* the initial /m/ and /l/ never belong to the same line and the alliterative /l/ is confined to the span between the two only occurrences of the superlative *most* (II_1 and IV $_1$*it is most*): II $_2$*less,* III $_1$*love – less,* $_2$*less,* $_3$*less – least,* $_4$*less littler.* As to the *m*-alliterations in the poem, the fourfold *more* of the whole first quatrain is crowned in the fifth line by the superlative *most mad and moonly* and supported by another labial triplet, I $_1$*forget – $_4$frequent – $_4$fail.* At the threshold of the final quatrain the chain of alliterative liquids is stopped by the couple IV $_1$*most – $_2$more* which in inverse order repeats the sequences I $_4$*more – II $_1$most.*

The triplet of successive alliterative /m/'s proves to be favored by Cummings, and a sentence of eleven syllables which opens another of his poems – *i met a man under the moon on Sunday* (p. 355) – displays three initial /m/'s and five /n/'s in other positions, twice in the salient glossolalic cluster /nd/ *(under, Sunday).*

In the poem "love is more thicker" the onset liquid of *less* underlies the nine-/l/ alliteration; correspondingly, the final sibilant of the same word prompts the six-/s/ alliteration in the even quatrains: II $_{3,4}$*sea –* IV $_1$*sane – $_1$sunly,* $_{3,4}$*sky.* The sole other appearance of the same initial sibilant – I $_3$*seldom* – carries in its first syllable a perhaps allusive metathesis of *less* before the latter's emergence in II_2 and multiple repetition in III_{1-4}. Jointly with *less, love* also takes part in the liquid alliteration; moreover, the two odd quatrains, opened by this noun, ostensively reiterate its final consonant, and no other words in the poem end with /v/: I $_1$*love – $_3$wave;* III $_1$*love – $_2$alive – $_4$forgive.* The semi-rhymes of the poem such as III $_2$*alive – $_4$forgive* heighten the reader's attention to the likeness of final consonants; III $_1$*love – $_2$alive,* two extreme members of the couplet, form a paronomasia tangible both in sound and in meaning. The correspondence between I $_1$*love* and $_3$*wave* is particularly notable in view of their similar syntactic position, not shared by the other nouns of the poem, as well as in view of the poet's surprising selection of the constant "wetness" as the *tertium comparationis* between a wave and love instead of their changeability, inconstancy, mobility, and similar properties familiar to poetic tradition.

The poem starts with the alliteration of grave nasals /m/ and ends with an alliteration of acute continuants /s/; the perceptive association with dark and light respectively (see above, p. 198) is semantically supported by the paronomastic contraposition of the lines – II $_1$*it is most mad and moonly* as the close of the introductory alliterative motif and IV $_1$*it is most sane and sunly* as the start of the epilogue; with a parallel change in sounds the narrative proceeds from mental and physical shadow into luminosity, with a concomitant semantic transition from II $_4$*deeper* to IV $_4$*higher.*

Besides the three alliterative consonants cited, there occur very few onset consonants in the "lexical" words of the poem. Among them only two sonorants – /r/ and /n/ – appear, each once in the poem in the second line of the two odd quatrains: I $_2$*recall,* III $_2$*never.* The few remaining onset consonants are each represented by one pair of semantically interconnected words or phrases: I $_1$*thicker* – $_2$*thinner,* III $_3$*bigger* – *least begin,* II $_4$*deeper* – IV $_2$*die.* If one takes into account the onset consonants of the two modal verbs also, the II $_2$*shall* raises to three the number of alliterative sibilants in the second quatrain (II $_{3,4}$*sea*), and IV $_2$*cannot* demands to be confronted with the second consonant in the initial cluster of the twice-occurring IV $_{3, 4}$*sky.* Contiguous words with initial vowels are brought together by the identity of adjacent sonorants: /n/ and /l/ in II $_2$*shall unbe* – II$_3$ and IV $_3$*than all* – *only;* /l/ in III $_1$*always* – $_2$*alive.*

As we have indicated in passing, the identity of two or more concatenated vowels under stress acts as an efficient unifier of a verbal and metrical sequence (one may recall how in the third quatrain the individuality and integrity of the concluding couplet is ensured by the chain of four lax /ɪ/'s under the last accent of each hemistich: III $_3$*bigger* – *begin* – $_4$*littler* – *forgive*). The opposition of laxness and tenseness serves to sharpen the contrast between the odd and even quatrains: almost all (over 84 percent) of the accented syllables at the end of the hemistichs are implemented by lax vowels in the odd quatrains and by tense ones in the even quatrains (or also by diphthongs in the fourth quatrain). The first quatrain follows this order in the first three lines but shifts to tense vowels in the fourth *(frequent, fail).* In one out of eight syllables the second quatrain abandons its tense vowels (II $_2$*less*).

Close attention to "love is more thicker" shows how sound correspondences acquire or enhance a semantic propinquity and how they act as kindred submorphemes upheld by a mysteriously complex and cohesive network of metrical, strophic, and compositional means (cf. Reinhart and Tamir-Ghez). The nonlecturer Cummings told his Harvard audience that "art is mystery" (1953: 82). The relative condensation, ostensibility, and self-containment of various parallelistic contrivances counterpose poetry to everyday language, but the significance of the relative differences does not permit us to absolutize the chasm between the two spheres, first and foremost because, as was announced in the epigraph to this book, "the dogged acceptance of absolutes" fetters the mind and benumbs the spirit.

We have pointed out, or rather in his quatrains the poet pinpointed, effective and meaningful pairs of rhyming or alliterative words, but the same consonances exist, somewhat deadened and hidden, in our ordinary speech: for instance, *through thick and thin, forgive and forget, deep-sea, sky-high,* etc. Our puns, whether deliberate or subliminal, stand nearer than one would think to paronomasias, which are a subjacent motivating power in verbal art. The paronomastic pair *Caroline - Scarlet* which we quoted from a jump-rope rhyme, as well as the ancient anagrams discovered by Saussure, such as the name *Scīpio* hidden in the Saturnian verse *Taurasia Cīsauna Samnio cēpit* (see Starobinski 1971: 29), are among the numerous examples of a play on proper names (due to the utterly particular position of names in our vocabulary), a play which the individual inventiveness of children and adults shares with folklore. The latter is ready, for example, to establish a paronomastic and mythopoeic connection between the name of a saint and the seasonal agricultural tasks and forecasts calendrically close to the saint's day, as in the Russian rural omen: "V den' *Mókija mók*ro i vsë léto *mók*roe" – 'If it is *wet* on the day of St. *Mok*ios (May 11), the whole summer will be *wet'* (Dal' II: 339).

Rhymes and other correspondences in the sound formation of words play a prominent, patent role in verbal art, but their latent participation in ordinary linguistic experience must also not be underrated (cf. Bolinger's initiatory study of 1950, "Rhyme, Assonance, and Morpheme Analysis," reprinted in 1965: 203 ff.; M. Bloomfield 1953; and Marchand 1957). Submorphemic etymology (see above, pp. 201 f.) is a vital facet of language. It is noteworthy that the writer of the book *How to Do Things with Words,* John L. Austin (1911-1960), a linguist no less than a logician, at the end of his life worked precisely on a synchronous, submorphemic processing of English lexical material and in conversation with Noam Chomsky asserted the relevance both of these affinities in language and of their investigation.

Valuable information on the speaker's submorphemic operations may be drawn from the "tip of the tongue" phenomenon. Roger Brown and David McNeil devoted a special study to this "state in which one cannot quite recall a familiar word", particularly a proper name, but comes close to it by recollecting words of similar sound shape or by testing *ad hoc* invented vocables because one remembers certain elements of the wanted name: "these more easily retrieved features of low-frequency words may be the features to which we chiefly attend in word-perception" (1966: 325). The number of syllables, the place of the stress, the beginnings and endings of words prove to be traits "favored by attention". One may add that sonorants also are readily recalled. Thus for instance, when one of the authors was unable to recall *Cornish,* the name of a street, he thought instead of *Congress* and *Corinth* and *Concord;* the inner sonorants *r* and *n* common to the 'target word' and to the three substitutes showed their presence in his mind, side by side with the initial consonant and with the syllabic and accentual mold of the searched-for name. The adhesiveness of speech-sound associations may be exemplified by the avoidance in moralistic talks of words bearing even a partial phonic resemblance to some vocables considered obscene.

Notwithstanding the varied proofs of speakers' and listeners' thorough attention to speech sounds, the pattern of ordinary language is nowhere near the autonomous, in fact guiding role sounds and their distinctive features play in poetry, which promotes the deliberate accumulation of similar sounds and sound groups to the constitutive device of the sequence (see above, p. 219). Robert Godel (1967) brought forward a telling example of two opposite approaches to the immediate repetition of one and the same sound group, e.g. a syllable, in a syntactic string: namely, the avoidance of such an iteration in ancient Latin prose and its use as a welcome sound figure in verse, which is rich in duplications such as *Dorica castra* (Virgil, Propertius, Ovid) or *hasta Tago* (Virgil), *hasta Tagen* (Statius), *ista Tages* (Lucan). Once more the spirit of poetry NUMERO DEUS PARI GAUDET.

XII. LANGUAGE AND POETRY

A dynamized tension between *signans* and *signatum* and in particular the direct interplay of the speech sound with meaning – is superimposed by Cummings on his poem and in general by poets upon their creations destined:

to overcome the palling flatness and univocity of verbal messages,

to curb the futile and impoverishing attempts aimed at 'disambiguation',

and to affirm the creativity of language liberated from all infusion of banality.

The passion of the linguist and poet Edward Sapir for the work of the poet and linguist Gerard Manley Hopkins, and particularly for his "almost terrible *immediacy* of utterance", a power spontaneously bound with a "wild joy in the *sheer sound* of words" (1949: 500), reflects both Hopkins' and Sapir's magic insight into the "inscape" of poetic creation. One recalls the nickname "medicine man" assigned to Sapir by Leonard Bloomfield (see Hockett 1970: 540).

That spell of the "sheer sound of words" which bursts out in the expressive, sorcerous, and mythopoeic tasks of language, and to the utmost éxtent in poetry, supplements and counterbalances the specific linguistic device of 'double articulation' and supersedes this disunity by endowing the distinctive features themselves with the power of *immediate* signification. Their *mediate* way of signification totally disappears in the poetic experiments of the early twentieth century, which are parallel to the abstract trend in painting and akin to the magic ingredient in oral tradition (cf. RJ V: 353f.; Liede II: 221ff.). Thus, in rereading the poem "Das grosse Lalulā" of Christian Morgenstern (1871-1914) in his book of *Galgenlieder* introduced by Zarathustra's saying – "a true man conceals in himself a child who wants to play" – one is struck by lines such as *Seiokrontro – prafriplo* and *Hontraruru miromente*, with their glossolalic *ntr*, as well as by the subsequent line *Entepente, leiolente*, which is quite close to counting-out rhymes: the *ente pente* of the *Abzählsreime*. And in fact it was precisely the counters of children's games (such as *éni béni, áni báni*) which inspired the versicle *"Vánja-bánja"* of the famous *Nebesnye verbljužata* 'The Heavenly Baby Camels' by the Russian avant-garde poet Elena Guro (1877-1913).

The ubiquity and mutual implication of Verb and Verbal Art impart a seminal unity to the forthcoming science of the two inseparable universals, *Language* and *Poetry*.

AFTERWORD

The relation of parts and wholes is the fundamental question which faces the science of language in the latter's manifold facets. Any attempt to disregard the mutual connection of parts in their interdependence with the whole displays the "dogged acceptance of absolutes" which, in the terms of Sapir's warning, "fetters" and "benumbs" the mind.

The recognition of the distinctive features and of their autonomous role in language requires their intrinsic analysis; but, on the other hand, the linguist is faced with the equally important and inalienable task of examining the relation of these features to the speech sound as a whole, in all the variety of its properties. All the constituents of the speech sound in its diverse phases from emission to the use and interpretation by the speaker and listener have to be examined and delimited with all the technical contrivances at our present disposal and with a consistent attention to the linguistic functions fulfilled by any component of the sound, because the *whole* of the *speech* sound is an artifact made for the aims of language. No phase of the speech sound can be dismissed by the investigator as quasi-irrelevant.

The study of all the attributes of the speech sound and in particular of the distinctive features must be based on a strict relativity principle which implies a vigilant search for the hierarchic patterning of the different elements. It is evident that a student of language may limit his research to a mere part of these elements. But he would be wrong if he forgot or negated the wider and vital task of integration which must inspire any linguistic analysis.

Any dealings with distinctive features prove to be insufficient so long as the question of their entire system and its underlying laws does not take into account the binary opposition constituting each feature. A catalog of mere contingencies is necessarily superseded by a logical model of the featural network. The hierarchical structure of single oppositions (with a superposed, "marked," opposite), of their combinations, and of their interrelations becomes the fundamental problem of analysis. This analysis is strongly corroborated by the recent discoveries of the relations between language and each of the two hemispheres of the brain and requires a further and deepening cooperation of linguists with the neurologists investigating these problems of dazzling significance.

The inquiry into the relation between the sound shape of language and the latter's grammatical structure must take into account the two differing functions of the distinctive features, sense-*discriminative* and sense-*determinative,* neither of which should be ignored.

Neither the divergences nor the convergences in the makeup of the distinctive features can be minimized. A rigorously relational approach to the features shows, for instance, that neither the hidebound concentration on convergence nor the biased negation of convergence does justice to such basic phenomena as the mutual affinity and diversity of vowels and consonants. Let us repeat that there is no autonomy without integration and no integration without autonomy.

The two essential focuses of linguistic investigation, one upon invariance and the other upon variation, are sterile separately from each other, and any one-sided exaggeration – one might even say monopolization – of one of the two facets with a disregard for the opposite one distorts the very nature of language. Any system is by definition always mutable, hence the notion of an individual or collective linguistic system, without variation, proves to be a contradiction in terms. The notion of context which furthers variation becomes ever wider and encompasses not only sequential and concurrent neighborhoods in the sound flow but also the diversity of speech styles. And on the other hand, the concept of invariance can no longer be confined to a single language, but the further logical step would be to view the sound patterns of single languages as varying implementations of universal invariants. Spreading efforts to expand the world inventory of distinctive features are enrooted in the unmotivated abandonment of the relational approach with respect to the comparative analysis of different sound patterns.

The growing sense for the interplay of variants and invariance introduces and strengthens the notion of dynamic synchrony and removes the traditional antinomy synchrony/diachrony. It becomes really outdated from a relativistic standpoint to confine one's treatment of linguistic matter to a mere description or a mere history. Also, such notional dualisms as competence/performance or innate/

acquired prove to be indivisible, as for instance may be exemplified by explanatory truisms such as "language cannot be learned without the capacity to learn it" and "language cannot arise without acquisition from the environment"; likewise, "a perceiver's and/or an emitter's performance is the implementation of his competence" and "competence means the competence of the perceiver and/or emitter to perform". The separation of the concepts, sound change and its diffusion, is an artificial one also, because any change in order to be achieved implies a personal repetition and an interpersonal diffusion.

The roles of the addresser and the addressee in verbal communication are two inseparable topics of investigation; and inner speech, an important variety of this double theme, means the assignment of the two roles to one and the same person. Both forms of speech (inner and outer) are two closely interconnected processes of communication, and cognition plays a substantial role in both of them. One must take persistently into account the activities of communication and cognition in both their *inter*personal and their *intra*personal aspects.

The distinctive features and their concurrent and sequential bundles (phonemes and syllables) differ from all other constituents of language through the lack of their proper, immediate signification. Their only *signatum* is that of 'mere otherness', or in Sapir's terms, they carry "no singleness of reference." Without having their own meaning they serve to differentiate the meanings of the grammatical units to which they pertain, morphemes and words. Their inner organization is built on the principle of most effective perception and recollection. And this merely mediate characteristic appears as their only load so long as language is taken in its narrowly rational application.

However, any distinctive feature is built on an opposition which, taken apart from its basic and conventional linguistic usage, carries a latent synesthetic association and thus an immediate, semantic nuance. This *immediacy* in signification of the distinctive features acquires an autonomous role in the more or less onomatopoeic strata of ordinary language. The habitual relation of *contiguity* between sound and meaning yields to a bond of *similarity*. This phenomenon goes beyond the limits of onomatopoeias proper and succeeds in creating submorphemic links between words of diverse origin. It is this similarity in sound and meaning which even assumes an active role in reviving or condemning lexical archaisms and in furthering viable neologisms.

The significance of the play on words *(jeu de mots)* in the life of language should not be underestimated: the vocalic association of the designations for *day* and *night,* with the light ~ dark contrast for a Slav, and with slower ~ quicker for a Frenchman, brings about, as Lévi-Strauss put it, *une petite mythologie* (cf. above p. 196, and 1976/1978).

The tension between two structural principles – contiguity and similarity – permeates the whole of language. If, as mediate building blocks of meaningful entities, the distinctive features serve to connect sound and meaning by virtue solely of contiguity, the inner sound symbolism peculiar to these features strives to burst forth and to sustain an immediate similarity relation, a kind of equivalence between the *signans* and the *signatum.* Besides the conventional *thései* relations, such a direct semantization of the sound shape comes into play.

And it is precisely 'play' and the mythopoeic transforms of language which help to dynamize the autonomous semantic potential of the distinctive features and of their complexes. Poetry, as a purposeful, mythopoeic play, is the fullest, universal accomplishment of the synthesis between contiguity and similarity.

The analysis of the two closely interconnected synthetic powers of poetry – that of similarity and contiguity and that of selection and combination – is a burning task faced by our science. Any fear of or reluctance about the analysis of the poetic transformation of language impairs the scientific program of those linguists who pull back from the pivotal problem of this vital transformation; and likewise it curtails the research of those literary scholars who, in treating poetry, pull back from the innermost problems of language.

Among the varied and intricate questions proffered by the sound shape of language, that of *the spell of the speech sounds* appears to acquire a particular attention. In her recent survey, Eli Fischer-Jørgensen rightly states that not only the "potential symbolic values" of the distinctive features but also their universal character has been widely documented. Certain instances, and in particular her comparison of West African linguistic data with her own experiments on Danish subjects, "show clearly that these values are not dependent on specific languages and cultures" (1978). The perceptual universality of these values shows certain limitations and an unevenness of distribution, due to the differences in the repertory of features in given languages. Therefore, the author wisely supports "the hypothesis of *almost* universal values". The frequent predilection of linguistic inquirers for 'absolute', exceptionless universals, as preferred to 'near' universals, clashes once

more with Sapir's warning against the "dogged acceptance of absolutes". Probability near to certainty but still less than 1.0 is as signal a
phenomenon as probability 1.0.

The inquiry into the acquisition of language, into the changes of
language, and into the aphasic losses - or in other words the inquiry
into the structuration, restructuration, and destructuration of language
- must deal primarily with lawful tendencies without any superstitious
fear of exceptions and without any prejudice which would assume that
there are only two possibilities: either an absolute rule or an absolutely
blind chance. The Saussurian vision of linguistic dust *(poussière linguistique)* far from disintegrating linguistics, widens its vistas in the
search for general laws. And just as Saussure's notion of linguistic dust
does not undermine his idea of system and its general laws, in the same
way, the "linguistic antinomies" discovered throughout centuries do
not authorize us to undermine the unity (or more exactly, the 'bi-unity')
of approach to language and to its sound shape in all its real multi-
formity, nor to close our eyes to the contradictions to be removed.

> January 1977 - November 1978
> Ossabaw Island, Georgia -
> Peacham, Vermont -
> Cambridge, Massachusetts

APPENDIX ONE

THE ROLE OF PHONIC ELEMENTS
IN SPEECH PERCEPTION

R. Jakobson's paper presented at the 18th International Congress of Psychology, Moscow, August 8, 1966, in Symposium 23: Models of Speech Perception, and reproduced in *Zeitschrift für Phonetik, Sprachwissenschaft und Kommunikationsforschung* 21, 1968, 9-20.

A Russian listener may be faced with an elliptical, unexpected utterance: four combinations "nonsyllabic plus syllabic." If he has identified the first two syllables as /ján'i/ and the further two vowels as /a/ and /ú/, the most probable guess will be that the sentence begins with the pronoun /já/ 'I' and the negative particle /n'i/ and that the subsequent two syllables belong to a verb with the 1. pers. sg. pres. desinence /ú/. NB: we resort to the usual "broad notation". The vowel /a/ of such verbal roots may be preceded by some thirteen and followed by some eighteen different nonsyllabic phonemes. The tentative grouping of the sequential input into words presents the decoder with the necessity of making his choice among 42 extant, phonemically distinct verbs since all of them fit into this pattern. He can do it only by detecting the phonemes in question: for instance, verbs in /ar'ú/ begin with eight diverse consonants, and in five verbs the initial syllable /pa/ may be followed by a different phoneme: /pajú, par'ú, pal'ú, pašú, pasú/.

Even if the predicate is accompanied by an object, e.g. /kós/, and the listener, anticipating the probable topic of the message, correctly decodes this monosyllable as the gen. or acc. pl. of /kazá/ 'goat', he is still confronted with 26 semantically and syntactically appropriate verbs, as long as the nonsyllabics of the verbal root have not been properly identified: /pajú/ 'water', /dajú/ 'give' or 'milk', /tajú/ 'conceal', /dar'ú/ 'grant', /par'ú/ 'whip', /var'ú/ 'cook', /mar'ú/ 'starve', /kar'ú/ 'scold', /pal'ú/ 'burn', /val'ú/ 'knock down', /sal'ú/ 'corn', /kal'ú/ 'slaughter', /man'ú/ 'beckon', /gan'ú/ 'drive', /ran'ú/ 'drop', /zavú/ 'call', /pasú/ 'graze', /važú/ 'guide' or 'convey', /našú/ 'carry', /mačú/ 'soak,' etc. – A further clause may be added to this message, e.g. /um'in'á iták xlapót pólan rót/ 'As it is I have a lot of trouble', yet the identification of the two phonemes at issue still remains indispensable as long as neither the context nor the situation (the non-verbalized context) provides the recipient with the necessary clue.

When the phonemes are recognized and the verb is identified as /dajú/, the decoder has still to choose between two homonyms – 'I milk' and 'I give' – since the vowels of both roots, which are distinct under stress (cf. /udój/ 'milking' and imp. /dáj/ 'give'), merge in unstressed position. The monosyllable /kós/ may be in turn a gen. plur. either of /kazá/ 'goat' or of /kasá/ 'scythe', because voiced and voiceless obstruents merge in final position. Hence as long as the context does not secure an unequivocal solution, the identically sounding clause admits at least three interpretations: 'I do not milk goats', 'I do not give goats', or 'I do not give scythes'. Again and again we must insist on the perceiver's probabilistic attitude toward the verbal input; he cannot do without phonemic discrimination, and to break the homonyms he looks for cues in the heteronymous and unsensical context. For the encoder homonymy is naturally devoid of any ambiguity, whereas the decoder may find no cue to decipher a homonym even in its verbal environment. Such questions as "Would you like hot ['warm' or 'peppery'] food?" and "Do you want a light ['light-color' or 'light-weight'] dress?" easily give rise to misunderstandings. When the young Majakovskij responded to Tolstoj's *Vojná i mír* 'War and Peace' by the punning name of his poem *Vojná i mír* 'War and the world' (1916) with an emphasis on a more international, universal scope of this epic, the subsequent reform of Russian spelling (1917) abolished the conventional, purely graphic difference between the homonyms *mír* 'peace' and *mír* 'world', and in view of the fact that both war and peace are treated on a world scale by Majakovskij, the context is unable to disambiguate the title of his poem.

It is evident that phonemic clues permit the listener to catch some word-and-clause contours before his complete identification of the verbal input. It is likewise obvious that the large number of redundancies enables the perceiver of a given message to skip some of its phonological as well as morphological and lexical components. Not only the production of our speech but also its perception may be elliptical to a high extent, and in the same way as the speaker easily translates any elliptical subcode into the optimal, explicit code of his language (labeled "full style" by Ščerba 1915), the listener in turn easily converts his "elliptical" perception into an explicit text.

In speech perception different levels of contextual constraint upon the phonemes, such as the syllable, the word, and the syntactical structure, appreciably restrict the range of expectations. The cognition of a verbal sequence involves not only instant and direct detection but also extrapolating anticipation, and on the other hand the retroactive power of immediate memory. Despite the deep embeddedness of phonemes in the formal and semantic environment, the number of strictly autonomous decisions which are required for the identification of phonemes in an utterance and cannot be deduced from any grammatical rules remains very sizable, as was exemplified by the Russian clause cited above and as may be corroborated by innumerable further illustrations.

The substantial difference between the encoding and decoding operations in verbal behavior is eloquently documented by the typology of aphasic disorders, and namely by the striking dissimilarity between the so-called motor, predominantly encoding, and the so-called sensory, primarily decoding impairments. It is particularly significant that the latter type of aphasia, in contradistinction to the former type, is characterized by the loss of those syntactical, morphological, lexical, and phonemic elements which are not determined by the context. In particular, the less some components of a phoneme are dependent on their simultaneous and sequential environment, the sooner they are subject to deletion (RJ II: 289 ff. and 307 ff.). Disturbances in phoneme-finding lay bare the strictly discriminatory selective operation as the immediate aim of the decoding process.

The universal ability of natives to discern the phonemic constitution of various utterances produced even at a most rapid speed faces the inquirers with a quite tangled problem. Although it has been repeatedly acknowledged that such fast consecutive discernment requires a latent conversion of the continuous flow of speech into an array of ultimate discrete linguistic elements, some impediments seemed to interfere with such an assumption. These controversies, however, have been actually engendered by the tenacious habit of treating the phoneme as a further indivisible linguistic unit, whereas the dissolution of the phoneme into distinctive features as its ultimate components dispels all the temporary inadequacies as soon as the distinctive features assume a cardinal position in our models of speech perception.

Contemporary research on the neurophysiological foundations of perception places particular stress on "the role of central factors in perception" and on the "centrally-induced control of sense data", as Bruner (1958) states. His illuminating study on neural mechanisms in perception adduces "the categorial nature of perceptual identification" and points out that "the equivalence of stimulus events is a function of certain invariances in relationship". In our perceptual faculty "we come to identify constancies, treating as equivalent objects that have been altered drastically in all respects save their defining attributes".

In Adrian's formulation (1954), "at some stage the complete report from the sense organs must be subjected to an editing which emphasizes the important items and sets the unimportant aside". A polarization method used by the nervous system changes our percepts into concepts.

The lessons of this research carry implications relevant for the insight of the role played by the distinctive features in speech perception. On the plane of psychological reality those features act as percepts which convert the continuum of their physical substratum into discrete polarized attributes. So long as these criterial attributes are present, the distinctive features maintain their identity regardless of intense contextual changes in the physical stimuli. Sapir ([1933] 1949) compared the elementary units of language with "notes, which, in the physical world, flow into each other in an indefinite continuum" but which, in terms of musical scale and composition are tangibly distinct entities "definitely bounded off against each other" (RJ II: 334ff.).

The transformation of physical items into a set of purely discriminative signals as the fundamental device of language and of speech perception was disclosed in Sweet's deliberations of the seventies (1877) on "the independently significant differences," and at the same time Baudouin de Courtenay (1877) pointed out the strictly relational character of these differences conceived as binary oppositions. The latter concept was further elucidated by Saussure (1916) and necessarily led these three linguists to the first inklings of distinctive features as the ultimate differential elements, endowed with "a purely oppositive, relative, and negative value" (according to Saussure; cf. Godel 1957). In a similar way Baudouin (1910; 1963: 246ff.) finished by interpreting the phoneme as a chordlike complex of elementary, indivisible components, and since they are discernible both on the motor and on the acoustical level, he labeled them "kinacousmata".

The last thirty years have witnessed a thorough development of these ideas and their application to concrete linguistic analysis (cf., e. g., RJ I and Muljačić's 1964 pithy outline). The scrutiny has shown a highly restricted repertory of distinctive features which occur in the languages of the world and a still narrower selection of these features for their use in any particular system of language. The coexistent features have proved to display rules of hierarchical patterning which are either universal or characterize a certain phonological type of languages or specifically one given language. New data on sound patterns of a widened range of languages, valuable though still fragmentary and waiting for a true linguistic analysis (see especially Ladefoged 1964), despite the claim of their collectors do not challenge description in terms of the propounded categories but suggest a more exact and capacious redefinition for some of them.

The number of features in any language is a small subset of the multiple of its phonemes, and the number of features within any phoneme is smaller than the total list of features displayed in the given language. The inventory of phonemes in turn, as was repeatedly stated, is a minor submultiple of the number of smallest meaningful units. Because the distinctive features, which are signals deprived of their own meaning and serving mainly to discriminate meaningful units, are limited in number, the listener is able to recognize and memorize these ultimate components of the speech sequence. The dichotomous scale imposed by them upon sound matter provides both the perception of speech and the acquisition of language with an efficient tool: the copresence of both polar terms in our mind makes binary opposition more effective than contingent duality, where neither of the two members can predict something about the other one (see Pos 1938). The mathematical foundations of such operative binary systems have been submitted to an enlightening analysis (see Ungeheuer 1959 and Bruck 1958). Sound signals with six simultaneous variables proved to be accurately identified by the listener only if he knew in advance what dimensions he had to focus on, and if each of them faced him with a binary selection (see Pollack & Ficks 1954). These conditions and consequences appeared to be similar to the perception of phonemes as bundles of concurrent distinctive features since "any minimal distinction in a spoken message confronts the listener with a two-choice situation" (see G. Miller 1956). In short, "the binary distinctions provide a way of simplifying the patterns on which the identifying mechanism acts" (Licklider 1952; cf. Wason 1961). Incidentally, the discrimination activities exerted by the central nervous system are generally supposed to involve a digital process, in particular a binary digit, especially for the identification of purely discriminative stimuli (cf. Žinkin [1958] 1968).

The more a message is creative, unusual and unlooked-for, the lower is the amount of redundancy and predictability and the greater must be the attention paid by the decoder to the minimal components of the utterance. When we start an outline of linguistic universals or a unilingual description by examining the groundwork of language, first and foremost we treat its semiotic rudiments, namely the distinctive features and the intrinsic laws of their combinability into bundles and sequences, with a consistent reference to the physical data processed and converted into "sense-discriminating" elements (*smyslorazličitel'nye*, according to the apt Russian designation used by Čistovič et al. 1965). On this level the meaningful morphological units remain merely distinguished but undefined and unclassified. The differentiation and specification of the diverse grammatical classes of morphemes and their combinations belong to the next, higher level of semiotic functions. The two aspects of grammar, and particularly of morphology, are termed by Sapir (1921) – "grammatical processes" and "grammatical concepts". That part of morphology which is concerned with processes must investigate the phonemic composition of morphemes and the formal differences between the grammatical classes of morphemes and words, namely differences in number, order, and selective set of phonemes and features. With the gradual improvement of linguistic analysis, paradigms change from mere catalogues into coherent systems of structured convergences and divergences. In accordance with this development, the difference between traditional *Formenlehre* and so-called morphophonemics vanishes and the former actually turns into the latter. This merger became imminent as soon as the earlier exclusive preoccupation of morphophonemics with phonemic alternations within identical morphemes was supplemented with an inquiry into phonemic syncretisms and dissimilarities within total classes of morphemes.

Thus, two different functions carried by the assemblages of distinctive features become patently demarcated; their basic, sense-discriminating capability is complemented by a sense-determining performance: the distinctive features and their assemblages serve to mark the unity and mutual diversity of various morphemic classes. Two autonomous and at the same time closely interconnected levels of linguistic analysis correspond to these two functions. The latter is posterior in children's gradual acquisition of language: in its early, holophrastic stage the infant raises the variety and combinability of distinctive features and their discriminative load before proceeding to the next stage – the rise and growth of syntax and morphology.

The far-reaching difference between the sense-discriminating and sense-determining, formative devices must be carefully taken into account in our scrutiny of speech perception. So far as distinctive features are used in their purely discriminative function (cf. the phonemic makeup of the Russian verbal roots discussed above) possibilities of utilizing grammatical cues for their identification by the speech perceiver decrease to a minimal degree.

"Only feature notation has linguistic significance" (Chomsky & Halle 1965); it must be particularly stressed that in contradistinction to the usual transcription of unresolved phonemes, the analytical feature notation shows what distinctions actually face the perceiver in the phonemic sequence.

In the 1930s the technical development of motor phonetics and the use of X-ray records for the study of speech production revealed the wide effects of coarticulation, which overthrow the division of the speech flow into distinct segments with definite articulatory boundaries (see Menzerath & Lacerda 1933). With the subsequent progress of acoustic studies and experiments, quite similar conclusions have been established on the physical level of speech sounds: evidence shows that it is not possible to assign observable acoustical boundaries to phoneme segments. A. M. Liberman et al. (1965) affirm: "There is no way to cut the acoustic signal along the time dimension so as to recover segments that will be perceived as separate phonemes; the acoustic representations of the phonemes overlap and intermix. ..." Chomsky's (1964) pointed critical remarks against certain grave shortcomings and discrepancies in recent phonological tenets convincingly denounce the treatment of phonemes as indivisible, ultimate units, but lose their edge when applied to the analysis of the distinctive features consistently defined in relational terms.

The quest to find coincidence between the boundaries of different concurrent features is due to the obsolete belief in the supremacy of phonemes and to an underestimation of the relative autonomy of features. Each feature presents its own boundaries and the temporal set of consecutive features displays an unswerving order. On the level of features sequential segmentation offers no intricacies. As Čistovič (1961–62) observed, the acoustic chain of distinctive features can be watched by the perceiver in their linear succession.

In the fascinating experiments of Čistovič et al. (1965), Russian phrases subjected to acoustical distortions engendered very instructive errors in their recognition by the listeners. E. g. /fs'ófpróšlam/ 'everything in the past' was grasped as /fxótplátnaj/ 'paid entrance'. Both the output and the input each comprises eleven phonemes; the vowels, two stressed and one unstressed, keep precisely the same place in both sequences; also the three sonorants of each sequence (r, l, m, and l, n, j) occupy an identical position. The auditor retained the voicelessness of the five obstruents; in the input three of them share at least one further distinctive feature with their counterpart in the output (/s'/ and /x/ are continuant, /f/ and /t/ diffuse, /š/ and /t/ acute). Among the eight nonsyllabics only two do not neighbor with vowels; they are also the only two which fully coincide in the output and input: /fs'ó/ – /fxó/ and /ófpró/ – /ótplá/. Apparently a special effort of attention and discrimination was paid by the decoder to consonants deprived of those formant transitions which favor a retrospective or anticipatory recognition. In short, even without having totally identified all the consonants heard, the perceiver nevertheless finds out and remembers certain of their features which enable him to assign each of these consonants to one or another class of phonemes (Čistovič 1955).

Various cases of overlapping collected by Bloch (1941) concern only the status of phonemes but find no analogues in application to features. Each feature displays its own binary opposition different from the oppositions displayed by the other extant features unless in certain contexts one of the features changes into another (diachronical overlap) or unless in certain elliptical subcodes of the given language both features merge (stylistic overlap).

The concurrent and sequential bits of information implemented in an utterance stand in a one-to-one relation with the distinctive features, provided that the nonelliptical, explicit phonemic code has been used by the utterer (compare with Halle & Stevens 1964). Certainly any distinctive feature undergoes manifold variations dependent on both the concurrent and the sequential phonemic environment (cf. Ivanov 1962). Under all these variations any given feature is, however, represented by its relational, polarized, topological invariant, as long as the feature is not obliterated in the utterance, and as long as the phonemic code is common to the encoder and decoder, so that the latter can promptly match the percept to the familiar model which exerts a normalizing tendency in his percepts (see Bruner 1958).

An instructive example of the relational invariance of a feature under the contextual variations is presented by Bondarko & Zinder (1966): the upward shift of pitch remains an unaltered invariant mark of the Russian consonantal opposition sharp ~ plain, whatever are its varying implementations conditioned by combinations with different concurrent and/or subsequent features (higher spectral level at least in one of the consonantal phases or an *i*-like formant transition to the following vowel). Further observations of the same authors prove once more the imperative necessity of matching the opposites solely within identical phonemic contexts *(ceteris paribus)*, e.g. the grave ~ acute continuants in the sequence *afa-asa, ufu-usu*. Although "on a relational basis the grave/acute opposition is still retained" in natural speech (Fant 1970), the artificial cutout of the prevocalic *f, s* from their vocalic environment distorts their authentic phonemic relation. Similarly the forcible cutout of an English interconsonantal lax *l* from its compulsory consonantal environment naturally impedes the perceptual discrimination (K. Stevens 1966).

The examples repeatedly adduced against the principle of invariance are hardly conclusive. The word *sólnce* 'sun' occurs in Moscow Russian with a reduction of /l/ into a downward formant transition of the preceding /ó/ (cf. Ščerba 1912 on the polyphthongal structure easily adopted by Russian stressed vowels). This *w*-like transition with the following cluster /nc/ has its counterpart in the intervocalic cluster of gen. /gárnca/ 'dry measure' where the vibrant, discontinuous /r/ remains opposed to the residual /l/. The "full style," however, restores the liquid phoneme of /sólnca/, whereas another variety of Moscow Russian simply discards any trace of /l/, gives rise to an automatic alternation /sónca/ – dim. /sólniška/, and rhymes /sónca/ – /akónca/ 'little window'. Another example has been taken from Malécot's (1960) article about the frequent American English pronunciation of forms such as *camp, can't, hint,* and *bunk* with an anticipatory vocalic nasality and an attenuation of the nasal consonant. As a rule the "vestigial nasal consonant" is present, and therefore neither the makeup of the sequence nor the invariance of the consonantal nasality feature is impaired. Nay, the reduction of the nasal consonant depends on the "speed of utterance", and the optimal, explicit code which underlies all the derived, elliptical subcodes reinforces the nasal consonant. The third case frequently discussed in this connection is the distinction of the intervocalic *t* and *d* in American English. Such pairs as *latter – ladder* or *writer – rider* are on the threshold of discriminability and subject to frequent confusions (see Oswald's 1943 experiments), especially in a slovenly fashion of speech (Sapir [1933] 1949). The more explicit is the code used, the stronger is the tendency to hold the lax and tense varieties apart. The most stable cue to the distinction of tense and lax phonemes remains the greater duration of the former. The tense consonant

in such forms as *latter, writer* displays a relative length of the consonant and relative shortness of the antecedent syllabic, in contrast with
the relative shortness of the consonant and relative length of the antecedent syllabic in *ladder* and *rider* (see Jakobson & Halle 1964). In
the speedier subcode this difference in quantitative relation between V
and C can be expressed chiefly or only by the varying duration of V,
but one must repeatedly caution against a feature analysis based on elliptical transforms of the optimal code!

It is evident that speech production and perception are two coupled
mechanisms, each of which affects the other. The articulatory process
involves an auditory feedback and proves to be disturbed when the latter is delayed (cf. Huggins 1966) and in a similar way speech perception is normally complemented by a motor feedback (cf. A. M. Liberman et al. 1965). However, this unquestionable sensorimotor coordination (cf. D. M. MacKay 1966 and Haggard 1966) can hardly justify any
speculation on the primacy of articulatory representation in speech
recognition. One can only agree with Gunnar Fant (1966) that "the
motor theory of speech perception has perhaps gained more interest
than it deserves". The participation of motor feedback is not at all an
indispensable condition for the identification and discrimination of
verbal messages. A passive acquisition of foreign languages usually
precedes their contingent active mastery. Russians in the Caucasus often learn to understand one of the local languages and to discern by
ear its sixty or seventy consonants without being able to reproduce
them or even grasp the articulatory model of such frequent Caucasian
phonemes as the glottalized stops. Many Russians and Poles when listening to Czech speech perfectly distinguish its sibilant vibrant /ř/
from the nonvibrant sibilants /ž, š/ and from the nonsibilant /r/ of the
Czech phonemic pattern without being able to mimic this sound or to
grasp its productional technique. Many foreigners of diverse languages, while discriminating and correctly identifying the interdentals
in English speech, fail to reproduce them, and substitute the native /s/
or /t/ for the voiceless, and /z/ or /d/ for the voiced interdental. To
approximate these English nonstrident continuants which are absent
in Polish, Poles often resort to their native noncontinuant strident phonemes, the affricates /c/ and /ʒ/: thus the Polish strident plosives
which deviate from the *consonantal* optimum in attenuating the reduction of energy (i. e. the consonantal optimum represented by the mellow plosives) are intended to reflect the English mellow constrictives
which attenuate the *nonvocalic* optimum (i. e. the maximally noisy pat-

tern of the strident constrictives; see Jakobson & Halle 1968). Opposite cases of foreign phonemes reproduced in pronunciation but confused in perception are most exceptional.

Many studies of children's language have disclosed that words which were clearly distinguished in their perceptual experience and memory remained homonymous in their own utterances so long as the phonemic distinctions involved were familiar to the child only on the sensory but not yet on the motor level. One of the numerous examples is Passy's story of the little French girl who still used only diffuse consonants and therefore substituted *toton* both for *garçon* and for *cochon* but protested resolutely when in jest adults called the boy *cochon* and the pig *garçon*, or when they used baby talk and named the pig or the boy both *toton*. "It's not *toton* but *toton*", was the girl's angry reply. From my own files: Bambo Śliwowski, a three-year-old boy of Warsaw, still substituted /a/ for the Polish /o/. When a friend of his parents repeated after him [dapaćáŋgu] instead of the regular [dopoćóŋgu] 'to the train', the outraged child retorted: "One can't say [dapaćáŋgu], one must say [dapaćáŋgu]!" The foreigners and children cited have stored in their memory an adequate table of phonemes and of their sensory actualizations without having grasped the corresponding vocal-tract configurations.

The beginnings of motor speech in a child's development may even be preceded by a stage of totally mute audition and comprehension (labeled *Hörstummheit* in German pedology). The infant easily discerns and grasps the utterances of his surroundings but is not yet equipped for speech production of his own. Finally, we are faced with the cogent cases of children who have thoroughly learned to understand language and master its grammar despite a congenital deprivation of speech (see Lenneberg 1962). Thus the idea of verbal perception by reference to production appears to be a one-sided exaggeration. Van Ginneken's (1907) emphasis on two polar psychological types of language users – one predominantly motor, and the other predominantly sensory – hints at an important variance in the hierarchy of these two levels.

In any case, both on the motor and on the sensory level every distinctive feature is plainly readable and displays the same polarity and invariance when viewed in rigorously relational terms. For example the grave ~ acute feature, acoustically defined as concentration of energy in the lower versus higher frequencies of the spectrum, finds its exact motor correlate in the opposition of the peripherally and medially located constriction. In general, as stated and shown by Fant (1970), "articulation and sound waves never go separate ways". Yet since the motor stage of any speech event is to the acoustical phenomenon as the means to its effect, the relations on the acoustical level seem to give a more efficient key to the generative invariances in relationship than vice versa. Any feature presents a much more conspicuous opposition of its alternatives on the acoustical than on the motor level, so that a listing of distinctive features in terms of their articulatory correlates without any acoustical correspondents inevitably remains an imprecise and inconclusive torso. Malmberg (1956) with his experience equally rich in linguistics and in the diverse aspects of instrumental phonetics prudently concludes that "as a rule, it is easier to find direct correlates of the structural linguistic units in the acoustical than in the physiological substance". In short, all the factual data militate against the conjectural assertion that articulatory movements mediate between the acoustical stimulus and perception (see A. M. Liberman 1957).

I should like to restate (see RJ I) that G. v. Békésy's portrayals of eardrum responses to the manifold Hungarian and German vowels reaffirm the invariant polarity of the distinctive features in a further stage of the speech event. The promising attempts to approach these features directly in terms of percepts (cf. Hanson 1966) suggest a close correlation between the physical stimuli and the perceptual dimensions. The "new emphasis on the role of central factors in perception" will undoubtedly lead to an intensive quest for the neurological stages of the speech event.

Two methodological principles may further the prospective inquiry into speech perception. They could be labeled *autonomy* and *integration*. Each level of language from its ultimate discrete components to the totality of discourse and each level of speech production and perception must be treated with respect both to intrinsic, autonomous laws and to the constant interaction of diverse levels as well as to the integral structure of the verbal code and messages (alias *language* and *speech*) in their permanent interplay. The necessary tie between these two fundamental principles warns the investigator against two traditional blunders. These are on the one hand *isolationism,* which deliberately disregards the interconnections of the parts and their solidarity with the whole, and on the other hand *heteronomy* (or, metaphorically, *colonialism*), which forcibly subjects one level to another's rules and denies the former's own patterning as well as its self-generating development. The same double principle can and must be extended to the

relationship between linguistics and psychology. The linguistic foundations of verbal structure and the psychological problems of speech
intention and perception demand not only a rigidly intrinsic analysis
but also an interdisciplinary synthesis.

APPENDIX TWO

ON THE SOUND SHAPE OF LANGUAGE:
MEDIACY AND IMMEDIACY[1]

by
LINDA R. WAUGH

0.   In our book, *The Sound Shape of Language* (pp. 1 ff. here), Roman Jakobson and I defined and illustrated a new dichotomy which we concluded was crucial for an understanding of the function of sound in language – namely, that of *mediacy* and *immediacy*. It is the purpose of this paper to present in an integrated and concise way the argumentation for this dichotomy.[2]

1.1   It has been recognized, at least since the time of the medieval doctrine *de modis significandi*, that language has two types of patterning: *articulatio prima et secunda* in the medieval terminology, "double articulation" (Martinet 1949, 1957) or "duality of patterning" (Hockett 1959, 1960, Hockett & Ascher 1964) in the modern rendition. Simply stated, language has two types of signs, one of which is purely differential or 'distinctive', and the other of which is directly significative and meaningful. In the case of the first type of sign (e.g., distinctive features – also phonemes as bundles of distinctive features), the *signatum* of the sign has nothing more than *'mere otherness'*. In the case of the second type (e.g., morphemes, words, phrases, sentences, and so forth)[3] the *signatum* has what Sapir called (1949:34) *"singleness of reference"*; it conveys a specific unit of information. The distinctive features (the smallest signs of the first type) are significative only in the sense that they differentiate or discriminate words of unlike meaning,

---

1. Roman Jakobson read and commented on an earlier draft of this paper. Earlier published versions include: "On the Sound Shape of Language", in the *Proceedings of the Deseret Conference on Languages and Linguistics (Annual Meeting)*, 198–215. Provo, UT: Brigham Young University, 1979; and "The Multifunctionality of the Speech Sound", in *Essays in Honor of Charles F. Hockett*, ed. by F. B. Agard et al., 288–302, Leiden: Brill, 1984.
2. Further use by Jakobson of this dichotomy can be found in 1974.
3. In what follows, I will use 'distinctive feature' and 'word' respectively to stand for these two types of signs.

that they carry '(mere) otherness': they are *sense-discriminative* only (see Jakobson, Fant, & Halle 1952; Jakobson & Halle 1956; Jakobson 1968; and pp. 57 ff. here). In fact, the attribute 'distinctive' in the term *'distinctive feature'* means the sense-discriminative properties of sound: those properties which are capable of differentiating between words of different meaning. The 'distinctive features' then are those attributes of sound which signal that a given word in which they occur is, with a probability near-to-one, different from any other word in the language endowed with a different property.

The proviso "with a probability near-to-one" is added here because of the possibility of *homonymy* (e.g., *pair* and *pear* in English) in a given linguistic system. Homonymy limits the sense-discriminative capacity of the features to a probability near to but not equal to one, but it does not cancel this vital function. There exists also the possibility of *doublets* - for example, English *either* (/i/) vs. *either* (/ay/) or Russian *škap* vs. *škaf* 'cupboard'. And yet, because of the sense-discriminative use of the features, there is a tendency for the doublets to be interpreted as evidencing some difference in meaning. In English, therefore, the difference between *either* (/i/) and *either* (/ay/) generally denotes a difference in style of speech or in social background (*either* with /ay/ is felt by many speakers to be more prestigious; witness also the song by Ira and George Gershwin: "You say eether and I say eyether ..."). In Russian, the use of word-final /f/ in a noun signals that the word is still felt as a foreignism. (For further discussion of these two functions of sound, see § 3.1 below.)

It is on the basis of the sense-discriminative capacity of the features that *neutralization* takes place in certain environments, for neutralization is nothing more than the suspension of this sense-discriminative capacity in a given environment - it is the loss of the ability of these features to be sense-discriminative; hence the loss of the features themselves. In Russian, for example, in word-final position, the voiced ~voiceless opposition in consonants is neutralized and an *"incomplete phoneme"* (see p. 31 f. here) results: //P//, //T//, //K//, //F//, //S//, etc. That these incomplete phonemes have no distinctive voicelessness is evidenced by the fact that there are no words in Russian which may be differentiated solely by the presence of absence of voice (e. g., [p] vs. [b]) in word-final position. The implementation of these incomplete phonemes by the redundantly voiceless member of the lost opposition is due to the unmarkedness of voicelessness as against voicing.

The neutralization of an opposition in given environments may lead to alternations in the shape of a given morpheme as it enters into certain combinations: e.g., in the Russian example given above a morpheme may evidence the non-distinctive (redundant) voicelessness of a consonant when it is word-final, in alternation with the distinctive voicelessness or voicing when it is word-medial. This is due entirely to the inner workings of the sense-discriminative system. However, such alternation is not a necessary prerequisite either for the sense-discriminative function of a given feature or for neutralization in a given environment. It is obvious that many languages (especially those with no inflectional system) show no such alternations and yet evidence neutralization. Moreover, in English the compact-diffuse opposition in nasal consonants is neutralized in word-initial position (e.g., [m] and [n] occur word-initially but not [ŋ]), although this has not led to any (major) alternations. And in German the neutralization of the opposition of [s] and [z] leads to alternations when it occurs word-finally but not when it occurs word-initially. On the other hand, the sense-discriminative function is a necessary prerequisite for such alternations. Thus, there is an implicational hierarchy, with the sense-discriminative use of the features being primary and relatively autonomous of alternations in given morphemes.

1.2   As is well known, while distinctive features signal that two words are different in meaning, they do not signal what the meaning difference is: distinctive features do not (at least in their primary usage) signal meanings, if by 'meaning' we mean 'information more specific than otherness' or 'singleness of reference'. And it is in this sense and in this sense only, that distinctive features are 'meaningless' and words 'meaningful': in accordance with the type of *signatum* which each type of sign has, not with the mere fact of having one. All linguistic signs, from discourse to the distinctive features, have a *signatum;* they only differ as to the type of *signatum.* Distinctive features, then, signal only 'differentiatedness': in that sense they have no singleness of reference and carry no unit of specific information; whereas words do have a singleness of reference and do carry a unit of specific information.

Since all the distinctive features have 'mere otherness' in their *signata,* it follows that for them the structure - i.e., the system of relations based on oppositional equivalences and differences - is found only in the *signans,* not in the *signatum* (cf. Jakobson 1972: 78). The *signatum* remains undifferentiated, being merely differential, while the *signans* is differentiated according to binary, oppositional, hierarchical laws of patterning. The distinctive features, then, reflect that area[4] of language where the oppositional structure inheres in the *signans* since the *signatum* gives only "differentiatedness". On the other hand, morphemes, lexical items, phraseology, word order, and so forth, all are part of that area where structure inheres in the *signatum,* according to various hierarchical laws of patterning, and where that structure is coordinated with formal properties as well. However, in this case the hierarchized differences in meaning are not necessarily correlated with consistently hierarchized differences in form – for example, in English, *walked/walks, brought/brings, went/goes, slept/sleeps, was/is,* and so forth, all evidence basically the same meaning opposition (past tense/present tense) but correlate it with a variety of different forms, depending on the lexical meaning of the verb. It is obvious that differences in form exist, but are variously related with the differences in meaning.

Since the distinctive features are only sense-discriminative, they have an *indirect,* a *mediated* relation to meaning: it is only through their use as the *signans* of another sign (for example, a word) that they may be associated with meaning, while the word itself has a *direct,* an *immediate,* a *non-mediated* relation to meaning. Thus, signs with a directly significative *signatum* are made up, in their *signans,* of signs which themselves do not carry meaning. This creates a dialectic tension, an inherent asymmetry, a sharp discontinuity between the *signans* and the *signatum* of any grammatico-semantic sign – a tension which is resolved by the unity of the sign on the one hand, but on the other hand allows for, e. g., the formation of a large vocabulary. We have in a very real sense 'tools to make tools': the general attribute of human beings which is valid for language structure as well.

This is not to say, however, that the distinctive features are merely the smaller units out of which the larger units are built. Clearly there is not a comparison of size to be made between distinctive features and grammatico-semantic features. In addition, in viewing the whole/part relationship which holds for linguistic signs in general (discourse/utterance/sentence/clause/phrase/word/morpheme/syllable/phoneme/distinctive feature) we see that, for the most part, wholes (e. g., words) in which structure inheres in the *signatum* – are made up of smaller parts (e. g., morphemes), which themselves are also directly

---

4. I am avoiding the use of the terms 'phonemics' or 'phonology' because they tend to lead to confusion, having been understood in various ways.

meaningful. There is, for these two, no disparity between the whole and its parts. It is only when one goes from the morpheme to the phoneme or the distinctive feature that the discontinuity occurs. Thus, in the whole/part hierarchy of signs noted above, the descent from morpheme to phoneme is not just (or not even) a descent from bigger to smaller, but from one type to another. In fact, it would be better to say that we are dealing here with two hierarchies: one beginning with discourse and descending to the morpheme and including all those signs which are directly meaningful; the other beginning with the syllable and descending to the distinctive feature and including all those signs which are only differential. Furthermore, the first hierarchy is basically in a whole/part relationship with the second, although some of the signs in the second hierarchy (e. g., phonemes, syllables) may be 'larger than' some signs in the first (e. g., morphemes) – since morphemes are potentially identifiable with a single distinctive feature or a combination of features (e. g., German *hatte/hätte:* past tense/subjunctive 2).

Moreover, these two hierachies are correlated with the two major types of patterning in language: the 'sense-discriminative system',[5] the area with signs like distinctive features, which have 'mere otherness', indirect signification, mediated relation to meaning, and oppositional structure in the *signans;* and the 'meaning system', the area with signs like words, which have 'singleness of reference', direct signification, non-mediated and thus immediate relation to meaning, and oppositional structure in the *signatum*. This opposition of 'sense-discriminative system' vs. 'meaning system' has, unfortunately, been widened metonymically to equate 'sense-discriminative system' with sound, or formal properties of signs, and 'meaning system' with meaning in general or meaning properties of signs. Yet it is not at all the case that form (or sound) is always correlated with 'mere otherness', either in language or in other semiotic systems. While some formal structure may, in other systems, also evidence duality (e. g., the genetic code, cf. Jakobson 1974 and pp. 67 ff. here), it is equally obvious that many 'formal' structures (e. g., systems of clothing, kinship systems, myths and folktales, food systems, and so forth) do not evidence 'duality' in the strict sense meant here. In these latter cases, while differences of form can of course be discerned, they are also directly meaningful. Thus, their analog is not with the sense-discriminative system at all but rather with the meaning system. And if we turn to language structure itself,

5. See fn. 3 above.

there also can be no straightforward equation of 'sound' (or properties of sound) with 'units of mere otherness', for many phonic properties are directly meaningful. This can be seen most clearly if we study such obviously meaningful elements as intonation contours (cf. Jurgens-Buning & van Schooneveld 1961; Ladd 1980; pp. 48f. here), emphatic stress, phrasing and pausing, and so forth. But it holds also for properties which look at first glance like the distinctive features and yet are quite different from them, not necessarily with regard to form but rather with regard to function *(signatum)*.

2.1   In the last few years, it has become clear through research done from such varied points of view as language structure, discourse analysis, variation theory, child language acquisition, speech perception, dichotic experiments, electric tracings of the brain, etc., that the speech sound *as a whole* is an *artifact* made for speech and invested with communicative import. In particular, it has been found that the speech sound is a multilayered, hierarchized signal with a variety of components which are invested with a variety of functions, only one of which is distinctiveness. In this sense the sound shape of language can be said to be *multifunctional*,[6] for the phonic properties which make up the speech sound, while they coexist in the sound, nevertheless evidence a variety of functions. In particular there exist redundant features, expressive (or stylistic) features, configurative (demarcative and culminative) features, and physiognomic features.[7] In addition, all of these, rather than having 'mere otherness', are *directly significative* in various ways.

   Far from being ancillary or superfluous, the *redundant* features (see Appendix One here; also pp. 39ff. here) indexically inform about the presence or absence of given distinctive features which are either simultaneous in the given bundle or adjacent in the given sequence (e.g., in English, nasality in the vowel informs about an adjacent nasal consonant). In this sense, the redundant features are inherently different from the distinctive features because they have "singleness of reference": they inform about specific distinctive features. And they do not have "mere otherness", because they are not used directly for the dif-

---

6. For a discussion of the multiple functions which language can have, see Jakobson 1960.
7. See Trubetzkoy 1969; Jakobson, Fant, & Halle 1952; Jakobson & Halle 1971; the present volume, p. 39ff.

ferentiation of two words or morphemes of otherwise identical sound shape. Nor are they relatively autonomous in their patterning: rather, their patterning is dependent upon that of the distinctive features. So, in the hierarchy of percepts contained in the sound, the distinctive features perform the primary function while the redundant features perform the secondary one. Of course in special modes of speech, especially in *elliptic speech*, the redundant features may substitute for the distinctive features.

In like fashion, the *configurative* features (see in particular Trubetzkoy 1969; also pp. 41 ff. here) fulfill a directly meaningful role, since they show either the unity (*culminative* features) or the limits (*demarcative* features) of the meaningful units such as morphemes, words, phrases, etc. which they occur in. They, like the redundant features, are indexical in function, but rather than being indexical to the distinctive features, they are indexical to given grammatical units. (It should be pointed out that the phonic properties which function as configurative features may also be used in a distinctive or redundant function in the same system.) It is in this sense that the word may exist as a 'phonic' phenomenon, given by specific properties in the sound. For example, in English, stress plays (in addition to its distinctive role) a culminative role in that it signals both the unity of the word and the number of words and word-groups in any given syntagm. In some languages, the device known as vowel harmony fills the similarly culminative role of indicating the unity of the word. In Czech, stress plays a demarcative role, indicating the beginning of the word. Of course, it is also possible to have negative signals of word boundaries: in Russian, the presence of a voiced consonant is a (negative) signal that no word boundary is present after the consonant, because (as said above) in word-final position neutralization of the voiced ~voiceless opposition occurs and voiced consonants cannot occur. (For further examples of configurative features, see Trubetzkoy 1969, and Jakobson, Fant & Halle 1952.)

Expressive (or *stylistic*) features indexically inform about, e.g., the placement of an item in a special subset of the vocabulary (loan words; exclamations) or the subjective attitude of the speaker (anger; despair; enthusiasm) – see pp. 43 ff. here. There existed in 19th century French, for example, an affected manner of speech whereby many Parisian women pronounced [ə] and [a] almost as [œ] and [æ] (Passy 1891: 248). Special items of vocabulary such as interjections often use sounds and clusters of sounds which don't occur otherwise in the language: e.g., interjections spelled as *tut, brr, phooey* in English. (Cf. Bolinger 1963:

122 f.) As Sapir pointed out (1949: 188), in certain North American Indian languages "sometimes sounds are found in songs which do not
otherwise occur in the language". Likewise, in Russian, the presence of
a non-palatalized consonant before /e/ signals special vocabulary
items such as loan words (e.g., /kafe/), acronyms (e.g., /nep/), or
names of letters of the alphabet (e.g., /be/). In English, vowel length
signals the subjective involvement of the speaker: *it's so-o-o-o big!*
Likewise, in English the aspirated release of a word-final tense stop
(e.g., [tʰɔpʰ], [nɔtʰ], [bækʰ]) is a signal of a special style of speech (such
as careful pronunciation, or emphasis of various degrees). In fact, at
least six different emotive variants have been discerned by Fónagy
(1976) for Hungarian sound sequences: anger, hate, sadness, joy, tenderness, irony.

The *physiognomic* features *(identifiers)* inform about and are overtly
indexical to the age, sex, geographical and ethnic origin, social class,
education, kinesthetic type, personality, and so forth of the speaker.
Here there are two major things to be discerned: what constituents in
the speech sound carry these types of information for the addressee,
and which of these are consciously or subliminally regulatable by the
addresser. For example, many speakers are adept at using (or on the
contrary not using) certain elements which communicate their geo-
graphic or ethnic origin (cf. Labov 1972). Likewise, the general pitch of
the voice, the specific ways of articulation, etc. may indicate a male or
female speaker.

These last types of features – the expressive and the physiognomic
– are not necessarily binary (whereas the distinctive, redundant, and
configurative features are all binary) and hence evidence "gradience"
(Bolinger 1961; also Labov 1964, 1972). But this does not allow us to
say that they are 'non-linguistic', just because they are not as structured
nor as compulsory nor (seemingly) as regulatable as the others. For, if
we mean by 'linguistic' in this context anything which sound in language can be used to convey, then they are just as linguistic as anything
else.

The barrier between each of these functions of phonic properties,
while it may not be absolute, is certainly basic enough to create great
difficulty when speakers try to change the properties from one function to another. Thus, in English, nasality in the vowels is redundant –
pointing, especially, to the distinctive nasality of a succeeding nasal
consonant (e.g., [ĩn] 'in' vs. [it] 'it' and [id] 'id') while in French it is
sense-discriminative (e.g., [bõarjē] 'bon à rien', [rjēnafɛr] 'rien à faire',

[bɔnami] 'bon ami') – for the distinctiveness of nasality in French, see Halle 1972: 189f., Tranel 1974, 1981 and Klausenberger 1974. And yet, anyone who has tried to teach French to native speakers of English knows how difficult it is for them to learn the sense-discriminative use of nasality. Likewise, in Russian, sharpness (palatalization) of /r'/ is distinctive, while in Norwegian it is configurative (demarcative, being word-final); Norwegians seem to be unaware of its presence at all and have great difficulty in discerning and especially in producing /r'/ as a sense-discriminative element.

2.2   The difference between these various functional phonic properties has also been confirmed by recent research on the brain (see Kimura 1967, Balonov & Deglin 1976, and Jakobson 1985: 163ff.; see also pp. 32ff. and 46ff. here). Not only is it the case that, as many linguists have claimed, speech is processed differently in the brain from all other auditory phenomena whether produced by humans, by animals, or by other environmental factors (see Balonov & Deglin 1976: 77ff.), but it also seems to be the case that the left hemisphere is particularly suited for the perception of distinctive and redundant features (Balonov & Deglin 1976; Zaidel 1978) while the right hemisphere is more suited to such auditory phenomena as the emotive and physiognomic features and other significative phenomena like intonation (Blumstein & Cooper 1972, 1974).

The recognition of all auditory stimuli outside of language is supervised solely by the right hemisphere (Balonov & Deglin 1976: 77ff.). Its inactivation does not affect the distinctive features, but has a totally destructive effect on all other auditory stimuli: noises of humans and animals, of industry, of transport, and of natural forces, as well as musical tones, chords, and melodies (cf. Gordon 1970; Mindadze et al. 1975), even in those cases when these auditory stimuli are quite familiar to the patient. Subjects with a temporarily inactivated right hemisphere were confused when faced with these types of auditory stimuli, which were perfectly recognizable as long as this hemisphere remained active. In addition, the inactivation of the right hemisphere renders the listener completely unable to recognize or even notice sentence intonations, especially the emotive ones, as well as the emotive and physiognomic features. Thus, patients with a temporarily inactivated right hemisphere lose the ability to distinguish between men's and women's voices or to tell whether two utterances belong to one and the same speaker or to two different people, as well as to identify even the most familiar individuals by sound only. Moreover, the patient also loses the ability to regulate his own voice in accordance with a given emotional situation (see Balonov & Deglin 1976: 164ff., 171ff.). The right hemisphere also acts as a 'brake' or 'censor': it exerts a 'damping' influence on the language centers of the left hemisphere (Balonov & Deglin 1976: 145ff., 182ff., 186).

The inactivation of the left hemisphere in its turn sharply obstructs the recognizability and reproducibility of distinctive features, redundant features, and the accentual design and internal structure of the word. The network of distinctive features loses its stability and equilibrium, and the disintegration of this system in turn reveals a hierarchical order in the deficits suffered by patients. The most common types of confusion between phonemes are limited to one single distinctive feature, and the various features manifest different degrees of resistibility. In particular, the features which are learned early in child language acquisition and which disappear latest in aphasics, are those which remain most viable under deactivation of the left hemisphere and are least prone to disappear (Balonov & Deglin 1976: 132, 142, 181). In addition, the hierarchical markedness relation within any given feature is also confirmed by these studies, with the unmarked value being more resistant than the marked.

Thus, when the left hemisphere is damaged or inactivated in some way, language, especially in its analytic mode, and in particular the distinctive features, their patterning, and their redundant supports are lost, but the emotive and physiognomic features remain. But, when the right hemisphere is inactivated or damaged, language in its more holistic mode is damaged and in particular the emotive and physiognomic features are lost, while the distinctive and redundant features remain. Moreover, tones (the sense-discriminative use of pitch) are best processed by the left hemisphere (van Lancker & Fromkin 1973), while intonation (the significative use of pitch) is best processed by the right hemisphere (Blumstein & Cooper 1972, 1974).

At the end of their very interesting monograph, Balonov & Deglin conclude with the following hypothesis:

"The mechanisms of sound production and the auditory functions of the right hemisphere prove to be considerably older than the mechanisms of sound production and the auditory function of the left hemisphere which secure speech articulation and the discrimination of speech sounds on the basis of distinctive features." (p. 194).

The asymmetric arrangement of the human brain and the development of the left dominant hemisphere have apparently been interconnected with the origin and growth of language, especially with *mediacy* (double articulation, duality of patterning), one of the dividing lines between human language and animal communication.

2.3 Sound is, by its very nature, *functional* or *semiotic* and not merely phonic: the same phonic property may perform different functions in different languages, and different phonic properties may perform the same function in the same language. Moreover, sound is *multifunctional*, being invested simultaneously with a variety of functions. But the fact remains that the functions which the various phonic properties fulfill are variously interrelated and that in the *hierarchy* of percepts contained in the speech signal, the distinctive features are *primary* while all the others are secondary: the distinctiveness function is not cancellable or optional, while the others are to a greater or lesser degree. An utterance without configurative features might make 'parsing' into words or phrases difficult, or an utterance without expressive features might sound flat and betray inattention on the part of the speaker; but utterances without distinctive features are confined to such restricted patterns as interjections, or intonation contours superposed on e. g., *mm* or *hm* (in English). In general, ideational, cognitive utterances don't exist without some distinctive features. In fact, even in elliptic speech where certain distinctive features are left out (elided), many still remain; and furthermore certain redundant features assume the distinctive function. Only a certain amount of ellipsis of the distinctive elements is possible, if communication is still to take place.

In their turn, speech sounds as a whole are multifunctional and semiotic: all aspects of the speech sound are endowed with a linguistic function. Every phonic element is potentially information-bearing and usable by members of a given speech community. The total speech sound is an *artifact:* all of its aspects are communicative and none are pre-given to language. This means that the dichotomy of *etic~emic* is a false one, as Claude Lévi-Strauss (1972) has noted: "Both the natural and the human sciences concur to dismiss an outmoded philosophical dualism. Ideal and real, abstract and concrete, 'emic' and 'etic' can no longer be opposed to each other. What is immediately 'given' to us is neither the one nor the other, but something which is betwixt and between, that is already encoded by the sense organs as by the brain." An 'emic' point of view which focusses only on distinctiveness and an 'etic' point of view which disregards the *raison d'être* of the speech components lose sight of the functional and communicative basis of the sound shape of language.

3.   While it is the case that the distinctive features are the sense-discriminative units *par excellence* and that generally speaking an immediate tie to meaning is vested in the redundant, configurative, expressive, and physiognomic features only, nevertheless in all languages, though to varying degrees and with certain differences between speakers, there is also the tendency for the distinctive features themselves to have a direct and immediate relation to meaning. The propensity for *immediacy* by the distinctive features also means that the essential disunity between the signs with 'mere otherness' and all others is, in a sense, counterbalanced and counteracted by the power of the former to have a meaning of their own.

A particularly important manifestation of this drive for immediate signification may be discussed under the heading of *sound symbolism,* although the term *sound iconism* would be more appropriate since there seems in this case to be an iconic (similarity) relation between sound and meaning. In particular, it has been found that there is a latent tendency, which may become patent in certain circumstances, for the sounds of given words to be congruent with their meanings. Such correspondences are very often built on the phenomenal interconnection between the different senses – on synesthesia, including the most difficult facet of 'colored hearing' (the relation between sound and colors). Given their synesthetic basis, it is not surprising that these iconic associations tend to be universal for the languages of the world. However, such universal tendencies can only be discerned with respect to the distinctive features (the phonemes, being bundles of features, may evidence too many different tendencies) and are best understood in terms of relational oppositions, since the features themselves are oppositional. Thus, the grave ~acute feature in the vowels, and to a certain extent in the consonants, tends to be associated with the oppositions bigger ~smaller,   thicker ~thinner,   darker ~brighter,   softer ~harder, heavier ~lighter, sweeter ~bitterer, slower ~quicker, less pretty ~prettier, less friendly ~friendlier, and, for some speakers, with black ~white, blue ~yellow (or, more generally, darker ~lighter colors). (See Köhler 1910–1915, Jespersen 1922b and 1933, Sapir 1927, Wellek 1931b, Chastaing 1958, 1961, and 1965a, Fónagy 1963, Peterfalvi 1970, Fischer-Jørgensen 1978). Such correspondences may underlie popular or folk etymology (more properly called synchronic etymology), may contribute to the life or death of certain words, or may led to a reanalysis of the meaning of given words in the light of the form or conversely of the form of given words in the light of the meaning. This can even create, as Lévi-Strauss has pointed out, *une petite mythologie* (1976). Grammaticalization of sound symbolism may also be found in sound-symbolic ablaut, e.g., in Yoruba, *bìrì* 'to be large' vs. *bírí* 'to be small', *sùrù* 'to be big' vs. *súrú* 'to be little', *gbòrò* 'to be wide' vs. *gbóró* 'to be narrow', *kìbìtì* 'to be of large size' vs. *kíbítí* 'to be of small size' (Westermann 1927 and 1937; the acute accent indicates high tone and the grave accent low tone). Sound symbolism is also, according to Jespersen (1922a) for example, more prevalent in children than in adults and more widespread in more recent stages of various language groups than in earlier stages – i.e., the symbolic (iconic) import of sounds is reinforced with each new generation. This has great importance for the problem of language origins and language evolution as well as for the differentiation of human and animal communication.

The constant dialectic between the purely sense-discriminative use of the distinctive features and their sound-symbolic use (especially when non-grammaticalized) was succinctly put by Benjamin Lee Whorf:

> "Language, through lexation, has made the speaker more acutely conscious of certain dim psychic sensations; it has actually produced awareness on lower planes than its own: a power of the nature of magic. There is a logic mastery in the power of language to remain independent of lower-psyche facts, to override them, now to point them up, now toss them out of the picture, to mold the nuances of word to its own rule, whether the psychic ring of the sounds fits or not. If the sounds fit, the psychic quality of the sounds is increased, and this can be noticed by the layman. If the sounds do not fit, the psychic quality changes to accord with the linguistic meaning, no matter how incongruous with the sound, and this is not noticed by the layman." (1956: 267f.).

A phenomenon similar to sound symbolism in its striving for an iconic relation between form and meaning is reduplication, which is "used to indicate such concepts as distribution, plurality, repetition, customary activity, increase of size, added intensity, continuance" (Sapir 1921), and may serve to impart a playful and at the same time disparaging tone to the utterance, as it does in Russian (with dissimilation of the initial consonant): *sifilis-pífilis* 'such a nothing as syphilis' or in English with the use of the phonestheme [šm]: *Brooklyn-schmooklyn, Joe-schmoe.*

Further tendencies of sounds toward independent signification can be noted under the general heading of *word affinities:* features, phonemes, collocations of phonemes which are common to a set of words with like meaning may come to be associated with that meaning: e. g., in the series of words *nip, clip, tip, dip, sip, grip, pip, quip, yip, flip, drip,* the post-vocalic stop is (synesthetically) sensed to be like a 'blow' and the (sound-symbolic) /ɪ/ seems to suggest a briefer focus upon the action (vs. /æ/ in *slap, clap, rap, tap, flap, lap*); cf. the use of /u/ to suggest foolishness (*rube, boob, galoot, loon, nincompoop, stooge, coo-coo, goof, spoof* – Bolinger 1965: 200), and of *fl-* as expressive of movement (*flow, flutter, flap, flake, flicker, fling, flit, flurry, flirt;* see Jespersen 1922a and Bolinger 1965). To this class of phenomena may be added the *sense-determinative* uses of the features, namely the restriction in English of word-initial [ð] to words of deictic meaning (e.g., *then, there, the, this, that, they,* etc.); or, as an example of its use in grammatical meaning, the compulsory presence in the Polish instrumental of the nasality feature (either in the nasal vowel or in the consonant /m/; Jakobson 1971: 178ff.). Such sound-meaning associations, especially in lexical meaning, can become the basis of a *sui generis* synchronic etymology labeled *"phonesthemes"* by Householder (1946), "secondary associations" by Hockett (1958), "phonetic symbolism" by Marchand (1959), "psychomorphs" by Markell & Hamp (1960–61), and "submorphemic differentials" by Bolinger (1965). Again, it has been pointed out that such associations may lead to the survival of certain members of the general class of words and to the addition of new members to the class.

An even more radical drive toward immediate signification is to be found in North American Indian *"abnormal types of speech"* (Sapir 1949: 179–196) – in which people with some defect (e.g., the hunchbacked, the cross-eyed, the left-handed, the greedy) are spoken of (or sometimes to) with the insertion of certain infixes in the utterance and with characteristic changes in consonants (so-called 'consonantal play'). The same types of substitutions are used when alluding to or quoting the 'speech' of such (sacred) animals as the Deer, Mink, Raven, Sparrow, and Wren. Analogous processes may also be used as literary devices in myths and songs: "Song texts often represent a mutilated form of the language, but study of the peculiarities of song form generally shows that the normal forms of speech are modified according to stylistic conventions, which may vary for different types of songs." (Sapir 1949: 188).

The alternation of the sound shape in American Indian usage is closely associated with world-wide process whereby words are variously modified because of *taboo*. On the one hand, such modifications camouflage the subject meant; on the other hand, to a certain degree they highlight the subject. Furthermore, the sound shape must not deviate too far from the tabooed shape, or else the taboo character is lost; and the replacement of the tabooed shape by the altered form is felt to be a way of avoiding possible danger, bad luck, or ill will. In some cultures, in addition, the taboo reaches the level of certain sounds or sound combinations which are then prohibited to either males or females *('male and female forms of speech')*. In Chukchee, for example, women regularly replace /r/ and /č/ by /š/, unless they are quoting male speech, in which case they do not make the substitutions (Bogoraz 1922: 665). In Gogo-Yimidjir (Australia) women always use the tense (voiceless) variants of the stops whereas men use the lax (voiced) variants (de Zwaan 1969: 216f.).

The strongest propensity of the distinctive features for autonomization and for immediate signification is found in the universal phenomenon of *poetry* (whether of children or adults) through such obvious phonic poetic devices as rhyme, semi-rhyme, alliteration, assonance, etc., through meter (whether based on number of syllables, number of stresses, or the like), through the general repetition of sounds, syllables, words, etc., through the division into lines, strophes, parts, etc., and through the general exploitation of the 'word affinities' noted above. Far from being subordinated to the meaning, in poetry sound plays a leading role, operates in full partnership with meaning, and may even help to create meaning. Such a leading role may also be present in 'ordinary' adult speech: *through thick and thin, forgive and forget, deep sea, sky high;* in slogans: *I like Ike;* in word play: *Focus Pocus* (the name of a camera store in Buffalo, N.Y.); in puns or spoonerisms: "Let me sew you to another sheet" (instead of "Let me show you to another seat"); and so forth. And, as has often been pointed out (Čukovskij 1971; Sanches & Kirschenblatt-Gimblett 1976) all sane children go through a stage where they invent rhymes, play with sound for its own sake, and tend to assign meanings to sounds directly. In many ways, adult speech and adult attitudes toward sound may be seen as the assignment of the primary role to mediated signification while in children its status remains unclear.

While sound symbolism, synesthesia, word affinities, consonantal play, and in particular poetic usage show the drive for autonomization through the direct association of sound shapes with meaning, a complementary phenomenon – the drive for autonomization through the use of the sound shape with no evident meaning attached – is exemplified by glossolalia, e.g., *kindra fendra kiraveca* of the Khlysty (Nečaev 1889: 140, cf. RJ 1966), and *kupóy shandré filé sundrukuma shandré lása hóya takí* of an American Presbyterian minister (Samarin 1972a: 77). It is also evident in this magical formula chanted for protection against mermaids (RJ 1966: 639f.):

> Au, au, šixarda kavda!
> Šivda, vnoza, mitta, minogam,
> Kalandi, indi, jakutašma bitaš,
> Okutomi mi nuffan, zidima …

Such usage is correlated with the magic function of language and thus complements, especially, taboo usage as well as mythic consonantal play (noted above). Moreover, in many cases, it is seen as a way for the human and the divine, the human and the superhuman, to communicate. One interesting phenomenon which awaits further explanation is the prevalence of clusters such as *nd, nt, ndr, ntr* in these various types of utterances by speakers of widely divergent linguistic backgrounds (see pp. 215ff. here). These mythic uses bear obvious resemblances to avant-garde poetry (e.g., Morgenstern's "Das große Lalulā", with lines like *Seiokrontro-prafriplo, Hontraruru miromente,* and *Entepente, leiolente*); to children's counting out rhymes (game preludes – e.g. *Inty, ninty tibbety fig, Howchy powchy domi nowday* – see Sanches & Kirschenblatt-Gimblett 1976: 92f.); to the verbal play which children seem to delight in and to use as a dynamic part of the acquisition process (see Weir 1962); and to magical phraseological expressions (e.g., *abracadabra,* cf. *salagadula michakaboula bibbidy bobbidy boo* from Walt Disney's "Cinderella").

All of these uses show the so-to-speak 'spell' of the speech sounds, the magical power which is associated with sound *per se.* And we see here that the drive for autonomization and *immediacy* of the distinctive features is associated with the mythical, the poetic, the magical, and the playful use of language in addition to its so-called 'ordinary' use.

4. While *mediacy* ('mere otherness' and indirect signification – double articulation, duality of patterning) separates language not only from systems of animal communication but also from many other human symbolic or semiotic systems, it is supplemented by those multi-

functional phonic properties which have direct signification, and it is complemented (or even superceded) by the tendency on the part of the distinctive features themselves to have *immediacy*. In this way, the vapid prospect of sound used solely as a device for 'mere otherness' and the rather mechanistic and absolutist dichotomy of 'sound' and 'meaning' is dispelled by the ongoing dynamic dialectic between 'mediacy' and 'immediacy', 'mere otherness' and 'singleness of reference', 'distinctiveness' and 'redundancy', 'sense-discrimination' and 'sense-determination', 'direct' and 'indirect' signification, 'structure in the *signans*' and 'structure in the *signatum*'. Such mutually intersecting dichotomies are examples of the pervasive asymmetry of patterning inherent in language, and are manifestations of both the *dynamic synchrony* and the *multifunctionality* which are part and parcel of linguistic structure.

REFERENCES

List of articles and books consulted and for the most part cited in this work.

Abrahams, H., 1955: "Börns tilegnelse af modersmålets fonologiske stof", *Nordisk Tidsskrift for Tale og Stemme*, 13-26.

Abrahams, R. D., 1969: *Jump-Rope Rhymes: A Dictionary*, Austin, Texas.

Abramson, A. S., 1962: *The Vowels and Tones of Standard Thai*, Bloomington, Ind.

—, 1976: "Laryngeal Timing in Consonant Distinctions", Haskins Laboratories, *Speech Research* 47, 105-112.

Abramson, A. S. & L. Lisker, 1969: "Laryngeal Behavior, the Speech Signal and Phonological Simplicity", *Actes du Xe Congrès International des Linguistes* IV, Bucarest, 123-129.

Ackrill, J. L., 1964: "Demos or Plato", *The Journal of Philosophy* 61, No. 20, 610 ff.

Adrian, E. D., 1954: "The Physiological Basis of Perception", Adrian et al. (eds.), *Brain Mechanisms and Consciousness*, Oxford.

Alarcos Llorach, E., 1968: "L'acquisition du langage par l'enfant", A. Martinet (ed.), *Le Langage*, Paris, 323-365.

Albright, R. W. & J. B., 1956: "The Phonology of a Two-Year-Old Child", *Word* 12, 382-390.

Allen, W. S., 1953: *Phonetics in Ancient India*, London.

—, 1965: "On One-Vowel Systems", *Lingua* 13, 111-124.

Alonso, A., 1939: "Examen de la teoria indogenista de Rodolfo Lenz", *Revista de filología hispanica* I.

Ammon, K. H., 1978: "Patholinguistische und experimentelle Befunde gegen die Motor-Theorie der Sprachwahrnehmung", G. Peuser (ed.), *Patholinguistika* 2, 27-34.

Andersen, H., 1968: "IE *s after *i, u, r, k* in Baltic and Slavic", *Acta Linguistica Hafniensia* 11, 171-190.

—, 1972: "Diphthongization", *Language* 48, 11-50.

Anderson, S., 1974: *The Organization of Phonology*, New York.

—, 1976: "Nasal Consonants and the Internal Structure of Segments", *Language* 52, 326-344.

Ansre, G., 1961: "The Tonal Structure of Ewe", *Hartford Studies in Linguistics* No. 1, Hartford Seminary Foundation.

Anttila, R., 1975: "Affective Vocabulary in Finnish: An(other) Invitation", *Ural-Altaïsche Jahrbücher* 47, 10-19.

Aoki, H., 1968: "Toward a Typology of Vowel Harmony", *International Journal of American Linguistic* 34, 142-145.

–, 1970: "Nez Perce Grammar", *University of California Publications in Linguistics* 62, Berkeley.

–, 1975: "The East Plateau Linguistic Diffusion Area", *International Journal of American Linguistics* 41, 183–199.

Applegate, J. R., 1958: *Outline of the Structure of Shilha*, Washington, D. C.

Arakin, V. D., 1973: *Samoanskij jazyk*, Moscow.

Argelander, A., 1927: *Das Farbenhören und der synästhetische Faktor der Wahrnehmung*, Jena.

Armstrong, J. D. & C. H. van Schooneveld (eds.), 1977: *Roman Jakobson: Echoes of His Scholarship*, Lisse.

Ashby, W. R., 1956: *An Introduction to Cybernetics*, New York.

Atzet, J. & H. B. Gerard, 1965: "A Study of Phonetic Symbolism among Native Navajo Speakers", *Journal of Personality and Social Psychology* 1, 524–528.

Austin, W. M., 1957: "Criteria for Phonetic Similarity", *Language* 33, 538–543.

Avram, A., 1962: "Obščaja i individual'naja sistemy v reči rebënka", *Revue de linguistique* 7, 243–250.

–, 1965: Review of H. Pilch, *Phonemtheorie* I, in *Word* 21, 487–493.

–, 1972: "Sur l'interprétation phonologique des voyelles nasales portugaises", H. Haarmann & M. Studamund (eds.), *Festschrift Wilhelm Giese*, Hamburg.

–, 1976: "Sur la valeur phonologique et la fonction morphonologique du timbre des consonnes finales en roumain et dans d'autres langues romanes", *Études romanes = Bulletin de la Société Roumaine de Linguistique Romane* 11, 5–16.

Balonov, L. J. & V. L. Deglin, 1976: *Slux i reč' dominantnogo i nedominantnogo polušarij*, Leningrad.

Baltaxe, C. A. M., 1978: *Foundations of Distinctive Feature Theory*, Baltimore, Md.

Bamgbosẹ, A., 1970: "Word Play in Yoruba Poetry", *International Journal of American Linguistics* 36, 110–116.

Bar-Adon, A. & W. F. Leopold, 1971: *Child Language: A Book of Readings*, New Jersey.

Baranovskaja, S., 1970: "O fonetičeskix korreljatax differencial'nyx priznakov", *Kuznecovskie čtenija*, Moscow.

Bar-Hillel, Y., 1957: "Three Methodological Remarks on *Fundamentals of Language*", *Word* 13, 323–334.

Bartoš, L., 1959: "Observations sur les réalisations phonétiques dans le langage d'un enfant de deux ans", *Sbórnik prací filosofické fakulty Brněnské university* VIII, *Řada jazykovědná* (A) Č. 7, 5–19.

Baskakov, N. A., 1966a: "Tjurkskie jazyki", *Jazyki narodov SSSR*, II, Moscow, 7–42.

–, 1966b: "Altajskij jazyk", *Jazyki narodov SSSR*, II, Moscow, 506–522.

Batmanov, U. A., 1946: *Fonetičeskaja sistema sovremennogo kirgizskogo jazyka*, Frunze.

Baucomont, J., F. Guibat, et al., 1961: *Les comptines de langue française*, Paris.

Baudouin de Courtenay, J., 1877: *Otčëty o zanjatijax po jazykovedeniju v tečenie 1872 i 1873 gg*, Kazan'.

–, 1881–82: "Otryvki iz lekcij po fonetike i morfologii russkogo jazyka", *Filologičeskie zapiski*, 1–88.

–, 1910: "Les lois phonétiques", *Rocznik Slawistyczny* III, 57–82.

–, 1922: "O relativnosti v oboru jazykovém", V. Mathesius & E. Radl (eds.), *Atheneum* II, Prague, 80–87.

–, 1963: *Izbrannye trudy po obščemu jazykoznaniju* I & II, Moscow.

—, 1974: *Dzieła wybrane,* I, Warsaw.

Beaunis, H. & A. Binet, 1892: "Sur deux cas d'audition colorée", *Revue Philosophique* 33, 448–461.

Beckner, M., 1976: "Function and Teleology", M. Grene & E. Mendelsohn (eds.), *Topics in the Philosophy of Biology,* Dordrecht, 197–212.

Bell, A., 1970: "Syllabic Consonants", *Stanford University Working Papers on Language Universals* # 4, B 1–B 49.

Bender, E. & Z. S. Harris, 1946: "The Phonemes of North Carolina Cherokee", *International Journal of American Linguistics* 12, 14–21.

Bennett, W. A., 1977: "Tensing and Neutralization in Modern French", *Phonetik, Sprachwissenschaft und Kommunikationsforschung* 30, 160–169.

Bentley, M. & E. J. Varon, 1933: "An Accessory Study of 'Phonetic Symbolism'", *American Journal of Psychology* 45, 76–86.

Benveniste, E., 1939: "Répartitions des consonnes et phonologie du mot", *Travaux du Cercle Linguistique de Prague* 8, 27–35.

— (ed.), 1964: "Lettres de Ferdinand de Saussure à Antoine Meillet", *Cahiers Ferdinand de Saussure 21,* 89–130.

—, 1966: *Problèmes de linguistique générale* I, Paris.

Berko, J. & R. Brown, 1960: "Psycholinguistic Research Methods", P. Mussen (ed.), *Handbook of Research Methods in Child Development,* New York, 517–557.

Berlin, B. & P. Kay, 1969: *Basic Color Terms,* Berkeley, Calif.

Berlin, C. I., S. S. Lowe-Bell, J. K. Cullen, Jr., C. L. Thompson & C. F. Loovis, 1973: "Dichotic Speech Perception: An Interpretation of Right-Ear Advantage and Temporal Offset Effects", *Journal of the Acoustical Society of America* 53, 699–709.

Bernard, J. & L. Sontag, 1947: "Fetal Reactivity to Tonal Stimulation: A Preliminary Report", *Journal of Genetic Psychology* 70, 205–210.

Bhat, D. N. S., 1973: "Retroflexion: An Areal Feature", *Stanford University Working Papers on Language Universals* # 13, 27–67.

—, 1974a: "A General Study of Palatalization", *Stanford University Working Papers on Language Universals* # 14, 17–58.

—, 1974b: "The Phonology of Liquid Consonants", *Stanford University Working Papers on Language Universals* # 16, 73–104.

—, 1974c: "Retroflexion and Retraction", *Journal of Phonetics* 2, 233–237.

Bhattacharya, G. N., 1937: "A Study in the Dialectics of Sphoṭa", *Journal of the Department of Letters,* University of Calcutta.

Bierwisch, M., 1971: *Modern Linguistics,* The Hague.

Biggs, B., 1971: "The Languages of Polynesia", *Current Trends in Linguistics* 8, The Hague, 466–505.

Binet, A. & Philippe, 1892: "Étude sur un nouveau cas d'audition colorée", *Revue Philosophique* 33, 461–464.

Blache, S., 1978: *The Acquisition of Distinctive Features,* Baltimore.

Bladon, R. A. W. & G. Fant, 1978: "A Two-Formant Model and the Cardinal Vowels", *Speech Transmission Laboratory Quarterly Progress and Status Report* 1, Stockholm.

Blanché, R., 1966: *Structures intellectuelles,* Paris.

Blesser, B., 1972: "Speech Perception under Conditions of Spectral Transformation I. Phonetic Characteristics", *Journal of Speech and Hearing Research* 15, 5–41.

Bloch, B., 1941: "Phonemic Overlapping", *American Speech* 16.

Blood, D. L., 1967: "Phonological Units in Cham", *Anthropological Linguistics* 9.

Bloomfield, L., 1930: "German [ç] and [x]", *Le Maître phonétique* 30, 27-28.
—, 1933: *Language,* New York.
—, 1939: "Menomini Morphophonemics", *Travaux du Cercle Linguistique de Prague* 8, 105-115.
Bloomfield, M. W., 1953: "Final Root-Forming Morphemes", *American Speech* 28, 158-164.
Blount, B. G., 1972: "Parental Speech and Language Acquisition: Some Luo and Samoan Examples", *Anthropological Linguistics* 14, 119-130.
Blumstein, S., 1973: *A Phonological Investigation of Aphasic Speech,* The Hague.
—, 1974: "The Use and Theoretical Implications of the Dichotic Technique for Investigating Distinctive Features", *Brain and Language* 1, 337-350.
—, 1978: *Acoustic Invariance in Speech,* Radcliffe Institute Working Paper, Cambridge, Mass.
Blumstein, S. & W. Cooper, 1972: "Identification versus Discrimination of Distinctive Features in Speech Perception", *Quarterly Journal of Experimental Psychology* 24, 207-214.
—, 1974: "Hemispheric Processing of Intonation Contours", *Cortex* 10, 146 ff.
Blumstein, S. & H. Goodglass, 1972: "The Perception of Stress as a Semantic Cue in Aphasia", *Journal of Speech and Hearing Research* 15, 800-806.
Blumstein, S. & K. N. Stevens, 1977: "Acoustic Invariance for Place of Articulation in Stops and Nasals across Syllable Contexts", paper presented at the 94th meeting of the Acoustical Society of America, Miami, Florida, Dec. 1977.
Boas, F., 1911: "Introduction", *Handbook of American Indian Languages* I, Washington.
—, 1938: "Language", F. Boas (ed.), *General Anthropology,* Boston & London, 124-145.
—, 1947: "Kwakiutl Grammar with a Glossary of the Suffixes", H. Yampolsky & Z. Harris (eds.), *Transactions of the American Philosophical Society* N. S. 37, Philadelphia.
Boas, F. & E. Deloria, 1941: *Dakota Grammar,* Memoirs of the National Academy of Sciences 23, Washington, D. C.
Bobon, J., 1952: *Introduction historique à l'étude des néologismes et des glossolalies en psychopathologie,* Paris & Liège.
Bogatyrëv, P. G., 1962: "O jazyke slavjanskix narodnyx pesen v ego otnošenii k dialektnoj reči", *Voprosy jazykoznanija* # 3, 75 ff.
Bogoraz, V. G., 1901: "Oblastnoj slovar' Kolymskogo russkogo narečija", *Sbornik otdelenija russkogo jazyka i slovesnosti,* I. Akademii Nauk, 68, No. 4.
— (Bogoras, W.), 1922: "Chukchee", *Handbook of American Indian Languages* II, Washington, D. C., 639-903.
—, 1934: "Luoravetlanskij (čukotskij) jazyk", *Jazyki i pis'mennost' narodov severa,* Moscow, 3, 5-46.
Bogorodickij, V. A., 1933: "Zakony singarmonizma v tjurkskix jazykax", Bogorodickij (ed.), *Ètjudy po tatarskomu i tjurkskomu jazykoznaniju,* Kazan', 58-73.
Bokarev, E. A. & G. A. Klimov, 1967: "Iberijsko-Kavkazskie jazyki", *Jazyki narodov SSSR,* IV, Moscow, 7-14.
Bolinger, D. L., 1946: "Thoughts on 'Yep' and 'Nope'", *American Speech* 21, 90-95.
—, 1949: "The Sign Is Not Arbitrary", *Boletin del Instituto Caro y Cuervo* V, 52-62.
—, 1950: "Rime, Assonance and Morpheme Analysis", *Word* 6, 117-136.
—, 1954: "Identity, Similarity, and Difference", *Litera* I, 5-16.
—, 1961: "Verbal Evocation", *Lingua* 10, 113 ff.
—, 1963: "The Uniqueness of the Word", *Lingua* 12, 113-136.

—, 1964: "Intonation as a Universal", *Proceedings of the Ninth International Congress of Linguists*, The Hague, 833-848.

—, 1965: *Forms of English*, Cambridge, Mass.

—, 1977: "Intonation and 'Nature'", paper for Burg Wartenstein Symposium No. 74 = *Fundamentals of Symbolism*, 1-22.

Bolton, H. C., 1888: *The Counting-Out Rhymes of Children, Their Antiquity, Origin, and Wide Distribution*, London.

Bondarko, L. & L. Verbickaja, 1965: "O markirovannosti priznaka mjagkosti russkix soglasnyx", *Zeitschrift für Phonetik, Sprachwissenschaft und Kommunikationsforschung* 18, 119-126.

Bondarko, L. V. & L. R. Zinder, 1966: "O nekotoryx differencial'nyx priznakax russkix soglasnyx fonem", *Voprosy jazykoznanija* # 15.

Bonfante, G., 1939: "Études sur le tabou dans les langues indoeuropéennes", *Mélanges de linguistique offerts à Charles Bally*, Geneva, 195-208.

Boor, H. de & P. Diels (eds.), 1961[18]: *Siebs Deutsche Hochsprache*, Berlin.

Bouda, K., 1953: "Die tschuktschische Frauensprache", *Orbis* 2, 33-34.

Böller, R. & E. Green, 1972: "Comprehension in Severe Aphasics", *Cortex* 8, 382-394.

Brackbill, Y. & K. Little, 1957: "Factors Determining the Guessing of Meanings of Foreign Words", *Journal of Abnormal and Social Psychology* 54, 312-318.

Bragina, N. N. & T. A. Dobroxotova, 1977: "Problema funkcional'noj asimmetrii mozga", *Voprosy filosofii* 2, 135-150.

Braunwald, S. R., 1971: "Mother-Child Communication: The Function of Maternal-Language Input", *Word* 27, 28-56.

Broadbent, D. E., 1954: "The Role of Auditory Localization in Attention and Memory Span", *Journal of Experimental Psychology* 47, 191-196.

Broecke, M. P. R. van den, 1976: *Hierarchies and Rank Orders in Distinctive Features*, Amsterdam.

Brough, J., 1951: "Theories of General Linguistics in the Sanskrit Grammarians", *Transactions of the Philological Society*, 27-46.

Brown, R. W., A. H. Black & A. E. Horowitz, 1955: "Phonetic Symbolism in Natural Languages", *Journal of Abnormal and Social Psychology* 50, 388-393.

Brown, R. & D. McNeil, 1966: "The 'Tip of the Tongue' Phenomenon", *Journal of Verbal Learning and Verbal Behavior* 5, 325-337.

Brown, R. & R. Nuttal, 1959: "Method in Phonetic Symbolism Experiments", *Journal of Abnormal and Social Psychology* 59, 441-445.

Bruck, R. H., 1958: "A Survey of Binary Systems", *Ergebnisse der Mathematik und ihrer Grenzgebiete*, NF 20.

Bruner, J. S., 1958: "Neural Mechanisms in Perception", H. C. Solomon et al. (eds.), *The Brain and Human Behavior* = Association for Research in Nervous and Mental Diseases, *Research Publications* 36 (French version in *Archives de Psychologie* 36, 1-28).

—, 1977: "From Communication to Language - A Psychological Perspective", *Cognition* 3, 255 ff.

Burkert, W., 1959: "Stoicheion", *Philologus* 103, 167-197.

Bühler, K., 1933: "L'onomatopée et la fonction représentative du langage", *Journal de Psychologie* 30.

Cairns, C. E., 1969: "Markedness, Neutralization, and Universal Redundancy Rules", *Language* 45, 863-885.

—, 1971: Review of N.S. Trubetzkoy, *Principles of Phonology*, in *Language* 47, 918-931.

Canonge, E. D., 1957: "Voiceless Vowels in Comanche", *International Journal of American Linguistics* 23, 63-67.

Capell, A. & H. E. Hinch, 1970: *Maung Grammar*, The Hague.

Caramazza, A. & E. Zurif (eds.), 1978: *Language Acquisition and Language Breakdown, Parallels and Divergences*, Baltimore.

Carlson, S., B. Granström & G. Fant, 1970: "Some Studies Concerning Perception of Isolated Vowels", Speech Transmission Laboratory, *Quarterly Progress and Status Report* 2-3, Stockholm, 19-35.

Cassirer, E., 1923: *Philosophie der symbolischen Formen* I, Berlin.

—, 1938: "Le concept de groupe et la théorie de la perception", *Journal de psychologie* 35, 368 ff. (English translation, 1944: "The Concept of Group and the Theory of Perception", *Philosophy and Phenomenological Research* V, 1 ff.).

Chafe, W. L., 1967: *Seneca Morphology and Dictionary*, Washington, D.C.

Chastaing, M., 1958: "Le symbolisme des voyelles: significations des 'i' " I & II, *Journal de Psychologie* 55, 403-423 & 461-481.

—, 1960: "Audition colorée: une enquête", *Vie et Langage* 105, 631-637.

—, 1961: "Des sons et des couleurs", *Vie et Langage* 112, 358-365.

—, 1962: "La brillance des voyelles", *Archivum linguisticum* 14, 1-13.

—, 1964: "L'Opposition des consonnes sourdes aux consonnes sonores et muettes: a-t-elle une valeur symbolique?" *Vie et Langage* 147, 367-370.

—, 1965a: "Dernières recherches sur le symbolisme vocalique de la petitesse", *Revue Philosophique* 155, 41-56.

—, 1965b: "Pop - fop - pof - fof", *Vie et Langage* 159, 311-317.

—, 1966: "Si les *r* étaient des *l*", (Part 1) *Vie et Langage* 173, 468-472; (Part 2) 174, 502-507.

Chatterji, S. K., 1964: "Glottal Spirants and the Glottal Stop in the Aspirates in New Indo-Aryan", Abercrombie et al. (eds.), *In Honour of Daniel Jones*, London, 407-414.

Chen, M. Y., 1972: "The Time Dimension: Contribution toward a Theory of Sound Change", *Foundations of Language* 8, 457-498.

Chen, M. Y. & W. S.-Y. Wang, 1975: "Sound Change: Actuation and Implementation", *Language* 51, 255-281.

Cherry, E. C., 1967: "Roman Jakobson's 'Distinctive Features' as the Normal Coordinates of a Language", *To Honor Roman Jakobson* I, The Hague, 60-64.

Chomsky, C., 1969: *The Acquisition of Syntax in Children from 5 to 10*, Cambridge, Mass.

—, 1971: "Write First, Read Later", *Childhood Education* 47, 296-299.

Chomsky, N., 1964: *Current Issues in Linguistic Theory*, The Hague.

—, 1967: "The General Properties of Language", Millikan & Darlay (eds.), *Brain Mechanisms Underlying Speech and Language*, New York, 73-88.

—, 1972: *Language and Mind*, New York.

—, 1975: *Reflections on Language*, New York.

—, 1977: *Dialogues avec Mitsou Ronat*, Paris.

Chomsky, N. & M. Halle, 1965: "Some Controversial Questions in Phonological Theory", *Journal of Linguistics* 1, 97-138.

—, 1968: *The Sound Pattern of English*, New York.

Chomsky, N. & E. Walker, 1976: "The Linguistic and Psycholinguistic Background", *Explorations in the Biology of Language*. Report of the MIT Work Group in the Biology of Language, Cambridge, Mass., 1975-1976.

Churchward, S., 1926: *A New Samoan Grammar,* Melbourne.

Claparède, E., 1900: "Sur l'audition colorée", *Revue Philosophique* 49, 515-517.

Clavière, J., 1898: "L'audition colorée", *Année Psychologique* 5.

Coetsem, F. van, R. Hendricks, & P. Siegel, 1979: "The Role of Function in Sound Change", *Festschrift William Moulton,* Princeton, N. J.

Cohn, R., 1971: "Differential Cerebral Processing of Noise and Verbal Stimuli", *Science* 172, 599-601.

Cohn, R.-G., 1977: "Mallarmé contre Genette", *Tel Quel* 69, 51-54.

Cole, R. A. & B. Scott, 1974: "Toward a Theory of Speech Perception", *Psychological Review* 81, 348-374.

Cooper, W. E., 1975: "Selective Adaptation to Speech", F. Restle et al. (eds.), *Cognitive Theory* I, New Jersey, 23-54.

Cooper, W. E., D. Billings, & R. Cole, 1976: "Articulatory Effects on Speech Perception: A Second Report", *Journal of Phonetics* 4, 219-232.

Coseriu, E., 1969: "Georg von der Gabelentz et la linguistique synchronique", G. Narr (ed.), *Tübingen Beiträge zur Linguistik* I, Tübingen.

Crothers, J., 1975: "Nasal Consonant Systems", Ferguson et al. (eds.), *Nasálfest,* Stanford, Calif., 153-166.

Crothers, J. & M. Shibatani, 1975: "On Some Fundamental Concepts of Phonology", Goyvaerts & Pullum (eds.), *Essays on the Sound Pattern of English,* Ghent, 505-536.

Crystal, D., 1970: "Prosodic Systems and Language Acquisition", *Prosodic Feature Analysis* III, 77-90.

—, 1973: "Non-Segmental Phonology in Language Acquisition: A Review of the Issues", *Lingua* 32, 1-45.

Cummings, E. E., 1953: *Six Nonlectures,* Cambridge, Mass.

—, 1972: *Complete Poems, 1913-1962,* New York.

Curry, F., 1967: "A Comparison of Left-Handed and Right-Handed Subjects on Verbal and Nonverbal Dichotic Listening Tasks", *Cortex* 3, 343-352.

Curtiss, S., 1977: *Genie - A Psycholinguistic Study of a Modern-Day "Wild Child",* New York.

Cutten, G. B., 1927: *Speaking with Tongues,* New Haven, Conn.

Cutting, J. E. & P. D. Eimas, 1974: "Phonetic-Feature Analyzers and the Processing of Speech in Infants", Haskins Laboratories , *Speech Research* 37/38, 45-63.

Cutting, J. E. & B. S. Rosner, 1974: "Categories and Boundaries in Speech and Music", *Perception and Psychophysics* 16, 564-570.

—, 1976: "Discrimination Functions Predicted from Categories in Speech and Music", Haskins Laboratories, *Speech Research* 47, July-Sept., 59-62.

Čerkasskij, M. A., 1962: "Ob osobennostjax fonologičeskogo stroenija tjurkskogo vokalizma", *Narody Azii i Afriki* 5, Moscow, 142-148.

Čistovič, L. A., 1955: "Vlijanie častotnyx ograničenij na razborčivost' russkix soglasnyx zvukov", *Telefonnaja akustika* I-II.

—, 1961-62: "Tekuščee raspoznavanie reči čelovekom", *Mašinnyj perevod i prikladnaja lingvistika* 6-7.

Čistovič, L. A., V. A. Koževnikov, et al., 1965: *Reč', artikuljacija i vosprijatie.*

Čistovič, L. A. et al., 1976: *Fiziologija reči. Vosprijatie reči čelovekom,* Moscow.

Čukovskij (Chukovsky), K., 1966[19]: *Ot dvux do pjati,* Moscow (English translation, 1971: *From Two to Five,* Berkeley, Calif.).

Dal', V., 1880-82[2]: *Tolkovyj slovar' živogo veliko-russkogo jazyka* I-IV, St. Petersburg-Moscow.

Darwin, C.J., 1971: "Ear Differences in the Recall of Fricatives and Vowels", *Quarterly Journal of Experimental Psychology* 23, 46-62.

—, 1974: "Ear Differences and Hemispheric Specialization", F. Schmitt & F. Worden (eds.), *The Neurosciences: Third Study Program*, Cambridge, Mass., 57-63.

Dave, R., 1977: "Retroflex and Dental Consonants in Gujarati", *Annual Report of the Institute of Phonetics*, University of Copenhagen, 27-155.

Debrunner, A., 1926: "Lautsymbolik in alter und neuester Zeit", *Germanische-Romanische Monatsschrift* 14, 321-338.

Delacroix, H., 1924: *Le langage et la pensée*, Paris.

Delattre, P.C., 1959: Review of L. Kaiser, ed., *Manual of Phonetics* (1951), in *Romance Philology* 13, 80-83.

—, 1966: *Studies in French and Comparative Phonetics*, The Hague.

—, 1967: "Acoustic or Articulatory Invariance?" *Glossa* I, 3-25.

—, 1968a: "From Acoustic Cues to Distinctive Features", *Phonetica* 18, 198-230.

—, 1968b: "Divergences entre nasalités vocalique et consonantique en français", *Word* 24, 64-72.

—, 1968c: "La radiographie des voyelles françaises et sa corrélation acoustique", *French Review* 42, 48-65.

—, 1969: "Coarticulation and the Locus Theory", *Studia Linguistica* 23, 1-26.

—, 1970a: "Des indices acoustiques aux traits pertinents", *Proceedings of the Sixth International Congress of Phonetic Sciences, 1967*, Prague, 35-47.

—, 1970b: "Rapports entre la physiologie et la chronologie de la nasalité distinctive", *Actes du Xe Congrès International des Linguistes* IV, Bucarest, 221-227.

—, 1971: "Pharyngeal Features in the Consonants of Arabic, German, Spanish, French and American English", *Phonetica* 23, 129-155.

Delattre, P.C., A.M. Liberman, & F.S. Cooper, 1964: "Formant Transitions and Loci as Acoustic Correlates of Place of Articulation in American Fricatives", *Studia Linguistica* 16, 104-121.

Delbouille, P., 1967: "Recherches récentes sur la valeur suggestive des sonorités", *Le Vers français au XXe siecle*, Paris.

Dell, F., 1973a: "E muet: fiction graphique ou réalité linguistique?" *Festschrift for Morris Halle*, New York.

—, 1973b: *Les règles et les sons: Introduction à la phonologie générative*, Paris.

Demos, R., 1964: "Plato's Philosophy of Language", *The Journal of Philosophy* 61, No. 20, 595 ff.

Dempwolff, O., 1934 & 1937: *Vergleichende Lautlehre des austronesischen Wortschatzes* I (1934), II (1937) = *Zeitschrift für eingeborene Sprachen*, Beihefte 15, 17.

—, 1939: *Grammatik der Jabem Sprache auf Neu Guinea*, Hamburg.

Dennis, M. & H. A. Whitaker, 1976: "Language Acquisition Following Hemidecortication: Linguistic Superiority of the Left over the Right Hemisphere", *Brain and Language* 3, 404-433.

Derkach, M., G. Fant, & A. de Serpa-Leitão, 1970: "Phoneme Coarticulation in Russian Hard and Soft VCV-utterances with Voiceless Fricatives", Speech Transmission Laboratory, *Quarterly Progress and Status Report* 2-3, Stockholm.

Derrida, J., 1967: *De la grammatologie*, Paris.

—, 1968: "Sémiologie et grammatologie", *Social Science Information* VII-3, 135-148.

Derwing, B., 1973: *Transformational Grammar as a Theory of Language Acquisition*, Cambridge, Eng.

Devine, A. M., 1974: "Aspiration, Universals, and the Study of Dead Languages", *Stanford University Working Papers on Language Universals* # 15, 1-24.

Diakonoff (D'jakonov), I. M., 1974: "Ancient Writing and Ancient Written Language: Pitfalls and Peculiarities in the Study of Sumerian", *Sumerological Studies in Honor of Thorkild Jacobsen*, Chicago, 99-121.

Diels, H., 1899: *Elementum*, Leipzig.

Diffloth, G., 1976: "Expressives in Semai", *Oceanic Linguistics Special Publication No. 13: Austroasiatic Studies* I, Honolulu, 249-264.

Dil, A., 1971: "Bengali Baby Talk", *Word* 27, 11-27.

Dłuska, M., 1937: "Polskie afrykaty", *Travaux du laboratoire de phonètique expérimentale de l'Université Jean-Casimir de Léopol* II.

Doke, M., 1935: *Bantu Linguistic Terminology*, London.

Dorman, M. F., M. Studdert-Kennedy, & L. J. Raphael, 1976: "Stop-Consonant Recognition: Release Bursts and Formant Transitions as Functionally Equivalent Context-Dependent Cues", Haskins Laboratories, *Speech Research* 47, 1-27.

Doroszewski, W., 1934: "Mowa mieszkańców wsi Staroźreby", *Prace filologiczne* 16, 249-278.

—, 1935: "Pour une représentation statistique des isoglosses", *Bulletin de la Société Linguistique de Paris* 36.1, 28-42.

Douglas, N., 1916: *London Street Games*, London.

Dukel'skij, N. I., 1962: *Principy segmentacii rečevogo potoka*, Moscow.

Durand, M., 1954: "Le Langage enfantin", *Conférences de l'Institut de linguistique de l'Université de Paris* 11.

Echeverría, M. S. & H. Contreras, 1965: "Araucanian Phonemics", *International Journal of American Linguistics* 31, 132-135.

Eckhardt, E., 1937: "Reim und Stabreim im Dienste der neuenglischen Wortbildung", *Englische Studien* 72, 161-191.

Ehrenreich, P., 1894: "Materialien zur Sprachenkunde Brasiliens, I", *Zeitschrift für Ethnologie* 26, 20-37.

Eimas, P. D., E. R. Siqueland, P. Jusczyk, & J. Vigorito, 1971: "Speech Perception in Infants", *Science* 171, 303-306.

Elizarenkova, T. Ja., 1961: "Differencial'nye èlementy soglasnyx fonem xindi", *Voprosy jazykoznanija* # 5, 22-33.

Elizarenkova, T. Ja. & V. N. Toporov, 1965: *Jazyk pali*, Moscow.

Erickson, D. M., 1976: *A Physiological Analysis of the Tones of Thai*, Ph. D. dissertation, University of Connecticut.

Erickson, D. M., M. Libermann, & S. Niimi, 1977: "The Geniohyoid and the Role of the Strap Muscles", Haskins Laboratories, *Speech Research* 49.

Ertel, S., 1969: *Psychophonetik: Untersuchungen über Lautsymbolik und Motivation*, Göttingen.

Erzsébet, P. D., 1974: "Synaesthesia and Poetry", *Poetics: International Review for the Theory of Literature* 11, 23-44.

Etienne, L., 1957: *L'art du contrepet*, Paris.

Fairley, I., 1968: "Syntax as Style: An Analysis of Three Cummings' Poems", *Studies Presented to R. Jakobson by His Students,* Cambridge, Mass., 105-111.

—, 1975: *E. E. Cummings & Ungrammar,* New York.

Fant, G., 1948: "Analys av de Svenska vokalljuden", *L. M. Ericsson Protokoll* H/P 1035, Stockholm.

—, 1949: "Analys av de Svenska konsonantljuden", *L. M. Ericsson Protokoll* H/P 1064, Stockholm, 38 ff. & Fig. 19.

—, 1950: "Transmission Properties of the Vocal Tract", Part I, *Quarterly Progress Report,* Acoustics Lab., MIT, July–Sept., 20-23; Part II, Oct.–Dec., 14-19.

—, 1952: "Transmission Properties of the Vocal Tract with Application to the Acoustic Specification of Phonemes", *Technical Report* # 12, Acoustics Lab., MIT, 1-16.

—, 1959: "Acoustic Analysis and Synthesis of Speech with Applications to Swedish", *Ericsson Technics* XV, No. 1, 1-106.

—, 1966: "Chairman's Introduction", *XVIII International Congress of Psychology, Symposium 23: Models of Speech Perception.*

—, 1967: "Auditory Patterns of Speech", *Proceedings of the Symposium on Models for the Perception of Speech and Visual Form,* Cambridge, Mass., 111-125.

—, 1968: "Analysis and Synthesis of Speech Processes", B. Malmberg (ed.), *Manual of Phonetics,* Amsterdam, 173-277.

—, 1969: *Acoustic Specification of Speech: Final Scientific Report* (1 Jan. 1966–31 Dec. 1966) (mimeographed).

—, 1970[2]: *Acoustic Theory of Speech Production,* The Hague.

—, 1973: *Speech Sounds and Features,* Cambridge, Mass.

—, 1976: "In Search of the Speech Code – Problems in Acoustic Theory of Speech Production", open lecture at University of Tokyo, December 4.

Farwell, C. B., 1973: "The Language Spoken to Children", *Papers and Reports on Child Language Development* 5-6, Stanford University, 31-62.

Ferdière, G., 1947: "Intérêt psychologique et psychopathologique des comptines et formulettes de l'enfance", *L'Évolution Psychiatrique* 3, 47-63.

Ferguson, C. A., 1963: "Assumptions about Nasals: A Sample Study in Phonological Universals", Greenberg (ed.), *Universals of Language,* Cambridge, Mass., 53-60.

—, 1964: "Baby Talk in Six Languages", *American Anthropologist* 66.

—, 1973: "Fricatives in Child Language Acquisition", *Papers and Reports on Child Language Development* 6, Stanford University, 61-85.

—, 1974: "Universals of Nasality", *Stanford University Working Papers on Language Universals* # 14, 1-16.

—, 1975: "Universal Tendencies and 'Normal' Nasality", Ferguson et al. (eds.), *Nasálfest,* Stanford, Calif., 175-196.

Ferguson, C. A. & C. B. Farwell, 1975: "Words and Sounds in Early Language Acquisition", *Language* 51, 419-439.

Ferguson, C. A. & O. Garnica, 1975: "Theories of Phonological Development", E. Lenneberg (ed.), *Foundations of Language Development* I, New York.

Ferguson, C. A., D. B. Peizer, & T. E. Weeks, 1973: "Model-and-Replica Phonological Grammar of a Child's First Words", *Lingua* 31, 35-65.

Firth, J. R., 1957: *Papers in Linguistics, 1934-1951,* Oxford.

—, 1968: *Selected Papers, 1952-1959,* Bloomington, Ind.

Fischer-Jørgensen, E., 1954: "Acoustic Analysis of Stop Consonants", *Miscellanea Phonetica* 2, 42-59.

—, 1958: "What Can the New Techniques of Acoustic Phonetics Contribute to Linguistics?" *Proceedings of the Eighth International Congress of Linguists*, Oslo, 433–478 (Report); 478–499 (Discussion).

—, 1966: "Form and Substance in Glossematics", *Acta Linguistica Hafniensia* 10, 1–33.

—, 1967: "Perceptual Dimensions of Vowels", *To Honor Roman Jakobson*, The Hague, 667–671.

—, 1968: "Voicing, Tenseness, and Aspiration in Stop Consonants, with Special Reference to French and Danish", *Annual Report of the Institute of Phonetics of the University of Copenhagen (ARIPUC)* 3, 63–114.

—, 1969: "Untersuchungen zum sogenannten festen und losen Anschluß", *Kopenhagener germanistische Studien* B 1, Copenhagen, 136–164.

—, 1972a: "Formant Frequencies of Long and Short Danish Vowels", *Studies for Einar Haugen*, The Hague, 189–200.

—, 1972b: "Kinesthetic Judgment of Effort in the Production of Stop Consonants", *Annual Report of the Institute of Phonetics of the University of Copenhagen (ARIPUC)* 6, 59–73.

—, 1972c: "PTK et BDG français en position intervocalique accentuée", *Papers in Linguistics and Phonetics to the Memory of Pierre Delattre*, The Hague, 143–200.

—, 1975: *Trends in Phonological Theory*, Copenhagen.

—, 1976: "Some Data on North German Stops and Affricates", *Annual Report of the Institute of Phonetics of the University of Copenhagen (ARIPUC)* 10, 149–200.

—, 1978: "On the Universal Character of Phonetic Symbolism with Special Reference to Vowels", *Studia Linguistica* 32, 80–90.

Flannery, R., 1946: "Men's and Women's Speech in Gros Ventre", *International Journal of American Linguistics* 12, 133–135.

Flournoy, T., 1900: *From India to the Planet Mars: A Study of a Case of Somnambulism with Glossolalia*, New York & London. (Translated from French: *Des Indes à la Planète Mars: Étude sur un cas de somnambulisme avec glossolalie*, Geneva, 1900.)

—, 1902: "Nouvelles observations sur un cas du somnambulisme avec glossolalie", *Archives Psychologiques* 1, 101–255.

Flydal, L., 1974: "Autour d'un dictionnaire de la prononciation française", *Norwegian Journal of Linguistics* 29, 1–33.

Foley, J., 1970: "Phonological Distinctive Features", *Folia Linguistica* 4, 87–92.

—, 1977: *Foundations of Theoretical Phonology*, Cambridge, Eng.

Foley, W. A., 1975: "Some Rules Involving Nasals and Their Implications", Ferguson et al. (eds.), *Nasálfest*, Stanford, Calif., 213–230.

Fónagy, I., 1956: "Über den Verlauf des Lautwandels", *Acta Linguistica* 6, 173–278.

—, 1963: *Die Metaphern in der Phonetik*, The Hague.

—, 1966: "Form and Function of Poetic Language", *Diogenes* 51, 72–110.

—, 1972: "A propos de la genèse de la phrase enfantine", *Lingua* 30, 31–71.

—, 1976: "Mimique buccale", *Phonetica* 33, 31–44.

Forchhammer, J., 1951: *Einführung in die allgemeine Sprechkunde*, Heidelberg.

Fortunatov, F. F., 1956: *Izbrannye trudy* I, Moscow.

Fox, C. W., 1935: "An Experimental Study of Naming", *American Journal of Psychology* 47, 545–578.

Fox, J. J., 1974: "Our Ancestors Spoke in Pairs: Rotinese Views of Language, Dialect and Code", R. Bauman & J. Scherzer (eds.), *Explorations in the Ethnography of Speaking*, Cambridge, Mass., 65–88.

–, 1975: "On Binary Categories and Primary Symbols", R. Willis (ed.), *The Interpretation of Symbolism*, New York, 99–132.

–, 1977: "Roman Jakobson and the Comparative Study of Parallelism", see Armstrong & van Schooneveld, 59–90.

Frachtenberg, L. J., 1920: "Abnormal Types of Speech in Quileute", *International Journal of American Linguistics* 1, 295–299.

–, 1922: "Coos", *Handbook of American Indian Languages* II, Washington, 297–429.

Francescato, G., 1970: *Il linguaggio infantile – Strutturazione e apprendimento*, Turin.

Frazer, J. G., 1935[3]: *Taboo and the Perils of the Soul*, New York & Edinburgh.

French, P. L., 1977: "Toward an Explanation of Phonetic Symbolism", *Word* 28, 305–322.

Fromkin, V. A., 1966: "Neuromuscular Specification of Linguistic Units", *Language and Speech* I, 1170–1199.

Fromkin, V. A. et al., 1974: "The Development of Language in Genie: A case of language acquisition beyond the 'critical period'", *Brain and Language* I, 81 ff.

Fry, D. B., 1974: "An Auditory Theory of Speech Production", *World Papers in Phonetics*, Tokyo, 21–36.

Fudge, E. C., 1967: "The Nature of Phonological Primes", *Journal of Linguistics* 3, 1–36.

Fujimura, O., 1967: "The Spectral Shape in the F2–F3 Region", W. Wathen-Dunn (ed.), *Models for the Perception of Speech and Visual Form*, Cambridge, Mass., 251–256.

Fuller, J. O., 1968: *Swinburne: A Critical Biography*, London.

Furfey, P. H., 1944: "Men's and Women's Language", *American Catholic Sociological Review* 5, 218–223.

Gabelentz, G. v. d., 1891: *Die Sprachwissenschaft, ihre Aufgaben, Methoden und bisherigen Ergebnisse*, Leipzig.

Galin, D., 1974: "Implications for Psychiatry of Left and Right Cerebral Specialization", *Archives of General Psychiatry* 31, 572–583.

Gallop, D., 1963: "Plato and the Alphabet", *The Philosophical Review* 72, 364 ff.

Gamkrelidze, T. V., 1974: "Order of 'rewrite rules' in Diachronic Phonology", *Linguistics* 126, 25–31.

–, 1975: "On the Correlation of Stops and Fricatives in a Phonological System", *Lingua* 35, 231–261; cf. the complete original Russian version, 1974: *Sootnošenie smyčnyx i frikativnyx v fonologičeskoj sisteme*, Moscow.

–, 1977: "Linguistic Typology and Indo-European Reconstruction", *Linguistic Studies Offered to Joseph Greenberg*, Saratoga, Calif., 399–406.

Gamkrelidze, T. V., T. Elizarenkova & V. V. Ivanov, 1977: "Lingvističeskaja teorija R. O. Jakobsona v rabotax sovetskix lingvistov", see Armstrong & van Schooneveld, 91–121.

Gamkrelidze, T. V. & V. V. Ivanov, 1973: "Sprachtypologie und die Rekonstruktion der gemeinindogermanischen Verschlüsse", *Phonetica* 27, 150–156.

Gaprindašvili, Š., 1970: "Voprosy teorii differencial'nyx priznakov", *Proceedings of the Sixth International Congress of Phonetic Sciences, 1967*, Prague, 351–355.

Garbell, I., 1965: *The Jewish Neo-Aramaic Dialect of Persian Azerbaijan*, The Hague.

Garvin, P. L., 1950: "Wichita I: Phonemics", *International Journal of American Linguistics* 16, 179–184.

–, 1971: "The Sound Pattern of Ponopean", *Travaux linguistiques de Prague* 4, 41–61.

Gazzaniga, M. S. & R. W. Sperry, 1967: "Language after Section of the Cerebral Commissures", *Brain* 90, 131–148.

Gendron, J. D., 1970: "Étude expérimentale des aspirées sonores en Malayalam", *Proceedings of the Sixth International Congress of Phonetic Sciences, 1967*, Prague, 365–369.

Genette, G., 1976: *Mimologiques*, Paris.

Genko, A. N., 1955: *Abazinskij jazyk*, Moscow.

Ginneken, J. van., 1907: *Principes de linguistique psychologique*, Paris.

Gleason, J. B., 1973: "Code Switching in Children's Language", T. E. Moore (ed.), *Cognitive Development and the Acquisition of Language*, New York, 159–167.

Goddard, I., 1974: "An Outline of the Historical Phonology of Arapaho and Atsina", *International Journal of American Linguistics* 40, 102–116.

Godel, R., 1957: *Les sources manuscrites du Cours de linguistique générale de F. de Saussure*, Geneva & Paris.

—, 1967: "Dorica castra: sur une figure sonore de la poésie latine", *To Honor Roman Jakobson* I, The Hague & Paris, 760–769.

Gołębiewski, P. K., 1931: "Le langage d'après St. Augustin", *Bulletin de la Société polonaise de linguistique* 3, 1–37.

Gombrich, E. H., 1961[2]: *Art and Illusion*, New York.

Gomperz, H., 1908: *Weltanschauungslehre II: Noologie*, Jena.

Gonda, J., 1940: "Some Remarks on Onomatopoeia, Sound-Symbolism, and Word-Formation", *Tijdschrift voor indische taal-land-en volkenkunde* 80, 135–210.

—, 1949–50: "The Function of Word Duplication in Indonesian Languages", *Lingua* 2, 170–197.

Goodglass, H., 1978: *Selected Papers in Neurolinguistics*, Munich.

Goodman, F. D., 1969: "Phonetic Analysis of Glossolalia in Four Cultural Settings", *Journal for the Scientific Study of Religion* 8, 227–239.

Goody, J. & I. Watt, 1963: "Consequences of Literacy", *Comparative Studies in Social History* 5.

Gordon, H., 1970: "Hemispheric Asymmetry in the Perception of Musical Chords", *Cortex* 6, 987–1010.

Gorlitzer, V. von Mundy, 1957: "Zur Frage der paarig veranlagten Sprachzentren", *Nervenarzt* 28, 212–216.

Goyvaerts, D. L. & G. K. Pullum, 1975: *Essays on the Sound Pattern of English*, Ghent.

Graham, L. & A. House, 1971: "Phonological Oppositions in Children: A Perceptual Study", *Journal of the Acoustical Society of America* 49, 559–566.

Grammont, M., 1901: "Onomatopées et mots expressifs", *Trentenaire de la Société pour l'Étude des Langues Romanes*, Montpellier, 261–322.

—, 1913[2]: *Le vers français: ses moyens d'expression, son harmonie*, Paris.

—, 1933: *Traité de phonétique*, Paris.

Greenberg, J. H., 1962: "Is the Vowel-Consonant Dichotomy Universal?" *Word* 18, 73–81.

—, 1963a: *Universals of Language*, Cambridge, Mass.

—, 1963b: "Vowel Harmony in African Languages", *Actes du Second Colloque International de Linguistique Nigro-Africaine, Dakar*, 33–38.

—, 1965: "Some Generalizations Concerning Initial and Final Consonant Sequences", *Linguistics* 18, 5–34.

—, 1966a: *Language Universals*, The Hague.

—, 1966b: "Synchronic and Diachronic Universals in Phonology", *Language* 42, 508-517.

—, 1969: "Some Methods of Dynamic Comparison in Linguistics", J. Puhvel (ed.), *Substance and Structure in Language*, Berkeley, Calif., 147-203.

—, 1970: "Some Generalizations Concerning Glottalic Consonants, Especially Implosives", *International Journal of American Linguistics* 36, 123-145.

Greenberg, J. H. & D. Kaschube, 1976: "Word Prosodic Systems: A Preliminary Report", *Stanford University Working Papers on Language Universals* #20, 1-18.

Grégoire, A., 1937 & 1947: I. *L'Apprentissage du langage, les deux premières années, Liège* (1937); II. *La troisième année et les années suivantes,* Gembloux (1947).

—, 1948: Review of *Kindersprache,* in *Lingua* 1, 162-174.

—, 1950: "La renaissance scientifique de la linguistique enfantine", *Lingua* 2, 355-398.

—, 1971: "L'apprentissage du langage", A. Bar-Adon & W. F. Leopold (eds.), *Child Language: A Book of Readings,* New Jersey, 90-95.

Groot, A. W. de, 1929: "Zum phonologischen System des Nordniederländischen", *Donum Natalicium Schrijnen,* Chartres, 549 ff.

Gudschinsky, S. G. & H. & F. Popovich, 1970: "Native Reaction and Phonetic Similarity in Maxakalí Phonology", *Language* 46, 77-88.

Guillaume, P., 1937: *Psychologie de la forme.*

Gump, P. V. & B. Sutton-Smith, 1965: "The 'It' Role in Children's Games", A. Dundes (ed.), *The Study of Folklore,* Englewood Cliffs, N. J., 329-336.

Guro, E., 1914: *Nebesnye verbljužata,* St. Petersburg.

Gvozdev, A. N., 1961: *Voprosy izučenija detskoj reči,* Moscow.

Haas, M. R., 1968: "Notes on a Chipewyan Dialect", *International Journal of American Linguistics* 34, 165-175.

—, 1969: "Internal Reconstruction of the Nootka-Nitinat Pronominal Suffixes", *International Journal of American Linguistics* 35, 108-124.

—, 1970: "Consonant Symbolism in Northwestern California", E. H. Swanson, Jr. (ed.), *Languages and Cultures of Western North America: Essays in Honor of Sven S. Liljeblad,* Pocatello, Idaho, 86-96.

Haggard, M. P., 1966: "Stimulus and Response Processes in Speech Perception", *XVIII International Congress of Psychology, Symposium 23: Models of Speech Perception.*

—, 1971: "Encoding and the REA for Speech Signals", *Quarterly Journal for Experimental Psychology* 23, 34-45.

Hála, B., 1941: *Akustická podstata samohlásek,* Prague.

—, 1956: *Nature acoustique des voyelles,* Prague.

Hála, B. & M. Sovák, 1947[2]: *Hlas. Řeč. Sluch,* Prague.

Hall, R. A., Jr., 1948: *French: Structural Sketch I,* Baltimore.

Halle, M., 1962: "Phonology in Generative Grammar", *Word* 18, 54-72.

—, 1970: "Is Kabardian A Vowelless Language?" *Foundations of Language* 6, 95-103.

—, 1972: "Theoretical Issues in Phonology in the 1970's", Rigault & Charbonneau (eds.), *Proceedings of the Seventh International Congress of Phonetic Sciences,* The Hague, 179-205.

—, 1976: "Roman Jakobson's Contribution to the Modern Study of Speech Sounds", L. Matejka (ed.), *Sound, Sign, and Meaning = Michigan Slavic Contributions* #6, Ann Arbor, 79 ff. (Reprinted in Armstrong & van Schooneveld, 123-143).

—, 1977a: "Language and Communication", *The Telephone's First Century - and Beyond*, New York, 37–59.

—, 1977b: "Tenseness, Vowel Shift, and the Phonology of the Back Vowels in Modern English", *Linguistic Inquiry* 8, 611–625.

Halle, M. & K. N. Stevens, 1964: "Speech Recognition: A Model and a Program for Research", Fodor & Katz (eds.), *The Structure of Language*, Englewood Cliffs, N. J.

—, 1971: "A Note on Laryngeal Features", MIT, Research Laboratory of Electronics, *Quarterly Progress Report* 101, 198–213.

Hanson, G., 1963: "A Factorial Investigation of Speech Sound Perception", *Scandinavian Journal of Psychology* 4, 123–128.

—, 1964: "A Further Factorial Investigation of Speech Sound Perception", *The Scandinavian Journal of Psychology* 5, 117–122.

—, 1966: "Distinctive Features and Response Dimensions of Vowel Perception", *XVIII International Congress of Psychology, Symposium 23: Models of Speech Perception*.

Harnad, S. et al. (eds.), 1977: *Lateralization in the Nervous System*, New York.

Harris, Z. S., 1951: *Methods of Structural Linguistics*, Chicago.

—, 1963: *Structural Linguistics*, Chicago.

Hartshorne, C., 1934: *The Philosophy and Psychology of Sensation*, Chicago.

Hattori, Sh., 1961: "Prosodeme, Syllable Structure, and Laryngeal Phonemes", *Bulletin of the Summer Institute in Linguistics* 1 (Tokyo, International Christian University), July, 1–27.

Haudricourt, A. G., 1950: "Les consonnes préglottalisées en Indochine", *Bulletin de la Société Linguistique de Paris* 46, 172–182.

—, 1961: "Bipartition et tripartition des systèmes de tons dans quelques langues d'Extrême-Orient", *Bulletin de la Société Linguistique de Paris* 56, 163–180.

—, 1972: *Problèmes de phonologie diachronique*, Paris.

Haugen, E., 1972²: *First Grammatical Treatise: The Earliest Germanic Phonology - An Edition, Translation and Commentary*, London (rev. ed.).

Havers, W., 1946: *Neuere Literatur zum Sprachtabu* = Sitzungsberichte der Akademie der Wissenschaften in Wien, Phil.-hist. Klasse, 223, Abh. 5.

Havránek, B., 1932: "Zur phonologischen Geographie (Das Vokalsystem des balkanischen Sprachbundes)", *Proceedings of the International Congress of Phonetic Sciences*, Amsterdam.

Hécaen, H., 1969: "Aphasic, Apraxic and Agnosic Syndromes in Right and Left Hemisphere Lesions", P. J. Vinken & G. W. Gruyn (eds.), *Handbook of Clinical Neurology* IV, Amsterdam & New York, 293–311.

Hécaen, H. & M. Albert, 1978: *Human Neuropsychology*, New York.

Hécaen, H., J. Dubois, & P. Marcie, 1969: "Critères neurolinguistiques d'une classification des aphasies", *Acta Neurologica Belgica* 67, 959–987.

Heffner, R-M. S., 1964: *General Phonetics*, Madison, Wisconsin.

Heise, D. R., 1965: "Sound-Meaning Correlation among 1,000 English Words: Semantic Differential Profiles for 1,000 Most Frequent English Words", *Psychological Monographs* 79, #8, 1–31.

Heller, L. G., 1964: "Expansion vs. Reduction Grammar: Separate, Reciprocal, or What?" *Proceedings of the Ninth International Congress of Linguists*, The Hague, 533–536.

Hellwag, C., 1781: *De formatione loquelae*, Tübingen.

Henderson, M. M. T., 1976: "Redundancy, Markedness, and Simultaneous Constraints in Phonology", *Language* 52, 314-325.

Henry, J. & Z., 1940: "Speech Disturbances in Pilagá Indian Children", *American Journal of Orthopsychiatry* 10, 362-369.

Henry, V., 1896: *Antinomies linguistiques*, Paris.

—, 1901: *Le langage martien. Étude analytique de la genèse d'une langue dans un cas de glossolalie somnambulique*, Paris.

Hering, E., 1964: *Outline of a Theory of the Light Sense*, Cambridge, Mass.

Hertz, R., 1973: "The Pre-Eminence of the Right Hand: A Study in Religious Polarity", R. Needham (ed.), *Right and Left*, Chicago, 3-31.

Herzog, G., 1946: "Some Linguistic Aspects of American Indian Poetry", *Word* 2, 82 f.

Hills, E. C., 1924: "Exclamations in American English", *Dialect Notes* V, Part 7, 253-285.

Hilmer, H., 1914: *Schallnachahmung, Wortschöpfung und Bedeutungswandel*, Halle.

Hjelmslev, L., 1939: "Forme et substance linguistiques", *Essais linguistiques* II, Copenhagen, 1973.

—, 1961²: *Prolegomena to a Theory of Language*, Madison, Wis.

Hockett, C. F., 1955: *Manual of Phonology*, Baltimore, Md.

—, 1958: *A Course in Modern Linguistics*, New York.

—, 1959: "Animal Languages and Human Language", J. S. Spuhler (ed.), *The Evolution of Man's Capacity for Culture*, Detroit.

—, 1960: "The Origin of Speech", *Scientific American*, 2-10.

—, 1961: "Grammar for the Hearer", *Proceedings of the Twelfth Symposium in Applied Mathematics*, Providence, R. I., 220-236.

—, 1965: "Sound Change", *Language* 41, 185-204.

—, 1967: "Where the Tongue Slips, There Slip I", *To Honor Roman Jakobson*, The Hague, 910-935.

—, (ed.), 1970: *A Leonard Bloomfield Anthology*, Bloomington, Ind.

Hockett, C. F. & R. Ascher, 1964: "The Human Revolution", *Current Anthropology* 5, 135-147.

Hoenigswald, H. M., 1948: "Declension and Nasalization in Hindustani", *Journal of the American Oriental Society* 68, 139-144.

Hoijer, H., 1942: "Phonetic and Phonemic Change in the Athapaskan Languages", *Language* 18, 218-220.

Hoijer, H. et al. (eds.), 1963: *Studies in the Athapaskan Languages*, Berkeley, Calif.

Holenstein, E., 1976a: *Linguistik. Semiotik. Hermeneutik*, Frankfurt.

—, 1976b: *Roman Jakobson's Approach to Language*, Bloomington, Ind.

—, 1977: "Jakobson's Contribution to Phenomenology", see Armstrong & van Schooneveld, 145-162.

Holmes, J. M., 1978: "'Regression' and Reading Breakdown", see Caramazza & Zurif, 87-98.

Hooper, J., 1976: *An Introduction to Natural Generative Phonology*, New York.

Hopkins, G. M., 1959: H. House (ed.), *Journals and Papers*, Oxford.

Hornbostel, E. M. von, 1927a: "Laut und Sinn", *Festschrift für C. Meinhof*, Hamburg, 329-348.

—, 1927b: "The Unity of the Senses", *Psyche* 7 (# 28), 83-89.

Houlihan, K. & G. Iverson, 1977: "Functionally-Constrained Phonology", presented at the Conference on the Differentiation of Current Phonological Theories, Indiana University.

Householder, F. W., 1946: "On the Problem of Sound and Meaning, an English Phonestheme", *Word* 2, 83 f.

—, 1962: "Azerbaijani Onomatopes", N. Poppe (ed.), *American Studies in Altaic Linguistics*, Bloomington, Ind., 115-121.

Howard, P. G., 1963: "A Preliminary Presentation of Slave Phonemes", H. Hoijer et al. (eds.), *Studies in the Athapaskan Languages*, University of California Publications in Linguistics 29, 42-47.

Hsieh, H.-I., 1971: "Lexical Diffusion in Child Acquisition", *Monthly Internal Memorandum*, The Phonology Laboratory, University of California, Berkeley, July, 38-54.

Huber, K., 1934: "Die Vokalmischung und das Qualitätensystem der Vokale", *Archiv für Psychologie* 91.

Huffman, F. E., 1976: "The Register Problem in Fifteen Mon-Khmer Languages", *Oceanic Linguistics Special Publication No. 13: Austroasiatic Studies* I, Honolulu, 575-589.

Huggins, A. W. F., 1966: "Delayed Auditory Feedback and the Temporal Properties of Speech Material", *XVIII International Congress of Psychology, Symposium 23: Models of Speech Perception*.

Humboldt, W. von, 1905: A. Leitzmann (ed.), *Werke*, Berlin.

Hurd, C. & P., 1971: "Nasioi Verbs", *Oceanic Linguistics* 9, 37-78.

Hurvich, L. M. & D. Jameson, 1957: "An Opponent Process Theory of Color Vision", *Psychological Review* 65, 384-404.

—, 1974: "Opponent Processes as a Model of Neural Organization", *American Psychologist* 29, 88-101.

Hyman, L. M., 1975: *Phonology: Theory and Analysis*, New York.

Ingram, D., 1978: "The Production of Word-Initial Fricatives and Affricates by Normal and Linguistically Deviant Children", see Caramazza & Zurif, 63-86.

Isačenko, A. V., 1968: *Spektrografická analýza slovenských hlások*, Bratislava.

Ivanov, V. V., 1962: "Teorija fonologičeskix različitel'nyx priznakov", V. A. Zvegincev (ed.), *Novoe v lingvistike* II, Moscow.

—, 1972: "Binarnye struktury v semiotičeskix sistemax", *Sistemnye issledovanija*, Annuary of the Academy of Sciences of the USSR, Moscow, 206-236 (English translation in R. J. Bogdan & I. Niiniluoto [eds.], *Logic, Language, and Probability*, Dordrecht, 196-200).

—, 1974: "On Antisymmetrical and Asymmetrical Relations in Natural Languages and Other Semiotic Systems", *Linguistics* 119, 35-40.

—, 1975: "K sinxronnoj i diaxroničeskoj tipologii prosodičeskix sistem s laringalizovannymi ili faringalizovannymi tonemami", T. Ja. Elizarenkova (ed.), *Očerki po fonologii vostočnyx jazykov*, Moscow, 3-58.

Ivić, M., 1965: *Trends in Modern Linguistics*, The Hague.

Ivić, P., 1965: "Roman Jakobson and the Growth of Phonology", *Linguistics* 18, 35-78.

—, 1972: "On the Nature of Prosodic Phenomena", *Phonetica Pragensia* 3, 117-121.

Iyer, K. A. S., 1947: "The Doctrine of Sphoṭa", *Journal of the Ganganatha Jha Research Institute* 5, 121-147.

Jaberg, K., 1930: "Spiel und Scherz in der Sprache", *Festgabe für S. Singer*, Tübingen, 67-81.

Jacob, F., 1970: *La logique du vivant*, Paris (English translation, 1973: *The Logic of Life*, New York).

−, 1974: "Le modèle linguistique en biologie", *Critique* 322, 197–205.

Jacobs, M., 1931: "A Sketch of Northern Sahaptin Grammar", *Publications in Anthropology* 4, Seattle, 103–107.

Jacobsen, W., 1969: "Origin of the Nootka Pharyngeals", *International Journal of American Linguistics* 35, 125–153.

RJ = Jakobson, R.: *Selected Writings* I², 1971 b; II, 1971 c; IV, 1966; V, 1979; VI, 1985 a; VII, 1985 b, The Hague.

−, 1923: *O cešskom stixe preimuščestvenno v sopostavlenii s russkim*, Berlin & Moscow (German translation, 1974: *Über den tschechischen Vers: Unter besonderer Berücksichtigung des russischen Verses*, Konstanz).

−, 1960: "Linguistics and Poetics", *Style in Language*, Cambridge, Mass., 350–377.

−, 1962: "Concluding Remarks", *Proceedings of the Fourth International Congress of Phonetic Sciences*, The Hague, xxv–xxix.

−, 1968: *Child Language, Aphasia, and Phonological Universals*, The Hague (translation of 1941: *Kindersprache, Aphasie und allgemeine Lautgesetze*, Uppsala [also in 1971²: *Selected Writings* I, The Hague]).

−, 1971 a: *Studies on Child Language and Aphasia*, The Hague.

−, 1972: "Verbal Communication", *Scientific American* 227, 72–80.

−, 1974: „Life and Language", *Linguistics* 138, 97–103.

−, 1975: "Glosses on the Medieval Insight into the Science of Language", *Mélanges Linguistiques Offerts à Émile Benveniste*, Paris, 289–303.

−, 1977: "Der grammatische Aufbau der Kindersprache", Rheinisch-Westfälische Akademie der Wissenschaften, *Vorträge* G 218 (followed by Diskussionsbeiträge).

−, 1978: "Mutual Assimilation of Russian Voiced and Voiceless Consonants", *Sign and Sound* (= *Studia Linguistica* 32, 1978), 107–110.

−, 1979: "K jazykovedčeskoj problematike soznanija i bessoznatel'nosti", *The Unconscious: Its Nature, Functions, and Method of Study* III, Tbilisi Georgian Academy of Sciences.

Jakobson, R., G. Fant, & M. Halle, 1952: *Preliminaries to Speech Analysis*, Cambridge, Mass.

Jakobson, R. & M. Halle, 1956: *Fundamentals of Language*, The Hague.

−, 1964: "Tenseness and Laxness", *In Honour of Daniel Jones*, London, 96–101.

−, 1968: "Phonology in Relation to Phonetics", B. Malmberg (ed.), *Manual of Phonetics*, Amsterdam, 411–449.

Jakobson, R. & L. R. Waugh, 1979: "An Instance of Interconnection between the Distinctive Features", B. Lindblom & S. Öhman (eds.), *Frontiers of Speech Communication*, Stockholm & London.

Jakovlev, N. F., 1928: "Matematičeskaja formula postroenija alfavita", *Kul'tura i pis'mennost' vostoka* I, Moscow, 41–64.

Janota, P., 1967: *Personal Characteristics of Speech*, Prague.

Jaquith, J. R., 1967: "Toward a Typology of Formal Communicative Behaviors: Glossolalia", *Anthropological Linguistics* 9.8, 1–8.

Jespersen, O., 1904: *Lehrbuch der Phonetik*, Leipzig.

−, 1918: "Nogle *men*-ord", *Studier tillegnade Esaias Tegner*, Lund, 49–55.

−, 1922 a: "Lydsymbolik", *Nordisk Tidskrift för Vetenskap, Konst och Industri* (II), Stockholm, 122–131.

−, 1922 b: *Language - Its Nature, Development and Origin*, London.

−, 1924: *The Philosophy of Grammar*, London.

—, 1933: "Symbolic Value of the Vowel *i*" [1922], in his *Linguistica,* College Park, Maryland, 283-303.

Johnson, R.C., N.S.Suzuki,&W.K.Ohls, 1964: "Phonetic Symbolism in an Artificial Language", *Journal of Abnormal and Social Psychology* 69, 233-236.

Jones, D., 1918: *An Outline of English Phonetics,* Cambridge, Eng.

—, 1962: *The Phoneme, Its Nature and Use* (revised edition), Cambridge, Eng.

Jones, L.G., 1967: "English Phonotactic Structure and First-Language Acquisition", *Lingua* 19, 1-59.

Joos, M., 1948: "Acoustic Phonetics", *Language Monograph* # 23, Baltimore.

Jurgens-Buning, J. E. & C. H. van Schooneveld, 1961: *The Sentence Intonation of Contemporary Standard Russian as a Linguistic Structure,* The Hague.

Jušmanov, N.V., 1937: "Fonetičeskie paralleli afrikanskix i jafetičeskix jazykov", *Africana* I, Moscow, 19-44.

Jünger, E., 1934: *Geheimnisse der Sprache. Zwei Essays,* Hamburg.

Kaczmarek, L., 1953: *Kształtowanie się mowy dziecka,* Poznań.

Kaiser, L., 1929: "La Langue d'Urk", *Archives néerlandaises de phonétique expérimentale* IV, 116ff.

Kajbarov, A.T., 1966: "Ujgurskij (novoujgurskij) jazyk", *Jazyki Narodov SSSR,* II: *Tjurkskie jazyki,* Moscow, 363.

Kania, J.T., 1972: "Phonetik der Kinder mit verzögerter Sprachentwicklung", K.Ohnesorg (ed.), *Colloquium Paedolinguisticum,* The Hague, 124-128.

Kaper, W., 1959: *Einige Erscheinungen der kindlichen Spracherwerbung erläutert im Lichte des vom Kinde gezeigten Interesses für Sprachliches,* Groningen.

Karcevskij, S., 1929: "Du dualisme asymétrique du signe linguistique", *Travaux du Cercle Linguistique de Prague* 1, 33-38.

—, 1931: "Sur la phonologie de la phrase", *Travaux du Cercle Linguistique de Prague* 4, 188-227.

Karlgren, B., 1915: *Étude sur la phonologie chinoise,* Stockholm.

—, 1962: *Sound and Symbol in Chinese,* Hong Kong.

Karwoski, T.F., H.S.Odbert,&C.E.Osgood, 1942: "Studies in Synesthetic Thinking II: The rôle of form in visual response to music", *Journal of General Psychology* 26, 199-222.

Kavanagh, J.F.&J.E.Cutting (eds.), 1975: *The Role of Speech in Language,* Cambridge, Mass.

Kaye, J.D., 1971: "Nasal Harmony in Desano", *Linguistic Inquiry* 2, 37-56.

Kenstowicz, M.&C.Kissebirth, 1977: *Topics in Phonological Theory,* New York.

Kent, R.D.&K.L.Moll, 1969: "Vocal-Tract Characteristics of the Stop Cognates", *Journal of the Acoustical Society of America* 46, 1549-1555.

Kerek, A., 1975: "The 'Sonority Hierarchy' in Child Phonology", presented at the Eighth International Congress of Phonetic Sciences, Leeds, 1975.

Key, H., 1965: "Some Semantic Functions of Reduplication in Various Languages", *Anthropological Linguistics* 7.3, 88-102.

Kim, Kong-On, 1977: "Sound Symbolism in Korean", *Journal of Linguistics* 13, 67-75.

Kimura, D., 1961: "Cerebral Dominance and the Perception of Verbal Stimuli", *Canadian Journal of Psychology* 15, 166-171.

—, 1967: "Functional Asymmetry of the Brain in Dichotic Listening", *Cortex* 3, 163-178.

—, 1973: "The Asymmetry of the Human Brain", *Scientific American* 228, 70-78.

Kimura, D.&S. Falb, 1968: "Neural Processing of Backwards-Speech Sounds", *Science* 161, 395-396.

King, F. L.&D. Kimura, 1972: "Left Ear Superiority in Dichotic Perception of Vocal Nonverbal Sounds", *Canadian Journal of Psychology* 36, 111-116.

Kiparsky, P., 1972: "Explanation in Phonology", *Goals of Linguistic Theory*, New Jersey, 189-225.

—, 1973: "Phonological Representations", Fujimura (ed.), *Three Dimensions of Linguistic Theory*, Tokyo, 1-136.

—, 1975: "Comments on the Role of Phonology in Language", see Kavanagh&Cutting, 271 ff.

—, 1976: "Abstractness, Opacity, and Global Rules", A. Koutsoudas (ed.), *The Application and Ordering of Grammatical Rules*, The Hague&Paris, 160-186.

Kiparsky, P.&L. Menn, 1977: "On the Acquisition of Phonology", J. Macnamara (ed.), *Language Learning and Thought*, New York.

Kirschenblatt-Gimblett, B. (ed.), 1976: *Speech Play*, Philadelphia.

Kjazimov, F., 1954: "Principy singarmonizma v azerbajdžanskom jazyke", *Izvestia O. L. Ja.*, Akademija Nauk SSSR, 13, No. 1.

Klausenberger, J., 1974: "Rule Inversion, Opacity, Conspiracies: French Liaison and Elision", *Lingua* 34, 167-179.

Klein, F., 1921: "Vergleichende Betrachtungen über neuere geometrische Forschungen", *Gesammelte Mathematische Abhandlungen* I, Berlin, 460 ff.

Klein, W., R. Plomp,&L. Pols, 1970: "Vowel Spectra, Vowel Spaces, and Vowel Identification", *Journal of the Acoustical Society of America* 48, 999-1099.

Klima, E. S., 1975: "Sound and Its Absence in the Linguistic Symbol", see Kavanagh&Cutting, 249-270.

Kok, E. P., V. S. Kočergina, L. V. Jakuševa, 1971: "Opredelenie dominantnosti polušarija pri pomošči dixotičeskogo proslušivanija reči", *Žurnal vysšej nervnoj dejatel'nosti* 21, 1012-1017.

Koller, H., 1955, 1959: "Stoicheion", *Glotta* 34, 161-174; and 38, 61-64.

Komenský, J. A., 1913: *Informatorium školy mateřské*, Brno.

—, 1966: *Panglottia, De rerum humanarum emendatione consultatio catholica* II, Prague.

Konn, D., 1969: "Types of Labial Vowel Harmony in the Turkic Languages", *Anthropological Linguistics* 11, 98-106.

Konovalov, D., 1908: *Religioznyj ekstaz v russkom mističeskom sektantstve*, Sergiev Posad.

Kořínek, J. M., 1937: "Zur lautlichen Struktur der interjektionalen Sprachgebilde. Ein Beitrag zur Erforschung der Beziehungen zwischen sprachlichen Gegensätzen und Emotion", *Slavia* 15, 43-52.

—, 1939: "Laut und Wortbedeutung", *Travaux du Cercle Linguistique de Prague* 8, 58-65.

Kowalski, T., 1929: *Karaimische Texte im Dialekt von Troki*, Kraków.

Köhler, W., 1910-1915: "Akustische Untersuchungen", *Zeitschrift für Psychologie* 54 (1910a); 58 (1910b); 64 (1912); 72 (1915).

—, 1913: "Psychologische Beiträge", *Archiv für Experimentale und Klinische Phonetik* I.

—, 1929: *Gestalt Psychology*, New York.

Kølln, H., 1971: "Linguistic Opposition", *Miscellanea Linguistica*, AUPO, Philologica Supplement, 5-8.

Krashen, S. D., 1976: "Cerebral Asymmetry", Whitaker & Whitaker (eds.), *Studies in Neurolinguistics,* New York, 157-191.

Krauss, M. E., 1964: "Proto-Athapaskan-Eyak and the Problem of Na-Dene: The Phonology", *International Journal of American Linguistics* 30, 118-131.

—, 1973: "Na-Dene", *Current Trends in Linguistics* 10.2, The Hague, 903-978.

Krech, E.-M., 1970: "Perzeptionsuntersuchungen zur Relevanz des Coup de Glotte im Deutschen", *Proceedings of the Sixth International Congress of Phonetic Sciences, 1967,* Prague, 503-506.

Krejnovič, E. A., 1958: "Opyt issledovanija struktury slova v korjakskom jazyke", Akademija Nauk SSSR, Institut Jazykoznanija, *Doklady i soobščenija* 11, 151-167.

Kristeva, J., 1977: "Contraintes rythmiques et langage poétique", in her *Polylogue,* Paris, 437-466.

Kruszewski, M. (N.), 1879: "Ob 'analogii' i 'narodnoj ètimologii' (Volksetymologie)", *Russkij filologičeskij vestnik* II, 109-120.

—, 1883: *Očerk nauki o jazyke,* Kazan.

Kuipers, A. H., 1960: *Phoneme and Morpheme in Kabardian,* The Hague.

Kumaxov, M. A., 1973: "Teorija monovokalizma i zapadnokavkazskie jazyki", *Voprosy jazykoznanija* #7, 54-67.

Kuznecova, A. M., 1965: *Izmenenija glasnyx pod vlijaniem sosednix mjagkix soglasnyx,* Moscow.

Labov, W., 1964: "Phonological Correlates of Social Stratification", *American Anthropologist* 66, 164-176.

—, 1970: "The Study of Language in Its Social Context", *Studium Generale* 23, 30-87.

—, 1972: "The Internal Evolution of Linguistic Rules", R. Stockwell & R. Macaulay (eds.), *Linguistic Change and Generative Theory,* Bloomington, 101-171.

Lacan, J., 1966: *Écrits,* Paris.

Ladd, D. R. Jr., 1980: *The Structure of Intonational Meaning,* Bloomington, Ind.

Ladefoged, P., 1964: *A Phonetic Study of West African Languages,* Cambridge, Eng.

—, 1971a: *Preliminaries to Linguistic Phonetics,* Chicago.

—, 1971b: "The Limits of Phonology", *Form and Substance,* Copenhagen.

—, 1972a: "Phonetic Prerequisites for a Distinctive Features Theory", *Papers in Linguistics and Phonetics in Memory of Pierre Delattre,* The Hague, 273-285.

—, 1972b: "Phonological Features and Their Phonetic Correlates", *Phonetica* 2, 2-12.

—, 1975: *A Course in Phonetics,* New York.

Ladefoged, P. & D. E. Broadbent, 1957: "Information Conveyed by Vowels", *Journal of the Acoustical Society of America* 29, 98-104.

—, 1960: "Perception of Sequence in Auditory Events", *Quarterly Journal of Experimental Psychology* 12, 162-170.

Ladefoged, P., K. Williamson, B. Elugbe, & S. A. A. Uwalaka, 1976: "The Stops of Owerri Igbo", *Studies in African Languages,* Supplement 6, 147-163.

Ladzekpo, S. K. & H. Pantaleoni, 1970: "Takada Drumming", *African Music Society* 4, 6-21.

Lafitte, P., 1962: *Grammaire basque,* Bayonne.

Lancker, D. van & V. A. Fromkin, 1973: "Hemispheric Specialization for Pitch and 'Tone': Evidence from Thai", *Journal of Phonetics* 1.

Langdon, M., 1971: "Sound Symbolism in Yuman Languages", J. Sawyer (ed.), *Studies in American Indian Languages,* Berkeley, Calif., 149-173.

—, 1978: "Animal Talk in Cocopa", *International Journal of American Linguistics* 44, 10-16.

Lange, O., 1962: *Wholes and Parts: A General Theory of System Behavior,* Oxford & London.

Lanham, L. W., 1969: "Generative Phonology and the Analysis of Nguni Consonants", *Lingua* 24, 155-162.

Lanyon-Orgill, P. A., 1944: *A Study of the Leuangiua Language,* London.

Larson, L. V., 1975: *The Opposition Tense-Lax in the German Vowel System,* M. A. thesis, Cornell University.

Lass, R., 1975: "How Intrinsic Is Content? Markedness, Sound Change, and 'Family Universals'", Goyvaerts & Pullum (eds.), *Essays on the Sound Pattern of English,* Ghent, 475-504.

Laycock, D., 1965: "Towards a Typology of Ludlings, or Play-Languages", *Linguistic Communications, Working Papers of the Linguistic Society of Australia* 6.

Lázaro Carreter, F., 1976: *Estudios de Poética,* Madrid.

Laziczius, G., 1935: "Probleme der Phonologie", *Ungarische Jahrbücher* 15, 495ff. (Reproduced, 1966, in *Selected Writings,* The Hague, 38ff.).

—, 1961: *Lehrbuch der Phonetik,* Berlin.

Lebrun, Y., 1970: "Clinical Evidence Against the Motor Theory of Speech Perception", *Proceedings of the Sixth International Congress of Phonetic Sciences, 1967,* Prague, 531-534.

Lecours, A. R. & F. Rouillon, 1976: "Neurolinguistic Analysis of Jargonaphasia and Jargonagraphia", Whitaker & Whitaker (eds.), *Studies in Neurolinguistics* II, New York, 95-144.

Lees, R. B., 1961: *The Phonology of Modern Standard Turkish,* Bloomington, Ind.

Lehiste, I. (ed.), 1967: *Readings in Acoustic Phonetics,* Cambridge, Mass.

—, 1970: *Suprasegmentals,* Cambridge, Mass.

Lekomceva, M., 1971: "Svjaznost' fonologičeskix priznakov i struktura fonologičeskix posledovatel'nostej", *Problemy strukturnoj lingvistiki,* Moscow.

Lenneberg, E. H., 1962: "Understanding Language without Ability to Speak", *Journal of Abnormal and Social Psychology* 65.

Léon, P., 1971: "Apparition, maintien et chute du'e-caduc', variantes combinatoires et expressives", *Studia Phonetica* 4, Paris.

Léon, P., H. Schogt, & E. Burstynsky, 1977: *La Phonologie: 1. Les écoles et les théories,* Paris.

Leopold, W. F., 1939, 1947: *Speech Development of a Bilingual Child.* I: *Vocabulary Growth in the First Two Years;* II: *Sound Learning in the First Two Years,* Evanston, Ill.

—, 1953-1954: "Patterning in Children's Language Learning", *Language Learning* V, 1-14.

—, 1956: "Roman Jakobson and the Study of Child Language", *For Roman Jakobson,* The Hague.

Lepschy, G., 1974: "Saussure e gli spiriti", R. Godel (ed.), *Studi Saussuriani,* Bologna, 181-200.

Lepsius, R., 1855: *Das allgemeine linguistische Alphabet,* Berlin.

Lesser, R., 1978: *Linguistic Investigations of Aphasia,* London.

Lévi-Strauss, C., 1958: *Anthropologie structurale* I, Paris.

—, 1963: *La Pensée sauvage,* Paris (1966: *The Savage Mind,* Chicago).

−, 1964: *Le cru et le cuit*, Paris.

−, 1971: *L'homme nu*, Paris.

−, 1972: "Structuralism and Ecology", *Barnard Alumnae* (Spring), 6-14 (reprinted in 1973 in *Social Science Information* 12.1, 7-23.

−, 1975: *La voie des masques* I-II, Geneva.

−, 1976: "Préface", to R. Jakobson, *Six Leçons sur le Son et le Sens*, Paris. (Eng. trans. by J. Mepham, *Six Lectures on Sound and Meaning*, 1978, Sussex).

Levy, J., 1974: "Psychobiological Implications of Bilateral Asymmetry", S. Dimond & J. Graham-Beaumont (eds.), *Hemisphere Function in the Human Brain*, London.

Lhermitte, F. & J. C. Gautier, 1969: "Aphasia", P. J. Vinken & G. W. Bruyn (eds.), *Disorders of Speech Perception and Symbolic Behavior* IV, *Handbook of Clinical Neurology*.

Li, Fang-Kuei, 1933 a: "Chipewyan Consonants", *Bulletin of the Institute of History and Philology of the Academia Sinica, Supplementary Volume* I, Peiping, 429-467.

−, 1933 b: "A List of Chipewyan Stems", *International Journal of American Linguistics* 7, 122-151.

−, 1946: "Chipewyan", H. Hoijer (ed.), *Linguistic Structures of Native America*, New York, 398-423.

Liberman, A. M., 1957: "Some Results of Research on Speech Perception", *Journal of the Acoustical Society of America* 29.

−, 1972: "The Specialization of the Language Hemisphere", Haskins Laboratories, *Speech Research* 31/32, 1-22.

Liberman, A. M., F. S. Cooper, K. S. Harris, & P. F. MacNeilage, 1963: "A Motor Theory of Speech Perception", *Proceedings of the Speech Communication Seminar, Stockholm 1962*.

Liberman, A. M., F. S. Cooper, et al., 1965: "Some Observations on the Efficiency of Speech Sounds", Haskins Laboratories, *Speech Research* 4.

Liberman, A. M., F. S. Cooper, D. P. Shankweiler, & M. Studdert-Kennedy, 1967: "Perception of the Speech Code", *Psychological Review* 74, 431-461.

Liberman, A. M., P. Delattre, & F. S. Cooper, 1952: "The Role of Selected Stimulus Variables in the Perception of the Unvoiced Stop Consonants", *American Journal of Psychology* 65, 497-516.

Liberman, A. M. & M. Studdert-Kennedy, 1977: "Phonetic Perception", R. Held, H. Leibowitz, & H.-L. Teuber (eds.), *Handbook of Sensory Physiology* VIII, Heidelberg.

Liberman, A. S., 1970: "Fonologičeskie problemy nemeckix spirantov", *Inostrannye jazyki v škole* I, 73-76.

−, 1971: "Fonema kak različitel'nyj priznak?" *Fonetika. Fonologija. Grammatika*, Moscow.

−, 1974: "The Order of Rules in Phonology and the Reality of Distinctive Features", *Linguistics* 126, 45-62.

Licklider, J. C. R., 1952: "On the Process of Speech Perception", *Journal of the Acoustical Society of America* 24.

Lieberman, P., 1970: "Towards a Unified Linguistic Theory", *Linguistic Inquiry* 1, 307-322.

−, 1975: *On the Origins of Language*, New York & London.

Lieberman, P. et al. 1972: "Phonetic Ability and Related Anatomy of the Newborn and Adult Human, Neanderthal Man, and the Chimpanzee", *American Anthropologist* 74, 287-307.

Liede, A., 1963: *Dichtung als Spiel, Studien zur Unsinnpoesie an den Grenzen der Sprache* I, II, Berlin.

Liestøl, A., 1964: *Runer frå Bryggen,* Bergen.

Lightner, T., 1965: "On the Description of Vowel and Consonant Harmony", *Word* 21, 244-250.

Liljencrants, J. & B. Lindblom, 1972: "Numerical Simulation of Vowel Quality Systems: The Role of Perceptual Contrast", *Language* 48, 839-862.

Lindau, M., 1975: "Phonetic Mechanisms of Vowel Harmony in African Languages", paper read at the Eighth International Congress of Phonetic Sciences, Leeds.

Lindblom, B., 1972: "Phonetics and the Description of Language", *Proceedings of the Seventh International Congress of Phonetic Sciences,* The Hague, 63-97.

—, 1975: "Experiments in Sound Structure", paper read at the Eighth International Congress of Phonetic Sciences, Leeds. To appear in his forthcoming book, *Experiments in Sound Structure,* London.

Lindblom, B., J. Lubker, & T. Gay, 1977: "Formant Frequencies of Some Fixed-mandible Vowels and a Model of Speech Motor Programming by Predictive Simulation", *Journal of Phonetics* 5.

Lindblom, B. & J. Sundberg, 1969: "A Quantitative Model of Vowel Production and the Distinctive Features of Swedish Vowels", Speech Transmission Laboratories, *Quarterly Progress Scientific Reports* 1/1969, Stockholm, 14-32.

Lipski, J. M., 1974: "On Universal Phonological Features", *Zeitschrift für Phonetik, Sprachwissenschaft und Kommunikationsforschung* 27, 420-431.

Lisenko, D. M., 1971: "Vlijanie konteksta na vosprijatie glasnyx", *Voprosy teorii i metodov issledovanija rečevyx signalov. Informacionnye materialy* 32, Leningrad, 52-59.

Lisker, L. & A. S. Abramson, 1964: "A Cross-Language Study of Voicing in Initial Stops: Acoustical Measurements", *Word* 20, 384-422.

—, 1971: "Distinctive Features and Laryngeal Control", *Language* 47, 767-785.

Locke, J., 1694: *Essay Concerning Humane Understanding,* Part III, London.

Lockwood, D. G., 1969: "Markedness in Stratificational Phonology", *Language* 45, 300-308.

Lombard, E., 1910: *De la glossolalie chez les premiers chrétiens et des phénomènes similaires,* Lausanne.

Lomtatidze, K. V., 1967: "Abazinskij jazyk", *Jazyki narodov SSSR,* IV, Moscow, 123-144.

Lorrain, F., 1975: *Réseaux sociaux et classifications sociales,* Paris.

Lotz, J., 1962: "Thoughts on Phonology as Applied to the Turkish Vowels", *American Studies on Altaic Linguistics* V.13, Indiana University, 343-351.

—, 1972: "Elements of Versification", Wimsatt (ed.), *Versification - Major Language Types,* New York, 1 ff.

Lounsbury, F. G., 1953: *Oneida Verb Morphology,* Yale University, New Haven.

Lucretius, 1851: J. S. Watson (trans.), *The Nature of Things,* London.

Lunt, H. G., 1952: *A Grammar of the Macedonian Literary Language,* Skopje.

—, 1973: "Remarks on Nasality: The case of Guaraní", *A Festschrift for Morris Halle,* New York, 131-139.

Luria, A. R., 1947: *Travmatičeskaja afazija,* Moscow.

—, 1958: "Brain Disorders and Language Analysis", *Language and Speech* I, 14-34.

—, 1960: "Differences between Disturbances of Speech and Writing in Russian and in French", *International Journal of Slavic Linguistics and Poetics* 3.

—, 1973: "Two Basic Kinds of Aphasic Disorders", *Linguistics* 115, 57-66.

—, 1974: "Language and Brain: Towards the Basic Problems of Neurolinguistics", *Brain and Language* 1, 1-14.

—, 1976: *Basic Problems of Neurolinguistics*, The Hague.

—, 1977: "The Contribution of Linguistics to the Theory of Aphasia", see Armstrong & van Schooneveld, 237-251.

Lyons, J. L., 1968: *Introduction to Theoretical Linguistics*, Cambridge, England.

MacKay, D. G., 1970a: "Spoonerisms: The Structure of Errors in the Serial Order of Speech", *Neuropsychologia* 8, 323-350.

—, 1970b: "Spoonerisms of Children", *Neuropsychologia* 8, 315-322.

MacKay, D. M., 1966: "The 'Active/Passive' Controversy", *XVIII International Congress of Psychology, Symposium 23: Models of Speech Perception*.

Macken, M. A., 1977: "Developmental Reorganization of Phonology: A Hierarchy of Basic Units of Acquisition", *Papers and Reports on Child Language Development* 14, Stanford University.

Mahling, F., 1926: "Das Problem der audition colorée", *Archiv für die gesamte Psychologie* 57, 165-302.

Mahnken, I., 1967: "Zur Frage der binären Oppositionen im Bereich prosodischer Erscheinungen", *Folia linguistica* I, 59-79.

Makarov, G. N., 1966: "Karel'skij jazyk", *Jazyki narodov SSSR*, III, Moscow, 61-80.

Malécot, A., 1956: "Acoustic Cues for Nasal Consonants: An experimental study involving a tape-splitting technique", *Language* 32, 274-284.

—, 1960: "Vowel Nasality as a Distinctive Feature in American English", *Language* 36.

—, 1966a: "The Effectiveness of Intra-Oral Air-Pressure Pulse Parameters in Distinguishing between Stop-Cognates", *Phonetica* 14, 65-81.

—, 1966b: "Mechanical Pressure as an Index of Force of Articulation", *Phonetica* 14, 169-180.

—, 1968: "The Force of Articulation of American Stops and Fricatives as a Function of Position", *Phonetica* 18, 95-102.

—, 1969: "The Effect of Syllabic Rate and Loudness on the Force of Articulation of American Stops and Fricatives", *Phonetica* 19, 205-216.

—, 1970: "The Lenis-Fortis Opposition: Its Physiological Parameters", *Journal of the Acoustical Society of America* 47, 1588-1592.

—, 1975: "The Glottal Stop in French", *Phonetica* 31, 51-63.

—, 1977: *Contribution à l'étude de la force d'articulation en français*, The Hague.

Malécot, A. & A. Chermak, 1966: "Place Cues for /ptk/ in Lower Cut-Off Frequency Shifts of Contiguous /s/", *Language and Speech* 9, 162-169.

Malécot, A. & G. Chollet, 1977: "The Acoustic Status of the Mute-e in French", *Phonetica* 34, 19-30.

Malinowski, B., 1922: *Argonauts of the Western Pacific*, London.

Malkiel, Y., 1978: "From Phonosymbolism to Morphosymbolism", *Fourth LACUS Forum*, Columbia, S.C.

Mallarmé, S., 1965: "Fragments", *Œuvres complètes*, Paris.

Malmberg, B., 1952: "Le problème du classement des sons du langage et quelques questions connexes", *Studia linguistica* 6, 1-56.

—, 1956: "Questions de méthode en phonétique synchronique", *Studia linguistica* 10.

—, 1962: "Le système consonantique du français moderne", *Acta Universitatis Lundensis*, N.S. 38, 3-73.

—, 1964: "Couches primitives de structure phonologique", *Phonetica* 11, 221-227.

—, 1968: "Linguistic Basis of Phonetics", B. Malmberg (ed.), *Manual of Phonetics*, Amsterdam, 1-16.

—, 1969: "Le trait distinctif - qualité absolue ou relative?" *Mélanges pour Jean Fourquet*, Paris, 185-190.

—, 1971: *Phonétique générale et romane*, The Hague.

—, 1972: "The Hierarchic Principle", *Proceedings of the Seventh International Congress of Phonetic Sciences, Montreal 1971*, The Hague, 1145-1149.

—, 1977: *Signes et symboles*, Paris.

Maltzmann, I., L. Morrisett & L. Brooks, 1956: "An Investigation of Phonetic Symbolism", *Journal of Abnormal and Social Psychology* 53, 249-251.

Manthey, F., 1937: *Die Sprachphilosophie des hl. Thomas von Aquin*, Paderborn.

Marçais, P., 1948: "L'articulation et l'emphase dans un parler arabe maghrélun", *Annales de l'Institut d'Études Orientales, Faculté des lettres de l'Université d'Alger* 7.

Marchand, H., 1957: "Motivation by Linguistic Form: English ablaut and rime-combinations and their relevancy to word-formation", *Studia Neophilologica* 29, 54-66.

—, 1959: "Phonetic Symbolism in English Word-Formation", *Indogermanische Forschungen* 64, 146-168, 256-277.

Markell, N. N. & E. P. Hamp, 1960-61: "Connotative Meanings of Certain Phoneme Sequences", *Studies in Linguistics* 15, 47-61.

Martin, S., 1962: "Phonetic Symbolism in Korean", N. Poppe (ed.), *American Studies in Altaic Linguistics*, Bloomington, Ind., 177-189.

Martinet, A., 1933: "Remarques sur le système phonologique du français", *Bulletin de la Société Linguistique de Paris* 34, 191-202.

—, 1937: *La phonologie du mot en danois*, Paris.

—, 1945: *La prononciation du français contemporain*, Paris.

—, 1949: "La double articulation linguistique", *Travaux du Cercle Linguistique de Copenhague* V *(Recherches structurales)*, 30-37.

—, 1955²: *Économie des changements phonétiques*, Paris.

—, 1957: "Arbitraire linguistique et double articulation", *Cahiers Ferdinand de Saussure* 15, 105-116.

—, 1972: "La Nature phonologique d'e caduc", *Papers in Linguistics and Phonetics to the Memory of Pierre Delattre*, The Hague.

Martinet, A. & H. Walter, 1973: *Dictionnaire de la prononciation française dans son usage réel*, Paris.

Masson, D. I., 1952: "Synesthesia and Sound Spectra", *Word* 8, 39-41.

Mathesius, V., 1931: "Zum Problem der Belastungs- und Kombinationsfähigkeit der Phoneme", *Travaux du Cercle Linguistique de Prague* 4, 148-152.

—, 1964: "On the Potentially of the Phenomena of Language", J. Vachek (ed.), *A Prague School Reader in Linguistics*, Bloomington, Ind., 1-32 (Paper of 1911 translated from Czech).

Mathesius, V. et al., 1931: "Projet de terminologie phonologique standardisée", *Travaux du Cercle Linguistique de Prague* 4, 309-323.

Matthews, G. H., 1970: "Some Notes on the Proto-Siouan Continuants", *International Journal of American Linguistics* 36, 98-109.

Mattingly, I. G., A. M. Liberman, A. K. Syrdal, & T. Halwes, 1971: "Discrimination in Speech and Nonspeech Modes", *Cognitive Psychology* 2, 131-157.

May, L. C., 1956: "A Survey of Glossolalia and Related Phenomena in Non-Christian Religions", *American Anthropologist* 58, 75-96.

McCawley, J., 1967: "Le rôle d'un système de traits phonologiques dans une théorie du langage", *Langages* 8, 112 f., and the English version of 1972: "The Role of Phonological Feature Systems in Any Theory of Language", Makkai (ed.), *Phonological Theory: Evolution and Current Practice*, New York, 522-528. References are to the English version.

—, 1974: Review of N. Chomsky & M. Halle, *The Sound Pattern of English*, in *International Journal of American Linguistics* 40, 50-88.

—, 1977: "Jakobsonian Ideas in Generative Grammar", see Armstrong & van Schooneveld, 269-284.

McNeil, D., 1970a: *The Acquisition of Language*, New York.

—, 1970b: "The Development of Language", P. Mussen (ed.), *Carmichael's Manual of Child Psychology*, 3rd ed., vol. I, New York, 1061-1161.

Meggyes, K. S., 1972: "The Synchrony of Different Developmental Stages in the Language of a Two-Year-Old Child", K. Ohnesorg (ed.), *Colloquium Paedolinguisticum, Brno, 14-16 Oct. 1970*, The Hague, 159-165 (summary of her Hungarian book *Egy kétéves gyermek nyelvi rendszere*, Budapest, 1971).

Meillet, A. & M. Cohen (eds.), 1924: *Les Langues du monde*, Paris.

Meinhof, C., 1912: *Die Sprachen der Hamiten*, Hamburg.

Meinhold, G., 1970: "Nasale und orale Vokale - Struktur und Perzeption", *Proceedings of the Sixth International Congress of Phonetic Sciences, 1967*, Prague, 641-644.

Mel'čuk, I. A., 1977: "3 osobennosti, 7 principov i 11 rezul'tatov grammatičeskix issledovanij Romana Jakobsona", see Armstrong & van Schooneveld, 285-308.

Melikišvili, I. G., 1970: "Einige universale Gesetzmäßigkeiten in dem System der Affrikaten", L. Dezső & P. Hajdú (eds.), *Theoretical Problems of Typology and the Northern Eurasian Languages*, Amsterdam & Budapest.

—, 1974: "K izučeniju ierarxičeskix otnošenij edinic fonologičeskogo urovnja", *Voprosy jazykoznanija* #3, 94-105.

—, 1976: *Otnošenie markirovannosti v fonologii*, Tbilisi (in Georgian with a detailed Russian summary: 146-162).

Mel'nikov, G. P., 1966: "Geometričeskie modeli vokalizma", *Problemy lingvističeskogo analiza*, Moscow.

Menn, L., 1971: "Phonotactic Rules in Beginning Speech", *Lingua* 26, 225-251.

Menyuk, P., 1971: *The Acquisition and Development of Language*, Englewood Cliffs, N. J.

Menzerath, P. & A. Lacerda, 1933: *Koartikulation, Steuerung und Lautabgrenzung*, Berlin.

Milewski, T., 1967: *Typological Studies in the American Indian Languages*, Kraków.

Milke, W., 1965: "Comparative Notes on the Austronesian Languages of New Guinea", *Lingua* 14, 330-348.

Miller, G., 1956: "The Perception of Speech", *For Roman Jakobson*, The Hague.

Miller, G. & P. Johnson-Laird, 1976: *Language and Perception*, Cambridge, Mass.

Miller, R. A., 1966: "Early Evidence for Vowel Harmony in Tibetan", *Language* 42, 252-277.

Millet, L'Abbé, 1938: *Etude expérimentale de la formation des voyelles*, Paris.

Mindadze, A. A., V. M. Mosidze, T. D. Kakuberi, 1975: "O 'muzykal'noj' funkcii pravogo polušarija mozga čeloveka", *Soobščenija Akademii Nauk Grunzinskoj SSR* 79, 457-459.

Miron, M. S., 1961: "A Cross-Linguistic Investigation of Phonetic Symbolism", *Journal of Abnormal and Social Psychology* 62, 623-630.

Molfese, D. L., R. B. Freeman, Jr., & D. S. Palermo, 1975: "The Ontogeny of Brain Lateralization for Speech and Non-Speech Stimuli", *Brain and Language* 2, 356-368.

Moravcsik, J. M. E., 1960a: "Being and Meaning in the 'Sophist'", *Acta Philosophica Fennica* 14.

—, 1960b: "SYMPLOKE EIDON and the Genesis of LOGOS", *Archiv für Geschichte der Philosophie* 42, 117-129.

Morgenau, H., 1961: *Open Vistas*, New Haven.

Morgenstern, C., 1905: *Galgenlieder*, Berlin.

Morgenstierne, G., 1941: "The Phonology of Kashmiri", *Acta Orientalia* 19, 79-99.

Morice, A. G., 1932: *The Carrier Language* I, St. Gabriel, Mödlung bei Wien.

Morrell, L. K. & J. G. Salamy, 1971: "Hemispheric Asymmetry of Electrocortical Response to Speech Stimuli", *Science* 174, 164-166.

Morrison, S. E., 1936: *Harvard College in the Seventeenth Century*, Vol. II, Cambridge, Mass.

Mosidze, V. M. & K. K. Akbardija, 1973: *Funkcional'naja simmetrija i asimmetrija polušarij mozga*, Tbilisi.

Mosiman, E., 1911: *Das Zungenreden, geschichtlich und psychologisch untersucht*, Tübingen.

Moulton, W. G., 1962: *The Sounds of English and German*, Chicago.

—, 1967: "Types of Phonemic Change", *To Honor Roman Jakobson* II, The Hague, 1393-1407.

Mueller, H., 1958: "Length as a Phoneme in the German Vowel System", *Journal of the Canadian Linguistic Association* 4, 35-37.

Muljačić, Ž., 1964: *Opća fonologija i fonologija suvremenog italijanskog jezika*, Zagreb.

—, 1973: *Fonologia generale*, Bologna.

—, 1977: "Phonologie théorique et phonétique", see Armstrong & van Schooneveld, 309-319.

Murphy, G., 1961: *Early Irish Metrics*, Dublin.

Nadoleczny, M., 1926: *Kurzes Lehrbuch der Sprach- und Stimmheilkunde*, Leipzig.

Nadžip, E., 1960: *Sovremennyj ujgurskij jazyk*, Moscow.

Nakazima, S., 1966-1973: "A Comparative Study of the Speech Developments of Japanese and American English in Childhood", *Studia Phonologica* 4-7.

Nečaev, V. V., 1889: "Dela sledstvennyx o raskol'nikax komissij v XVIII veke", *Opisanie dokumentov i bumag, xranjaščixsja v moskovskom arxive ministerstva justicii* VI, part II, 77-199 (Suppl. # 2, Fragments from the poetic creations of the Khlysty, 169-179).

Needham, D. & M. Davis, 1946: "Cuicateco Phonology", *International Journal of American Linguistics* 12, 139-146.

Neffgen, H., 1903: *Grammatik der Samoanischen Sprache*, Vienna & Leipzig.

—, 1918: *Grammar and Vocabulary of the Samoan Language*, London.

Nettl, B., 1953: "Observations on Meaningless Peyote Song Texts", *Journal of American Folklore* 66, 161-164.

Neville, H., 1974: "Electrographic Correlates of Lateral Asymmetry in the Processing of Verbal and Nonverbal Auditory Stimuli", *Journal of Psycholinguistic Research* 3, 151-163.

Newbrand, H. L., 1951: *A Phonemic Analysis of Hawaiian*, M. A. Thesis, University of Hawaii.

Newman, S. S., 1933: "Further Experiments in Phonetic Symbolism", *American Journal of Psychology* 45, 53-75.

—, 1939: "Personal Symbolism in Language Patterns", *Psychiatry* 2, 177-182.

—, 1947: "Bella Coola, I: Phonology", *International Journal of American Linguistics* 13, 129-134.

—, 1971: "Bella Coola Reduplication", *International Journal of American Linguistics* 37, 34-38.

Nichols, J., 1971: "Diminutive Consonant Symbolism in Western North America", *Language* 47, 826-848.

Nida, E. A., 1949: *Morphology*, Ann Arbor.

—, 1964: *Toward a Science of Translating*, Leiden.

Nikolaeva, T., 1977: *Frazovaja intonacija slavjanskix jazykov*, Moscow.

Noreen, A., 1903, 1907: *Vårt Språk* I, II, Lund.

Obendorfer, R., 1976: Review of Eli Fischer-Jørgensen, *Trends in Phonological Theory*, in *Norwegian Journal of Linguistics* 30, 239 ff.

Obrecht, D. H., 1968: *Effects of the Second Formant on the Perception of Velarization Consonants in Arabic*, The Hague.

Ó Cuív, B., 1966: "The Phonetic Basis of Classical Modern Irish Rhyme", *Ériu* 20, 94-103.

Oftedal, M., 1975: Review of E. Ternes, *The Phonemic Analysis of Scottish Gaelic*, in *Phonetica* 32, 130-140.

Ohala, J. J., 1975: "Phonetic Explanation for Nasal Sound Pattern", Ferguson et al. (eds.), *Nasálfest*, Stanford, Calif., 289-316.

Ohnesorg, K., 1948: *Fonetická studie o dětské řeči*, Prague.

—, 1955: "Kapitola ze srovnávací fonetiky dětské řeči", *Sborník prací filosofické fakulty Brněnské university* IV A, 95 ff.

—, 1959: *Druhá fonetická studie o dětské řeči*, Brno.

—, 1966: "Le vers enfantin", *Teorie verše* I, Brno.

—, 1970: "En marge de quelques problèmes pédophonétiques", *Proceedings of the Sixth International Congress of Phonetic Sciences, 1967*, Prague, 697-699.

—, 1972: "Une contribution à la pédophonétique comparée", K. Ohnesorg (ed.), *Colloquium Paedolinguisticum*, The Hague, 187-192.

Oksaar, E., 1971: "Zum Spracherwerb des Kindes in zweisprachiger Umgebung", *Folia Linguistica* 4, 330-358.

Olmsted, D. L., 1971: *Out of the Mouth of Babes*, The Hague.

Orr, J., 1944: "On Some Sound Values in English", *British Journal of Psychology* 35, 1-18.

—, 1945: "Note on Professor Thorndike's Paper", *British Journal of Psychology* 36, 14.

Osgood, C. E., 1937: "The Ethnography of the Tanaina", Yale University, *Publications in Anthropology* # 16.

—, 1963: "Universals and Psycholinguistics", J. Greenberg (ed.), *Universals of Language*, Cambridge, Mass.

Osthoff, H. & K. Brugmann, 1878: *Morphologische Untersuchungen auf dem Gebiete der indogermanischen Sprachen* I, Leipzig.

Oswald, V. A., 1943: "'Voiced *t*' - a Misnomer", *American Speech* 18.

Oyama, T. & J. Haga, 1963: "Common Factors between Figural and Phonetic Symbolism", *Psychologia* 6, 131–144.

Öhman, S. E. G., 1966: "Coarticulation in VCV Utterances: Spectrographic Measurements", *Journal of the Acoustical Society of America* 39.

Pačesová, J., 1968: *The Development of Vocabulary in the Child*, Brno.

—, 1970: "Some Thoughts on Language Development in Czech-Speaking Children", *Sborník prací filosofické fakulty Brněnské university, Řada jazykovědná* (A), 18, Brno, 5–23.

Painter, C., 1971: "Vowel Harmony in Anum", *Phonetica* 23, 239–248.

—, 1973: "Cineradiographic Data on the Feature 'Covered' in Twi Vowel Harmony", *Phonetica* 28, 97–120.

Palermo, D. S., 1975: "Developmental Aspects of Speech Perception: Problems for a Motor Theory", see Kavanagh & Cutting, 149–154.

Panov, M. V., 1967: *Russkaja fonetika*, Moscow.

Pantaleoni, H., 1972: *The Rhythm of Atsiã Dance Drumming among the Anlo (Eve) of Anyako*, Ph. D. Dissertation, Wesleyan University, Conn.

Parsons, T. & R. F. Bales, 1955: *Family, Socialization, and Interaction Process*, Glencoe, Ill.

Passy, P., 1891: *Étude sur les changements phonétiques et leurs caractères généraux*, Paris.

Patočka, J., 1964: *Aristoteles, jeho předchůdci a dědicové*, Prague.

—, 1976: "Roman Jakobsons phänomenologischer Strukturalismus", *Tijdschrift voor filosofie* 38, 129–135.

Pauliny, E., 1961: *Fonologia spisovnej slovenčiny*, Bratislava.

—, 1966: "The Principle of Binary Structure in Phonology", *Travaux Linguistiques de Prague* 2, 121–126.

—, 1978: "Differencial'nye priznaki glasnyx slovackogo jazyka", *Voprosy jazykoznanija* # 1, 76–80.

Pawley, A., 1960: "Samoan Phonology in Outline", *Te Reo* 3, 47–50.

—, 1966: "Polynesian Languages", *Journal of the Polynesian Society* 75.

Peirce, C. S., 1965[2]: *Collected Papers*, Vol. 1–5, Cambridge, Mass.

Perkell, J. S., 1965: "Cineradiographic Studies of Speech, Implications of a Detailed Analysis of Certain Articulatory Movements", *Proceedings of the Fifth International Congress on Acoustics*.

Pesot, J., 1973: *Les onomatopées; structure acoustique et catégories perceptuelles*, Mémoire de l'Université de Montréal.

Pestovskij, B. A., 1925: "Kalmyckie pesni", *Bjulleten' Sredneaziatskogo gos. universiteta*, Tashkent, 75–80.

Peterfalvi, J.-M., 1965: "Les recherches expérimentales sur le symbolisme phonétique", *American Journal of Psychology* 65, 439–473.

—, 1970: *Recherches expérimentales sur le symbolisme phonétique*, Paris.

Petrova, T. E., 1968: "Orokskij jazyk", *Jazyki narodov SSSR*, V, Leningrad, 172–190.

Pétursson, M., 1976: "Aspiration et activité glottale", *Phonetica* 33, 169–198.

Peuser, G., 1977: *Sprache und Gehirn. Eine Bibliographie zur Neurolinguistik*, Bonn.

—, 1978: *Aphasie*, Munich.

Pike, K. L., 1943: *Phonetics,* Ann Arbor.

—, 1947: "Grammatical Prerequisites to Phonemic Analysis", *Word* 3, 155-172.

—, 1967[2]: *Language in Relation to a Unified Theory of the Structure of Human Behavior,* The Hague.

Pillai, M. S., 1960: "Tamil - Literary and Colloquial", Ferguson & Gumperz (eds.), *Linguistic Diversity in South Asia = International Journal of American Linguistics* 26: 3, Part III, 27-42.

Piotrovskij, P. G., 1966: *Modelirovanie fonologičeskix sistem i metody ix sravnenija,* Moscow.

Pipping, H., 1922: *Inledning till studiet av de nordiska sprakens ljudlära,* Helsinki.

Pisarkowa, K., 1975: *Wyliczanki polskie,* Kraków.

Pisoni, D. B., 1975: "Dichotic Listening and Processing Phonetic Features", F. Restle et al. (eds.), *Cognitive Theory,* Vol. I, New Jersey, 79-102.

Plomp, R., 1970: "Timbre as a Multidimensional Attribute of Complex Tones", R. Plomp & Smoorenburg (eds.), *Frequency Analysis and Periodicity Detection in Hearing,* Leiden, 397-414.

—, 1975: "Auditory Analysis and Timbre Perception", Fant & Tatham (eds.), *Auditory Analysis and Perception of Speech,* London, 7-22.

Polivanov, E. D., 1916: "Po povodu zvukovyx žestov japonskogo jazyka", *Sbornik po teorii poètičeskogo jazyka* I, Petrograd.

—, 1928: *Vvedenie v jazykoznanie dlja vostokovednyx vuzov,* Leningrad.

—, 1929: "Obrazcy ne-iranizovannyx (singarmonističeskix) govorov uzbekskogo jazyka", *Izvestija Akademii Nauk SSSR,* Seventh Series, 511-537.

Pollack, I. & L. Ficks, 1954: "Information of Elementary Multidimensional Auditory Displays", *Journal of the Acoustical Society of America* 26.

Polland, S. B. & B. Hála, 1926: *Artikulace českých zvuků v roentgenových obrazech,* Prague.

Poppe, N., 1960: *Vergleichende Grammatik der altaïschen Sprachen* I, Weisbaden.

Pos, H. J., 1938: "La notion d'opposition en linguistique", *XI Congrès International de Psychologie.*

—, 1939: "Perspectives du structuralisme", *Travaux du Cercle Linguistique de Prague* 8, 71-78.

Postal, P., 1968: *Aspects of Phonological Theory,* New York.

Posti, L., 1965: "Über das Quantitätsystem im Estnischen", *Congressus Secundus Internationalis Fenno-Ugristarum* I, Helsinki, 408-418.

Preston, M. S., 1971: "Some Comments on the Developmental Aspects of Voicing in Stop Consonants", D. L. Horton & J. Jenkins (eds.), *Perception of Language,* Columbus, Ohio, 236-246.

Pribram, K., 1971: *Languages of the Brain: Experimental Paradoxes and Principles in Neuropsychology,* Englewood Cliffs, N. J.

Pukui, D. & S. Elbert, 1965: *Hawaiian-English Dictionary,* Honolulu.

Pulgram, E., 1961: "French /ə/ - Statistics and Dynamics of Linguistic Subcodes", *Lingua* 10, 305-325.

Pulleyblank, E. G., 1972: "The Analysis of Vowel Systems", *Acta Linguistica Hafniensia* 14, 39-62.

Quintilianus, 1963: = *M. Fabii Quintiliani Institutionis Oratoriae* with an English translation by H. E. Butler, London & Cambridge, Mass.

Ramasubramanian, N. & R. B. Thosar, 1971: "Synthesis by Rule of Some Retroflex Consonants", *Language and Speech* 14, 65-85.

Raphael, L. J., 1972: "Preceding Vowel Duration as a Cue to the Perception of the Voicing Characteristic of Word-Final Consonants in American English", *Journal of the Acoustical Society of America* 51, 1296 ff.

Raphael, L. J. & F. Bell-Berti, 1975: "Tongue Musculature and the Feature of Tension in English Vowels", *Phonetica* 32, 61-73.

Rardin, R., 1969: "On Finnish Vowel Harmony", MIT Research Laboratory of Electronics, *Quarterly Progress Reports* 94, 226-232.

Read, C., 1971: "Pre-School Children's Knowledge of English Phonology", *Harvard Educational Review* 41, 1-34.

Reformatskij, A. A., 1955: "O sootnošenii fonetiki i grammatiki", *Voprosy grammatičeskogo stroja*, Moscow.

—, 1966: "Ierarxija fonologičeskix edinic i javlenija singarmonizma", *Issledovanija po fonologii*, Moscow.

—, 1970: *Iz istorii otečestvennoj fonologii*, Moscow.

Reichard, G., 1945: "Composition and Symbolism of Cœur d'Alene Verb Stems", *International Journal of American Linguistics* 11, 47-63.

Reichard, G., R. Jakobson & E. Werth, 1949: "Language and Synesthesia", *Word* 5, 224-233.

Reinhart, T., 1976: "Patterns, Intuitions, and the Sense of Nonsense", *PTL - Journal of Descriptive Poetics and Theory of Literature* 1, 85-103.

Renou, L., 1941: "Les connexions entre le rituel et la grammaire en sanscrit", *Journal Asiatique* 233, 105-165.

Revzin, I., 1970: "Nekotorye zamečanija v svjazi s dixotomičeskoj teoriej v fonologii", *Voprosy jazykoznanija* 3, 58-70.

Rice, K. D., 1978: "A Note on Fort Resolution Chipewyan", *International Journal of American Linguistics* 44, 144 f.

Rigsby, B. & M. Silverstein, 1969: "Nez Perce Vowels and Proto-Sahaptian Vowel Harmony", *Language* 45, 45-59.

Ringen, C. O., 1976: "A Concrete Analysis of Hungarian Vowel Harmony", paper presented at the CUNY Conference on Vowel Harmony.

Robbins, R. H., 1966: "The Warden's Wordplay: Toward a Redefinition of Spoonerisms", *The Dalhousie Review* 46, 457-465.

Romportl, M., 1973: *Studies in Phonetics*, Prague.

Rood, D. S., 1975: "The Implications of Wichita Phonology", *Language* 51, 315-337.

Roper, C., P. Dixon, E. Ahern, & V. Gibson, 1976: "Effect of Language and Sex on Universal Phonetic Symbolism", *Language and Speech* 19, 388-397.

Ross, A. S. C., 1937: "An Example of Vowel Harmony in a Young Child", *Modern Language Notes* 52, 508 f.

Rossi, M., 1972: "L'intensité spécifique des voyelles", *Proceedings of the Seventh International Congress of Phonetic Sciences*, The Hague, 574-588.

Roussey, C., 1899-1900: "Notes sur l'apprentissage de la parole chez un enfant", *La Parole* 1.

Ruegg, D. S., 1959: *Contributions à l'histoire de la philosophie linguistique indienne*, Paris.

Ruesch, J. & G. Bateson, 1951: *Communication: The Social Matrix of Psychiatry*, New York.

Ruhlen, M., 1973: "Nasal Vowels", *Stanford University Working Papers on Language Universals* # 12, 1-36.

—, 1974: "Some Comments on Vowel Nasalization in French", *Journal of Linguistics* 10, 271–276.

—, 1975–1976: *A Guide to the Languages of the World,* Stanford University.

—, 1977: "The Geographical and Genetic Distribution of Linguistic Features", *Linguistic Studies Offered to Joseph Greenberg* I, Saratoga, Calif., 137–160.

Rūķe-Draviņa, V., 1952: "Einige Beobachtungen über die Frauensprache in Lettland", *Orbis* I, 55–73.

—, 1977: "Child Language Studies", see Armstrong & van Schooneveld, 403–409.

Ryle, G., 1960: "Letters and Syllables in Plato", *The Philosophical Review* 69, 431 ff.

Sahlins, M., 1976: "Colors and Cultures", *Semiotica* 16, 1–22.

Salus, P. H. & M. W., 1974: "Developmental Neurophysiology and Phonological Acquisition Order", *Language* 50, 151–160.

Samarin, W. J., 1967: "Determining the Meanings of Ideophones", *Journal of West African Languages* 4, 35–41.

—, 1970: "Inventory and Choice in Expressive Language", *Word* 26.

—, 1972a: *Tongues of Men and Angels,* New York.

—, 1972b: "Variation and Variables in Religious Glossolalia", *Language in Society* 1, 121–130.

Samuels, M. L., 1972: *Linguistic Evolution,* Cambridge, Eng.

Sanches, M. & B. Kirschenblatt-Gimblett, 1976: "Children's Traditional Speech Play and Child Language", B. Kirschenblatt-Gimblett (ed.), *Speech Play,* Philadelphia, 65–110.

Sanctius Brocensis, Franciscus (Francisco Sanchez de Las Brozas), 1976: *Minerva,* trans. & ed. by F. Riveras Cardenas, Madrid. (Also E. del Estal Fuentes [ed.], 1975: *Acta Salmanticensia: Filosofia y Letras,* No. 92, Universidad de Salamanca.)

Sapir, E., 1910: "Song Recitative in Paiute Mythology", *Journal of American Folklore* 23, 445–472.

––, 1911: "Diminutive and Augmentative Consonantism in Wishram", *Handbook of American Indian Languages,* Bulletin 40, Pt. I (§ 53 in F. Boas "Chinook").

—, 1921: *Language. An Introduction to the Study of Speech,* New York.

—, 1922: "The Takelma Language of Southwestern Oregon", *Handbook of American Indian Languages,* BAE-B 40, 1–296.

—, 1927: "Language as a Form of Human Behavior", *The English Journal* 16, 413–433.

—, 1949: D. Mandelbaum (ed.), *Selected Writings,* Berkeley, Calif., especially: "Language" [1933], 7–32; "Sound Patterns in language" [1925], 33–45; "The Psychological Reality of Phonemes" [1933], 46–60; "A Study in Phonetic Symbolism" [1929], 61–72; "Grading: A Study in Semantics" [1924], 122–149; "The Grammarian and His Language" [1924], 150–159; "The Status of Linguistics as a Science" [1929], 160–166; "Abnormal Types of Speech in Nootka" [1915], 179–196; "Male and Female Forms of Speech in Yana" [1929], 206–212; "Review of Poems of Gerard Manley Hopkins" [1921], 500–502; "Speech as a Personality Trait" [1927], 533–543; "The Unconscious Patterning of Behavior in Society" [1927], 544–559; "Symbolism" [1934], 564–568.

Sapir, E. & M. Swadesh, 1960: *Yana Dictionary,* Berkeley, Calif.

Sapir, J. D., 1975: "Big and Thin: Two Diola-Fogny Meta-Linguistic Terms", *Language in Society* 4, 1–15.

Sasanuma, S., 1975: "Kana and Kanji Processing in Japanese Aphasics", *Brain and Language* 2, 369-383.

Saussure, F. de, 1916: *Cours de linguistique générale,* Lausanne & Paris. We refer to the pages of R. Engler's critical edition: I/1967 and II/1974, Wiesbaden.

Schaerlaekens, A. M., 1977: *De taalontwikkeling van het kind,* Groningen.

Schane, S. A., 1968: *The Phonology and Morphology of French,* Cambridge, Mass.

—, 1973: "[Back] and [round]", *A Festschrift for Morris Halle,* Cambridge, Mass., 174-184.

Scherzer, J., "Five Cuna Linguistic Games", *Penn-Texas Working Papers in Sociolinguistics* # 6.

Schmidt, W., 1926: *Die Sprachfamilien und Sprachenkreise der Erde,* Heidelberg.

Schooneveld, C. H. van, 1978: *Semantic Transmutations: Prolegomena to a Calculus of Meaning,* Bloomington, Ind.

Schuchardt, H., 1897: "Keltorom. *frog-, frogn-* Lautsymbolik", *Zeitschrift für romanische Philologie* 21, 199-205.

Scollon, R., 1978: "Variable Data and Linguistic Convergence", *Language in Society* (to appear).

Scott, N. C., 1964: "Nasal Consonants in Land Dayak (Bukar-Sadong)", *In Honor of Daniel Jones,* London, 432-436.

Sebeok, T., 1962: "Coding in the Evolution of Signalling Behavior", *Behavioral Science* 7, 430-442.

Sechehaye, A., 1908: *Programme et méthodes de la linguistique théorique,* Paris.

Sedlak, P., 1969: "Typological Considerations of Vowel Quality Systems", *Stanford University Working Papers on Language Universals* # 1, 1-40.

Segalowicz, S. J. & F. A. Gruber (eds.), 1977: *Language Development and Neurological Theory,* New York.

Shankweiler, D. & M. Studdert-Kennedy, 1967: "Identification of Consonants and Vowels Presented to Left and Right Ears", *International Journal of Experimental Psychology* 19, 59-63.

Shaumyan, S. K., 1965: *Strukturnaja lingvistika,* Moscow.

—, 1968: *Problems of Theoretical Phonology,* The Hague.

—, 1977: "Roman Jakobson's Contribution to the Study of Slavic Historical Phonology and Phonetics", see Armstrong & van Schooneveld, 421-433.

Sheets, J., 1977: "Hominid Dental Evolution and the Origins of Language", *Man* 12, 518-526.

Shimizu, K., 1975: "A Comparative Study of Hemispheric Specialization for Speech Perception in Japanese and English Speakers", *Studia Phonologica* 9, 13-24.

Shupljakov, V., G. Fant, & A. de Serpa-Leitão, 1969: "Acoustical Features of Hard and Soft Russian Consonants in Connected Speech: A Spectrographic Study", Speech Transmission Laboratory, *Quarterly Progress and Status Report* 4/1968, 1-6.

Siertsema, B., 1958: "Problems of Phonemic Interpretation: Nasalized Sounds in Yoruba", *Lingua* 7, 356-366.

Sievers, E., 1901[5]: *Grundzüge der Phonetik zur Einführung in das Studium der Lautlehre der indogermanischen Sprachen,* Leipzig.

—, 1924: *Ziele und Wege der Schallanalyse; zwei Vorträge,* Heidelberg.

Silverstein, M. (ed.), 1971: *Whitney on Language,* Cambridge, Mass.

Singh, S., 1974: "A Step Towards a Theory of Speech Perception", *Preprints of the Speech Communication Seminar,* Vol. 3, Stockholm, 55-66.

—, 1976: *Distinctive Features: Theory and Validation*, Baltimore.

Slis, I. H., 1975: "Consequences of Articulatory Effort on Articulatory Timing", Fant & Tatham (eds.), *Auditory Analysis and Perception of Speech*, London.

Smith, A., 1966: "Speech and Other Functions after Left (Dominant) Hemispherectomy", *Journal of Neurology, Neurosurgery and Psychiatry* 29, 467-471.

Smith, N. V., 1973: *The Acquisition of Phonology*, Cambridge, England.

Sokolov, A. N., 1959: "Issledovanija po probleme rečevyx mexanizmov myšlenija", *Psixologičeskaja nauka v SSSR* I, Moscow, 488-515.

—, 1968: *Vnutrennjaja reč' i myšlenie*, Moscow.

Sommerfelt, A., 1928: "Remarques sur la valeur expressive des voyelles", *Norsk Tidsskrift for Sprogvidenskap* I, 30 f.

—, 1929: Review of C. & U. Stern, *Die Kindersprache*, in *Norsk Tidsskrift for Sprogvidenskap* III, 271-273.

Soubramanian, V. I., 1962: "Phonemic Outline of a Dialect of Malayalam", *Indian Linguistics* 23, 99-116.

Sovijärvi, A., 1938: *Die gehaltenen, geflüsterten und gesungenen Vokale und Nasale der finnischen Sprache*, Helsinki.

Sparks, R. & N. Geschwind, 1968: "Dichotic Listening in Man after Section of Neocortical Commissures", *Cortex* 4, 3-16.

Specht, F., 1940: "Die äußere Sprachform als Ausdruck der seelischen Einstellung", *Die alten Sprachen* V, 112 ff.

—, 1944: *Der Ursprung der indogermanischen Deklination*, Göttingen.

Spellacy, F. & S. Blumstein, 1970: "The Influence of Language-Set on Ear Preference in Phoneme Recognition", *Cortex* 6, 430-439.

Sperry, R. W. & M. S. Gazzaniga, 1967: "Language Following Surgical Disconnection of the Hemispheres", *Brain Mechanisms Underlying Speech and Language*, New York, 108-124.

Spicer, J., 1975: *The Collected Books*, Los Angeles.

Spitzer, L., 1927: "Singen und Sagen - Schorlemorle", *Zeitschrift für vergleichende Sprachforschung* 54, 213-223.

Spreen, O., 1968: "Psycholinguistic Aspects of Aphasia", *Speech and Hearing Research* 11, 453-466.

Sprigg, R. K., 1961: "Vowel Harmony in Lhasa Tibetan: Prosodic Analysis Applied to Interrelated Vocalic Features of Successive Syllables", *Bulletin of the School of Oriental and African Studies* 24, 116-138.

Springer, S. P., 1973: "Hemispheric Specialization for Speech Opposed by Contralateral Noise", *Perception and Psychophysics* 13, 391-393.

Springer, S. P. & M. S. Gazzaniga, 1975: "Dichotic Testing of Partial and Complete Split Brain Subjects", *Neuropsychologia* 13, 341-346.

Stankiewicz, E., 1964: "Problems of Emotive Language", *Approaches to Semiotics*, The Hague, 239-264.

—, (ed.), 1972: *A Baudouin de Courtenay Anthology: The Beginnings of Structural Linguistics*, Bloomington, Ind.

—, 1977: "Poetics and Verbal Art", *A Perfusion of Signs*, Bloomington, Ind.

Stanley, R., 1967: "Redundancy Rules in Phonology", *Language* 43, 393-438.

Starobinski, J., 1971: *Les mots sous les mots: Les anagrammes de Ferdinand de Saussure*, Paris.

Stebnickij, S. N., 1934: "Nymylanskij (korjackij) jazyk", *Jazyki i pis'mennost' narodov severa*, Moscow, 47-84.

Stevens, K. N., 1966: "On the Relations between Speech Movements and Speech Perception", *XVIII International Congress of Psychology, Symposium 23: Models of Speech Perception.*

—, 1973: "Further Theoretical and Experimental Bases for Quantal Places of Articulation for Consonants", MIT Research Laboratory of Electronics, *Quarterly Progress Report* 108, 247–252.

—, 1977: "Acoustic Invariance for Place of Articulation in Stops and Nasals Across Syllable Contexts", paper presented at the 94th meeting of the Acoustical Society of America, Miami, Florida, Dec. 13–16.

Stevens, K. N. & S. E. Blumstein, 1975: "Quantal Aspects of Consonant Production and Perception: A Study of Retroflex Stop Consonants", *Journal of Phonetics* 3, 215–233.

—, 1976: "Context-Independent Cues for Place of Articulation in Stop Consonants", paper presented at the 91st Meeting of the Acoustical Society of America.

Stevens, K. N. & D. H. Klatt, 1974: "Role of Formant Transitions in the Voiced-Voiceless Distinction for Stops", *Journal of the Acoustical Society of America* 55, 653–659.

Stevens, S. S., 1934: "Tonal Density", *Journal of Experimental Psychology* 17, 585–592.

—, 1950: "A Definition of Communication", *Journal of the Acoustical Society of America* 22, 689–690.

—, 1951: "Mathematics, Measurement, and Psychophysics", S. S. Stevens (ed.), *Handbook of Experimental Psychology,* New York, 1–49.

Stevens, S. S. & H. Davis, 1938: *Hearing: Its Psychology and Physiology,* New York.

Stewart, J. M., 1967: "Tongue Root Position in Akan Vowel Harmony", *Phonetica* 16, 185–204.

Stimson, H., 1966: "A Tabu Word in the Peking Dialect", *Language* 42, 285–294.

Stokoe, W. C., Jr., 1975: "The Shape of Soundless Language", see Kavanagh & Cutting, 207–228.

Straka, G., 1963: "La division des sons du langage en voyelles et consonnes peut-elle être justifiée?" *Travaux de linguistique et de littérature* I, Strasbourg, 17–99.

Strang, B. M. H., 1968[2]: *Modern English Structure,* New York.

Studdert-Kennedy, M., 1974: "The Perception of Speech", *Current Trends in Linguistics* 12, The Hague, 2349–2385.

—, 1976a: "Speech Perception", *Contemporary Issues in Experimental Phonetics,* New York, 243–293.

—, 1976b: "Universals in Phonetic Structure and Their Role in Linguistic Communication", Haskins Laboratories, *Speech Research* 48, 43–50.

Studdert-Kennedy, M. & D. Shankweiler, 1970: "Hemispheric Specialization for Speech Perception", *Journal of the Acoustical Society of America* 48, 579–594.

Stumpf, C., 1907: "Zur Einteilung der Wissenschaften", *Abhandlungen der Königlichen Preussischen Akademie der Wissenschaften,* Berlin.

—, 1926: *Die Sprachlaute,* Berlin.

Summerfield, L. & M. Haggard, 1977: "On the Dissociation of Spectral and Temporal Cues to the Voicing Distinction in Initial Stop Consonants", Haskins Laboratories, *Speech Research* 49.

Sunik, O. P., 1968a: "Ul'čskij jazyk", *Jazyki Narodov SSSR,* V, Leningrad, 149–171.

—, 1968b: "Udègejskij jazyk", *Jazyki Narodov SSSR,* V, Leningrad, 210–232.

Swadesh, M., 1937: "The Phonemic Interpretation of Long Consonants", *Language* 13, 1–10.

—, 1947: "On the Analysis of English Syllabics", *Language* 23, 137–150.

Swanton, J. R., 1911: "Tlingit", *Handbook of American Indian Languages* 1, 159-204.

Sweet, H., 1877: *A Handbook of Phonetics*, Oxford.

—, 1899: *The Practical Study of Languages: A Guide for Teachers and Learners*, London.

—, 1906³: *A Primer of Phonetics*, Oxford.

—, 1913: *Collected Papers*, Oxford.

Szemerényi, O., 1964: "Structuralism and Substratum: Indo-Europeans and Semites in the Ancient Near East", *Lingua* 13, 1 ff.

—, 1967: "The New Look of Indo-European Reconstruction and Typology", *Phonetica* 17, 65-99.

—, 1973: "Marked-Unmarked and a Problem of Latin Diachrony", *Transactions of the Philological Society*, 55-74.

—, 1977: "Sprachtypologie, funktionelle Belastung und die Entwicklung indogermanischer Lautsysteme", *Acta Iranica*, Leiden, 339-393.

Šaraf, G., 1927: "Palatogrammy zvukov tatarskogo jazyka sravnitel'no s russkim", *Vestnik Naučnogo Obščestva Tatarovedenija* 7, Kazan', 65-102.

Ščerba, L. V., 1912: *Russkie glasnye v kačestvennom i količestvennom otnošenii*, St. Petersburg.

—, 1915: "O raznyx stiljax proiznošenija i ob ideal'nom fonetičeskom sostave slov", *Zapiski Neofilologičeskogo Obščestva pri Petrogradskom Universitete* VIII.

Šerech, J., 1952: "Über die Besonderheiten der Sprache der Frauen (Domaine slave)", *Orbis* I, 74-81.

Širokov, O. S., 1973: "Struktura čukotskogo singarmonizma", *Problemy strukturnoj lingvistiki*, Moscow, 586-599.

Tamir-Ghez, N., 1978: "Binary Oppositions and Thematic Decoding in E. E. Cummings and Eudora Welty", *PTL = Journal of Descriptive Poetics and Theory of Literature* 3, 235-248.

Taranovsky, K., 1965: "The Sound Texture of Russian Verse in the Light of Phonemic Distinctive Features", *International Journal of Slavic Linguistics and Poetics* 9, 114-124.

Tarte, R. D., 1974: "Phonetic Symbolism in Adult Native Speakers of Czech", *Language and Speech* 17, 87-94.

Tarte, R. D. & L. S. Barritt, 1971: "Phonetic Symbolism in Adult Native Speakers of English", *Language and Speech* 14, 158.

Taylor, I. K., 1963: "Phonetic Symbolism Re-examined", *Psychological Bulletin* 60, 200-209.

Taylor, I. K. & M. M., 1962: "Phonetic Symbolism in Four Unrelated Languages", *Canadian Journal of Psychology* 16, 344-356.

—, 1965: "Another Look at Phonetic Symbolism", *Psychological Bulletin* 64, 413-427.

Teeter, K., 1959: "Consonant Harmony in Wiyot", *International Journal of American Linguistics* 25, 41-43.

Telegdi, Z., 1970: "Humboldt als Begründer der Sprachtypologie", L. Dezsö & P. Hajdú (eds.), *Theoretical Problems of Typology and the Northern Eurasian Languages*, Amsterdam, 25-34.

Terent'ev, V. A., 1969: *Jazkovye universalii i lingvističeskaja tipologija*, Moscow.

Ternes, E., 1973: *The Phonemic Analysis of Scottish Gaelic*, Hamburg.

Teuber, H.-L., 1967: "Lacunae and Research Approaches to Them: I", C. H. Millikan & F. L. Darley (eds.), *Brain Mechanisms Underlying Speech and Language*, New York, 204-216.

—, 1974: "Why Two Brains?" Schmidt & Worden (eds.), *The Neurosciences* III, Cambridge, Mass., 71-74.

—, 1976: "The Brain and Human Behavior", invited evening address at the 21st International Psychological Congress, Paris, July 20.

Thom, R., 1972: *Stabilité structurelle et morphogénèse*, Reading, Mass.

—, 1974a: *Modèles mathématiques de la morphogénèse*, Paris.

—, 1974b: "La linguistique, discipline morphologique exemplaire", *Critique* 322, 235ff.

Thompson, L. C. & M. T., 1972: "Language Universals, Nasals and the Northwest Coast", *Studies in Linguistics in Honor of G. L. Trager*, The Hague, 441-456.

Thomson, A., 1909: "Die Eigentöne der Sprachlaute und ihre praktische Verwendung", *Indogermanische Forschungen* 24, 1-9.

—, 1934: "Bemerkungen über die š-Laute", *Zeitschrift für slavische Philologie* 11, 345ff.

Thorndike, E. L., 1945: "On Orr's Hypothesis Concerning the Front and Back Vowels", *British Journal of Psychology* 36, 10-14.

Thun, N., 1963: *Reduplicative Words in English: A Study of Formations of the Types tick-tock, hurly-burly, and shilly-shally*, Uppsala.

Todorov, T., 1972: "Le sens des sons", *Poétique* 11, 446-462.

—, 1977: *Théories du symbole*, Paris.

Tompa, J., 1968: *Ungarische Grammatik*, The Hague.

Tonkova-Yampol'skaya (Jampol'skaja), R. V., 1969: "Development of Speech Intonation during the First Two Years of Life", *Soviet Psychology* 7, 48-53 (Translated from *Voprosy psixologii* 14, 1968, 94-101).

Toporov, V. N., 1970: "About the Phonological Typology of Burushaski", R. Jakobson & S. Kawamoto (eds.), *Studies in General and Oriental Linguistics*, Tokyo, 632-647.

Tranel, B., 1974: *The Phonology of Nasal Vowels in Modern French*, Ph. D. Dissertation, University of California, San Diego.

—, 1981: *Concreteness in Generative Phonology*, Berkeley.

Traugott, N. N. & S. I. Kajdanova, 1975: *Narušenie sluxa pri sensornoj alalii i afazii*, Leningrad.

Trautmann, M., 1884: *Die Sprachlaute im Allgemeinen und die Laute des Englischen, Französischen und Deutschen im Besonderen*, Leipzig.

Trojan, F., 1970: "Bericht über die Ergebnisse der Enquête zu Jakobsons Gesetz vom Schichtenbau des Sprachlautsystems", *Proceedings of the Sixth International Congress of Phonetic Sciences, 1967*, Prague, 925-929.

Trubetzkoy, N. S., 1926: "Studien auf dem Gebiete der vergleichenden Lautlehre der nordkaukasischen Sprachen", *Caucasica* 3, 7-36.

—, 1929: "Zur allgemeinen Theorie der phonologischen Vokalsysteme", *Travaux du Cercle Linguistique de Prague* 1, 39-67.

—, 1931a: "Die phonologischen Systeme", *Travaux du Cercle Linguistique de Prague* 4, 96-116.

—, 1931b: "Die Konsonantsysteme der ostkaukasischen Sprachen", *Caucasica* 8, 1-52.

—, 1931c: "Gedanken über Morphonologie", *Travaux du Cercle Linguistique de Prague* 4, 160-163 (English translation in 1969: *Principles of Phonology*, Berkeley, Calif., 305-308).

—, 1934: "Das morphonologische System der russischen Sprache", *Travaux du Cercle Linguistique de Prague* 5, part 2.
—, 1936: "Die phonologischen Grundlagen der sogenannten 'Quantität' in den verschiedenen Sprachen", *Scritti in onore di Alfredo Trombetti*, Milan, 155–176.
—, 1939a: *Grundzüge der Phonologie* = *Travaux du Cercle Linguistique de Prague* 7. Our citations refer to the page numbers of the English translation: *Principles of Phonology*, Berkeley and Los Angeles, 1969.
—, 1939b: "Aus meiner phonologischen Kartothek: Das phonologische System der dunganischen Sprache", *Travaux du Cercle Linguistique de Prague* 8, 22–26 & 343–345.
—, 1975: *Letters and Notes*, The Hague.
Truby, H. M., 1971: "Prenatal and Neonatal Speech, 'Pre-Speech', and an Infantile Speech Lexicon", *Word* 27, 51–101.
Tryon, D. T., 1970: *Conversational Tahitian*, Berkeley, Calif.
Tsuru, S. & H. S. Frics, 1933: "A Problem in Meaning", *Journal of General Psychology* 8, 281–284.
Tucker, A. N., 1962: "The Syllable in Luganda", *Journal of African Languages* 1, 122–166.
Tucker, A. N. & J. Tompo Ole Mpaayei, 1955: *A Maasai Grammar*, London.
Turner, V., 1967: *The Forest of Symbols*, Ithaca, N. Y.
Twaddell, W. F., 1935: *On Defining the Phoneme* (= *Language Monographs* 16), Baltimore, Md.
Twisleton, E., 1873: *The Tongue Not Essential to Speech*, London.
Tynjanov, Ju., 1924: *Problema stixotvornogo jazyka*, Leningrad.
Tzeng, O., D. Hung, & W. S.-Y. Wang, 1977: "Speech Recoding in Reading Chinese Characters", *Journal of Experimental Psychology: Human Learning and Memory* 3, 621–30.

Uldall, H. J., 1944: "Speech and Writing", *Acta Linguistica* 4, 11–16.
Ultan, R., 1970: "Size-Sound Symbolism", *Stanford University Working Papers on Language Universals* # 3, 1–31.
—, 1971: "A Case of Sound Symbolism in Konkow", J. Sawyer (ed.), *Studies in American Indian Languages*, Berkeley, Calif., 295–301.
—, 1973: "Some Reflections on Vowel Harmony", *Stanford University Working Papers on Language Universals* # 12, 37–67.
Underhill, R., 1976: *Turkish Grammar*, Cambridge, Mass.
Ungeheuer, G., 1959: "Das logistische Fundament binärer Phonemklassifikationen", *Studia Linguistica* 13, 69–97.
—, 1962: *Elemente einer akustischen Theorie der Vokalartikulation*, Berlin.
Usnadze, D., 1924: "Ein experimenteller Beitrag zum Problem der psychologischen Grundlagen der Namengebung", *Psychologische Forschung* 5, 24–43.
Uspenskij, B. A., 1967: "Problemy lingvističeskoj tipologii v aspekte različenija 'govorjaščego' (adresanta) i 'slušajuščego' (adresata)", *To Honor Roman Jakobson* III, The Hague & Paris, 2087–2108.

Vachek, J. (ed.), 1964: *A Prague School Reader in Linguistics*, Bloomington, Ind.
—, 1968: *Dynamika fonologického systému současné spisovné češtiny*, Prague.
—, 1976: *Selected Writings in English and General Linguistics*, The Hague.

Vahlen, I., 1854: *Ennianae poesis,* Leipzig.

Valéry, P., 1957: *Œuvres* I, Paris.

Vallier, D., 1975: "Malévitch et le modèle linguistique en peinture", *Critique* 31, 284-296.

—, 1979: "Le problème du vert dans le système perceptif", *Semiotica.*

Vandamme, F., 1968: "Is Transformational Grammar a Contribution to the Theory of Innate Ideas?" *Studia philosophica Gandensia* 6, Ghent, 93-108.

Vanderslice, R. & P. Ladefoged, 1972: "Binary Suprasegmental Features and Transformational Word-Accentuation Rules", *Language* 48, 819-838.

Vanvik, A., 1971: "The Phonetic-Phonemic Development of a Norwegian Child", *Norsk Tidsskrift for Sprogvidenskap* 24, 270-325.

Velten, H. V., 1943: "The Growth of Phonemic and Lexical Patterns in Infant Language", *Language* 19, 281-292.

Vendryes, J., 1924: "À propos de la racine germanique **tend-* 'allumer, brûler'", *Mélanges offerts à M. Charles Andler,* Strasbourg, 383-387.

—, 1953: Compte rendu de M. Cohen, *Sur l'étude du langage enfantin,* in *Bulletin de la Société Linguistique de Paris* 49, No. 139, 25-27.

Vennemann, T. & P. Ladefoged, 1973: "Phonetic Features and Phonological Features", *Lingua* 32, 61-74.

Vertogradova, V. V., 1967: *Strukturnaja tipologija sredneindijskix fonologičeskix sistem,* Moscow.

Vinarskaja, E. N., 1971: *Kliničeskie problemy afazii,* Moscow.

Vinogradov, G., 1930: *Russkij detskij fol'klor,* Irkutsk.

Vogt, H., 1954: "Contact of Languages", *Word* 10, 365-374.

—, 1963: *Dictionnaire de la langue oubykh, avec introduction phonologique,* Oslo.

Volkonskij, S. S., 1913: *Vyrazitel'noe slovo,* St. Petersburg.

Vygotsky, L. S., 1962: *Thought and Language,* Cambridge, Mass. (a version translated and revised by the editors, E. Hanffmann & G. Vakar, of the Russian original, 1934: *Mysl' i jazyk,* Moscow & Leningrad).

Wallace, A. F. C., 1961: "On Being Just Complicated Enough", *Proceedings of the National Academy of Sciences* 47, 458-464.

Wallis, J., 1653: *Grammatica linguae anglicanae,* Oxford.

Wallon, H., 1945: *Les origines de la pensée chez l'enfant* I, Paris.

Wandruszka, M., 1952: "Der Streit um die Deutung der Sprachlaute", *Festgabe Ernst Gamillscheg,* Tübingen, 214-227.

Wang, W. S.-Y., 1967: "Phonological Features of Tone", *International Journal of American Linguistics* 33, 93-105.

—, 1969: "Competing Changes as a Cause of Residue", *Language* 45, 9-25.

Ward, I. C., 1936: *An Introduction to the Ibo Language,* Cambridge, England.

Wason, P. C., 1961: "Response to Affirmative and Negative Binary Statements", *British Journal of Psychology* 52.

Waterson, N., 1970: "Some Speech Forms of an English Child: A Phonological Study", *Transactions of the Philological Society,* 1-24.

—, 1971a: "Child Phonology: A Prosodic View", *Journal of Linguistics* 7, 179-211.

—, 1971b: "Child Phonology: Comparative Studies", *Transactions of the Philological Society,* 34-50.

LW = Waugh, L. R., 1976a: *Roman Jakobson's Science of Language,* Lisse.

—, 1976b: "Lexical Meaning: The Prepositions *en* and *dans* in French", *Lingua* 38, 69-118.

—, 1977: *A Semantic Analysis of Word Order*, Leiden.

—, 1978: "Remarks on Markedness", Dinnsen (ed.), *Current Phonological Theories*, Bloomington, Ind.

—, 1979a: "Markedness in Phonological Systems", *The Fifth Lacus Forum* 1978, Columbia, S.C.

—, 1979b: "Marked and Unmarked - A Choice between Unequals in Semiotic Structure", to appear in *Semiotica*.

—, 1979c: "The Context-Sensitive Meaning of the French Subjunctive", in L. Waugh & F. van Coetsem (eds.), *Cornell Contributions to Linguistics: Semantics and Syntax*, Leiden.

—, 1979d: "The Multifunctionality of the Speech Sound", in Makkai (ed.), *Essays in Honor of Charles F. Hockett*.

Webster, J.C. & R.B. Chaney, Jr., 1967: "Information and Complex Signal Perception", *Models for the Perception of Speech and Visual Form*, Cambridge, Mass., 246-251.

Weeks, T., 1974: *The Slow Speech Development of a Bright Child*, Lexington, Mass.

Weinreich, U., W. Labov, & M. Herzog, 1968: "Empirical Foundations for a Theory of Language Change", W. Lehmann & Y. Malkiel (eds.), *Directions for Historical Linguistics*, Austin, Texas, 97-195.

Weir, R.H., 1962: *Language in the Crib*, The Hague.

—, 1966: "Some Questions on the Child's Learning of Phonology", Smith & Miller (eds.), *The Genesis of Language*, Cambridge, Mass., 153-168.

Weiss, J., 1963a: "Role of 'Meaningfulness' vs. Meaning-Dimensions in Guessing the Meanings of Foreign Words", *Journal of Abnormal and Social Psychology* 66, 541-546.

—, 1963b: "Further Study of the Relation between the Sound of a Word and Its Meaning", *American Journal of Psychology* 76, 624-630.

—, 1964a: "The Role of Stimulus Meaningfulness in the Phonetic Symbolism Response", *Journal of General Psychology* 70, 255-263.

—, 1964b: "Phonetic Symbolism Reexamined", *Psychological Bulletin* 61, 454-458.

—, 1966: "A Study of Ability of English Speakers to Guess the Meanings of Non-Antonym Foreign Words", *Journal of General Psychology* 72, 97-106.

Weiss, M. & A.S. House, 1973: "Perception of Dichotically Presented Vowels", *Journal of the Acoustical Society of America* 53, 51-58.

Wellek, A., 1931a: "Der Sprachgeist als Doppelempfinder", *Zeitschrift für Ästhetik und allgemeine Kunstwissenschaft* 25, 226-262.

—, 1931b: "Zur Geschichte und Kritik der Synästhesie-Forschung", *Archiv für die gesamte Psychologie* 79, 325-384.

Werner, H., 1966: *Comparative Psychology of Mental Development*, New York.

Werner, O., 1972: *Phonemik des Deutschen*, Stuttgart.

Wertheimer, M., 1958: "The Relation between the Sound of a Word and Its Meaning", *American Journal of Psychology* 71, 412-415.

Wescott, R., 1965: "Speech-tempo and the Phonemics of Bini", *Journal of African Languages* 4, 181-190.

—, 1970: "Types of Vowel Alternation in English", *Word* 26, 309-343.

—, 1971a: "Linguistic Iconism", *Language* 47, 416-428.

—, 1971b: "Labio-velarity and Derogation in English: A Study in Phonosemic Correlation", *American Speech* 46, 123-137.

−, 1973: "Tonal Icons in Bini", *Studies in African Linguistics* 4, 197–205.

−, 1975: "Tonal Iconicity in Bini Colour Terms", *African Studies* 34, 185–191.

Westermann, D., 1907: *Grammatik der Ewe-Sprache*, Berlin.

−, 1927: "Laut, Ton und Sinn in westafrikanischen Sudan-Sprachen", *Festschrift Meinhof*, Hamburg, 315–328.

−, 1937: "Laut und Sinn in einigen westafrikanischen Sprachen", *Archiv für vergleichende Phonetik* I, 154–172, 193–211.

Westermann, D. & I.C. Ward, 1933: *Practical Phonetics for Students of African Languages*, London.

Whitney, W.D., 1875: *Life and Growth of Language: An Outline of Linguistic Science*, New York.

−, 1876: *Language and the Study of Language*, New York.

Whorf, B.L., 1956: *Language, Thought, and Reality*, New York.

Williamson, K., 1965: "A Grammar of the Kolokuma Dialect of Ijo", *West African Language Monograph* 2, London.

Willis, R., 1830: "On the Vowel Sounds, and on Reed Organ-Pipes", *Transactions of the Cambridge Philosophical Society* 3, 231–268.

Wilpert, P., 1950: "Die Elementenlehre des Platon und Demokrit", *Natur Geist Geschichte - Festschrift für Aloys Wenzl*, Munich, 49–66.

Wilson, R.D., 1966: "A Criticism of Distinctive Features", *Journal of Linguistics* 2, 195–206.

Winteler, J., 1876: *Die Kerenzer Mundart des Kantons Glarus in ihren Grundzügen dargelegt*, Leipzig.

Winter, W., 1959: "Über eine Methode zum Nachweis struktureller Relevanz von Oppositionen distinktiver Merkmale", *Phonetica* 4, Supplement.

Wise, C.M. & W. Hervey, 1952: "The Evolution of Hawaiian Orthography", *Quarterly Journal of Speech* 38, 311–325.

Witting, C., 1959: *Physical and Functional Aspects of Speech Sounds, with Special Application to Standard Swedish*, Uppsala.

Woo, N., 1970: "Tone in Northern Tepchuan", *International Journal of American Linguistics* 36, 18–30.

Wood, C.C., W.R. Goff & R.S. Day, 1971: "Auditory Evoked Potentials during Speech Perception", *Science* 173, 1248–1251.

Wood, S., 1975: "Tense and Lax Vowels - Degree of Constriction or Pharyngeal Volume?" Lund University Phonetics Lab., *Working Papers* 11, 109–134.

Woodfield, A., 1976: *Teleology*, Cambridge, England.

Wurm, S.A., 1972: *Languages of Australia and Tasmania*, The Hague.

Xolodovič, A.A., 1954: *Očerk grammatiki korejskogo jazyka*, Moscow.

Yilmaz, H., 1967 & 1968: "A Theory of Speech Perception", *Bulletin of Mathematical Biophysics* 29 (1967), 793–825 (I), and 30 (1968), 455–479 (II).

Zaidel, E., 1978: "Auditory Language Comprehension in the Right Hemisphere Following Cerebral Commissurectomy and Hemispherectomy: A Comparison with Child Language and Aphasia", see Caramazza & Zurif, 229–276.

Zarębina, M., 1965: *Kształtowanie się systemu językowego dziecka*, Wroclaw.

Zaxařin, B.A., 1975: "Fonemy Kašmiri (poiski i rešenija)", T.Ja. Elizarenkova (ed.), *Očerki po fonologii vostočnyx jazykov,* Moscow, 142-171.

Zelenin, D., 1929-1930: *Tabu slov u narodov vostočnoj Evropy i severnoj Azii = Sbornik Muzeja antropologii i ètnografii* VIII-IX, Leningrad.

Zimmer, K.E., 1967: "A Note on Vowel Harmony", *International Journal of American Linguistics* 33.

Zinder, L.R. et al., 1964: "Akustičeskaja xarakteristika različija tvërdyx i mjagkix soglasnyx v russkom jazyke", *Voprosy fonetiki* 69, 28-36.

Zollinger, H., 1979: "Correlations between the Neurobiology of Colour Vision and the Psycholinguistics of Colour Naming", *Experientia* 35.

Zurif, E.B. & M. Mendelsohn, 1972: "Hemispheric Specialization for the Perception of Speech Sounds: The Influence of Intonation and Structure", *Perception and Psychophysics* 11, 329-332.

Zurif, E.B. & P.E. Sait, 1970: "The Role of Syntax in Dichotic Listening", *Neuropsychologia* 8, 239-244.

Zwaan, J.D. de, 1969: *A Preliminary Analysis of Gogo-Yimidjir,* Canberra.

Žinkin, N.I., 1968: *Mechanisms of Speech,* The Hague (trans. from 1958: *Mexanizmy reči,* Moscow-Leningrad).

Žirmunskij, V.M., 1962: *Deutsche Mundartkunde,* Berlin (1956: *Nemeckaja dialektologija,* Moscow- Leningrad).

Živov, V.M., 1974: "Problemy sintagmatičeskoj fonologii v svete fonetičeskoj tipologii jazykov", *Voprosy jazykoznanija* # 4, 57-70.

Zuravlëv, A.P., 1974: *Fonetičeskoe žnacenie,* Leningrad.

INDEX OF NAMES

INDEX OF LANGUAGES

INDEX OF TOPICS DISCUSSED

Mouton de Gruyter
celebrates its 25th anniversary

Special Jubilee Offers

Roman Jakobson
Selected Writings
Eight text volumes and a complete bibliography of his writing with a new introduction by L. Waugh

Hardcover. Previous price: € 1242.00 (price for 9 volumes bought separately) Now: US$ 298.00 / € 298.00 / sFr 513,–
Save 75% when purchasing as a set
• ISBN 3-11-017361-1

The series Selected Writings represents the whole range of Roman Jakobson's fields of research.

Volume I: Phonological Studies
2nd expanded ed. 1971. 25 x 16,5 cm. x, 776 pages.

Volume II: Word and Language
1971. 25 x 16,5 cm. 752 pages.

Volume III: Poetry of Grammar and Grammar of Poetry
Edited and Foreword by Stephen Rudy. 1981. 25 x 16,5 cm. xviii, 814 pages.

Volume IV: Slavic Epic Studies
1966. 25 x 16,5 cm. xii, 642 pages.

Volume V: On Verse, Its Masters and Explorers
Edited by Stephen Rudy and Martha Taylor.
1979. 25 x 16,5 cm. viii, 623 pages.

Volume VI: Early Slavic Paths and Crossroads
Edited by Stephen Rudy.
Part 1: Comparative Slavic Studies. The Cyrillo-Methodian Tradition.
Part 2: Medieval Slavic Studies.
1985. 25 x 16,5 cm. xxxiv, 942 pages.

Volume VII: Contributions to Comparative Mythology. Studies in Linguistics and Philology, 1972–1982
Edited by Stephen Rudy and Linda R. Waugh. Foreword by Linda R. Waugh.
1985. 25 x 16,5 cm. xxiv, 405 pages.

Volume VIII: Major Works 1976–1980
Completion Volume I
Edited by Stephen Rudy.
1988. 25 x 16,5 cm. xxiv, 685 pages. Figures.

Roman Jakobson. 1896–1982
A Complete Bibliography of His Writings
Edited by Stephen Rudy

1990. 23 x 15,5 cm. xii, 188 pages. Hardcover.

Prices are subject to change

WALTER DE GRUYTER GMBH & CO. KG
Genthiner Straße 13 · 10785 Berlin
Telefon +49-(0)30-2 60 05-0
Fax +49-(0)30-2 60 05-251
www.deGruyter.de

Mouton
de Gruyter
Berlin · New York